This Book belongs to
Margaret alexandra davis
in winter Park, Florida

Miracle of Love

ALSO BY RAM DASS

Be Here Now
The Only Dance There Is
Grist for the Mill
Journey of Awakening

Miracle of Love

STORIES ABOUT NEEM KAROLI BABA

BY Ram Dass

A Dutton Paperback

E. P. DUTTON

NEW YORK

For information contact:
E. P. Dutton, 2 Park Avenue,
New York, N.Y. 10016

Library of Congress Cataloging in Publication Data
Ram Dass.
    Miracle of love.
    1. Neem Karoli Baba.   2. Hindus in India—
Biography.   I. Title.
BL1175.N43R35   1979   294.5'6'10924   79-10745

ISBN: 0-525-47611-3

Published simultaneously in Canada by
Clarke, Irwin & Company Limited, Toronto and Vancouver

Production Manager: Stuart Horowitz
Designed by Jos. Trautwein

10 9 8 7 6 5 4 3 2 1

First Edition

For
Maharajji
whose presence reveals
how subtle is the path of love.

love is the answer . . .

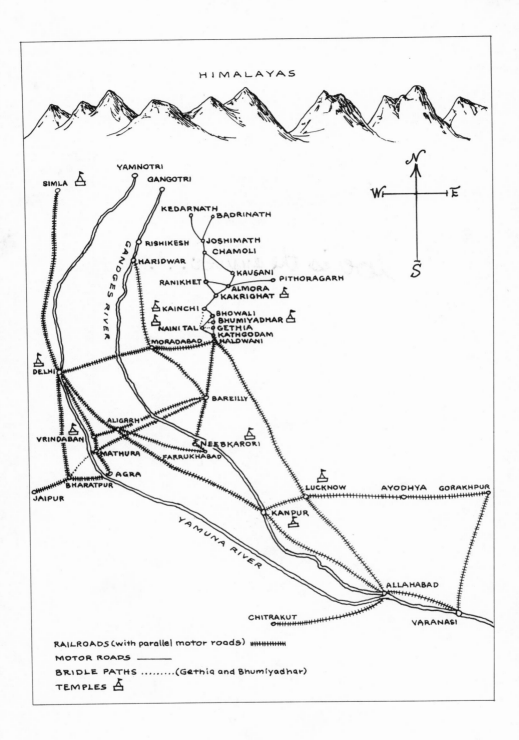

HIMALAYAS

N
W — E
S

SIMLA YAMNOTRI GANGOTRI

KEDARNATH BADRINATH

RISHIKESH JOSHIMATH
HARIDWAR CHAMOLI

GANGES RIVER

RANIKHET KAUSANI
ALMORA PITHORAGARH
KAKRIGHAT

KAINCHI BHOWALI
BHUMIYADHAR
NAINI TAL GETHIA
KATHGODAM
MORADABAD HALDWANI

DELHI

BAREILLY

ALIGARH

VRINDABAN NEEBKARORI
MATHURA FARRUKHABAD

AGRA LUCKNOW AYODHYA GORAKHPUR

BHARATPUR
JAIPUR KANPUR

YAMUNA RIVER

ALLAHABAD

CHITRAKUT VARANASI

RAILROADS (with parallel motor roads) ++++++++++
MOTOR ROADS —————
BRIDLE PATHS .... (Gethia and Bhumiyadhar)
TEMPLES

Contents

Introduction

"When the Flower Blooms . . ."

IN 1967 I met my guru. That meeting changed the course of my life, for through him I came to perceive my life in spiritual terms. In him I found new depths of compassion, love, wisdom, humor, and power, and his actions stretched my understanding of the human possibility. I recognized in him an alliance of the human and the divine.

After our initial meeting I remained in India, as close to him as I was allowed to be, for five more months before returning to America. Before leaving India I had received his *ashirbad* (blessing) for a book, which until that moment I had had no thought of writing. Back in the West, I found many kindred souls open and ready to share what I had received; and his blessing and their thirst gave rise to *Be Here Now*.

In 1970 I returned to India and remained with him, off and on, from February 1971 until March 1972, when my visa expired and I was evicted from the country. However, with him or away from him, he remained the source and impetus for my spiritual awakening.

From the beginning, I had wanted to share him with others, but initially he forbade me bringing people directly to him. A relatively few (several hundred) Westerners nevertheless found their way to him and were touched at the core of their beings as I had been. On September 11, 1973, he died, or, as the Indians would say, he left his body.

In the succeeding years, I have found that the absence of his body has not diminished his influence upon my life. To the contrary, with each passing year I have increasingly experienced his presence, his guidance, his love, and, each time I have taken myself too seriously, his cosmic giggle. This suggested the possibility that others who had never "met" him in the body could similarly be touched by him. This suspicion has been confirmed by a surprisingly large number of people who have reported that through books, lectures, tapes, and personal contact with devotees, they have experienced him in a way that has graced their lives.

I speak of him as "my guru," but in fact I never think of him or our relationship in such a formal way. For me, he is very simply *Maharajji,* a nickname (which means "great king") so commonplace in India that one can often hear a tea vendor addressed thus.

Those of us who were with Maharajji meet again frequently in India or in the West. The conversation invariably turns to recollections of him. Story after story pours forth, and each story is punctuated with silence, laughter, or expostulations as we savor its depth and elegance. In those moments the space becomes rich with the living spirit and we know that he is among us.

In my travels I have now met thousands of awakening beings whose open-hearted receptivity makes me want to share the intimacy with Maharajji to which stories about him give rise. And yet thus far only a very few stories about him, primarily concerning my personal experiences with him, have appeared in print. It was in order to rectify this situation that the present book was undertaken.

Immediately after his death, I encouraged several Westerners in their plan to travel throughout India collecting stories. They were able to obtain some four hundred anecdotes, but, at the time, they found many of the Indian devotees reticent to speak about him. He had always frowned upon their talking much about him, and they were still feeling that restriction. In 1976 two of us were again in India and found, to our delight, that many of the Indian devotees—who, of course, had known him far more extensively and over the course of many more years than we had—were now willing to freely share their treasure of stories. At that time we collected twelve hundred stories. Since then, with the help of another Westerner, we have added an additional four hundred stories gathered from East and West, thus bringing the total number of stories, anecdotes, and quotations based on interviews with over a hundred devotees to over two thousand.

Of course, even a hundred devotees are altogether but a fraction of the thousands who were touched by Maharajji in the course of his life, each of whom holds some precious memory and piece of the puzzle. But lest we would drown in such an ocean of recollection, at a certain point I made an arbitrary decision to stop gathering and begin to organize what we already had.

The devotees whose stories are included are from a wide range of social and cultural positions. Interviews were gathered from important officials in their offices and from sweepers on the streets. We taped discussions of women from the Himalayan hill villages as they squatted warming their hands around a coal brazier in the late afternoon. We listened to reminiscences in living rooms, streets, temple compounds, while sitting around fires under the stars, in cars, hot tubs, airplanes, and on long walks. Stories were offered by Hindu priests as they puffed on their *chillums* (hashish pipes), by professors, police officials, farmers, industrialists, by children and their mothers, who spoke while stirring their bubbling pots over wood and charcoal fires. Always there was the same feeling of shy joy at sharing such a private, precious memory with another. These gatherings to speak about him were indescribably gracefull.

Having gathered these stories, our next question was how to present this formidable body of material. For three years I had been working with this problem, writing and rewriting. My initial effort was more in the way of a personal chronology, but I found that such a structure did not easily include all the material, and, additionally, it demanded the inclusion of much that seemed irrelevant. So I started again, this time incorporating my personal experiences as merely additional stories and grouping selected stories around various topical headings. The result is the present compilation.

These stories, anecdotes, and quotations create a mosaic through which Maharajji can be met. To hold the components of this mosaic together I have used the absolute minimum of structural cement, preferring to keep out my personal interpretations and perspective as much as possible.

But this strategy of sharing with you the material in its purest form makes precious little compromise for your motivation, for I have excluded the usual seductive story lines that would make you want to read further. I did not want to manipulate your desire to want to read about Maharajji; rather, I merely wanted to make whatever was available to me, available to you. As you will see, Maharajji demanded that all of us make some considerable effort to have his *darshan* (the experience of his presence). I feel that it is in the spirit of his teachings to demand that those readers who would have his darshan through this book make a similar "right" or "real" effort (in the sense spoken of by Buddha in the eightfold path and by George Gurdjieff).

So if you approach this book with the desire to meet him and have his darshan in a way that could profoundly alter your life, as it has ours, then you will want to work with this book slowly and deeply. I can only assure you that in my opinion each story carries some teaching and is worthy of reflection. You will neither want to nor be able to read this book through from cover to cover in one or even a few sittings. Rather, like fine brandy, these recollections must be sipped slowly and the taste and aroma allowed to permeate deeply into your mind and heart. And remember to listen to the silence into which the stories are set, for the true meeting with Maharajji lies between the lines and behind the words. For this effort, you will be amply rewarded through meeting a being of a spiritual stature rarely known on this earth.

It is difficult to separate Maharajji and his teachings from the environment in which I knew him. His form, in its larger sense, is for me India and the beautiful Kumoan Hills and the Ganges—it is his devotees and all their tenderness and bickering; it is his temples and the photographs of him. His teachings were the love of the Earth Mother that I first experienced in the Indian villages—and my dysentery and visa hassles, and the sacred cows and the rickshaw rides, the teeming markets and misty jungle walks. And yet, while the drama of being with him was played out on the rich stage of India, the value of the setting seemed merely as a reservoir of experiences through which the teachings could occur. He himself did not seem particularly Indian, no more Eastern than Western. Although we met him in Hindu temples, he did not seem any more Hindu than Buddhist or Christian.

He used all the stuff of our lives—clothing, food, sleep; fears, doubts, aspirations; families, marriages; sicknesses, births, and deaths—to teach us about living in the spirit. By doing this, he initiated a process through which we could continue to learn from the experiences of our lives even when we were not with him. This accounts at least in part for the continuity in his teachings that we have all experienced since his death.

I hope that through working with these stories, you can tune your perceptions in such a way as to meet and begin a dialogue with Maharajji through the vehicle of your own daily life events. Such a moment-to-moment dialogue, carried on in one's heart, is a remarkable form of alchemy for transforming matter into spirit through love.

I have been hanging out with Maharajji in just this way. And I can't begin to tell you . . .

Soquel, California
March 1979

Acknowledgments

THE MATERIAL in this volume is culled from over two thousand stories about Maharajji gathered during five years from more than one hundred devotees. To these devotees who shared their treasured memories, I wish to express my deep love and appreciation. Some of them felt that no book could or should be written about a being with qualities as vast, formless, and subtle as Maharajji's, and yet they contributed their stories nevertheless. I honor them for this kindness and I hope that in my zeal to share experiences of Maharajji with others who were not fortunate enough to have met him, I have not misused their trust.

Some devotees tell me that stories told by other devotees are not factually accurate. I have no way of ascertaining the authenticity of any single story. All I can report is that those of us who gathered the stories were impressed by the credibility of those of us who told the stories.

Though the responsibility for this manuscript lies *solely* with me, I am delighted to acknowledge a lot of loving help from my friends:

1. Anjani, foremost among these, donated over four months of full-time effort at a point when my confidence in this project was seriously

flagging. Her love for Maharajji touched this manuscript in so many ways.

2. K. K. Sah sent me thick letters from India with page by page and, at times, line by line suggestions for improving the manuscript and avoiding embarrassing cultural errors. His devotion and loving efforts have fed me greatly.

3. Chaitanya helped gather stories in 1973 and again with me during an eventful tour of India in 1976. He critiqued an earlier form of the manuscript, and kindly allowed me to include his poem, "Subtle Is the Path of Love."

4. Saraswati (Rosalie Ransom) toured India and the United States with tape recorder in hand to enrich our story library immeasurably.

5. Krishna Das (Roy Bonney), Rameshwar Das, and Pyari Lal Sah agreed to share riches from their treasury of photographs.

6. Lillian, Sandy, and Jyoti so lovingly typed the manuscript.

7. Ram Dev, Subrahmanyum and Girija, Krishna and Mira, and Soma Krishna provided helpful critiques at early stages of the work.

8. Bill Whitehead edited this book with a sensitivity both to the devotee's intimate love of Maharajji and the reader's newness to him. He remained patient over three years with what seemed to me like changes required from on high, but must have seemed like the machinations of just another neurotic author to him.

I anticipate that many of Maharajji's devotees may not find in this book the Maharajji that they know in their hearts. I can only beg their forbearance, for this book is for those who have never met Maharajji. For those who have, no book is necessary.

At moments the audacity of this undertaking almost overwhelmed me. Knowing the way Maharajji works, however, I proceeded with the faith that there is no way this book could manifest without his blessing.

The symbol ᨆ (Ram), which appears throughout this book, is taken from Maharajii's handwritten diary.

A moment with the Beloved
And the river changes its course.

"... the Bees Come"

WE CAME TO Maharajji's feet, impelled by our yearning for the living spirit and drawn by his light. We came from Europe and Great Britain, the United States and Canada, Australia and South America. As Herman Hesse said of the fellow travelers in his *Journey to the East,* each had his or her own special reason for making the journey but all also shared a common goal. We came with our varying hues of cynicism and faith, open- or closed-heartedness, sensuality or asceticism, intellectual arrogance or humility. To each, Maharajji responded uniquely: now fiercely, now

When the flower blooms, the bees come uninvited.
—RAMAKRISHNA

tenderly; now through ignoring us or sending us away, now through making much over us; now through reading the mind and heart; now through playing dumb. He did what was necessary to quiet the mind and open the heart so that the thirst that had drawn us all to him could be slaked.

I was traveling with a young Western fellow in India. We had come to the mountains in a Land Rover I had borrowed from a friend, in order to find this

1

fellow's guru to get some help with his visa problem. I was in a bad mood,
having smoked too much hashish, been in India "too long," and not
particularly wanting to visit a "guru" anyway.

[*The following is adapted from the book,* Be Here Now.]

We stopped at this temple and he asked where the guru was. The Indians
who had gathered around the car pointed to a nearby hill. In a moment he was
out of the car and running up the hill. They were following him and appeared
delighted to be able to see the guru. I got out of the car. Now I was
additionally upset because everybody was ignoring me. I ran after them,
barefoot, up this rocky path, stumbling all the way. I didn't want to see the
guru anyway and what the hell was this all about?

Around a bend of the path I came to a field overlooking a valley, and in the
field under a tree sat a man in his sixties or seventies with a blanket around
him. Surrounding him were eight or nine Indians. I was aware of the beautiful
tableau—the group, the clouds, the green valley, the visual purity of the
foothills of the Himalayas.

My traveling companion ran to this man and threw himself on the ground,
doing dunda pranam *(full-length prostration). He was crying and the man*
was patting him on the head. I was more and more confused.

I stood to the side, thinking, "I'm not going to touch his feet. I don't have
to. I'm not required to do that." Every now and then this man looked up at me
and twinkled a little. His glances just made me more uncomfortable.

Then he looked at me and started speaking in Hindi, of which I understood
very little. Another man, however, was translating. I heard him ask my
friend, "You have a picture of Maharajji?"

My friend nodded, "Yes."

"Give it to him," said the man in the blanket, pointing at me.

"That's very nice," I thought, "giving me a picture of himself," and I
smiled and nodded appreciatively. But I was still not going to touch his feet.

Then he said, "You came in a big car?"

"Yes." (I hadn't wanted to borrow the car in the first place, not wanting the
responsibility, so the car was a source of irritation for me.)

He looked at me, smiling, and said, "You will give it to me?"

I started to say, "Wha . . ." but my friend looked up from the ground
where he was still lying and said, "Maharajji, if you want it, you can have it.
It's yours."

And I said, "No, now wait a minute. You can't give away David's car like
that." The old man was laughing.

In fact, everyone was laughing—except me.

Then he said, "You made much money in America?"

*I reviewed all my years as a professor and smuggler and very proudly said,
"Yes."*

"How much did you make?"

*"Well," I said, "at one time"— and I sort of upped the figure a bit further
to inflate my ego—"twenty-five thousand dollars."*

*The group converted that into rupees, and everybody was awed by this
figure. All of this was of course bragging on my part. I had never made
twenty-five thousand dollars. And he laughed again and said, "You'll buy a
car like that for me?"*

*I remember what went through my mind at that moment. Although I had
come from a family of Jewish fund-raisers, I had never seen such hustling as
this. "He doesn't even know my name and already he wants a seven-thousand-
dollar vehicle," I thought.*

*"Well, maybe . . ." I said. The whole thing was by now upsetting me
very much.*

*And he said, "Take them away and give them food." And so we were
given magnificent food, and then we were told to rest. Sometime later we were
back with Maharajji and he said to me, "Come here. Sit." So I sat down
facing him and he looked at me and said, "You were out under the stars last
night." (This, of course, was the English translation of what he said.)*

"Um-hum."

"You were thinking about your mother."

*"Yes." (The previous night a few hundred miles away I had gone outside
during the night to go to the bathroom. The stars had been very bright and I
had remained outside, feeling very close to the cosmos. At that time I had
suddenly experienced the presence of my mother, who had died nine months
previously of a spleen condition. It was a very powerful moment, and I had
told no one about it.)*

She died last year."

"Um-hum."

"She got very big in the stomach before she died."

Pause . . . "Yes."

*He leaned back and closed his eyes and said (in English), "Spleen, she died
of spleen."*

*What happened to me at that moment I can't really put into words. He
looked at me in a certain way and two things happened. They do not seem like
cause and effect, but rather appeared to be simultaneous.*

*My mind began to race faster and faster to try to get leverage—to get a hold
on what he had just done. I went through every super-CIA paranoia I'd ever
had: "Who is he? Who does he represent? Where's the button he pushes to*

make the file appear? Why have they brought me here?" None of it would jell.

It was just too impossible that this could have happened this way. My traveling companion didn't know about any of the things Maharajji was saying, and I was a tourist in a car. The whole thing was just inexplicable. My mind went faster and faster.

Until then I had had two models for psychic experiences. One was: "Well it happened to somebody else, and it's very interesting and we certainly must keep an open mind about these things." That was my social-science approach. The other one was: "Well, I'm high on LSD. Who knows how it really is?" After all, I had had experiences under the influence of chemicals in which I had created whole environments.

But neither of these categories applied to this situation, and as my mind went faster I felt like a computer that has been fed an insoluble problem—the bell rings and the red light goes on and the machine stops. My mind just gave up. It burned out its circuitry, its zeal to have an explanation. I needed something to get closure at the rational level and there wasn't anything.

At the same moment I felt this extremely violent pain in my chest and a tremendous wrenching feeling, and I started to cry. I cried and cried and cried, but I was neither happy nor sad. It was a kind of crying I had not experienced before. The only thing I could say about it was it felt as if I had finished something. The journey was over. I had come home. (R.D.)★

राम

In the words of Dada, "We all think we are chasing the guru, but really, you see, he is chasing us."

All I knew about the hardships of India made me sure I didn't want to go there, yet in October of 1971 I found myself at JFK Airport with two friends, waiting to board a plane for Bombay. A large crowd of our New York "spiritual" group had come to see us off, or, as I suspected, to make sure we actually got on the plane. We were all three in varying states of panic, wondering what we were doing. Both the panic and the confusion were to intensify a hundredfold when we actually arrived in India.

We three, like nearly all the group of Westerners we eventually joined around Maharajji, first heard of him through Ram Dass. Yet, though my life totally changed after the night I first heard Ram Dass lecture, I did not feel drawn to go to India. Partially, the mystique of what going to India represented in those days made it seem presumptuous for me to even consider

---

★ (R.D.) denotes story concerning Ram Dass.

the trip. Nor was it clear to me that the power of the awakening I had experienced was, in fact, a connection with Maharajji—that he could possibly be my guru. We had all heard how difficult it was to find him. And what if he sent me away as he had others?

Now, three years later, I was going to India, but I still hadn't the temerity to chance rejection—I was going to see some south Indian saints and perhaps later "visit" up north, if there seemed any hope of being received.

Coming off the plane in Bombay, we were met by an airline representative (in India, a feat in itself), who advised us that we had reservations on an afternoon flight to New Delhi and that tickets were waiting for us at the counter. This was a stunner, but after a twenty-six or twenty-eight-hour flight we were too dazed to feel more than mild wonder. After all, we were in India—anything could happen here. (This mystery of tickets and reservations to Delhi was never solved in any "reasonable" way.) In Delhi, we thought of going to the American Express office to ask for messages, as we had planned to do in Bombay. After all, since we were here, there must be a message. There was: "Go to Jaipuria Bhavan in Vrindaban. Maharajji expected soon." It was signed, "Balaram Das." We didn't know who that was.

We learned that Vrindaban was not far from Delhi and that we could get there by an afternoon train. Somehow we never thought of pausing in the relative Westernness of Delhi. The message said go and go we did. We thereby learned the first great lesson of India: Never travel by third-class unreserved coach! It was the equivalent of a three-hour ride on a New York City subway at rush hour, with the addition of sunshine, dust, and engine smoke pouring in the open windows.

Eventually, we battled our way off the train at Mathura, and in the glowing dusk of the Indian plain, whose beauty we could not then appreciate, we found a bus to take us to nearby Vrindaban. There we were put down in the large bazaar of what to all appearances was a thirteenth-century village of winding alleys full of people, rickshaws, dogs, pigs, and cows. By now it was dark and most of the illumination came from lanterns in the shops lining the streets. We asked for directions to "Jaipuria Bhavan" in our nonexistent Hindi and were directed first up one alley and then down another. It grew later and the shops were beginning to close. Our panic grew with our exhaustion and hunger, for even if we came upon the hostel we would not recognize it, for every sign was in Hindi. We began to envision ourselves huddling for the night among the cows in some doorway.

Then suddenly approaching us appeared a Westerner—someone whom I'd met the year before in California. In hysterical relief, I threw my arms around him, but he, an old-timer in India, was totally calm in the face of our emotion. Oh, yes, Jaipuria Bhavan was just there, around the next bend.

During the next few days, the small Western satsang (community of spiritual seekers) began gathering at Jaipuria Bhavan, awaiting Maharajji's arrival at his Vrindaban ashram (monastery). Many of them we knew from America, including the mysterious "Balaram Das," whom we'd known as Peter. We heard their stories of Maharajji with relief and anticipation. He didn't sound so fierce and terrifying after all. Then word came that he was here! The next morning we could go to have his darshan.

I arrived at the ashram a little late with Radha, nervously clutching my borrowed sari and the offering of flowers and fruit. We circumambulated the temple and pranammed (bowed) to Hanumanji*, then approached the gate in the wall between the temple garden and the ashram. How well I remember that green wooden door! When we knocked, the old chaukidar (gate-keeper) opened it a crack and peered out at us. Then, as each time afterward for as long as I was in India, I wondered if he would let us in. But he stepped back, pulling the door open for us. I looked through, down the vista of the long verandah along the front of the ashram building. At the far end, Maharajji was sitting alone on his wooden bed. When I saw his great form, my heart jumped so that I staggered against the gate. That first sight of him is still piercingly clear in my memory.

Radha had already rushed through and I ran after her, losing my sandals along the way. It was all so simple and familiar—bowing at his feet, giving the fruit and flowers (which he immediately threw back in my lap), weeping and laughing. Maharajji was bouncing, smiling, and crowing in English, "Mother from America! Mother from America!" During that first darshan, though Maharajji spoke mainly in Hindi, I understood everything without the interpreter who stood nearby. And I recognized the love that had poured through Ram Dass, that had irresistibly drawn me to India: Here was the source.

जय

Everybody else was all excited, but I was pretty skeptical about the whole thing. Still, I was the first one off the bus and found myself running immediately into the temple. Even though I'd never been there, I somehow knew all the turns to make in order to get to where Maharajji was. As I came around the corner he started bouncing up and down and exclaiming all these things in Hindi that totally confused me. I came to him and bowed down at his feet.

*Definitions of Sanskrit and Hindi appear in the Glossary.

He began to hit me really very hard. I had both a sense of great confusion and a feeling of the most incredible at-oneness that I've ever felt in my life. He was so totally different from what I had expected yet so familiar at the same time. At that moment I felt all the suffering, all the pain from the last several years dissolve completely. And though the pain was to come back again in the future, the love I felt at that moment made it all a lot less painful later.

I had heard of Maharajji while wandering in India, and I finally found him in Allahabad. My first meeting was in the early morning. Maharajji was in a room on the bed, with a Ma (Indian woman devotee) sitting before him on the floor. There was fruit on the bed. Then out from under the big blanket came this hand. He took some big apples and kept bouncing them off the Ma's chest, but she was totally absorbed in meditation. I sat watching, then suddenly Maharajji looked directly at me. He was like a tree, so grounded, so organic. He flipped me a banana and it landed right in my hand. I wondered what I should do with the banana, a sacred object. I figured it would be best to eat it.

I had come to India from the United States as a devotee in a very intense religious sect—the guru was the *guru, the final and great savior. After only two weeks in his presence, I was clearly disillusioned about him and began to wander about India on my own—still hoping to find the one true and pure guru somewhere. Several times in my wanderings someone would tell me of Maharajji and that he was nearby. But I would not go, as I felt no particular pull. Finally I was down near Bombay, still seeking the true guru, when an old friend showed up. He looked so clear and light that before we even spoke I determined to go to wherever it was he had just come from. He had just left Maharajji in Vrindaban. I packed my bags and was gone that afternoon. Twenty-four hours later I was before Maharajji. There were a number of Westerners there. Maharajji did not speak to me but he kept looking very intently at my heart* chakra (*psychic energy center in the heart area of the body*), *and what I kept hearing, as a voice within me, was that my search was over. I had come home.*

I was sitting for several months in Buddhist meditation in Bodh Gaya. About two-thirds of the way through the second month, this funny-looking little man started to appear in the upper-right-hand corner of my awareness. Every so often he'd smile. I wondered who he was and just watched him come and go. Later I began to suspect that it was Maharajji, whom I'd heard about the year before.

At the end of the retreat I opened a copy of The Hundred Thousand Songs of Milarepa *and a picture of Maharajji fell out. When we finally got to Vrindaban where he was supposed to be, we found the gates of the temple locked. Feeling very sad that I had come all this way only to find the gates locked, I went across the street and sat on the culvert.*

All of a sudden I felt as if Maharajji had come leaping over the wall, for I was completely surrounded and filled with the greatest love I had ever experienced. I burst into tears. People passing by saw this crazy, long-haired Westerner sobbing his guts out. They just looked at me and smiled and continued on.

I didn't know what was going on, but I had the clear sense of being home. There was absolutely no question that I was exactly where I wanted to be. A month before I couldn't have imagined such an experience, but here I was, so relieved, so happy. My heart seemed to have burst open.

Shortly afterward we were allowed into the temple. Maharajji asked me all the usual questions, like who I was and where I was from and what I did. And then suddenly I found myself bowing, with my head at his feet—and feeling totally right about it. And he was patting me on the head, saying something like, "Welcome, glad to see you made it. Welcome aboard." All I wanted to do was to hang onto his feet, and I didn't care at all that this wasn't in any way consistent with my self-image.

My wife had met Maharajji and had come to get me in America and bring me back to meet him. When we first went to see Maharajji I was put off by what I saw. All these crazy Westerners wearing white clothes and hanging around this fat old man in a blanket! More than anything else I hated seeing Westerners touch his feet. On my first day there he totally ignored me. But after the second, third, fourth, fifth, sixth, and seventh day, during which he also ignored me, I began to grow very upset. I felt no love for him; in fact, I felt nothing. I decided that my wife had been captured by some crazy cult. By the end of the week I was ready to leave.

*We were staying at the hotel up in Nainital, and on the eighth day I told
my wife that I wasn't feeling well. I spent the day walking around the lake
thinking that if my wife was so involved in something that was clearly not for
me, it must mean that our marriage was at an end. I looked at the flowers, the
mountains, and the reflections in the lake, but nothing could dispel my
depression. And then I did something that I had really never done in my adult
life. I prayed.*

*I asked God, "What am I doing here? Who is this man? These people are
all crazy. I don't belong here."*

*Just then I remembered the phrase, "Had ye but faith ye would not need
miracles."*

"Okay, God, I don't have any faith. Send me a miracle."

*I kept looking for a rainbow but nothing happened, so I decided to leave the
next day.*

*The next morning we took a taxi down to Kainchi to the temple, to say
good-bye. Although I didn't like Maharajji, I thought I'd just be very honest
and have it out with him. We got to Kainchi before anyone else was there and
we sat in front of his* tucket *(wooden bed) on the porch. Maharajji had not yet
come out from inside the room. There was some fruit on the tucket and one of
the apples had fallen on the ground, so I bent over to pick it up. Just then
Maharajji came out of his room and stepped on my hand, pinning me to the
ground. So there I was on my knees touching his foot, in that position I
detested. How ludicrous!*

*He looked down at me and asked, "Where were you yesterday?" Then he
asked, "Were you at the lake?" (He said "lake" in English.)*

*When he said the word "lake" to me I began to get this strange feeling at
the base of my spine, and my whole body tingled. It felt very strange.*

He asked me, "What were you doing at the lake?"

I began to feel very tight.

Then he asked, "Were you horseback riding?"

"No."

"Were you boating?"

"No."

"Did you go swimming?"

"No."

*Then he leaned over and spoke quietly, "Were you talking to God? Did
you ask for something?"*

*When he did that I fell apart and started to cry like a baby. He pulled me
over and started pulling my beard and repeating, "Did you ask for
something?"*

That really felt like my initiation. By then others had arrived and they were around me, caressing me, and I realized then that almost everyone there had gone through some experience like that. A trivial question, such as, "Were you at the lake yesterday?" which had no meaning to anyone else, shattered my perception of reality. It was clear to me that Maharajji saw right through all the illusions; he knew everything. By the way, the next thing he said to me was, "Will you write a book?"

That was my welcome. After that I just wanted to rub his feet.

॰ॐ॰

It was in London. I was on a bus with many empty seats. Then an old man carrying a blanket got on the bus and chose to sit on the window seat beside me, so that I had to stand up to let him in. This annoyed me somewhat, but as he sat down he gave me such a sweet, gentle smile that I forgot my annoyance and sat thinking to myself, "What a sweet old man." Before the bus came to the next stop on its route I turned to look at him again—but he was gone!

The bus had not stopped again since he had gotten on. How could he have gotten off without my standing to let him pass?

Later I went to India on the advice of a friend who had been there, and I saw a picture of Maharajji—it was the same man! I located Maharajji and found out that on the day I had seen him on the bus in London carrying a specific plaid blanket, a woman in India had given Maharajji just such a blanket, which he was wearing that same day.

THE INDIANS ALSO came to Maharajji with varying degreees of desire and readiness. But for them it was different. They had grown up in a culture in which holy beings abounded, and the parents of most of them had had gurus. For the family, the guru was a combination of grandfather, worldly and spiritual guide, and reflection or manifestation of God. They often treated Maharajji more as a man and less as a God, and yet at the same time they could surrender more easily to him. For them, surrender was not a personal matter of ego as it was for us. In the group of stories about initial meetings described by some of Maharajji's closest Indian devotees, both the differences of culture and the similarity of opening and love are apparent.

I have known Maharajji since I came into this world. My father and mother were both devotees—my father since 1940 and my mother since 1947. Because our parents were devotees and because he was always being discussed in our family, we were all born devotees of him.

ॐ

I first met Maharajji in Bhowali many years ago. Maharajji frequently visited a certain Ma's home there. I told her that I had heard about him but had never met him, and I asked her to tell me the next time he came. After a week or so Maharajji came at night. In the morning a message came for me and I went at once. I found him lying on a cot. He looked at me, then closed his eyes for a moment. He knew at once who I was, who I had been before, and what I was going to do in this world. In a few seconds, he said, "I am very pleased to see you," which he repeated many times. Maharajji had walked from Nainital to Bhowali during the night. He said, "You have brought me here! I shall see you again in Haldwani." Then Maharajji boarded a bus for Almora. (In those days he traveled mostly by bus, not by car.) People warned me not to take him seriously: "Neem Karoli is a big liar. He very seldom tells the truth. You can't depend on him."

In any case, I went to Haldwani. After a few days someone came to my room and told me that Maharajji had come to Haldwani and gave me his address. I saw him then and have been with him ever since.

ॐ

I first met Maharajji in 1950 when I rode with my boss and Maharajji from Nainital to Haldwani. My boss, a government minister, was already a devotee of Maharajji's and had offered him this lift. But I was smoking and acting as if Maharajji was just another person. In 1958, after the death of my mother, I was in Bhowali with my father, on vacation. We spent a night in the government rest house there and my father became ill in the night, in much pain. They called the Bhowali doctor who gave him an injection but to no avail. The next day, doctors from Nainital came and said that he needed an emergency gall bladder operation. That same day I went to consult doctors at the nearby TB sanitorium. Preparations were then underway for a puja (ritual of prayer) to celebrate the opening of a small Hanuman temple built by the doctor there who was a devotee of Maharajji. I stayed on to watch. Maharajji arrived but stayed hidden. I grew curious to meet him. I heard that Maharajji had put someone in a trance, so I watched a while from a distance before leaving.

That evening a messenger from the Nainital bus station came to me and told me to visit a certain Baba Neem Karoli. Since there are so many babas, I dismissed the message. But at night I went to the bus station and inquired as to who had sent this message, but no one knew. This aroused my curiosity even more. I asked where I could find this Baba Neem Karoli and went there. Maharajji said to me, "Your name is so-and-so and your father is very ill."

"Yes."

"You thought he might die, but God has cured him. Doctors have told you that he should be operated on. But he shouldn't be. He'll be all right."

Maharajji gave me two or three mangos for my father, which I fed to him and he began to improve. After a few days Maharajji again called me. I went but didn't touch his feet. I was planning to return to Delhi and Maharajji said, "You're going to Delhi. You drive too fast. Take your father carefully and he'll be all right." This touched my heart and I touched Maharajji's feet. My father never had the operation and became very healthy, with no relapse.

श्री

Since I wasn't married, I was living with my brother and his wife. When Maharajji came to them I went into the farthest room so I wouldn't have to be involved with such people, for I thought, "Sadhus [renunciates] are no good." After some time Maharajji came into the room where I was. He walked in, sat down, and said, "Sadhus are no good." After that I just became a devotee.

ONE OF Maharajji's closest devotees for the last twenty years gives the following account:

In 1935 I was on vacation from school and went to Dakshineshwar on a religious pilgrimage. When I reached the place where there were many Shiva temples, a man appeared before me whom I had not noticed to be there before.

"My son," the man said, "You are a Brahmin? I shall give you a mantra."

"I will not take it," I said, "I do not believe in it."

"You must take it," he insisted, and so I relented.

Thereafter, I faithfully recited the mantra daily. Many years passed.

It was June 1955. I had some close friends who were like members of the family. Every Sunday we'd chat in the evening at our house. Around 9:00 P.M. I saw my wife, aunt, and mother going out. I asked them where they were going, and they said just to an adjacent house, that some baba was visiting. One of the fellows with me said cynically, "Does he eat? I can arrange food for him." (This fellow was a hunter.)

My wife said, "You should not say things like that."

In ten minutes they returned. They reported that he had been sitting in a dirt hut with an oil lamp and had told them to go. When they didn't go, he said, "Go! Your husband's Bengali friends have come. Go and serve them tea. I shall come in the morning."

In the morning my wife and I went over together. Maharajji was on a small cot in a tiny room. As we entered he sprang up and took my hand, saying, "Let's go." We left so fast that my wife had to remove her sandals to keep up. He took us to our own house and said, "I shall stay with you." When the women from the other house came to take him back he would not go.

Later he questioned me: "You are a devotee of Shiva?"

"Yes."

"You already have a mantra." It was at that moment that I realized it had been Maharajji who had given me the mantra twenty years before.

॥ॐ॥

My first meeting with him in Kanpur was short and sweet—perhaps only two minutes. I pranammed to him. He asked me who I was and gave me his blessing and left abruptly. Where he went, nobody could say.

I met him again ten months or a year later in Lucknow. One by one, he sent the many people who were sitting with him away until only we three were left. Then he asked my sister-in-law, "What do you want?" She said she'd come only to pay her respects.

Then he asked me, and I replied, "I only need your blessings, nothing more."

Then he said to my wife, "You have come with positive questions. Why don't you ask them?"

In fact she had come with some questions, which she hadn't even confided in us. But she had made a decision beforehand not to ask the questions herself. She wanted Maharajji to answer them unasked, and she wanted it done in private, so she didn't speak. She couldn't answer that she didn't have questions, but because of her decision she couldn't ask them. So Maharajji said to her, "You want me to answer your questions without your asking. And you want me to tell you when you are alone. You are putting a sadhu to a very hard test. Tomorrow I will come to your house in Kanpur and answer your questions." We sat there a few minutes more and then he said, "Go!" As we *were leaving a doubt came to my mind that Maharajji had just sidetracked us by saying he'd visit us tomorrow and answer the questions.*

At about ten o'clock that evening a message came to our house for a Maharajji devotee who was visiting us. The message was that Babaji (familiar form of Baba) was coming to the devotee's house and he should return home right away. We accompanied him. As soon as I pranammed to Maharajji, he said, "You doubted my integrity! Never doubt a sadhu—the burden is on him, not on you. You have not to doubt." I apologized to him. I had indeed doubted. Then he said, "All right, tomorrow I'll come to your place."

So the next morning he came over. As this was his first visit, I really didn't know what to do. Others told me that nothing is to be done—just provide a big pillow on a bed for him to lean on and offer some food or fruit or milk. He'll take whatever he feels like. It's his sweet will.

When he arrived I escorted him to the sitting room. He said, "No, I won't sit there. Let the others sit there; you take me to that small room!" I was surprised and confused, since I did not know which small room he was referring to. He gave a description of the room and walked through the house as if he knew where the room was. I was following him, not leading him, in our house. He went straight to the room and said, "Here I want to sit." He said, "Call Ma" (my wife). She came, and he then answered all the questions she had in her mind. "Is there any question to which I haven't replied?" he asked. She had to say that there were no more.

जय

An ICS (Indian Civil Service) commissioner of Lucknow used to drink ferociously. The superintendent of police said to Maharajji that they should go visit him. Maharajji agreed, and when they arrived the commissioner had a bottle hidden behind him. Maharajji yelled from the car, "What's the matter?"

The commissioner was furious. He screamed at the superintendent: "Who have you brought here? He has no manners! Get him out of here."

The superintendent opened his holster and was about to shoot the commissioner for talking to Maharajji that way. But Maharajji blew up: "What are you doing? He is a great saint! You see only his outside. I'll never come with you again."

The commissioner later became a great devotee. He would come for darshan but sit outside by the shoes for he felt that was his place. He eventually became head of the Administrative Officer School in Allahabad.

He suffered from thrombosis. At the end he suffered great agony but kept Ram mantra (repetition of Ram, a name of God) going and was very gay. The superintendent was in tears when he visited him near the end, and he asked, "Should I call your wife and son?"

The commissioner said, "No, this is not a time of attachment. At this time, all I have to do is remember Ram and Maharajji. Good-bye. We'll meet again." And he died.

I had wanted to meet Maharajji for a long time but could never catch him. Finally a friend came and took me in his company car to where Maharajji was supposed to be. There were four rooms and Maharajji was in the far room. I went in. The minute I entered, Majarajji said, "Get out, you!"

So I went out and sat down but wouldn't leave. I sat for many hours. Finally my friend had to return the car because it was closing time. Although my house was quite distant, I was determined to stay and have Maharajji's full darshan. Finally someone took pity and said, "You aren't doing it right. When some people start to go in, you go in with them, and if he throws you out, wait and try again with the next people." I did so and was twice thrown out. Finally, the third time, Maharajji said, "Come sit here. What is your name and what do you do?" Then he said, "Okay, now go."

But I said, "I'm not going. I haven't had darshan yet. I haven't had a chance to discuss my problems with you."

Maharajji said, "Go now and come at 6:00 A.M." So I went home but I couldn't sleep, and at 2:00 A.M. I got up and did puja. I was afraid Maharajji would leave before I got there. When I arrived at the house at 6:00 A.M. Maharajji had already left, but they said he would return. After some time he did come back and then Maharajji and I spent many hours together. In fact, the rest of my life has been spent with Maharajji.

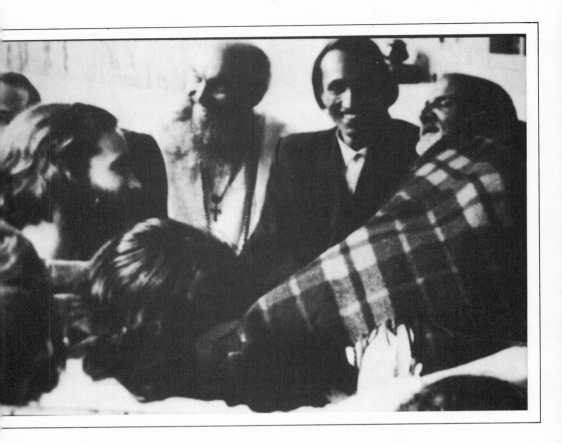

Darshan

A MEETING OF THE SPIRIT

Not everyone who met Maharajji was "opened" or "awakened" at the initial visit. Many came, enjoyed a pleasant visit, and left apparently unaffected. They seemed to have "no business" with Maharajji, that is, they were either unready to be touched so deeply, or the vehicle of the guru or this particular guru was not their way.

Balaram (to a new arrival on the verandah at Vrindaban): "Have you had Maharajji's darshan yet?"
"I don't know. Is he the fat one sitting over there?"

Then there were those who while experiencing no dramatic "zap," yet responded to some subtle thread that drew them back to Majarajji again and again.

I was astonished to watch the way in which tough people would melt as they stayed around Maharajji.

17

For many of us who were either dramatically opened initially or subtly drawn, the desire that became uppermost in our lives was to be with Maharajji. We had become "devotees," for when we were with him we were experiencing being "at home" in the heart of God. Little wonder that his presence became so addictive and that we would leave home and go to any lengths to be with this spiritual pied piper who was teaching us to dance and play in the fields of the Lord.

But to assume that just because you wished to be with Maharajji, you could be, did not take into account the nature of this man's behavior. He moved about unpredictably. And whenever he stayed in any one place for even a few days, people would arrive in a continuous stream from morning till night. Some came barefoot with naked babies from nearby farms; others came by jet and taxi.

I was standing in the front yard of a humble house in a little village in the hills when Maharajji arrived unexpectedly. I was told to remain outside, so I had the opportunity to watch the people come. They seemed to appear almost out of nowhere, arriving from all directions. They were running, some of the women wiping the flour from their hands on their aprons, others carrying their babies half dressed. The men had left their shops unattended. Some were pulling flowers from the trees as they came to have something to offer . . . But they came with an expectancy, with a joy, with a reverence, that could not be mistaken. (R.D.)

ॐ

True, many wanted something worldly from the "miracle baba," but beyond that they wanted once again to taste of the nectar of being with him.

Many of us vacillated in our reactions to this constant demand upon Maharajji. At one moment we saw ourselves and the other devotees and seekers as so many vultures around a piece of raw meat or like flies crawling over a piece of sugar. At those times we tried to protect him, and often we held back so as not to contribute to the scene.

But at other times we would realize how totally Maharajji had control of the situation. When he felt that people were, as he put it, "eating his head," he would simply go into a back room and close the door, or send everyone away, or get in a car and leave without a backward glance. Once, after traveling many months to see Maharajji, we at last found

him at a devotee's home in Delhi. We were allowed into the back room
with him for a few minutes and then were sent out to have tea with
many others. About fifteen minutes later Maharajji walked out of the
inner room and right by us, not more than two feet from our faces, with
not the least turn of the head or signal of recognition. He went to a car
in which a driver was waiting, he got in, and the car left for a destination
unknown. Such a person was clearly not at our mercy!

So Maharajji kept continually on the move, in a totally unpredictable
fashion. Within a temple compound he would move from place to place,
at one moment freely available, while at the next closeted in some room
with the door securely bolted.

Were that his only movement, devotees could settle in near the temple
and just visit each day and wait for the moments when he would appear.
But his movement was not limited to a single compound. Rather, he
wandered from village to village, from the mountains to the plains, from
one end of India to the other, from temples to private homes to jungle
ashrams. In the middle of the night he might leave unannounced for a
destination unknown. Or he might board a train and supposedly be des-
tined for a certain city, only to leave the train at some other station,
sometimes so quickly, even as the train was moving, that devotees who
had followed him were left behind.

The intense desire of the devotees to be with Maharajji, combined
with his elusive and unpredictable behavior, gave rise to the most intricate dramas of hide and seek, labeled by one waggish devotee as the
"great grace race."

Being a devotee of Maharajji was like participating in a continuous
and unending treasure hunt, limited only by economic resources or family
responsibilities. The pot of gold was, of course, darshan with Maharajji.
And gold it was! One Indian devotee put it succinctly when he said,
"Even sexual intercourse with my wife cannot equal darshan with Maharajji."

The Indian devotees had an intricate communication system that allowed them at least thirty percent of the time to trace Maharajji and
know of his whereabouts within a day of his arrival in any town or
village. We Westerners were not so lucky, and so we had to use our
wits, our intuitions, our cunning—and our unmitigated gall—to get to
his feet. Our percentage of success was perhaps not so impressive as that
of the Indian devotees, but our style and our dramatic entrances and
exits certainly were.

I was having Maharajji's darshan and all of a sudden Tukaram walked up. I asked Tukaram how he had gotten in and he said, "Oh, I jumped over the wall." And I thought, "Oh, God! Well, I won't be here for long." Then Krishna Priya climbed in. The chaukidar saw her clambering over the wall and since he didn't want to take the blame for letting them in, he went to tell Maharajji. The gate-keeper said, "Baba, these people climbed over the wall. I'm sorry. I did the best I could to keep them out." Maharajji's initial reaction to the chaukidar's report was rage: "Get 'em out! Get 'em all out!" I got thrown out, too. We Westerners shared the guilt among us. We came back the next day for darshan and discovered that overnight the wall had been doubled in height.

MANY LEVELS—MANY CHANGES

WHEN YOU FINALLY arrived at the right place at the right time and were told, "Yes, he's here," and found yourself seated before him, what was it like? Even the tongues and hands of the gods and goddesses of speech, music, and poetry could not do justice to those occasions. So how could I? Like the blind men with the elephant, each devotee met a different Maharajji.

When Maharajji came out you never knew what to expect. He could do the same thing a week in a row until you'd think, "Well, he'll come out at 8:00." Then he might not come out all day, or he might just go into another room and close the door and be in there for two days. You had to learn to expect the unexpected.

One day he came out and all he said all day long was "Thul-Thul, Nan-Nan," repeating these words to himself like a mantra. Days went by like this and somebody finally said, "Maharajji, what are you saying?" And it turned out to be an old Behari dialect and all it meant was "Too big, too big, too little, too little." When he was finally asked why he was saying this, he said, "Oh, all you people, you all live in Thul-Thul, Nan-Nan; you live in the world of judgment. It's always too big or too little."

ॐ

You can never know, as you sit before Maharajji, who it is that he is working with in the course of a darshan. He may be talking with one person

*while another is being deeply moved in some special way. You yourself can't
know what you are receiving from him.*

जय

*One aspect of being with Maharajji that struck me and a lot of people was
the multileveled nature of the experience. We would just be sitting with him and
seemingly nothing much would be happening. We'd be having tea, and
sometimes he would throw some fruit around, or somebody would come and say
a few words. It was all very low-key, but we'd be watching everything that he
would do, taking the most extreme delight in the tilt of his head or the
movement of his arms. At the same time that we would experience an
incredible light joy, we'd also have the sensation that we were in the midst of a
raging fire.*

जय

*People are sitting quietly around Maharajji, concentrating. Maharajji faces
the opposite direction of a person when he picks up on a loose thought and
then he rolls to face the person. With an expression of annoyance and love, he
raises one finger or shakes his fist. If someone is meditating, he tweaks his nose
or pulls his beard. He turns to a person and tells her that she is very good.
Another he maligns, telling all sorts of bad stories. Again he turns to another
and says, "Go. You wicked person!"*

AND THE WORDS and apples and tea and silences and laughter were all
washed in a continuous river of love that poured forth from Maharajji.
The devotees who "knew" were equally as happy with Maharajji's insults as with his praise, for it was all palpable love and food for the
spirit.

We took our cue in this respect from one of Maharajji's long-term,
trusted devotees, called "Dada," who served Maharajji with a singleness
of purpose that awed us. When Maharajji would compliment him, Dada
would say, "Ha, Baba," meaning, "Yes, Baba," and when Maharajji
would shout insults at him, sometimes upbraiding him from morning
till night, he would reply, in exactly the same tone, "Ha, Baba!" Obviously, fame and shame were one to him, at least when Maharajji was
the source. No longer could Maharajji get Dada angry or guilty; over
the years it had all been burned out. For Dada, it was all grace.

Sometimes Maharajji would talk to one person and everyone else would listen, perfectly content just to be present.

THERE WAS THE sport of watching the newcomers arrive, skeptical, with questions, and then seeing their hearts gently open and their soft, flowerlike quality emerge under the tender care of the master gardener. We would sit in those groups as Maharajji turned this way and that, attending now to a person at his side and the next moment to a devotee far distant who was just entering the temple; and as he changed the mood of the group from easy laughter to fierce intensity in a moment and then back again. One felt at such times as if Maharajji were the puppeteer and we the puppets.

Maharajji's company was very special. He was always natural, like a child, a saint in the traditional manner. He set no conditions nor expected any particular behavior from his devotees. He was rarely affected by the outside. He could converse with half a dozen people simultaneously with a camera held a foot from his face. He had no form. He performed no rituals or puja. He followed no orthodox customs such as ritual bathing. Yet his presence was more than inspiring; it was enlightening. While meditating in or near his presence, even though he'd be talking and joking loudly, one quickly reached the place of clear light, a place difficult to achieve without his grace and power.

TIMELESS DARSHANS

MAHARAJJI OFTEN counseled the Indian devotees to sit in silence; just to sit, listen, and absorb. But around Maharajji that was difficult to do, for there was a continuous and compelling drama going on around him: who came, who went; what they said; what food was being distributed; who got to sit closest to him; how he was working with each person; which person he petted and which he yelled at; how he moved about on the tucket. One Indian told us that those of us who did not speak Hindi were lucky, because it kept us from getting too involved. When there was a little silence or when you could detach yourself from the melodrama, you could just bask in the timeless grace of his presence.

The minute you meet him, if you are ready, he will plant himself within you—the seed. And time is nothing.

ॐ

You'd forget everything when you were with him. There would be nothing but Maharajji—total, effortless worship. That's the real puja.

ॐ

Sometimes we would sit up so late at night in Kainchi, talking with Maharajji, that we would lose all sense of time until we would hear someone taking their morning bath, and we would realize that the whole night was gone.

ॐ

It was one of those darshans, where you think somebody must have put LSD in the tea.

ॐ

We would bask in his radiance.

ॐ

Actually you can be more truly with Maharajji when you are away from his form. At a distance you can concentrate on him undisturbed.

DARSHANS OF INTIMACY

FOR OTHERS WHAT stands out is the precious intimacy that comes from experiencing another being within the same space that your own being occupies, the whisper of a lover who knows your innermost heart.

Maharajji never preached, never lectured; he spoke within your heart. With him one automatically knew everything. It came through the heart, not by reading books.

Ten or twenty of us would sit in the back of the ashram at Kainchi, talking with Maharajji. One of us would say, "But, Maharajji, what about so-and-so?" asking some question about God or life. Maharajji would start talking and pretty soon everybody would be in tears. Sometimes he'd start talking about Christ and start crying himself.

He and I never really had much going on the verbal level. But inside, I felt so much love that I'd hang around; when I'd leave I wouldn't go very far—and I would always come back. It was like that with a lot of people.

Maharajji reached each person's heart in a way special to that person. Everyone's experience with him was different. You cannot explain what it is like to be with him. It is a thing to be felt in your heart.

He was so gentle that you weren't afraid of him at all. But sometimes you'd think that there must be a lion in there.

Three or four young Western women were at Krishna's birthday. While everyone was singing kirtan *in the temple before* Lakshmi–Narayan, *they went over to Maharajji's window, which was shuttered from inside, and began softly singing a song about the baby* Krishna *(an incarnation of Vishnu),* Devakinandana Gopala. *After some time, Maharajji opened the shutters and angrily told them to go away and slammed the shutters again. This scene was repeated several times while the young women continued softly singing. Finally Maharajji again opened the shutters, only this time he had tears streaming down his face and he listened in a state of* bhava *(spiritual emotion) for quite some time.*

Remember where Casteneda talks about stopping the world? Sometimes Maharajji would do things to you and you'd feel like he'd just stopped the world. Sometimes you'd be listening and sometimes not, and then suddenly Maharajji would do something and you'd hang suspended. There was one period in my life when I used to keep whole scrapbooks all about horses. No one else knew about them. And once when my mind was somewhere else, Maharajji turned to me and asked me about horses. My mind just stopped.

Every time my mind wandered Maharajji would catch me. He would never miss. When I wavered from the concentration in the least bit, he would catch me and put me back.

Maharajji was sitting on the tucket and he leaned over and kissed Kabir on the head. That kiss affected everyone who was there. It made people feel really warm inside.

Every time Maharajji would hug somebody, everybody in the room would go, "Ahhhhh . . ."

DARSHANS OF LOVE

All the love and affection and kindness that came from Maharajji—you cannot get these from man.

How can you describe what it was to be with Maharajji? It is like trying to describe the sweetness of a fruit or the fragrance of a rose.

You never have met one so lovable, so kind, so sweet. How could you not love him?

You almost wanted to give up your breath to him if you could.

A devotee asked me if I had ever been caught by Maharajji's glance in a way that, as he briefly looked at me, I forgot everything but knew only Maharajji's love. The devotee said it is a wonderful and rare thing when he looks at you in that way, and you are very fortunate if you can hold his gaze in that state.

He could go through your heart with just a look or a movement. The slightest thing could feel as if it were piercing you.

I was leaving for Nepal the next day. It was evening and we were sitting in the back of the ashram. Maharajji never actually mentioned my leaving the next day because I had received a "quit India" notice, but at the end of the darshan he just held my eyes with his. It was the guru's glance, a look of absolute, universal, total compassion; it was love beyond words. Not long, but just—my being in his being. And that filled me with such—what's the word for that feeling?—grief or longing or . . . I felt in that look infinite compassion, and even though the glance didn't last very long, its power still comes through to me, particularly at very difficult times.

I was only about sixteen when I first met Maharajii. It was a bhandara *(feast) and many people were there. When I met him I was filled with such bhava, transported, it seemed, by divine love. Maharajii instructed me to serve the devotees at the bhandara. There were many to be fed, and we worked long hours, but that feeling never left me.*

ॐ

When asked what he experienced on meeting Maharajji, one man replied, "It is not something that can be said. It must be experienced. The love, the affection, the compassion, the grace of knowing him . . ."

TALKING AT DARSHANS

He would talk, talk with no limit and with no rhyme or reason. If he was abusing someone, he would go on shouting with no end. But he was hearing everything. What an intoxication! He would behave like a very abnormal man, doing all sorts of nonsense, shouting and abusing.

But what made you stay there? You wouldn't be conscious of time and space. You never questioned where you were or why you were there. Days and months would pass with him, and they seemed like a moment. Sometimes I wasn't aware that I had not eaten or slept for days, and he made me do things I wouldn't do in the normal course. If I wanted to leave him, he'd make me stay; if I wanted to stay another night, he'd force me to go.

ॐ

He was always rattling on like a child, talking about this and that, most of which wasn't translated. It was like seeing a fine foreign movie where you don't really need the subtitles!

ॐ

In some instances he would say a thing only once. If you didn't catch it, it was gone.

One Westerner was sitting in front of the Hanuman murti in Vrindaban. She was very much longing to see Maharajji, but in those days he was refusing to allow Westerners in for darshan. She sat there, head bowed, singing some kirtan. Just then there was some flurry of excitement. She looked up and there, standing directly in front of her, smiling so very sweetly, was Maharajji. Then to her delight he cocked his head and said in English, "Too much!"

Several Westerners were recalling Maharajji's "hit parade" of English phrases. A few were: coconut; right face, quick, march! left, right, go!; sit down; bus has come; sometimes; damn fool; commander-in-chief; thank you; stand up; water.

When you were with Maharajji you talked about what he wanted to talk about. If you started your topic, Maharajji would ignore it or change it.

There was no conversation around Maharajji other than with him.

Maharajji talked about irrelevancies as if they were very important.

Maharajji would talk to one and be hitting another and only the one who was supposed to would understand.

Maharajji showed great interest in everything, just like an ordinary man. He had no pretensions, yet nobody could decieve him.

WITH THE Westerners the talk usually included a series of routines. With many of them Maharajji developed special routines, and the particular individual would be called to the front, day after day, to perform the same dialogue. To one young woman he would ask each day the same questions: "What are Indian women like? Why are they good?"

She would reply each day with the same answer: "Because they are devoted to their husbands."

To another devotee he would ask again and again, "Will you marry?"

The devotee would always reply, "Maharajji, how can I marry. I'm so useless."

To another, "What is your name?"

"Chaitanya Maha Prabhu" (the name of a great Indian saint), which Maharajji would then repeat and cock his head appreciatively.

He had trained us well as performing humans. One devotee commented about all this: "Maharajji had his zoo and we were all inmates."

And then there was *arti,* the ceremony of light. It is a ceremony for honoring the guru. A flame is waved before the guru, and it is accompanied by a chant that enunciates the guru's many qualities. Under the tutelage of K. K. Sah (one of the long-time Indian devotees), we had learned the entire Sanskrit chant and how to perform the ceremony in order to "surprise" Maharajji. When we finally performed the arti, Maharajji was seemingly so delighted that he made us perform it over and over again, even though while we did it he talked continuously to one or another of those gathered about him. And from that time on, whenever a new group of Indian devotees came to pay their respects we were trotted out from the rear of the ashram to perform arti and thus show how spiritual the Westerners really were. Through these many repetitions we learned much. Initially we had wanted to please and impress Maharajji. Later the prayer became just more spiritual materialism. But through that constant repetition, we came to appreciate how a ritual can take on a life of its own and generate a spiritual power independent of the specific reason for which it is being performed at any one time.

CHIDING AND PLAYFULNESS AT DARSHANS

One of Maharajji's devotees was eighty years old and very spry, like a mountain goat. One day he came in for Maharajji's darshan when a young, distant relative of his was also there. The relative pranammed to the old devotee but didn't get up. Maharajji turned to the elder and said, "If you had money, he'd get up and touch your feet."

Once a devotee wore a new and expensive sari to darshan. Maharajji said, "You know, Ma, I went to this wealthy family for a visit, but they wore such simple clothes that you couldn't tell the difference between the rich ones and the poor ones. So simple and clean."

One evening, Maharajji was out squatting on a dirty street when along came some "important" people—poets, judges, and officials. As they stood around Maharajji, he asked them, "Why don't you sit?" With some hesitation they sat down on the street. Immediately Maharajji arose. "Okay, let's go."

I had purchased some apples in Mathura to take as prasad (an offering, usually food, which became consecrated when accepted by Maharajji) for Maharajji. They were costly and I had hand-picked them. When I offered them, Maharajji said, "Put them away. I'll eat them later." I wouldn't do it, because of my pride, so I peeled the first and it was rotten, and so with the second and third and fourth. Maharajji looked at me and said, "I told you to put them away." I discovered later that the other five were fine.

I was working in Agra and whenever Maharajji came to Vrindaban I would take him ten or fifteen rupees' worth of prasad. I would see others coming with so much more that, one Sunday, I felt quite bad because I could only bring so little. Monday morning I was waiting to touch his feet before going off to work and I thought to myself, "With my limits, my ten rupees are worth ten thousand of someone else's." Just then Maharajji came out of his room saying,

"Strange people come to me and offer ten rupees and say they have offered ten thousand."

ॐ

There was one expression he would never allow me to catch with my camera. He'd be sitting normally and then all of a sudden he would straighten up and look directly down at you, his eyes wide open and intense. I tried for months to catch that expression. I'd take a photograph, but in the time it took to advance the reel he'd return to normal, giggling and laughing. He'd look at me and smile with delight at my frustration. (I wish I'd had motor-drive!)

ॐ

Once he walked over to me and took my bamboo staff and began to do this Chaplinesque dance with it. He moved it back and forth as if he had never seen a stick before, as if he were a large monkey. He started playing with it and moving it around; then he just threw it away and walked down the road! That was the end of that darshan! I was the only one who saw this happen.

ॐ

One morning the coals in the brazier in front of Maharajji had gotten really low, so they piled some wood on it and of course the wood started to smoke and wouldn't light. So Maharajji said they should pour some kerosene on it, which they did, but still it didn't light. Big clouds of smoke were coming up. Maharajji was leaning forward, looking, and then all of a sudden POW! The flames leaped right up to the roof. Maharajji jumped back, as delighted as a child, giggling and clapping his hands. He was so thrilled.

ॐ

One day I got to the ashram very early and I was just sitting over on the porch. Some man arrived carrying a gun. Of course Maharajji said, "Bring it over. Let me see that rifle." So the man opened up the barrel and checked the chamber to make sure it wasn't loaded. Even though it was a shotgun, broken in the middle, he wanted to make sure it wasn't loaded. Maharajji took it and opened it up, and then he snapped it shut and held it up to his shoulder as you would to shoot it. He played a while, opening it up and snapping it shut, then gave it back to the man and sent him away. After the man had left, he asked, "Why does he carry a gun?"

I said, "I don't know." My standard answer.

And Maharajji said, "He carries it because he's afraid of things."

PURITY OF DARSHANS

In the winter of 1971 it started getting very crowded and Maharajji began telling people to go to different places. I was told to go to Puri. He also said I could go and see Goenka (a well-known Buddhist meditation teacher) on the way back. I had been feeling that I really needed to learn something about meditation, so I went to Bodh Gaya and stayed there for forty days. During that time my mind was exceeedingly clear, like nothing I'd ever experienced before.

When I came back to Dada's house Maharajji was there. I don't know if I was experiencing my love for him in a new way or if my heart was closed. Maybe both. But all I was seeing was a man doing all these different things, and I felt none of that love connection I had felt before. There was a clearness and an openness but none of that emotionality and warmth. I stayed there two or three days and kept waiting for the return of that feeling I'd felt before. And I saw all these people opening in a way that I missed. I prayed to Maharajji and it still didn't change.

I decided I'd go to the Sangam (holy place at the confluence of three sacred rivers). While I was there, I prayed that after bathing my heart would open again. And as I was bathing I felt my heart open wide. I got out and everywhere I looked, everything was glowing. I got into a rickshaw to go back to Dada's house—and I realized that I had no prasad. And the route from the Sangam to Dada's doesn't go by any bazaars. We did pass a calendar walla (vendor) with those devotional calendar pictures. I looked at all the pictures but they were so gauche. Just as I was giving up, I looked down at my feet and there on the ground in the dust was a picture of Ram embracing Hanuman, which was so exquisite. I bought the picture and went on to Dada's house. I was late so I didn't think there would be time for me to reach Maharajji and present the prasad. But as I came through the door a path opened up right to Maharajji. I was so opened up from the meditation course and the Sangam that I gave the prasad without my ego. It was the purest act I'd ever done around

Maharajji. Something was taking place, but I was not "doing" it. I put the picture on the tucket and sat down. Maharajji picked it up and looked at it. Tears started coming out of his eyes, and I started to cry, too. Then he stood up and stormed out of the room, giving the picture to Dada. A few weeks later this picture was up in the Vrindaban temple, right next to the murti.

The point of the story is that because I was able to do that selflessly, he was able to accept it fully. At other times I came with all kinds of prasad and I would really want him to accept it in a certain way—and he would hardly look at it. I'd polish up the apples for hours, hold them on the bus, say mantras over them; I was trying to be pure. But this time I wasn't trying to be pure; the purity was simply there.

TOUCHING HIS FEET

"I TAKE THE DUST from the lotus feet of the guru to cleanse the mirror of my mind." So begins a sacred ode to Hanuman. Touching, holding, rubbing the guru's feet has always had profound significance in the Hindu tradition. For out of the guru's feet comes the spiritual elixir, the soma, the nectar, the essence of the sacred Ganges River—the subtle *pran,* or energy that heals and awakens. To touch the feet of such a being is not only to receive this grace, but it is an act of submission, of surrender to God, for that is what the guru represents on earth.

But for those of us around Maharajji, the theories connected with the spiritual value of touching the guru's feet had little if anything to do with the matter. Rather it was the strangest pull of the heart. A mother, who with her husband had come to India from the United States out of concern for the well-being of her son who was deeply devoted to Maharajji, stayed on for some time. At the conclusion of her visit she reports the following:

Then as the time came that we had to return to the States, I began thinking about the last darshan I would have. I realized that I really wanted to touch Maharajji's feet. I didn't know why I wanted to but I did. I figured that if I went ahead and did it, it would upset my husband, but I thought, "So it upsets him. It is still my decision!" At my last darshan I touched Maharajji's feet. To my surprise so did my husband!

*How vividly I recall, after my first meeting with Maharajji, how all my
disdain and arrogance disappeared before an almost overwhelming desire
literally to be at his feet. It was perhaps the second or third visit with
Maharajji when the opportunity presented itself. I was watching the man next
to me. The expression on his face suggested that he was experiencing waves of
rapture, and as I watched him out of the corner of my eye I felt jealous. We sat
next to each other, cross-legged, before a large, heavy chest-high wooden table.
The man, the principal of a school in the vicinity, was probably in his late
fifties. He was dressed in a heavy woolen suit with socks (his shoes had been
left outside the door of the temple), a tie, a muffler, and, in the fashion
common to the men of the hill country in this late November, a woolen hat.
Before us, sitting on the table cross-legged, was Maharajji, well-wrapped in a
bright plaid blanket, so that only his head showed above the blanket and a bare
foot stuck out beneath. It was this foot that was the source of both the rapture
and the jealousy, for the man was massaging the foot with great tenderness and
love, and I was yearning to be in his place. How bizarre to find myself sitting
in a tiny Hindu temple halfway around the world, jealous because I could not
rub an old man's foot!*

*As I reflected on this strange turn of events, Maharajji talked now to one
and now to another of the twenty or so people gathered in the small room at
the back of the temple compound. He spoke in Hindi, which I did not
understand, but he seemed to be asking one a question, scolding another, joking
with a third, and giving instructions to a fourth. In the midst of these
conversations I saw him move ever so slightly, and his other foot appeared
beneath the blanket just beside me.*

*I suspected that only people who had been around him for some time were
allowed to massage his feet—and I was the newest comer—but I decided I
couldn't be faulted for trying. So slowly my hands went up and touched the
foot and began to massage. But instead of waves of bliss, my mind was full of
the sharp edges of doubt and confusion as to whether I should use my fingers or
my palms. Just as suddenly as the foot appeared, it was withdrawn back under
the blanket. My mind was filled with self-recrimination about my own
impurity.*

*As the visit went on, Maharajji took me more and more out of my self-
consciousness and into a space that had no familiar boundaries. I was
experiencing waves of confusion, bordering on hysteria. And that was the
moment the foot reappeared before me. And again I reached for it. But this
time my mind was too overwhelmed to analyze procedure. I just clung to the
foot as a drowning man to a life preserver. (R.D.)*

ॐ

There was one particular moment I remember in Kainchi. I was sitting in front of Maharajji's tucket, rubbing his feet for the longest time, wondering if I was pure enough to be doing this. Then I went beyond thoughts, going deeper and deeper into that love until there wasn't any concern about rubbing Maharajji's feet or even my love for Maharajji. I was just "swimming" in his feet.

ॐ

Sita would always sit on my right, and being a greedy, obnoxious Leo, I'd push my way up front and grab Maharajji's foot. Sita would always want the same foot, so I'd have a shoving match with her. She'd say, "Get away from here. You don't belong here." And she'd throw her shoulder down to block me. Sometimes Maharajji would give his foot to me and sometimes to her.

ॐ

I very rarely touched his feet, because I felt he was too pure.

WHAT WAS IT about the darshans that captured us? Was it the many levels and changes, or the moments of timelessness, or perhaps the intimacy and love? Or was it the talking and chiding and humor, or maybe the purity? Then, of course, perhaps it was the touching of the feet. Or was it all of them . . . or none of them? Was the connection perhaps a subjective one, beyond our dualistic experiencing? Maharajji, who are you? Are you other than our very selves?

There is no answer. There is no question, really. There is just darshan, which is grace.

Krishna Das (Roy Bonney)

Take Chai

"Take *chai* [tea]."
"But Maharajji, I've already had chai."
"Take chai."
"Okay."
"Go take *kanna* [food]."
"Maharajji, I just ate an hour ago."
"Maharajji wants you to take kanna now."
"Okay."
"Maharajji sent these sweets over for you."
"But I couldn't eat another thing."
"It's Maharajji's wish that you have these sweets."
"Okay."
"Maharajji sent me to give you chai."
"Oh, no! Not again!"
"I am only doing my duty. It is Maharajji's wish."
"Okay."
"A devotee has just arrived from Delhi with a large bucket of sweets.
Maharajji is distributing it. He wants you to come."

37

"Oh, my God, I'll explode."
"It prasad."
"Thank you, Maharajji. (Oh, no, not the apples too!) Ah, thank you, Maharajji."

While many experienced Maharajji's qualities of timelessness or love at darshans, everybody who came before him felt his concern that they be fed. Often even before you could sit down he would insist that you "take prasad." People just never went away from him hungry.

I stopped at a gasoline station in Berkeley, California, run by a Sikh fellow. I thought I'd practice my Hindi with him. When he found out that I stayed at the temple at Kainchi, the first thing he said was, "Oh, you belong to that baba. I visited him. He gave me puris [fried bread]. Nobody else gives you food just for nothing."

MANY OF THE poor people in the areas around the temple or on pilgrimages came to depend upon the food that was freely given for their survival; but for the rest of us, such excessive feeding and continuous preoccupation with food seemed to indicate that the food represented something more.

My first impressions focused on all the food that was present. I had just come down from Nepal, where I had been on a strict Buddhist meditation trip for a long time, and I saw all these people sitting down and stuffing their faces! I thought, "Oh, they don't know where it's at. Look at the gluttons!" Then I sat down to eat . . . and in a few days I was stuffing my face. I had never before experienced such a feeling as that. Literally I could not get enough to eat. It was as if I were feeding my spirit.

ॐ

He offered the pera (a sweet) *back to me to eat, and oddly enough I turned it down. What was in my mind was that I felt completely filled and someone else should have it. So he gave it to someone else.*
At another darshan he had filled my hands with peras, which I promptly ate. Shortly thereafter he started to give me another huge handful, which I turned down, thinking that I'd had my share. An Indian behind me became upset and told me I should never turn down Maharajji's prasad, that I should

always take what he offers to me. Then, of course, I felt bad. Next Maharajji offered me another handful, which I joyfully received.

✳

I arrived at the temple in November and lived there continuously until the end of March. During all that time I was fed well, daily, and yet not a penny was ever asked of me in compensation. I couldn't understand it. Here I was a relatively wealthy Westerner, and the Indians had such a hard time economically, and yet they would not accept payment. So I just kept sneaking money into the box at the temple. (R.D.)

✳

I was trying to hide somewhere around the temple, across the courtyard from where he came out the door. And when he came out, I got pushed by the people right up to the tucket. I tried always to be far away and hide myself, so when I got pushed near to him I tried to hide behind the column, but people pushed me and pushed me. And Maharajji came out. I was scared and crying. And Maharajji gave me a pear. When I ate the pear it made me feel like there was water all over inside me. It was like eating love alive. Since that day this pear has always been in my mind, and nothing has ever matched this feeling. I have never eaten another pear since that day.

✳

One time, when my daughter was young and still with us, we stopped in Bhowali en route to Kainchi for darshan. She wanted jelebees (a sweet), but there were none. I said, "When we get to Kainchi, there will be some." But when we got there, we found that it was a Hindu fast day—Ekadashi (literally "eleventh day" in lunar month)—and so only boiled potatoes were served. As we entered Maharajji's room, to our surprise a man arrived with a large basket full of jelebees.

Maharajji said, "Give some to that girl first," pointing to my daughter.
He knows everything!

✳

A sadhu once came to the temple and upbraided Maharajji: "You do nothing for people. You don't feed or help people."

Maharajji said, "Give him a room and food and money," yet all that the devotees felt like doing was beating this sadhu. They got him around a corner to do so, but Maharajji yelled at them. After the sadhu had eaten, he became very quiet. Maharajji said, "The thing you people don't understand is that he's hungry. He hasn't eaten for three days. What else could he do but what he did?"

तम

Once I said, "Why do you feed so many people and why so much? I could eat four chapattis [flat, unleavened bread] and stay alive."

Maharajji answered, "We have an inner thirst for food. We don't know of it. Even if you don't feel you can eat, your soul has a thirst for food. Take prasad!"

THE NATURE OF the food that was served around Maharajji is worthy of note, for though it satisfied our souls, our intellects were often appalled. The usual diet at the temple consisted of white rice, puris and potatoes (both fried), and sweets of almost pure white sugar. The diet was starch, grease, and sugar, and much black tea. All the sensitivity that the Western preoccupation with diet had awakened in us screamed at this diet. And yet, this was "prasad." Did you reject prasad, or did you give up your dietary models? What did you do when the love came in the form of starch, grease, sugar, and tea? Greasy potatoes were one thing; a blessing from the guru, however, was an entirely different matter.

I previously believed that a saint should observe certain restrictions as to food. Also, I never took tea or coffee, and I ate a very simple, small diet. I never took medicines. I wondered how people could take so many pills. After Maharajji left I caught a cold. At first the doctors thought it was flu, then they said it was a more serious disease. So I had to take fifteen pills a day to cure it. It was all Maharajji's play. The doctors also told me to put on weight so from 6:00 A.M. to 10:00 P.M. I ate. I wondered how I could eat so much when previously I had eaten only two chapattis at a meal. All my old ideas vanished.

This was similar to what happened when I came to Kainchi, prior to which time I never drank tea. On the first day at Kainchi I did not take it, and on the second day when Maharajji asked me if I would drink tea, I didn't reply. The third morning he asked me, "Do you want tea? You don't want it. Here, you should drink tea. It's a cold place!" So this time I drank tea, and since that day I take anything—tea, coffee, whatever.

WHEN MAHARAJJI spoke about diet he generally ignored the nutrition issues that so concerned some of us, but he did suggest that we "eat simple foods." And he also advised us to eat food that was indigenous to the area in which we were living. And then to various devotees he gave specific instructions about diet, advising one to forego wine, meat, eggs, hot spices, "because they lead to an impure heart." Yet to another he said, "What is this concern with what is meat and what is not. When you can live without meat, well and good. When you cannot live without it, then you should have it." Some he counseled to "eat alone, silently, simply, or with a few people"; to others his instructions concerned the value of fasts three times a month, although when you were around him he interrupted any fast you might attempt. From this confusion of instructions, most of us came away with the feeling that he was counseling us to trust our intuitions rather than get too caught in rules. At least, that's what we wanted to hear.

Because he fed us all so unstintingly with love and attention, as well as food, we sought ways to reciprocate. Yet his life was so simple that there was nothing to give, so most people brought flowers or food, especially fruits and sweets. These he would then distribute by his own hand or touch the food and then have it distributed. Such touching, or blessing, by such a being as Maharajji, converted the food vibrationally from a physical material into prasad. In the absence of the physical form of such a being as Maharajji, food is offered in the heart and the mind of the devotee before partaking. If food is offered purely, the beings to which it is offered accept an essence from the food. Then we eat what is left, which has become prasad. In the West, this would be similar to our saying grace before eating.

Maharajji also showed a continuous concern for the quality of the food that was being distributed from the kitchens at the temple. He would call the cooks and examine the food. If it was poorly made, he would yell; if it was unnecessarily extravagant, he would yell.

When I was living up on the hill in that little kuti *(hut), Maharajji would send me away with a box of food every evening. But when he gave it to me he always checked the entire box, putting his hands all through it.*

†पू

Maharajji would tell the Mothers that the vibrations with which food was cooked could definitely affect your state of mind. He would say that if you truly made your food prasad, it would purify you. But even a very pure man, if he ate food that was prepared without proper consciousness—that food would create confusion in his mind. He said that eating purely prepared food made a yogi great.

†पू

At the market I bought some clusters of green berries to give to Maharajji. They were kind of dirty so I very carefully washed them. Then I put them back into the bag. But you know how it is with Indian bags. It broke and the berries fell all over the ground, so I carefully washed them again, berry by berry. It took a long time. Finally I brought them to Maharajji; everybody else, of course, had also brought fruits. But the minute I put them down Maharajji appeared very excited. He spread them all out very carefully, studied them, ate many of them himself, and distributed the rest as something particularly precious. I felt that he sensed the love and care with which I had prepared the berries.

†पू

For some time, Maharajji would eat only the food prepared by one particular Ma. She told me that if one day she was too busy and someone had helped her with it, he would refuse to eat it. She said that she would sometimes lie to him just so he would eat the food—she would say that she had cooked the food by herself without help. Still he would push it away. He seemed to be able to feel the difference.

†पू

My Brahmin grandfather took his food alone, as was the tradition. The food was specially prepared for him by my wife. He had started to eat when Maharajji arrived, so father ordered more food prepared. My wife wanted to give Maharajji a special item of food that she had made for grandfather, so she gave some to Maharajji. Father got angry.

"How can you give Maharajji other than freshly prepared food?" he asked my wife.

Then Maharajji called him and said, "The freshly prepared food was eaten by the sadhu. The special food offered out of such pure love was eaten by God."

Most of the time Maharajji ate alone and distributed all that we devotees brought to him. But it was each person's dearest desire, when we brought the fruit or other food that Maharajji eat some of it himself. And when he did, it felt like such a precious moment, one in which Maharajji had accepted a token of your love.

Once when I brought a soft apple and peeled it and cut it up and held it up before him as I had seen the Indians do, he reached down and took a few pieces from my hand . . . and I experienced that ecstasy you might feel if a wild bird or deer had come and eaten out of your hand. (R.D.)

राम

Maharajji was sitting in the back in Kainchi, by the showers, late one afternoon. We were offering him pomegranate seeds, most of which he was eating one by one; others he was handing out to the people around him. One of the Indians started giving him some of them back to him. Maharajji continued eating them obliviously and passing them out. The next thing you knew it had developed into this great little game. People were passing the pomegranate seeds under the tucket, passing them back so that I could keep giving him more. He ended up eating all the seeds, though they had recirculated several times. We shared the delightful conspiracy of feeding and "fooling" him.

राम

I purchased a dozen oranges to take to Maharajji. We arrived at the tiny temple where Maharajji was visiting and where many Indian devotees already had gathered and were crammed into his room. As soon as our presence was made known, we were pushed to the space just in front of the wooden table on which Maharajji sat. I offered the oranges to him. There was already much fruit and some sweets on the table. But then something happened that surprised me. Maharajji started to go at my oranges as if he had never seen food before. As each orange was opened he would grab it and eat it very rapidly. And before my eyes he consumed eight oranges. I was being fed the other four, at Maharajji's insistence, by the school principal.

Later I asked KK, a close Indian friend, about this peculiar behavior. KK explained that Maharajji was "taking on karma*" from me and that this was a technique by which he often did that. (R.D.)*

THE MEANING OF "taking on karma" is that a very high being, such as Maharajji, can work with subtle vibratory patterns and can take from devotees patterns with which they have been stuck for this lifetime or many lifetimes. For example, such a being could take away your sorrow or your ill fortune.

This process, which is a familiar one among Indian saints as well as sorcerers and medicine men from many parts of the world, can be done in a variety of ways. Often the medicine man works with a lock of hair or the feces or urine of the person suffering the effects of some negative forces, either inside or outside themselves. In India, such karmic healers often work with things the devotee gives them. Shirdi Sai Baba, a very great saint of India, would ask his devotees for *annas,* small coins worth less than a penny. These he would handle continuously until he had extracted the negative condition from the devotee into himself. This negative material he then could release from himself by other yogic processes. Another well-known guru in India asks his devotees for cigarettes and smokes from morning till night, year in, year out, often three or four cigarettes at a time. Maharajji's way was to eat the karma, and he seemed to have no limit to his capacity. One woman, a long-standing devotee, told the following story:

Once in Bhumiadhar, where Maharajji was staying the night, we had all taken our evening meal and had retired at 10:30 P.M. Around 1:00 A.M. Maharajji started yelling that he was very hungry and that he must have dal *(lentils) and chapattis. I awoke and reminded him that he had already eaten. But he insisted that he must have dal and chapattis. Who can understand the ways of such a being. So I woke Brahmachari Baba (the priest) and he built a fire and prepared the food. It was ready about 2:00 A.M. and we watched*

Maharajji consume the food with great hunger. Then we all retired again. At about 11:00, the next morning, a telegram arrived saying that one of Maharajji's old devotees had died down on the plains (about 150 miles away) the previous night at 2:00 A.M. When the telegram was read to Maharajji he said, "You see, that's why I needed chapattis and dal." This aroused our curiosity, because we didn't see at all. We pressed him but he would say nothing more. Finally after two or three days of our persistence he said, "Don't you see? He [the man who had died] had been wishing for chapattis and dal, and I didn't want him to carry that desire on through death for it would affect a future birth."

Sometimes when visiting homes he would come to the door and say he was very hungry and ask if he could eat. In very poor homes where there might not be any food, he would just say he was very thirsty and ask for water.

In Lucknow, Maharajji took some public-works officials in a car to the poorest part of town where these officials do not take proper care of the roads and sanitation. From one of the shacks he called forth a Moslem (whom Maharajji called "a Musselman") and they embraced, and then Maharajji said, "I'm very hungry."

"But Maharajji, I have no food."

"Ap! Wicked one! You have two rotis [flat bread] hidden in the roof!"

The man was surprised that Maharajji knew, and he got them. Even though Maharajji and the officials had just eaten, he ate one with relish and handed the other to the officials including the Hindu Brahmins, who would never eat food prepared by a Moslem, and said, "Take prasad!"

ॐ

When Maharajji came to the Lucknow temple for the last time, he would say to each person who came (if he or she could afford to do so), "Go! Get sweets," and when they would return with sweets, he'd distribute them, almost fifteen hundred rupees' worth that day. One doctor bought a thousand rupees' worth of sweets, and the personal problem causing him concern was solved.

In the period between 1939 and 1949, when Maharajji would come into a town such as Nainital, all the women would prepare food in the hope that he would come to their homes. They did it out of a mixture of loving service and the feeling that it was a blessing to feed such a saint. And KK, who followed him from early morning until late at night, once watched him consume twenty full meals in one day. Another reported watching him take ten meals in a row. And if you have been to India and understand the graciousness of the Indian home, where the guest is treated as God, you will appreciate the immense portions and the persistence in feeding. An Indian meal is more than ample for a normal human being.

But perhaps Maharajji's immense capacity represented something other than dietary requirements.

One morning Maharajji said to the people at the ashram, "You people can't feed me or take care of me. I'm going to Ma. She'll feed me." And he left for the ashram of Ananda Mayee Ma, a great woman saint of northern India. During the entire trip he was saying, "She'll feed me. I'm going to see Ma. She'll feed me." Then he burst into the darshan room like a child of five, with his blanket flying in all directions. She was sitting there and he was saying, "Ma! Feed me. Feed me, Ma!" She exploded in laughter. A huge meal was brought to him and the two of them passed it out to all the devotees.

AGAIN AND AGAIN Maharajji enjoined us to "feed people." His concern was not merely for his own devotees but with all people who hunger. He would say, "God comes to the hungry in the form of food." And to the cooks he would say, "Making food is a service to God. People need food to stay alive."

He used to say that you should serve everything, every creature. "It is all God's creation. Serve everyone, whether he be a dacoit [thief] or anything else. If he comes to you hungry, give him food." So often he said, "Everyone has a right to be fed."

MAHARAJJI'S OWN BEHAVIOR set a dramatic example for us. Besides feeding all who came to have his darshan, he was continually arranging for large *bhandaras* (celebrations consisting of mass free feedings for all comers, including the wealthy, the poor, the beggars, the lepers). The people were fed when they arrived, for Maharajji instructed, "A starving person should not have to wait. Such a person should be fed when he is hungry."

At these great bhandaras, which often served a thousand or more, many devotees would vie to help in the preparation and distribution of the food. Here judge and merchant, teacher and politician, could all be found peeling potatoes, stirring the huge pots, or ladling out the *halva* or rice with huge spoons.

The *Kumbha Melas* were even more festive occasions. These are gatherings of hundreds of thousands of sadhus, saints, and seekers who come from all over India in order to bathe in the confluence of three rivers— the Ganges, the Yamuna, and the Saraswati, an underground spiritual river, at an auspicious astrological moment. It is like a huge spiritual fair that goes on for a month or more. At the *melas* Maharajji's tent usually served 250 to 500 a day for at least a month. That is a lot of potatoes to be peeled!

During these celebrations Maharajji demanded hard work of the devotees, and many saw these experiences as training in discipline. One devotee describes the experience this way:

At the mela, they prepared khichri *(a rice and dal mixture), but the serving spoon was very heavy and soon the servers, growing tired, began to serve only small portions. As a result, the beggars would stand in line again and again to get enough to eat. Finally one of Maharajji's devotees got very angry and just then Maharajji arrived from* Chitrakut *(a place sacred to devotees of Ram). He yelled at them all and said they could not serve food with anger and that they should give plenty to everyone.*

ANOTHER, pointing out that the devotees were not even praised for working hard, said:

No matter how hard people worked at the melas and bhandaras, Maharajji would say, "You people are playing and going about doing nothing. You are always sleeping."

ALTHOUGH PEOPLE WERE continually bringing food to Maharajji, which he distributed, sometimes there were more to receive than there were givers. It was at these times that the discerning eye caught Maharajji manifesting what is known as the *"siddhi* [power] of Annapurna." *Annapurna* is the Goddess of Grain, the aspect of the Divine Mother that feeds the universe. One who has Annapurna's siddhi can keep distributing from a store of food, yet it will remain full.

On a feast day at the temple when I was quite young, they were giving out special sweets. Maharajji gave me a small leaf cup of these sweets that he had been keeping especially for me. Then he said, "You give those sweets back to me." So I gave them to him, because I had such faith in him. He just put the leaf cup under his blanket and began distributing those sweets from under his blanket. I don't know how he did it, but he gave a handful to each person in that huge crowd of at least a thousand people. I was so surprised. I couldn't understand how he could be distributing so many more sweets than the number of sweets I had given to him, so, being just a kid, I stuck my hand under his blanket and took out the leaf cup to see. Maharajji turned to me and said, "Now the magic is finished."

ॐ

A man brought some oranges to Maharajji and put them in an empty basket by his side. Maharajji started giving the oranges to the people in the room and then to others in the temple. The man had brought eight oranges, and Maharajji gave out forty-eight.

ॐ

At the mela, many came to the tent and Maharajji told us to prepare tea for all those people. No one wanted to tell Maharajji that they had run out of milk. Finally someone did, and Maharajji said, "Go and get a container of water from the Ganga and keep it covered with cloth." All that day and until midnight that night, there was plenty of good tea with milk.

ॐ

Maharajji called me over to sit with him while he was throwing prasad *(food offerings). He was eating small biscuits from a small plate with only a few biscuits. Maharajji started giving me biscuits, taking them out of the biscuit plate with his hand. He kept taking more out, until both my hands were full and I couldn't separate them because of the amount of prasad. Earlier I had been upset observing Maharajji, thinking, "Prasad should be given, not thrown." He knew that, and this is why he called me back and started giving me prasad into my hands.*

जय

Maharajji once called me in Allahabad to tell me he had come down to Vrindaban. When I arrived at the Vrindaban ashram, there were only a few people there. One woman came for darshan, bringing a bag of wonderful apples. You can't imagine how big and luscious-looking they were. Maharajji began distributing them and I thought surely he would give me one as well. But he didn't. He gave a few to the other devotees and the rest he gave back to the woman. She wouldn't give me one, either. Oh, how tightly she tied them back up in her bag!

Shortly afterward, Maharajji crossed the yard and went into a room alone and sat on the tucket in there. Then he called me in alone. I don't know from where it came, but he put his hand down beside him on the tucket and handed me an apple—even bigger, more luscious than those the woman had given him. And then he handed me another apple. I don't know where they had come from because I had seen for myself that he hadn't kept any from the woman!

जय

I was accompanying Maharajji from Allahabad to Vrindaban by train, when in the station, before we boarded the train, I saw the loveliest large juicy oranges. For a moment I was tempted to stop and buy some, but I passed by. Once we were in the train, my attention was diverted just for a short time, and when I looked again at Maharajji he had beside him such a huge basket of oranges! I don't know where they had come from, but they were better than those I had seen in the station.

When Maharajji handed me one orange I put it in the right breast pocket. The second orange I put in the left breast pocket. They created such bulges that I looked like a woman! Then he handed me a third, which I put in one pants pocket, and a fourth, in the other pocket. And he kept on giving me more, so that I had to catch them in my shirttails—front and back. He gave me so many oranges I could hardly move! I started giving these sweet oranges out to others, saying, "This is the best prasad I have to offer today." To this day I don't know how he came by those oranges.

जय

At the Kumbha Mela in 1966 Maharajji was sitting on the bank of the Ganga with two or more sadhus. He told us to bring him a lot of Ganga water. He held it for a few minutes and then told us to distribute it. It was milk.

To ALL BUT the closest devotees, Maharajji tended to mask these powers and would often use a cover story to make it appear as if he had nothing to do with the additional food.

When Maharajji established a Hanuman temple on a site that had previously been a burial ground, a great bhandara was held to set free the "wandering spirits." Late at night it was discovered that the ghee *(clarified butter) had run out. The man in charge of stores went to Maharajji and told him that there was a shortage of ghee, although many people were still coming to be fed. How were they to provide? Maharajji replied, "Go there and check among the empty cannisters! You'll find somewhere a full tin." Although the man knew that they were all empty, as he himself had checked and counted them, he went. And, indeed, he found a full tin there among the empties.*

ﹰﻟﻖ

One man stayed with Maharajji for many years as a sort of attendant. He'd keep Maharajji's clothes, help him bathe and fetch water, and so forth. He performed much service and slept at Maharajji's feet to be always nearby. His practice was to keep fast on Tuesday, taking only milk. On one Tuesday, Maharajji offered him food but he refused, saying he'd take milk. The whole day passed and he wasn't given any milk.

Late at night Maarajji asked him if he'd eaten or drunk milk. He said no, he was fasting, but milk he'd had. Maharajji said, "You're lying! Tell the truth! No one gave you milk." Maharajji's shouting woke the ashram. Maharajji questioned the cook and found that no one had remembered to give him his milk, and by now none was in the ashram. Maharajji got up and went to his room. He called the man in and told him to lock the door. Maharajji asked the time; it was after midnight. Maharajji said, "You haven't eaten all day. It's after midnight. Can you eat now? It's Wednesday." The man said he could. Maharajji reached into his dhoti *(cloth used to cover lower part of a man's body) and took out five parathas (fried bread) and two types of vegetables. Maharajji said, "It's God's prasad, Ram's prasad." The man started to leave so he could eat it outside, but Maharajji stopped him and told him to eat it there. When he was finished, Maharajji produced a small amount of* khir *(a sweet rice pudding). This the man also ate and then started out of the room to get water. Maharajji again stopped him: "Where are you going? Here's water." Water was kept near Maharajji's bed for his use in the night, but the man wouldn't use Maharajji's vessels. Maharajji poured the water into his mouth. Then Maharajji told him not to tell anyone about the evening.*

OFTEN THIS PROCESS of disguise would involve incredible abuse and yelling at devotees (shifting attention, as any good magician would do), thus creating in them great guilt, as if it were their own sloppiness that had led to the misplacement of the food. Later he would be very tender with them, and they sensed that he had used them but not abused them.

One time they ran out of ghee at Hanuman Ghar, and Maharajji asked a devotee, in secret, to get some water in a bucket and put it in the woods. Then he said, in his usual direct manner, "I have to go piss," and he went out. When he returned, he was yelling. He went over to a sadhu and berated him for not watching the supply. He said thieves were going to steal the ghee. "Look," Maharajji said, "they have put a tin of ghee out here in the woods." And they brought in the bucket filled with ghee.

ॐ

A devotee was serving at a bhandara at Kainchi. They were starting to run out of malpuas *(sweet puris), as the feast had continued for ten days. When the people came, they began to give them chapattis and dal, but no malpuas. Then sixty or seventy women arrived from distant villages, not just to see Maharajji but because they desired malpuas. Maharajji said, "Give them malpuas." A devotee told Maharajji that there were no more, and Maharajji upbraided him, saying, "You are a thief. There were plenty of malpuas. You've stolen them. Take the keys from him. I don't want him in the temple anymore. He should not have the keys to the storeroom. He has probably hidden the malpuas somewhere." When someone checked the storeroom, there were plenty of malpuas. Later Maharajji was so loving and tender to the accused devotee.*

ॐ

I was in Allahabad with Majarajji at mela time. Maharajji said there were some Ma's who had come from Nainital and added, "Let's go to the mela grounds and find them." We took a taxi, which Maharajji dismissed once we arrived. It was dark and many thousands of people were crowded there. Maharajji sent me and a friend to look, but we were fearful of losing him, so we made only a cursory inspection and rushed back, saying that we could not find the Ma's. Finally Maharajji said he would go. In the third tent that he investigated, he found them just as they were finishing a puja to Maharajji. They had been doing this puja every day for thirty days, hoping for his darshan. This was the final day. They had even made an image of Maharajji.

Maharajji walked in and stood at the back of the tent, then he brought the Ma's to another devotee's house and sent us out for milk and sweets. We were students and did not want to spend all our money, so we said to each other, "After all, how much can a Ma drink?" We brought small amounts of sweets and milk, for which Majarajji berated us and threw us out. We sat on the porch, repentant. Later he called us into his room and asked, "Do you think I needed you to get sweets?" And there in the room were buckets and buckets of sweets, and Maharajji made us eat and eat.

THE RETIRED superintendent of prisons of Lucknow, a very old and respected devotee, tells of his experience with Maharajji. The story is very special in that it reflects the faith of his wife, which was sufficient to allow her to let Maharajji's siddhi of Annapurna work through her.

He would put you in the wrong, catch you unprepared, then help you. One night in Nainital we had returned to our house for the evening meal, after having been with Maharajji much during the day. There were four of us, and my wife had prepared just enough food for our family. Then my small daughter heard Maharajji passing by on his way from the government house and she went out and said, "Maharajji, we live here. Come to our house."

I called her and said, "Don't bother Maharajji. We have been with him much today." Also I realized that we had only a little food.

But Maharajji said, "No, I must go to your house," and he came in, bringing about twenty people. After a very few minutes he said to me, "These people are hungry. Give them food." I wouldn't say no because I knew his strength, so I went toward the kitchen. Maharajji yelled, "And hurry up!" In the kitchen I whispered to my wife the dilemma we were in. We had only enough vegetables in the small pot for the four of us, and the market was far below and already closed.

My wife, who had more faith than I, said, "Don't worry. Maharajji will take care of it. Here, take this small pot (which she had covered) and don't remove the cover to look inside. And there is a large serving spoon. Just serve the people and I will make the puris." I did as she said, not looking inside. I knew it was going to be very odd.

To each person I gave one or two large spoonfuls, then asked each, "Do you want more?" Some said yes and I gave it to them. Everyone got as much vegetable and puri as they wanted.

Maharajji was smiling. Then he said, "Everyone has taken. Everyone is full. This is a very big feast."

A NUMBER OF stories of the "early days" have filtered down about Maharajji. How much is fact and how much is fiction is uncertain. Here is a delightful example:

The village children of the area often came to the lake, herding their cows and goats. One day, seeing no one around, they hung their lunch bundles in the low-hanging branches of the trees and went off to play. They returned to find their lunches missing and Maharajji sitting contentedly under the tree. He smiled at the children, and in exchange for their food he pulled puris and laddus (a sweet particularly favored by Hanuman) from under his garment. The children ate to their hearts' content.

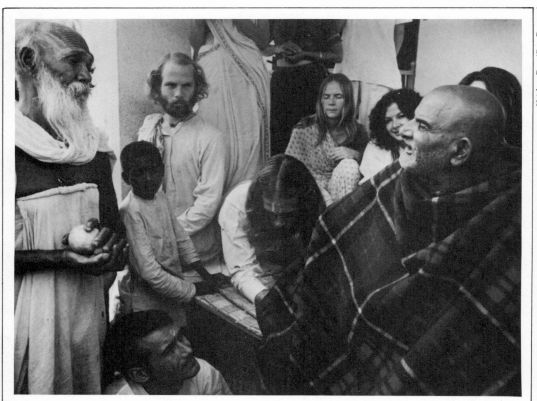

Krishna Das (Roy Bonney)

Under Maharajji's Blanket

THE WAY IN WHICH guru and devotee relate to one another varies immensely from devotee to devotee. In the holy books it is said that a devotee might see the guru in the roles of father, mother, child, friend, master, lover, or God. And there were devotees who saw Maharajji in each of these ways. But the essence of the way in which Maharajji's Indian devotees felt toward him is perhaps better captured by the word *baba* than by the term *guru*. Baba can mean "grandfather" or "elder." It is a term of respect used with either an older person or a spiritual person. The sadhus, or wandering renunciates, of India are usually called baba, and so is the old street cleaner. Its softness and familiarity better capture the quality of the play between Maharajji and his devotees.

FOR SOME of them, he was seen primarily as the grandfather of the family:

The fatherly affection he'd give can't be gotten from anyone else.

FOR OTHERS their "baba" was their dear friend:

When you love somebody you play anything with them. That's what I did. I never thought differently.

ॐ

We'd travel together often and just talk about this and that.

FOR MANY he was a wise advisor:

I'd just come, ask him my questions, and go.

TO SOME he was just another saintly sadhu:

He was just an ordinary baba. He'd come often, and we would give him a little sweet or a glass of water. He'd sit on a bare cot. And we felt so much bloated with pride because "we fed a baba today."

ॐ

My family has always had saints like Maharajji connected with them.

BUT FOR many he was a guardian angel, as if from another realm:

While with him I always felt protection, from anywhere, from all things.

ॐ

Maharajji picks us from one spot and places us at another.

ॐ

Whenever we feel difficulty from any ordeals in our life, we always remember him. Then he always helps us, either directly or by giving some strength to others to help us.

Aɴᴅ ꜰᴏʀ some, God:

Whoever had his darshan, even from behind, is saved.

☈

Maharajji is the havan *(sacrificial fire) accepting and burning my karma.*

☈

He's beyond anything you could say of him.

☈

You see, he is God. That's of course who he is.

Aʟʟ ᴛʜᴇꜱᴇ categories are too specific. Really, for most devotees he was now one and now another of these, or he was all of them. Quite simply, he was their "baba."

I didn't care about his miracles. I only knew that he was my baba.

☈

One woman never thought of Maharajji as a great saint with powers. He said that he didn't have them, so she believed him. She thought of him as a saintly, good, and kind person, who gave her love and affection and peace of mind. Her husband thought that Maharajji was God himself. In Maharajji's presence both of them would forget their problems.

☈

I have never been afraid of him. Never. It was not out of fear of him that I was tense and alert around him—but out of fear for him. For instance, if you have a flower garden and are caring for it, you are not afraid of the flowers but of the horse and the cow who may trample or eat it or of the gardener who may forget to water it. I was afraid, you see, that someone's carelessness might cause him inconvenience or pain; like your mother would feel if you came home from school and she was not there—she'd worry about who would feed and take care of you. It was like that.

Aᴍᴏɴɢ ᴛʜᴇ Westerners there was also considerable heterogeneity in the ways of seeing Maharajji and being with him. Although many of us had extremely intimate relations with Maharajji, nevertheless, the more formal term "guru," with its emphasis as a vehicle for spiritual liberation, would seem a more appropriate label than "baba." Because gurus were not commonplace in the culture from which we had come, we tended to invest more heavily in the guru mythos. We didn't particularly want a grandfather or another friend. We wanted God or at least a divine intermediary. And that's how most of us saw Maharajji. In these quotations some differences among us become apparent:

(One Western devotee speaks to another.) I didn't need to be around him a lot. It was okay for everyone else who had to be around him constantly. I think that my traveling with you was good because you were a perfect complement to me. You had to be near Maharajji, you had to sit at his feet; you had to pick up every little detail, hear every little story. And I really loved that; it was really beautiful—but for me all of that got in the way; that was not what I needed. I just needed the essence, the seed, the feeling.

गुरु

I remember one day we had eaten very well, as usual, and we all napped afterward. But there was a feeling of what the Sufis call baraka *(blessing or spiritual power). When we woke up we were disoriented, but it felt so delightful. A lot of the real work for me was in that feeling I got after coming and taking prasad and relaxing. It was in this way that I experienced the actual baraka, or blessing, taking place.*

गुरु

I was crying all the time because Maharajji wouldn't take me to him, inside his arms, into the temple and fly me up into the sky. After that first contact with him I became extremely eager, almost crazy, to be inside his blanket.

So I always tried to bargain, to find some way that I could get him to take me. And I realized very quickly that there was no way to do anything that could make him take me.

I never felt that the words were really important. The true guru is within. And Maharajji was a manifestation that I needed to see in order to understand that truth.

Because of the longing for him and the sense of being in the presence of my own divine holy God-Mother—I always felt Maharajji to be as my Mother; Maharajji was like the Ma for me. Maharajji's relation to God was totally internal and subtle.

It was just so fine to be who you are—to be yourself. The playfulness was so infinite, the heart-opening so wide.

IN THE FOLLOWING comparison between the behaviors of two of the devotees, another dimension of difference becomes clear.

When Devotee A was in the temple it was predictable that if any Westerner were allowed near Maharajji, he would be the one. There was no limit to the ingenuity he employed to remain in Maharajji's presence for every possible second. If Maharajji told people to go away, A would be the last to leave and then might go immediately around the back of the building, pick a flower off a tree, and arrive from the other side, as if he were just arriving for the first time. When others were being told to go, he would often hide so as to avoid being included in the expulsion edict. It developed into an elaborate game, in which Maharajji was a participant.

A was a master of his game. He seemed to have a special sense that told him where Maharajji would be any moment, and he managed to be there, waiting. Others tried to compete in this game but none approached A's totally one-pointed (or, depending upon how you saw it, totally selfish) behavior. Others were hampered by guilt or compassion for others—feelings which, if mentioned, elicited only an uncomprehending look from A.

Devotee B was an entirely different story. If Maharajji sent us to help in the kitchen, B would remain peeling potatoes long after others had given up and drifted back to Maharajji. He would stay until the last potato was peeled and then look for more work. Although he had been trained as an attorney in the United States, his service and humility at the temple were so outstanding that soon he was in charge of kitchens and storerooms. He remained in the temple performing the purest service for five years, until he was evicted by the government. No job was too menial and there was no evidence of personal pride about his humility, nor any effort to get attention for his work. It was truly as if he came closest to God through his service. He hardly ever came near Maharajji, and when he did it was usually only to touch his feet and then go back to his duties.

Devotees like A often infuriated other devotees because they seemed to be monopolizing Maharajji, while devotees like B aroused respect and sometimes guilt in others. Yet intuitively we knew that each in his own way was a pure devotee, and Maharajji obviously loved them both.

As varied as were all the ways of seeing and being with Maharajji, so were his reactions. He responded to each according to his or her capacity to absorb. In the infinitely changing nature of Maharajji's behavior, each person found what he or she needed. Because he stood nowhere he was like a mirror, showing each devotee the baba or guru that they projected. Often with one act he fed simultaneously the disparate needs of a dozen devotees.

Who can say with these saints? They are like the sky. Maharajji's mind was completely clear. He would seem to have no thoughts; only that which Bhagavan (God) willed would come into his mind. Like a cloud it would come and then—whup—oh, such action that thought would produce! And again, like a cloud it would pass. His mind was always clear.

तुम

He used to speak to the devotee according to the person's own depth, according to what line of devotion the person was following.

ॐ

If you were clever or deceptive Maharajji ignored you, but if you were simple and open he'd help you.

ॐ

Maharajji, when he liked a person, expressed it from the heart. When he didn't want to see the face of a person, he would cover his face with a blanket.

ॐ

Maharajji did not reveal himself to everybody. He could see into the soul of a person; where we would see a nice sort of chap, he would see the person's inner workings. To some people he would just give prasad and send them away.

ॐ

Whether a person had been with Maharajji for twenty-five years or was a rank newcomer, all were given the same consideration. There were no favorites, and no one was indispensable.

ॐ

On one occasion a caravan of army trucks stopped at the gate, and hundreds of soldiers came and stood in line. Maharajji was talking to a farmer sitting beside him. One by one the soldiers and officers came forward, bent over and touched Maharajji's feet, looked at him for another moment, and then turned away. That experience was all most of them seemed to want. But every so often one would come forward who seemed different—perhaps seeming to have a bit more light or perhaps seeming to suffer more. Many times I watched as such a person bent forward. Maharajji would hit him on the head, or give him a flower, or interrupt his conversation to say something to him, such as, "Your mother will be all right," or "You shouldn't fight with your superiors," or

"You love God very much." We could see only the tiniest fraction of what Maharajji saw.

The soldiers wanted pictures of Hanuman (the protecting deity of the Indian army) and of Maharajji, to carry as protection in war. Maharajji said, "The army has good and simple and spiritual men." It was not as if Maharajji were "deciding" to do this or that; rather, the nature of the seeker was eliciting from him, as from a mirror, this or that response. (R.D.)

राम

The first time I saw Maharajji was at a mela, and I was asked to come to Chitrakut. The first thing that impressed me was that he was like a mirror. In Chitrakut there were so many people and they were talking about all his doings, and I was never interested but said that I thought he was like a mirror. When they then told Maharajji, he was very happy to hear that I thought this.

राम

I would talk with Maharajji about all matters, including such things as science or humans going to the moon. He was like a mirror; he had nothing to do with any of it. But he showed interest, and the next time you spoke of it he would follow what you were saying. He used to say, "I remember everything."

MAHARAJJI DID not seem to be "deciding" how to react to any devotee and in fact advised others to . . .

> *SEE GOD IN EVERYONE. IT IS*
> *DECEPTION TO TEACH BY INDIVIDUAL*
> *DIFFERENCES AND KARMA.★*

NEVERTHELESS, when pressed, he could "explain" his behavior:

Once I was chastising Maharajji for giving photos to people who were worldly and didn't care about him. He said, "You don't understand me. If I

★ This quote, and those set in this manner throughout the book, are direct quotes of Maharajji.

tell a man he is a great bhakta *[devotee], I am planting a seed. If a person already has the seed planted and growing, why should I plant another?"*

I said, "You are telling these drunkards, liars, and dacoits that they are real bhaktas. They will just go home and carry on their old behaviors."

Maharajji said, "Some of them will remember what I said of them, and it will make them want to develop this quality in themselves. If ten out of a hundred are inspired in this way, it is a very good thing."

जय

A devotee once said to Maharajji, "Maharajji, why do you tell people to do something and then blame them for it?"

"If I tell them to jump off a cliff, should they do it? I just tell them what is going on in their minds."

ALL OF THIS seemed to be a process whereby Maharajji was using devotees in the service of the awakening of one another.

When the Indians were feeling resentful of the Westerners, Maharajji would say, "They are very sincere and very pure, and that's why I love them. The Westerners all test me. You [Indians] all have blind faith."

जय

Maharajji once said of the Westerners, "For Westerners, just being in India is a form of renunciation. They have given up so much to be here. Once they believe, they believe fully, with their whole hearts and souls, like children."

NOT ONLY DID his response differ from person to person, but it varied over time for each individual as well. It was as if each time you came before Maharajji were the first time. And if the same conversation happened again and again, which was often the case, it was because the devotee remained caught in the same place, visit after visit. But each time the devotee would let go of the aspect of his thinking and behavior in which he or she was stuck, then he or she would find a whole new Maharajji.

One of Maharajji's favorite styles of dealing with devotees, especially the Indians, was abuse. And he was a master of it. Most of the West-erners did not understand Hindi well enough to appreciate the peppery language Maharajji used, and most of the translators took it upon them-selves to clean up his language for him. The Indians had become accus-tomed to his way of talking and actually interpreted it as a form of en-dearment.

Maharajji always hit the people he liked.

तेरा

If he called you names, like saying you were wicked or depraved, you knew he liked you.

तेरा

He'd abuse people, calling them troublemakers, telling them they danced naked, drank too much, were rowdies or sherabis *(winos).*

तेरा

A relative used to give me trouble all the time, but I would say nothing. Troubled, I went to Maharajji and he knew right away, saying that this man was bothering me. He said, "It is good if somebody abuses you, good in a spiritual way also. A person progresses if someone abuses him. Don't be worried. A day will come when this man will come and bow his head before you."

One day it happened. He came to me, saying, "I made all these mistakes; I gave you unnecessary troubles . . ."

BESIDES THE abuse there was a great deal of teasing and chiding.

"Dada has his God today! Tea and cigarettes," said Maharajji to Dada, who only laughed.

तेरा

Dada used a corner of his own dhoti to wipe Maharajji's mouth. Someone criticized Dada and said he should not do this. Then a woman brought milk and there were a few drops around Maharajji's mouth after he drank. Maharajji turned to Dada and asked, "Why are you leaving this?" and grabbed Dada's dhoti himself to wipe his mouth in front of everyone.

One woman laughingly remembered the intimate friendship she had with Maharajji. She told how he loved to tease and "pull people's legs." She described how he would play in this way with the Westerners. Before a large group of Indians he would ask them some questions, and they would give some reply. Then Maharajji would turn to the woman and wink, saying in this way, "See how naive these people are; they don't know anything." And the Westerners would be taking everything he said as deep mysterious truth, while he laughed at their simple innocence.

A family came for the darshan of Maharajji. They had bought a box of sweets for him in Nainital, and during the drive to Kainchi they began saying to each other how much they would like to sample a sweet or two. Finally they did so and then rearranged what was left so it would not appear that one was missing before the box was presented to Maharajji. Immediately Maharajji recoiled and refused even to touch the box. "Take it away, take it away, it is contaminated! Throw it out! Let the dogs eat it! No, the dogs wouldn't even touch this—it is polluted. Throw it out!"

There was a sweets-maker who used to come to Maharajji full of devotion and bring many sweets for all whenever he visited. Maharajji praised him and rewarded him. After some time he began to become inflated with pride and self-importance. One day in particular, after an absence of some time, he brought a prasad—a small box of sweets, half the size of what people usually bring—and this from a sweets-maker. Maharajji looked at him askance, emptied out the sweets, and gave the small box to a devotee nearby and said, "Don't give him a big box of puris. Here, put some puris in this instead."

┠ᴍᴎ

"Would you like to drink this water?" Maharajji asked me. It was unclean and from a Moslem source. He knew I was a Brahmin and would not drink it, and he never forced me against my nature. Often he would say to people, "Offer that to S," knowing I would not take it. Then Maharajji would say, "No, don't give it to him, he won't take it."

┠ᴍᴎ

I had been in Bombay on a religious pilgrimage, where I stayed with a family in their home. The head of the family had to take a drink of alcohol every evening for his heart condition. He offered me some, and I ended up getting quite drunk on Scotch.

Later, when I returned to Maharajji, he was talking to me about a sadhu who had gone to America. Maharajji asked, "What do they feed him in America?"

"I don't know, Maharajji, but I'm sure it's very pure food."

"They feed him milk," said Maharajji.

"That's good."

"Do you know what they put in the milk?"

"No."

He leaned forward and said to me in a mock conspiratorial voice, "Liquor!"

"No!"

"Yes!"

"Oh, no!" I exclaimed as though he had just described the most horrendous breach of behavior.

To which Maharajji replied, "Oh, yes," and looked at me significantly.

I broke up. He had just nailed me to the wall. (R.D.)

ONE OF THE beauties of the relationships between the abusing, chiding Maharajji and the devotees was that many of them weren't afraid to fight back. And he seemed especially to enjoy those who stood up to him.

I was able to speak in this brutal way because, knowing him since I was six, I never reflected about the respectable way to talk with him; there was no feeling of "bigness" or "elderness" between us. Once, for example, he was just pulling on my nose and I said to him, "Don't do that! If you can make it longer, then you can do it; otherwise, don't touch my nose."

Maharajji said, "Okay, I won't touch it. But I can bless you on the top of your head."

I said to him that whatever he did with me, he must do in the right way. So he patted me on the head. This was the way I could talk to him. This is what I am missing these days, since he left his body.

ॐ

The last time I saw Maharajji was in Vrindaban. We had traveled since early morning to get there and arrived shortly before noon, but he didn't come out of his room until after 3:00 P.M. When he emerged he immediately began yelling at me, telling me to go away, saying that he didn't want to see my face. "Jao [Go]!"

I yelled right back at him, asking what had I done to him. I had traveled all morning and waited all day to see him and this was his greeting. "No!" I said, "I won't go."

He kept on yelling and finally called the chaukidar to throw me out. The chaukidar came, hands folded, speaking politely but persistently. I yelled at Maharajji: "Just let me see how this man will touch me! How he will throw me out! I won't go."

You know, finally Maharajji called me to him. He patted me on the head and said a few mantras, just as he had done the first time I saw him. Now he was smiling so beautifully. He told me that his shakti *(spiritual energy) would always be with me and that now I should go. By then I was filled by him, and I said that he didn't have to tell me to go. I was leaving on my own now, because I had received his darshan.*

ॐ

My mother is a great devotee of Maharajji, and she even rebuked Maharajji when she thought it proper. Maharajji said of her, "See, she can do this. Only people with a pure heart can do such things!" Then again, sometimes

Maharajji rebuked her for coming. "Oh! Why have you come? You should go home. You've come without the permission of your son!"

ॐ

I never knew who Maharajji was. Once when I wouldn't leave, Maharajji said, "You have eaten my brain. Please go from here." Maharajji would insult me: "Go away. I won't talk to you." I would reply, "I won't go until my work is done."

ॐ

I didn't want to go to Madras with Maharajji. He asked me to go, but I had no clothing. Maharajji said he was going, and I said I would only go to the station and say good-bye. So I went inside his railroad coach because I wanted to pranam. But he just wouldn't talk to me; he turned away and wouldn't even look at me. I wouldn't get off, and after the train started, Maharajji began laughing. Then I had to go with him.

ॐ

In those days Maharajji never stayed too long in one place—seldom more than two or three days—so I wasn't able to get his darshan more than a few times. Then I left Kanpur for Calcutta for twenty years, where I was very busy and had no connection with Maharajji. When I returned to Kanpur I remembered Maharajji, wondering where he was and growing annoyed at myself for not seeking him. I left my meals for two months. My wife asked me why I was angry, why I wouldn't eat grains, but I never told her the reason. I was deeply annoyed with myself.

Once in Allahabad a man asked that I have the darshan of a very good saint. Without knowing the saint's name, I was taken to Dada's house. Maharajji saw me and said, "Why have you not eaten your meals for two months?"

I replied, "Why have you not given me darshan? I may be mad, but you are a saint—you shouldn't be mad." Like a child I spoke very rudely to him.

Someone asked me, "Are you going to have a fight with Maharajji?"

I said, "Yes, of course. Why shouldn't I fight? He is like my father and I his son. Why shouldn't we fight? Don't interfere."

Maharajji said, "Please don't interfere. He is my very old devotee."

The people went away and Maharajji turned to me and said, "Now go home. I will come to your house tomorrow morning and I'll take my meal there."

I said, "All right, when you take your meal at my place, only then will I start taking grains. If you don't come, I will not."

Maharajji said, "Come tomorrow."

I said, "No, Maharajji. I have no reliance on your words. You tell me to come for you tomorrow, but you may not be here then. Then what will my position be? I won't go. I'll sleep tonight here on the verandah or on the grass."

Maharajji said, "No. There's no place for you to sleep here."

I said, "It doesn't matter, Maharajji. I'll sleep outside the gate on the public road with one or two bricks for a pillow. Then in the morning I'll catch hold of you."

Maharajji said, "Oh, no. You must rely on me. I will definitely go with you. You go!"

Maharajji insisted, giving me his firm word. He then sent someone after me to drive me home. This man asked me to wait for half an hour. I sat down. Several people who had overheard my discussion with Maharajji told me that Maharajji often gives a blank check that is never cashed. He may or may not come.

I told them that I would come the following morning, and if Maharajji didn't come with me, I would take the oath that I would not even drink water until he came.

As I was saying this Maharajji immediately came from inside: "Wait, wait. I'll go with you just now."

We climbed into two cars and drove to my house, arriving at about eleven at night. No fresh food was available, but Maharajji ate of the leftovers from dinner, taking a little of whatever was offered. He said, "I've taken. Now you eat. Start eating grains and don't fast." Then he left. This is the story of Maharajji's blessing upon me. By and by it increased.

OFTEN THE quality of the play between Maharajji and devotees was truly childlike.

Maharajji would plead with me like a spoiled child. "Oh, Ma, please sing bhajan [devotional song]." He would quote the song, "A well without water, a cow without milk, a temple without a lamp, so is a man without bhajan."

It was the day of Rakshabandhan, *the day of tying protection ribbons on the wrists of your brothers. Earlier, I had bought ribbons for my brothers and for Maharajji as well. I left the ones for my brothers at home but had Maharajji's in my purse. I'd never spent this day with Maharajji and I very much wanted to tie the ribbon around his wrist, but I felt shy doing it in front of so many people. When we were alone for a moment he let me tie it on his wrist. Just then someone came into the room and Maharajji said to him, very shyly, "Mother is tying the Rakshabandhan."*

Maharajji had been in his room all morning, giving darshan to many people. After many hours Dada whispered to Maharajji, as a father to a child, "Come, Maharajji, you have been in here all morning and have never once gone to urinate."

Maharajji put the blame squarely on Dada's shoulders: "It's all your fault. You didn't remind me!"

Maharajji once seemed to make a great effort to pick up a dead fly on a piece of paper. Finally he held it out for Dada to take. As Dada reached for it the fly flew away, and Maharajji said angrily, "I went to all that trouble, and you let it go!"

"Baba," said Dada, "it was in your hand, not mine." Maharajji just laughed.

In 1968, at Kainchi, Maharajji would spend most of the day sitting on Dada's bed. He would say, "Dada keeps awake, so I must stay up, too." At 3:00 A.M. he came to Dada's room, knocking. "You wake me, so today I wake you!"

"But it's 3:00 A.M.," protested Dada, *"and I wake you at 5:00."* Maharajji just laughed and came in.

तुम

Once the Ma's came to Maharajji, saying, *"Maharajji, come take your bath."*
"Go away," he replied. *"I don't want to. Come, KK, we'll go to Vrindaban!"*

तुम

Maharajji was lying down, sick with a cold. Mrs. Soni, who had never seen him lying sick like that, rubbed his feet and said, *"Oh, Maharajji, your feet are so cold."*
"Are they, Ma?" He was like a little child.
It was a new moon, which is auspicious to see. So just as one would with a child, she said, *"Maharajji, come to the door and look at the new moon and you'll be better."*
"Will I, Ma?" She helped him to the door, coaxing him. *"Ma, I don't see it."*
"There it is."
"Where, Ma?" Finally: *"Oh, I see it."*
Then she said, *"Now you'll be all better tomorrow."* She helped him back to bed, and the next day he was better.

तुम

One devotee said that although she had a camera she had never taken pictures of Maharajji. She would lend her camera to others. One day it was loaded and in her possession. She was alone with Maharajji and decided to try to take pictures.
"He tried to pull my leg. You know—posing this way and that, turning his head to the right, the left, pretending to meditate. It was such fun." She pointed out several photos of Maharajji, now on the ashram walls, which were taken at the time.

Only we were allowed to be with him at all times—while he was eating, bathing, or going to the latrine. He was so delightful! Sometimes he was like a small child—so playful and joyful. Sometimes he would seem so helpless.

A man would come to Kainchi dressed in his camouflage jungle clothes and tell Maharajji stories of his hunting exploits. Mahrajji called the man "hunter" in English. The man once skillfully described crawling stealthily through the grass in search of a tiger, slowly parting the grass ahead of him as he crawled. As he related the incident he acted out his part. All this time, Maharajji sat in seemingly rapt attention, with apprehension proper to the mood of the story. "Then suddenly," said the hunter, "there in front of me was a tiger!"

At this, Maharajji leaped backward on his tucket, just as a child would do. Maharajji was so gleeful at such a good story.

Once when Westerners arrived Maharajji yelled with childlike delight, "Here they come! They've come to see me."

> *WHERE DID YOU GET THAT?*
> *NOBODY HAS GIVEN ME ANY.*

THERE IS A LONG history of Maharajji's association with dacoits, or robbers. To the extent that a person had a pure or spiritual spark, Maharajji would point to it and fan it—regardless of the person's social status. At the same time, he did not condone thievery, and he dealt harshly with it when it came to his attention. Besides meeting the lawless element of society in jails, which he often visited, he met them on the road in culverts. In his earlier days when he wandered the jungle, the huge ditches under the roads that were designed to hold the monsoon rains served well as shelter in the night. And here he found individuals who became, in one way or another, his devotees.

Maharajji slept in many culverts. So did dacoits. They would go in and push aside the cobwebs and all. There is one huge culvert near Mathura under a bridge where robbers go and await their prey. Maharajji would stay there and the dacoits would say, "Baba, are we going to get any money tonight? You'd better say yes or we'll kill you."

Maharajji says that's why he knows all the bad guys.

Dacoits would get free education in Nainital. The children would come to see Maharajji, and Maharajji would say of their fathers, "Their hearts are pure sometimes." Someone showed Maharajji a picture of a dacoit with rudraksham *beads (sacred beads of Shiva). "How sincere," Maharajji commented. "He did bad things but he was pure in his duty."*

A policeman lead a captive through town and was being very cruel to him. Maharajji said, "Don't do that."

The policeman was very abusive to Maharajji, but Maharajji replied, "You should be more kind. You never know when you will be in the same position."

The next day the policeman was arrested for bribery and taken in chains through the town.

Maharajji was visiting a jail during Ram Lila *(a festival during which the Ramayana is enacted daily), and the inmates were acting out the Ramayana, dressed in appropriate costumes. The jail superintendent was arrogantly telling Maharajji who was in prison for what and for how long—even while the inmates were enacting characters from the Ramayana. The superintendent's old father came, and Maharajji had him do arti to the fellow who was playing Ram and also touch his feet. This humbled the superintendent.*

A woman and her sister were taken by Maharajji to visit a juvenile jail in Bareilly. The convicts had constructed a dais for Maharajji to sit on, but they were required to remain some distance from him. They sang kirtan, with folded hands. Maharajji gave some money to the superintendent for sweets for everyone but told him not to tell where the money had come from. As they were leaving they saw some young boys, sitting in their cells.

One of the women with Maharajji asked, "Maharajji, can't you do something for them?"

Maharajji was in tears. "Do you want to take that responsibility?"

Once Maharajji was arrested as a loiterer and put in jail. Three or four times during the night he unlocked the cell to go out and urinate, much to the perturbation of the jailer. In the morning, the jailer told his superior of the trouble Maharajji had caused him. The superior realized who Maharajji was and apologized, brought him food, and let him go. He became a great devotee of Maharajji.

Maharajji frequently used the expression "Central Jail" in reference to his body and to the ashrams. Maharajji used this expression even before J became superintendent of police of the Central Jail. Maharajji used to visit an Anglo-Indian devotee who was in the Fategarh Central Jail. While visiting J's home, Maharajji would ask for prison food and they would serve him the prisoners' fare. He would eat it, then visit the prisoners. A few of these people, who were from all walks of life, even considered themselves devotees.

Dada and Gurudatt Sharma were with Maharajji in a jeep on their way to the temple at Bhumiadhar. As they drove up to the temple they saw some men who were apparently trying to break in. Maharajji grew very excited and said, "They're after Hanumanji! Let's go! Let's go!"

The dacoits ran off down the road. Maharajji jumped out of the jeep, dropped his blanket, and took off down the road after them, running full speed.

Dada and Gurudatt Sharma tried to keep up but kept getting in each other's
way, and by the time they caught up with Maharajji he was already returning.
He was laughing and happy. "I chased them, Dada. I scared them! I yelled so
loud that they peed in their pants. I did good, Dada. Didn't I do good?"

ॐ

Once an inspector who had been accused of taking a bribe, the Central
Excise Commissioner, and Maharajji were sitting together. Maharajji asked
the inspector, "You take bribes, don't you?"
    The man trembled and wept. Maharajji asked the Commissioner, "He will
be thrown out and go to jail?"
    The boss replied, "I don't know."
    Maharajji then said, "If he's thrown out, his children and wife will die."
    The man was acquitted. Maharajji would get people to make confessions
publicly, and thereby clear their conscience, and then he would seek compassion
for them.

ॐ

It was a hot summer night and Maharajji and some devotees were sitting
outside on the lawn at D's house. Maharajji was sitting in the only chair. All
the members of the top-class gentry encircled him. I sat at a distance, watching.
Then two people came, one dressed in the traditional formal attire of an
advocate and one in a dhoti. Both pranammed and took a seat beside me, but
Maharajji ignored them and talked to those in the circle. The two newcomers
were very impatient and the advocate wanted to leave. I felt much trouble in
them, for if you are before a saint, why run? The advocate pressed the man in
white, who stood up and got Maharajji's attention. He said he had a request.
    Maharajji said, "Go on."
    He continued, "My friend [advocate] is in great trouble."
    So Maharajji said to the advocate, "You are not an advocate, are you?"
    He replied, "True, I am not."
    Maharajji asked, "What is your trouble?"
    The man couldn't answer but his friend in white said, "He was involved in
murder."
    "Did you not commit murder?" asked Maharajji.
    "No."

"Was not the murder arranged by you?"

"Yes."

Maharajji looked as if he were viewing a slide before his eyes. Maharajji said, "What harm did he do you? Was he not a simple and honest man?"

"Yes, but he was a hurdle in my way."

Maharajji said, "He had three or four children. It is a heinous crime. Are you not sorry?"

"Yes."

"You will not do it again in your life?"

"No."

"Now you can go," Maharajji said.

The man in the dhoti asked, "Will he be acquitted?"

Maharajji said, "Yes, he will be pardoned."

Maharajji said to the murderer, "Think of the man's wife and helpless children. Who will look after them?" The man was trembling.

"Look after the children," Maharajji continued, "and help them, and you will realize later what you have done." The judge for the case had already written a decision, but late at night he got up and changed the judgment to acquittal.

ૐ

During Maharajji's absence a number of bags of cement were stolen from the Vrindaban ashram. As soon as he returned he called for the gardener.

"How many bags of cement did you steal?"

"No, Maharajji, I didn't take them."

"Tell me," Maharajji continued, "how much money did you get for them?"

"Nothing."

Maharajji stood up and slapped the gardener on the face so hard that he fell to the ground. Then Maharajji walked away, leaving him there. Five minutes later, Maharajji inquired of others, "How is he now? Call him."

The gardener again came before Maharajji.

"Did you steal them? How many rupees?"

The gardener confessed and said that he received 250 rupees for the cement.

Maharajji turned to the man in charge of the ashram accounts and said to him, "Give him another 250 rupees," and to the gardener, "Now, go!"

The gardener was fired and sent away. Some time later he returned and touched Maharajji's feet and begged to have his old job back again.

Maharajji said, "You've come back! This time I'll put you in Central Jail."

The gardener was sent to the Lucknow temple, where Mahotra, a retired prison official, was the manager.

जय

A policeman and a dacoit were both visiting Maharajji. Each was massaging a leg. Maharajji said to the dacoit, "There is a bounty out for you and anyone who brings you in gets a reward, isn't that true?"

"I don't know, Maharajji," the dacoit replied.

Then Maharajji turned to the policeman, "Do you recognize him?"

"No, Maharajji."

Such was his play.

Subtle Is the Path of Love

WHEN MAHARAJJI gave one American devotee the name of Chaitanya
Maha Prabhu, he told him that his name meant "consciousness of God
within the heart." Later Chaitanya wrote a poem that delicately suggests
the precious moments and feelings we shared in Maharajji's presence.

You move through woods
before you reach the temple
    and cross a flowing stream.
Gentle, so gentle . . .
        Perhaps he's there;
        perhaps not.
Either way you're sure of sweets, and other nourishment
that promises so much.
And like your dreams
not even sleep is required; all is provided free.
The only limitation is—doubt—
nothing else.

For here there is no need of you; you are free
to come and go. Free to see
all that was once relation
wander in a place beyond your expectation.

How can anyone describe what happened?
        I never asked any questions.
        Didn't relax.
        It's not as if I suddenly became a child.
When others sang
I'd catch my hands
        and watch.
If you asked I'd have to say
        nothing happened—nothing at all.
I don't know how much was prepared
before I came:
        He merely looked at me . . .
        and, like the wind,
                was everywhere
                suddenly
                everything.

He was the edge of cliffs
biding me to leap.
The leap itself
its river-sound and rock space.
Fear he was, and longing
the hesitation, trust
the standing still.
        And no matter where I fall
        he holds me.

True, it is strange
        to inhabit the earth so lightly,
to have one's proper name
        drop away
like a leaf you hid behind . . .
to have a new name tremble awkwardly
        over your lips . . .
to find the voice behind the lips
        suddenly singing.

It's hard being dead
at first, when the world no longer seems strong
        enough to hold you
and you long to know the time, what
        day it is,
                his name.
He is tender with you then, and all doors
are open to you.
He lets you go on wishing
your own wishes; nothing is required.
You are free
to test your world
like a broken toy
against his playful emptiness. Perhaps
this is all you need, a contrast
        with your world . . .
some sweets, a place to be, a show to watch . . .
Enough—to be no longer who you used to be
Enough—
        But subtle is the path of love.
        No answers and no questions.

Each day with him has its own momentum.
The only thing missing is a beginning.

The change can be total.
Here where love is
stronger than electricity,
and candles burn more slowly
than the candles you know.
Here, where days neither begin nor end—quiet days,
neither inside nor out, neither with others
nor alone.

So simple. So strange.
Being free to go, you're drawn to stay. Still,
he may not look at you for months. Never ask
your name or offer another to you.
Your anxious hands may never catch
the fruit he throws so quickly without seeing you.
His feet may seem too close to the earth
for you to kiss—no matter.
As you remain with him you
Grow used to the stars and
rise dark mornings so you can hurry to him . . .

Those things that combine to distract you will vanish
in your readiness to be always in his presence.
The shame it evokes, and the hope,
are the lovers you first
spy on. He lets you watch them create each other
while he just lives there in such sweetness
that their differences commingle in his light.

And soon, their power over you
flies like fruit from his open hands, and
they close forever
over what you thought you were.
Here in this orchard of the heart
he feeds you all you bring him,
though you may never realize how.

So simple, so strange.
And still you think,
Have I tricked myself again?
What do I want,
*   and why?*
What keeps me here—
*   is this his so-called power?*
If only I could leave, I would. Perhaps,
I've strayed among the cliffs too long—
perhaps, I'm lost . . .
*   What's happened to my future?*
This isn't what I want
or is it?

So simple. So strange.
He sat upon a wooden bed and looked
unreal and far away.
When I first saw him
*   I looked at him*
*   he didn't look at me.*
I made no difference in his world.
Everything was new to me then
*   even his elbows made me laugh.*

And his loving eyes gazed openly
into my hidden world.
Asking nothing, being all.

Those were the graceful days.
We did nothing at all.
He used to say we were good for nothing
but the five-limbed yoga: eating, drinking, sleep,
    gossip, and moving about.
Alone among friends
we ate with our hands
    and tossed our leaf plates in the river.

How like himself
he was
    opening doors
    sitting where he sat
    walking here and there
    saying what he pleased
    laughing when he laughed
       and we laughed with him.
Letting all distinctions, like the future,
    which before had moved so restlessly ahead,
    conform to the folds of his blanket.
So much
is being with him
    his presence being all.
"Don't throw anyone out of your heart,"
    he said. "Love people and feed them."

So simple. So strange.
He let us walk with him and hold his hand.
Put flowers on our heads and pulled our beards.
He'd send us away
and call us back, married us
and named our children—
Who could he be?

Oh, what a funny old man
his clothes were falling off.
We came to be here now
and he said, "Come back tomorrow."

What is it that touches the purest secret in us
lets us enter
          where all is distance?

Is it truth
so familiar it seems to live alone?
—the tense urge that lovers are . . .
the space between two thoughts . . .
a letting go . . .
The gift
          flowers endlessly . . .
forever turning us toward love's beginnings
to where
          we no longer are.
Only absence left
to remind us.

Thoughts arise and pass away.

There is nothing I can do.
No thoughts
no deeds
    can save me.
I sing. I dance
with hands held high in adoration.
I play my part . . . all other roles
    being taken;
the unseen and the seen.
So it has been.
So it will be.

A trusting heart
consumes all lies.

O Beloved,
there are no distinctions;
the whole universe is strung upon you.
This garland I place at your feet—
    let me give you flowers . . .
my child, my lover,
you cold old stone
monkey man . . .
There is nothing I can do to touch you.
Still, I will.
Brother among brothers
sister father friend,
why pull your blanket from my hands?

To help me is such a trifling matter.
The pain is too much to bear.

But I bear it. I bear all. There is nothing else.
let me give you flowers . . .

Forever let my love be unfulfilled
Forever let me yearn for you

Can I ever forget that I never remember you?

Subtle is the path of love.

So simple. So strange.

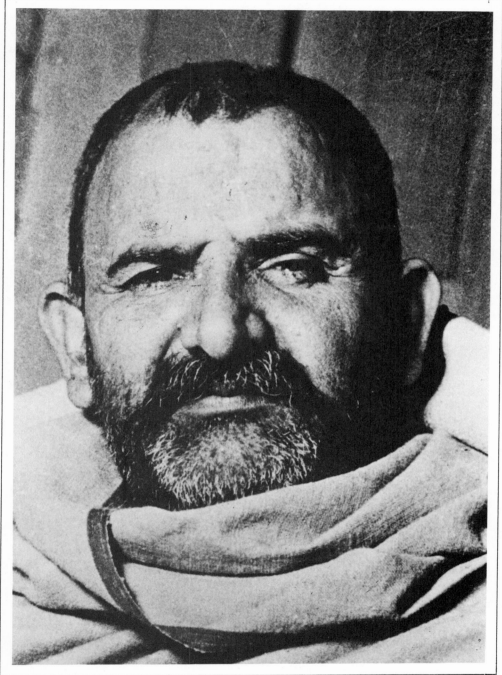

Faith ... No Fear

ALL THE COLORFUL melodrama that transpired wherever Maharajji went; all the various ways the devotees thought of and reacted to Maharajji, and his many faces in response; the anger and abuse, the chiding, the tenderness—all of this filled the time and space when we were around him, and yet . . . we knew that this was a part, but not the essence, of the relationship. It was not acts or words or opinions, but something far more subtle that Maharajji was transmitting to us. It was deep within ourselves that Maharajji was gently transforming us.

There was no aspect of life that was not touched by him.

You know, you could go to Maharajji filled with many problems. You'd sit with him a while and they would all be solved.

He would create an entire situation just to teach you. He never gave lectures or taught from scriptures, but he taught through incidents and situations.

Maharajji guided us on all levels—spiritual, mental, and material. He gave instructions in how to raise children and in being a good marriage partner and in business. But these were not specific rules or instructions. He guided by changing the heart.

I was invited by a group of high-powered folks at Esalen to join them in studying with a Sufi teacher in South America. I was very uncertain about the whole matter, so I wrote to KK in India and asked him to find out from Maharajji whether I should go to Chile for these studies. Then the answer came back from KK: "Maharajji says that you can go and study with a Sufi saint if you desire."

As I read the letter something happened in my heart and I suddenly felt absolutely certain that I didn't want to go, and so I didn't. On my next visit to India, when discussing this letter with KK, he told me, "When I asked Maharajji, he said, 'If he wishes, let him go . . .' And then he said, 'Why would he want to go?' But then quickly he added, 'Don't write that last part in the letter.' " (R.D.)

It was at this deeper level that we felt Maharajji to be the shepherd and ourselves to be a part of the flock. Through this unspoken process we developed faith where previously there had been fear. Our faith was that in the midst of the changing uncertainties of the universe, if we kept Maharajji in our hearts, if we just stayed under his blanket in trust, then it would be all right.

Devotees who had been with Maharajji for many years often reflected a fearlessness in the manner in which they lived, as the result of their faith in his protection. Some he specifically taught to be fearless.

Maharajji once called me over and said, "Ram Dass, you are to fear nothing." (R.D.)

ॐ

Once, when my finances were in disarray, Maharajji came to my place and said I should not have anxiety. I said to him I wasn't calling for any anxiety—though I was indeed anxious. "No, no, no. You should not have any anxiety."

It is strange. I am still that same person, but even in a crisis I feel it will be set right sooner or later. Maharajji does it: I have had no anxiety.

My wife says, "You are completely changed. Even serious matters you take lightly."

He didn't say that he would do so, but at that moment he took my anxiety.

ॐ

Maharajji had taken all my responsibilities on his shoulders. He told me, "Don't be afraid of anything. No one can do anything against you!" When he was physically before us we were not so courageous, but now I am more courageous day by day. Now his power is working. Now I see him in dreams but only for a moment. I have faith that he is working for his devotees.

ॐ

KK had much fear—suppression of the soul. Maharajji said, "You are afraid. You are so simple and they are clever and they fool you. You are afraid of Brahmins. But you will not be afraid of anybody."

KK replied, "For this, I want the grace of your blessing."

Then Maharajji patted him on the back two or three times, and after that everyone noticed a change in KK.

ॐ

One time I was reported to the officials for packing underweight fruit boxes. I was innocent, but the charge had me worried. Maharajji chastised me:

"*Coward! Never be a coward! Be brave! Coward! Why do you fear? Don't you know me? I am with you!*" Then he reminded me of how Ram protected his devotees. He said that he too would always protect his devotees. Even if they committed hundreds of murders, he would give them complete protection.

THERE WAS no dearth of examples, for those who needed them, to demonstrate that faith in Maharajji was well placed.

Well, I was staying in Kainchi. I went to Maharajji and said, "Now I have to go. It is my fruit season and I have to be there. Otherwise I will incur a great loss."

I am a worldly man, you know. My fruit must be picked and sent off to Bombay and such places. Every day I remained in Kainchi, it was getting riper and would soon be too ripe to send away.

Maharajji said, "No, no you will stay here. You will go tomorrow."

Fifteen days passed in this way. Then, finally, Maharajji said, "Tomorrow I will send you. Be sure about it."

So the next day I came here and the fruit was all overripe. I thought, "Well, Maharajji has given me a loss." All the fruit was overripe, and I could only send it off to the local markets at Kanpur or Allahabad—not to Bombay, where we got better prices.

And what happened? There was a great slump in the market! Those people who had sent their fruits to Bombay, Calcutta, or Madras couldn't even make up the freight charges! And I, who had sent my fruit to local markets, got more than my expectations. I had been so very much annoyed with this Maharajji who had unnecessarily detained me in Kainchi. Who knows his works?

ૐ

The enemies of a certain family had for some reason surrounded the family's house and locked them inside for three days and nights. If they stayed inside any longer they would starve, and if they went outside they would be beaten by these wicked ones. While the family inside was discussing their dilemma, they heard some shouting at their door: "Open up! Open up! Come out and fight! Are you caste or are you cowards? Come on!" They peeked outside and saw Maharajji waving a stick and shouting. They all grabbed sticks and ran out to Maharajji. When the attackers saw the family armed with sticks and being led by this fat man, they ran away.

Maharajji then said, "Telephone so-and-so and so-and-so. Tell them that I am here."

Within half an hour, police generals and government ministers were sitting in the living room of the man's house. Thereafter the attacks on the family ceased.

उॐ

A man's eight-month-old child was standing on a thirty-foot balcony. A servant and the child's brother were there playing with a kite when the child fell to the marble floor thirty feet below. The mother tried to catch the child but couldn't. The child didn't move, but still there seemed to be no broken bones. Suddenly the child laughed, and the doctors could find nothing wrong at all and said that this was impossible. Some days later, Maharajji came to their house and said, "You were worried. You still didn't realize who you have on your shoulders, protecting you. The baby didn't fall on the ground. It fell on my lap."

उॐ

While in Madras one day, Maharajji said, "I want to show my eyes to a good doctor. Who is a good doctor here?" I told him that there was a specialist nearby. Maharajji said, "All right. I'll show my eyes to him." That evening I found that this doctor was out of town, so I fixed an appointment with another specialist for 10:30 in the morning.

When I explained the situation to Maharajji, he asked who the other doctor was, and when I told him his name Maharajji said, "Nay, nay! I want to see the first doctor, not this other one."

Maharajji told me to come to him after three days. This was a long time and I was impatient. After two days the first doctor had returned, so I made an appointment for Maharajji. I went immediately to the dharmashala (hostel) *to tell him, but Maharajji's luggage was just being carried out. When I told him the doctor had come, he laughed and said, "Today I'm going to Rameshwaram." He refused to let me accompany him.*

Nearly a month later, on my way to Bombay, I broke my spectacles. A specialist there made new spectacles for me, but within five minutes of putting them on I got a serious headache. The specialist checked everything and said they were all right but it would take a few days to get used to them.

I returned to Madras, but I still couldn't put on those specs for more than a few moments. I decided to show them to a specialist in Madras and wondered which one I should go to—the first doctor or the second. Now, the second was

*very quick and always available, while the first was very busy and one had to
wait for hours to see him. But I remembered what Maharajji had said, so I
made an appointment with the first one. When I told my son, he asked to come
along for a check-up. The doctor tested my eyes and found that the new specs
the Bombay doctor had given were the wrong prescription. That was corrected.
When he examined my son's eyes he found the cornea was torn—serious
enough for an immediate operation. Although he missed his final examinations
at college, my son's eyes were saved. This is what Maharajji's lila (play;
game) of a month earlier had been about.*

ॐ

*A devotee from Allahabad said he had met Maharajji forty years before. He
was traveling at night and he had become totally lost, when he suddenly saw a
cave with a light in it. As he approached the cave he discovered Maharajji
sitting there. Maharajji gave him food and after the meal said, "You are lost.
Go in that direction." In about fifteen paces the devotee suddenly saw the
village. But when he turned around, the cave and the terrain of the cave were
no longer there.*

ॐ

*Maharajji often called one devotee, a poor man, to accompany him on long
pilgrimages. The devotee always agreed without a complaint, although he often
had to borrow money to finance these trips. Once Maharajji asked him to come
to Badrinath. Before leaving, the man pointed to the small picture of Maharajji
on their puja table and told his wife that if for any reason she wanted to
communicate with him while he was gone she should address herself to
Maharajji's photo, since the two would be together. A few days later, high in
the Himalayas, Maharajji suddenly turned to this devotee and said, "Why
have you come here?"*

The devotee replied that he had come at Maharajji's request.

*Maharajji said, "At your home there is no dal, no flour, nothing. Your wife
is very worried because there is nothing to eat and you are far away. You
should have at least provided bread for them to eat!"*

*But Maharajji's presence had an intoxicating effect upon people. Their
worries vanished and they felt that he was taking care of everything for the
best. Half an hour after he had berated the devotee for leaving his wife without
food, Maharajji shouted out, "Food has come! They have got food. The
Kashmiri mother gave it to them. Don't worry."*

When he returned, the devotee questioned his wife. She said that when the food had finally run out she had gone to Maharajji's picture and told him that there was no more food in the house. Within a few minutes a rich neighbor, who treated her like a daughter, came to the house with bags of flour, rice, dal, and so forth. She went to the picture and thanked Maharajji.

राम

Once Maharajji saved me from a snake bite. I was passing the winter in a tiny room in Haldwani, where I was talking with someone, when suddenly I left off in mid-sentence for no accountable reason. I turned around and looked into my room. It was very strange. A snake was crawling into the room, and once inside it crawled under a gunny sack. I thought: Why was it that I turned around just then? It must be Neem Karoli Baba's doing (even though, physically, Maharajji was hundreds of miles away). I also thought that it must be a poisonous snake. Otherwise there would be no reason for Maharajji to show it to me. I very carefully put the snake in a cannister and released it outside. About five years later, I was complaining to Maharajji that he wasn't helping me in any way or protecting me; I was having too many troubles. Maharajji said, "Why? I saved your life once. I saved you from the snake." I had known in my mind that he had done it. Such things do not happen by accident.

राम

One dark, rainy night at Kainchi, Maharajji woke up several devotees and said there was a jeep half a mile up the road that was stuck. He said to take tea to the passengers. The devotees went running because he told them to hurry. Maharajji wanted them to go up where there was no path. They found the jeep with four women and a man, stranded there with no blankets. Maharajji sent even more devotees up to the jeep, saying to them, "That tea will be cold. Bring them more tea." When the people were finally brought to the temple, Maharajji said, "I used to visit the home of these women thirty years ago and they gave me a blanket and were kind." He gave them blankets and they remembered him from before.

राम

Normally when Maharajji was away, he would send his blessings from where he was. He wouldn't go to the phone. But while I was away for six *months in 1967, he visited my family in Kanpur practically once a month. While I was in Germany, my colleague and I were thinking of buying a car for the time and selling it later. We'd already decided on the car, which we were determined to buy on Sunday. On Saturday we didn't normally get any mail delivery, but this day before the sale a letter came from my wife. She said, "Maharajji has come today. He says that you are going to buy a car and that you shouldn't do that. If you have any such intentions, Maharajji's orders are to give them up." I told my friend that the deal was off and that if he bought it I wouldn't travel with him.*

How did Maharajji do this? He came one morning to visit my family and he asked my wife to write that letter. He said, "He'll do something foolish! Forbid him!" He went away and after two hours came again and asked her if she had written the letter. She hadn't. He said, "Well, I'm going to stay here until you write that letter and post it. Otherwise it will be too late." Only when it was posted did Maharajji leave. It could have reached us on Monday, but it came in time. That was the first and last time the mail ever came on Saturday afternoon. That was his grace. But why did he bother to come all the way from Kainchi to tell my wife? If he wanted, there were enough people right in front of him to bother with. Why did he think of me?

ॐ

Once in Haridwar, a man was bathing in the river and lost his footing. The man was tossed about and carried in a whirlpool like a log. He was quite a bit older than his wife (he was fifty-two and she fifteen when they married), who was much devoted to him. After taking Maharajji's name she jumped into the river and pulled her husband ashore. When they went to the place where Maharajji was, people there told them that Maharajji had been impossible and very abusive and would not let anyone near him. The woman went up and gently tapped at the door. He sweetly asked her in and inquired after her nose ring (which she had lost in the river). (The loss of a nose ring is a bad omen for an Indian woman, suggesting her husband's death.) When her husband came along, Maharajji said, "You were going down the river like a piece of wood being whirled around." Apparently the changes in Maharajji's behavior, the abusiveness, had been involved in saving the man.

ॐ

Maharajji takes care of all his devotees in so many ways. One day a devotee was on his way to Kainchi and en route stopped at a roadside food stand and ate some fried pakoras. (*In those days, he ate pakoras every day.*) *When he arrived at Kainchi, the first thing Maharajji said was, "Do you eat pakoras? You've been eating those things for a long time now! Why do you eat them? You'll ruin your stomach." From that day onward, this devotee never again ate pakoras from the bazaar.*

ᵣᵀᵧ

A woman devotee was sitting in the corner of the room near a strange man. Maharajji said to her, "Come sit here. The bad karma of other people can affect a person."

ᵣᵀᵧ

A doctor from Bombay who attended many VIPs, including Nehru, was a somewhat stiff person (though he often gave massages to others). Another devotee was present when the doctor was visiting Maharajji. Maharajji saw the doctor coming and went into another room. He said, "I'll not see him." Then from the other room Maharajji yelled, "You couldn't save Nehru. What's wrong?"

The doctor said, "When I gave him the massage he got better, but then his nerves got very bad." The other devotee asked the doctor if he had traveled outside India.

"Yes, for twelve months attending VIPs."

She asked him how he knew Maharajji.

He replied, "I never believed in saints. In the Independence movement of 1942 I was a revolutionary and there were orders out to shoot me. I was in Kanprayag, near Badrinath. I was at a small dharmasalla, and while I was bathing Maharajji was upbraiding a swami nearby. As I passed by, Maharajji caught hold of me and said, 'You are hungry. Go into that room.' In the room there were two leaf plates of fresh puris and potatoes, which Maharajji told me to eat. When I finished all I could eat, Maharajji said, 'Take more with you. Now run. Within an hour the police will be here. Go to Tibet. But don't go by this route, go by that one.' But I had some doubts about Maharajji and left a friend behind to wait and see. In an hour a district superintendent of police who knew Maharajji came with a search party inquiring for the doctor. Maharajji asked him, 'Who would come at this hour?' And as they started to proceed toward Tibet, Maharajji warned them not to: 'This is the season for avalanches, and if you go on an avalanche will kill you. Go back.' So they went back."

जय

One day, when Maharajji was at a village near Neeb Karori, a woman
came to get water from the well. Maharajji laughed. When a devotee asked
why he laughed, he said that the woman and her husband lived in a village
three miles away and in six hours her husband was going to die from seeking
this same water that she was fetching. "He is going to become thirsty and he is
going to go to the water jug and be bitten by a cobra. But, Maharajji added, if
the devotee wanted to, he might be able to save him." The devotee immediately
sent two or three men, who ran all the way and stopped the man just as he
was going for the water. Indeed, there was a cobra there and the man was
saved.

जय

A forester from Agra came to Kainchi en route to Calcutta, and Maharajji
told him, "Don't leave today."
"But Maharajji, I have to go. I have an interview."
Maharajji insisted. The forester was sulky but didn't go. The next day in
the papers he read that India's worst train accident in living memory had
involved the train he would have been on.

जय

In 1943 Maharajji came to Fatehgarh, where there was an old couple whose
son was away fighting in Burma. When Maharajji came to their house they
gave the little they had to Maharajji. They had only two cots. Maharajji said,
"I'll sleep now." They gave him one of the cots and a blanket. The old
couple stayed up the whole night watching Maharajji. He was groaning and
moving in the bed until 4:00 A.M. At 4:30 Maharajji became quiet; then he
took the bedsheet and wrapped something in it. He told the old man, "It's very
heavy. Don't try to see what's in it. You should throw it into the Ganga
where it is deep. No one should see you or you'll be arrested." As he was
taking it to the Ganga he felt it and it was full of bullets.
When he returned, the old man was told by Maharajji, "Don't worry. Your
son is coming in a month." When the son came some weeks later, he said he
had almost died. His company had been ambushed by the enemy and by chance

*he had fallen into a ditch. All night, bullets were flying left and right. At 4:00
A.M. the Japanese saw that they had killed everyone, and so they retreated. At
4:30 the Indian troops came. The son was the only survivor. (It was the same
night Maharajji had visited the parents that this ambush occurred.)*

ॸ

One day Maharajji asked to be driven from the plains to the distant
mountain town of Bhimtal. He went straight to a devotee's house and told the
people there to go to the old pilgrimage rest cabin at the Shiva temple and
bring back whomever was staying there. For years no one had stayed in the
dilapidated rest cabin, so the devotees thought it very unusual when they found
one of the doors locked from within. They knocked and shouted but no one
answered. Then they returned and reported to Maharajji.

Maharajji left that house and went to see another devotee, where he again
sent people to the rest house with instructions not to return without its
occupant. They caused a great commotion at the door until finally an old man
opened the window. He tried to send the devotees away but they persisted,
until finally the man and his wife were taken to Maharajji. Immediately
Maharajji started shouting, "Do you think you can threaten God by starving
yourselves? He won't let his devotees die so easily. Take prasad!" He called
for puris and sweets, but the man refused them. Maharajji insisted, and finally
they both ate.

The couple had come from south India on a pilgrimage to Badrinath and
other holy places. They were from a very rich family but had decided to leave
home and family behind to devote their remaining years to prayer. They had
resolved always to pay their own way and never to beg. As they were
returning from Badrinath, all their money and possessions had been stolen.
They had only enough money for bus fare to Bhimtal, where they found the
deserted rest cabin. They resolved to stay there and die, since that seemed to be
the Lord's will. They had been locked inside without food for three days before
Maharajji forced them out. Maharajji insisted that they accept money for their
trip back to Madras. They said that they would not beg. Maharajji said they
were not begging and they could mail the money back when they reached home.
They accepted the money and were sent off.

*O Kabir, why be afraid of anyone when the Lord Himself protects you?
What does it matter if a thousand dogs bark fiercely when you are seated
on an elephant?*

Key to the Mind

STORIES SHOWING Maharajji's deep concern for his devotees and his protectiveness of them also suggest awesome powers of mind. It seemed as if he knew everything about his devotees, whether we were near to him or far away. It is little wonder that we could become fearless, knowing that he was literally watching over us.

I was with Maharajji during the time of the partition and there were so many refugees from Pakistan that there was hardly a space to place a foot. Maharajji and I were picking our way through the crowd, and one woman came and bowed before him and requested that he come and bless a newborn baby some distance from where we were. Maharajji agreed.

Further along, the same woman was complaining bitterly of the destruction of Lahore. Maharajji immediately chastised her with a rhetorical question: "Didn't that saint in Lahore tell you six months ago that this was going to happen?"

राम

Sometimes when many people came to him he would relate each person's personal history, including what their forefathers had done, as if he had been well acquainted with that person for a very long time.

Since Maharajji would sometimes not let us Westerners come to him until the afternoon, one morning a group of us went to visit the tiny ashram that at one time had been the residence of another great saint of that area, Sombari Maharaj. It was a good visit. En route back in the forenoon, we encountered a hill that the VW bus just couldn't climb with all of us in it, so we got out to push—that is, all of us except for the two young women in the party, who didn't bother to get out.

We easily got the bus up the hill, but I was rankled by the fact that the young women had not helped us. I was too well-bred to say anything; inside though, I was angry and remained silent for the remainder of the drive to the temple. As we entered the temple Maharajji said, "Ram Dass is angry." But I had hidden it well and everyone disagreed with Maharajji and said that, on the contrary, I had been very pleasant. But Maharajji was not to be deterred. "No," he said, "Ram Dass is angry because the young women wouldn't get out and help push." (R.D.)

Once when Maharajji was sitting in a room with no windows, he said, "Oh, so-and-so is coming just now!" Within a few moments, this person entered the room.

Maharajji told me all sorts of things. He said, "You have been playing hockey with the Mother." He was referring to the fact that I had been at Sri Aurobindo's ashram for a while and had played hockey with the Mother.

In the 1940s a Moslem ICS (Indian Civil Service) officer's son who was studying in England had had a heart attack, and his mother had gone to see her son there. Maharajji was visiting the house of a devotee who never asked anything of Maharajji; but in this case he asked Maharajji about the boy, as they were family friends. Before he could put the question to Maharajji, Maharajji said, "What? He's asking about that boy who is studying in England. What do you want to ask? The mother has gone there. You've seen her off at the airport. As soon as she arrived the son began to improve." Then Maharajji got up and said, "Let's go. This is how the mind travels." (It was confirmed later that the boy did begin to improve once his mother arrived.)

Maharajji asked a man if he'd ever before seen such a place as Kainchi—so beautiful and peaceful and ideal for meditation, with its mountains and river and forests. The swami replied that he'd once seen a similar place in Kandy (Sri Lanka). Maharajji, who had never been there, surprised the man by describing that place, down to the smallest details.

Our eldest daughter had appeared in some competitive examinations for employment in the government of India. After the exams we went to see Maharajji in Vrindaban. As we were pranamming to him, Maharajji addressed her and said, "You have spoiled five of your exam papers!"

She said, "Yes."

Maharajji said, "Don't worry. You'll still come out successful and you'll get your job."

And she did.

Our family is large but not rich, yet with his blessings we've been carrying on quite well. I got my job in the bank by his grace. After I had my job interview I went to see him. He told me all the questions I was asked and said, "You'll be selected." In fact, I had come out at the top of the list.

ॐ

Maharajji turned to me one day and said, "Do you still send money to that Benares pundit *[religious scholar]?"*

"Yes, Maharajji, I do," I replied.

Maharajji had never met this pundit nor had I ever told Maharajji that I regularly sent money to him. This pundit was a reciter of the Ramayana and he lived off donations from his listeners. Maharajji knew all things and he would look after people he'd never met.

ॐ

A devotee who worked for the railroad brought a couple for the first time to see Maharajji. The wife was told by Maharajji in private, "You have been supporting a poor ten-year-old child. That is very fine of you to do." When she came out of the room she was quite astounded, because no one, not even her husband, knew that she was supporting the child.

ॐ

Before we eat we offer our food to a picture of Maharajji. Once my wife forgot to put salt in the curry. "I forgot, but Maharajji will forgive me." Fifteen days later, Maharajji came and my wife sat at his feet. The first thing he said to her was, "You gave me curry without salt."

ॐ

One of the young men from a family in Kanpur was in the military fighting in the China War. The report came that he had died and the brother came to tell Maharajji. Maharajji said, "No, he has not died." No one believed Maharajji, and the widow married again in six months and the file of the war department was closed. After some time, the man returned.

ॐ

In 1968, after I had been at the temple for some time, I had to go to Delhi. At that time, I was trying to be a very pure yogi. In Delhi I did all my business with dispatch and then had time for a vegetarian lunch before returning to the mountains. At the end of the meal I was served two biscuits with tea. I didn't think they were proper yogi food, but they were cream-filled and I couldn't resist. But since I was barefoot and in my ulfie *(sadhu clothing) and was being treated as a sadhu even in the restaurant, I ate the cookies surreptitiously. Upon my return to Maharajji his first words were, "How did you like the biscuits?" (R.D.)*

ऊँ

Since I was one of the few Westerners who spoke Hindi, he'd talk with me. Sometimes we'd gossip, and he'd pull one or two dazzlers. He'd mention somebody that I'd never mentioned to anybody else and say, "What was the story with this person?" I'd do a double take! And he'd laugh and giggle and then look at me and smile. Much of the time when I was sitting with Maharajji I would find myself turning into a giggling idiot. I'd roll around and sometimes virtually fall over, and he'd give me a great big hug.

THE GURU MUST KNOW EVERYTHING ABOUT YOU.

I KNOW EVERYTHING. WHY DO I KNOW?

NOT ONLY WAS Maharajji watching over us, but he could easily see within us as well. And that was quite a different matter.

To realize that someone has access to the secret compartments of your mind is unnerving. It gives rise to a type of intimacy that is unparalleled in most of our human relationships. Those of us who are close to another person often sense what the other is feeling. When we have come to know the way another thinks we may even be able to guess what is on his or her mind. But there are so many tiny, subtle thoughts; and many of these are censored almost the moment they come to mind because they would be socially unacceptable or even unacceptable to our own conscious image of ourselves. To realize that someone has access even to these thoughts immediately puts you at an extraordinary disadvantage, as if your opponent had broken your code. You are so vulnerable. But of course it is also incredibly exciting to meet another consciousness in such an intimate way. And with Maharajji, added to this was a quality of unconditional love coming from the other, as if he were saying to you, "I know all about you and I love you."

The most precious things about Maharajji cannot be described in stories—like massaging his legs. If I had a useless thought as I was massaging him, he'd pull my hand away; and then, when I would recenter my mind, he'd put my hand back. In those subtle ways he would teach you.

The first time my wife met Maharajji was among a crowd at the India Hotel. Maharajji had not spoken to her, and after some time she was thinking that she should be home preparing tea for me, which she did every day at that time. Maharajji was distributing sweets and suddenly he turned to her and said, "You go home now. Your husband is waiting for his tea."

When I first was new to him, he had just had his head shaved and I thought how I'd love to kiss him right on the top of his head. And one darshan, shortly after that, he took me into his room. Giggling and laughing, he sort of doubled over and in so doing presented me the top of his head. There was nothing I could do but to kiss it, and I recognized at that moment that my desire was being granted.

I always talked to Maharajji in my mind. When he was embarrassing somebody, I'd think, "Oh, Maharajji, don't do that." Then he'd look at me and respond, so I knew he was hearing me.

One day when I was sitting by the tucket waiting for him to come out and give darshan, the thought occurred to me that I would like to have my heart beat at exactly the same rate and same time as Maharajji's. Just as soon as I thought that there was a great commotion from within the building, a slamming of doors, and suddenly Maharajji burst through the outer doors onto the porch. He briskly took his seat on the tucket and sat directly in front of me, his chest only some six inches away. I could feel my heartbeat and remained in constant consciousness of my heart beating in tune with his for some time. Although Maharajji was lively and talked with many people, he kept his body turned in this position close to me. Then my mind began to wander—and immediately Maharajji flipped around so that he was sitting on the far side of the tucket, facing away from me. Stunned, the thought flashed through my mind, "Maharajji, if that really happened, look at me." Quick as a flash he glanced directly at me and then away once more. He didn't look at me again for the rest of the darshan.

Maharajji played with my desires so subtly. I might spy an apple on his bench before he would appear for darshan. And I'd think how much I'd like that apple and how long it was since I'd had an apple. Then Maharajji would appear and he'd seem to make a point of throwing me that very apple. But of course he would be throwing other devotees other pieces of fruit, so you could never be sure. I'd always just think, "Isn't that interesting?"

Once when I was living high up in the hills behind the temple, where it was very cold, I heard from some newly arrived devotees about a space blanket used by the astronauts that was very warm and weighed only a few ounces. In my cold hut I kept thinking about how nice it would be to have such a blanket. The next morning I came to the temple and was having tea with another devotee, who was cleaning out his rucksack. He threw this thing at me and said, "Here, why don't you take this? It's a space blanket that I never use." When such things kept happening to me, I thought that if Maharajji was going to gratify all my desires I ought to start asking for more important things, like a little compassion.

In Bareilly Maharajji said to come to the station in the morning to meet him. There was a large flood and I thought, "Maharajji won't come, but I'll go to the station anyway." Maharajji came, however, and the first thing he said was, "You were thinking I couldn't come because of the flood."

If I would think to myself that a fellow devotee was less of a saint than he thought himself to be, Maharajji would immediately ask me, "So-and-so isn't as much of a saint as he thinks he is, is he?"

I told my wife I didn't want to go see Maharajji, because he'd only say to take prasad and go. But she insisted. That day he didn't ask me to go. I hadn't taken food but he let me stay until 11:00 P.M. As everyone stood up, Maharajji said, "From today, don't tell anyone I don't allow you to sit here."

I was sitting there praying for an opportunity to get away from the satsang to do some sadhana *(spiritual practice), when Maharajji said, "Go to Nepal." It turned out that my visa had expired the day before.*

Sometimes you'd be sitting behind him and he would appear unconcerned with you. Then some thought would arise in your mind and he would answer you directly or make some gesture or say something to someone else that would be an answer to the thought. Sometimes he would be in the room with you talking seriously, and in mid-sentence he'd turn around, open the window, and begin to talk to another person outside about what was on his mind.

Maharajji could give you a whole teaching just in a glance. You'd be sitting there, going through some incredible suffering in your mind. He would just look at you and your whole being would change. I don't know if he was actually doing anything or whether it was just the way he looked at you, but you knew that the universe was right and that you were taken care of. At other times you'd be going off on some mental tangent, when with just the slightest glance from Maharajji you would be totally demolished.

ॐ

A husband and wife tell the following story:

HUSBAND: *I was working in Calcutta in the smallpox program. It was one of those times when I was having a tiny pang of remorse. I went through the streets of Calcutta and I saw all the beggars, thought about their suffering, and as usual got into my argument with God about suffering. "It's really not necessary," I kept telling him.*

At that time I was reading the Phaedo, *Plato's account of Socrates' death, which ends with Socrates and his disciples discussing whether Socrates should postpone taking the hemlock, and Socrates says to bring it in, because it doesn't make any difference. The disciples are all crying and he tells them, "Listen, there are only two possibilities: either there is something after death or there is nothing after death. If there is nothing after death, then thank God at last I'm going to get a good sleep. And if there is something after death, then at least I have the chance of having a good conversation." Then they brought the hemlock, which he took and died.*

So I reasoned that if Socrates, in all his wisdom, at the time of his death didn't know the nature of life, then I really shouldn't feel so despondent that a simple soul like me didn't understand. Thus I was consoled.

WIFE: *At the same time my husband was in Calcutta, I was in Delhi looking for Maharajji. We finally found him at the home of the Barmans in New Delhi (this was his last visit to New Delhi before he left his body). We were sitting with him in the afternoon on the same day he had arrived. Maharajji looked at me and simply said, "Socrates." Later on that same day he looked at me again and said, "Socrates."*

I discussed this with the devotees accompanying me, trying to figure out what he had meant. Perhaps it was that I looked or thought like Socrates, but we couldn't quite figure it out. My husband came home from Calcutta, and after telling him that I had seen Maharajji I said, "You know, he said the strangest thing to me and we still don't understand what it means. He looked at me and called me 'Socrates.' What do you think it means?" Then my husband told me what he'd been thinking and we figured out that it was exactly the same day my husband just described.

†ᵢᵤ

Dada said, "Mind reading and telling the future and knowing who was coming and so forth—such things were always happening around Maharajji. There was nothing special about them."

THIS AWESOME capability of knowing the human mind allowed Maharajji not only to know the thoughts and acts of others but to be able to enter into the mind of another person and bring about change from within.

Maharajji once told me, "The key to the mind is in my hand and I can turn it in any direction."

†ᵢᵤ

During the English occupation an Englishman had reserved a first-class compartment on the train, and when he went to his compartment he found Maharajji there. He went to the conductor and said that there was a very disreputable looking man in his compartment and would they please remove him. The conductor came and looked and said, "I'm sorry. That's a saint and I can't remove him."

So the Englishman, now even more upset, sent for the chief conductor. When the chief conductor came, he said the same thing. So at the next major station the Englishman decided to remove the man himself, but the minute he went into the compartment he forgot his anger and mission and sat quietly and peacefully for the rest of the trip. Finally Maharajji said, "This is my village," and the train was stopped and he and his party got off.

†ᵢᵤ

I think it was he who made me go with him. I used to go with him but I never wanted to go.

ॐ

The Ma's, as they were called, were women whose greatest pleasure was in taking care of Maharajji. Once a doctor had said Maharajji should take certain pills at 10:00 A.M. On this particular morning the Ma's brought the medicine ten minutes late. Maharajji said fiercely, "If you people don't take better care of me, I'll turn your minds against me"—which was the worst threat he could make.

ॐ

I was the station master at Mount Abu and Maharajji had promised to come there sometime. When I was off duty it was my policy never to go into the station. But this one day I had been in a long conversation with a friend, and as I left I wanted somehow to break my policy by cutting through the station in order to save time getting home. Just as I got into the station and was rushing through, the Bombay Mail arrived, and there was Maharajji tapping at the window.

ॐ

A number of us Westerners were meditating together at a Buddhist ashram in Bodh Gaya. After a time, some of us were ready to take a break and go on to Delhi, several hundred miles away, to celebrate Shiva's birthday. One of the women in the group, who had come to India overland by charter bus, reported that the bus driver wanted to hang out with us, too. So thirty-four of us left Bodh Gaya and met the bus in Benares and started to drive to Delhi.

One of the men in the group, Danny, had left the courses briefly in the middle to visit Allahabad, in order to experience a Kumbha Mela. He had returned deeply impressed and bringing us each small medallions depicting the monkey, Hanuman, which he had purchased on the mela grounds.

When it turned out that the bus route went right by Allahabad, Danny pressed us to visit the mela grounds. I protested that the mela was now over and it would just be an empty piece of riverbank. But he pointed out that it was one of the most sacred spots in India. Some of us were tired, for it was only our first day out in the world after such sustained meditation practice, and all we really wanted was to get to the dharmasalla where we planned to stay *overnight. The thought of even driving the few miles out of our way to get to the river was not appealing, and yet it was a very holy place. I weighed the merits of the alternatives and finally agreed that we should go to the river for a brief stop to watch the sunset.*

As we approached and drove down into the mela grounds, which were now quite deserted, the driver asked where he should park. Danny pointed to a place that he said was near a Hanuman temple and also was the spot where he had purchased the small medallions.

As the bus was pulling up to that spot, someone yelled, "There's Maharajji!"

Sure enough, walking right by the bus with Dada, there he was. We all scrambled off the bus and rushed to his feet. I was having a hysterical crying-laughing fit. I remember kissing his feet in bliss and at the same moment my mind being aware that the spot of sand on which he was standing smelled strongly of urine.

Dada later told us that as the bus came into view, Maharajji had said, "Well, they've come."

Maharajji instructed us to follow them, and the bus followed the bicycle rickshaw to Dada's house on the suburban street of this great university city. Within minutes we were given food, and arrangements were made for us to lodge at a nearby estate with another devotee. I was told that since morning the servants had been preparing food under Maharajji's orders in anticipation of our coming. But if that were so, which of us thought he was making a decision in the bus about whether to visit the mela grounds? Apparently all was not as I "thought" it was. (R.D.)

ONLY MAHARAJJI knew why he remembered whom he did when he did. Apparently, however, it was not all in his hands, for many devotees found that by thinking about him, they drew his attention, or even his physical presence.

Said one Ma, "If the devotion is strong enough, the guru is drawn by the devotee."

A Frenchman was staying in Ananda Mayee Ma's ashram and asked HRJ about this Neem Karoli Baba, wanting his darshan. HRJ said that if he were to remember Maharajji for only ten minutes, Maharajji could be there. The Frenchman closed his eyes and repeated "Neem Karoli Baba, Neem Karoli Baba," and after ten minutes, unexpectedly, Maharajji came to Ma's ashram. He went over to the Frenchman and asked, "Why are you remembering me? I've come. What do you want?"

ॐ

I was in the habit of arising at around 2:00 A.M. and sitting up a while in meditation. I told no one of this activity. One morning as I came for darshan, the Ma's rushed over to me in great glee, all talking at once. What they were telling me was that in the middle of the night, as they were sitting with Maharajji, he had turned to them and said, "S [referring to me] has just awakened. She is thinking of me very much."

ॐ

One day I came from Snowview to Tallital, hoping to see Maharajji. I was wondering how I could find him, since sometimes he stayed in one house, sometimes in another. Just as I passed by the house in which he was staying, someone came out and caught hold of me. Maharajji knew that I was coming and sent this person to intercept me and bring me to him.

ॐ

One Tuesday morning I planned to visit Maharajji at Kainchi, but a call came for me and I had to go to Nainital for business. I figured I could still take the last bus to Kainchi, but when the time came I missed the bus. At about 8:00 P.M. I got a lift to Bhowali, but by that time there was no way to get to Kainchi. I felt some depression and went home. I was thinking in this way when there was a knocking at my door. I told my son to tell whomever it was that I was tired and to ask their name. Just then I heard some shouting: "I am Baba Neem Karoli!" This was about 9:00 P.M. Maharajji told me, "You always bother about this and that! Why are you bothering?" He took his dinner at my home and then got into the jeep and returned to Kainchi.

ॐ

The acting superintendent of police, hearing that he was not going to be confirmed, was very upset and decided to resign. At about 8:00 P.M. he was with his wife when an orderly came and said, "There is a man outside sitting on the road, calling for you." He knew it was Maharajji.

Maharajji said to him, "You were crying. You were thinking of resigning. How foolish."

An old man who for years worked as a prison guard became extremely ill. At one point, his doctor gave him only twenty-four hours to live, but the man remembered Maharajji, meditated on him, and refused to die. On the third day, Maharajji arrived in the city and went to the home of another devotee. He said to him, "There's an old man living near here. He's thinking of me very much and he's very sick. We must visit him."

Upon entering the sick man's room, they found him in very grave condition. Maharajji placed his foot near the man's head. The dying man pranammed to Maharajji and then left his body.

Maharajji said to the other devotee, "He was remembering me very much. Darshan was given, then finished! The end!"

I AM HERE AND I AM IN AMERICA.
WHOEVER REMEMBERS ME, I GO TO.

CHAOS AND CONFUSION

WHEREVER MAHARAJII was, there was chaos and confusion. Sometimes two people were sent to do the same task, other times one was sent to undo what the first was in the process of doing. Maharajji would tell one person one thing and another something opposite; when confronted with such inconsistencies he would deny all. Such confusion served a number of obvious purposes. First, it veiled his powers so that no one could be quite certain what had just happened. And the confusion also allowed each person to hear what he or she needed to hear from among the conflicting bits of information. Such inconsistencies served to loosen the minds of those devotees with problems of rigid thinking. From another point of view one could understand the confusion as a reflection of the fact that Maharajji was not just one person. As a mirror, he was the reflection of whomever was thinking upon him, and he was conscious on many planes at once. Thus, one statement, such as "I can do nothing," might be followed moments later by the statement, "I hold the keys to the mind. Everyone is my puppet." Appreciating this dimension of Maharajji made one delight in the confusion.

Two long-time devotees were told that they would be able to find Maharajji at a certain temple on the banks of the Ganga. They went there immediately and found him. He acted as if he'd never seen them before. "Who are you? Where do you come from? What work do you do? Why have you come here?" he inquired of each of them. They patiently answered him until finally he said, "Sit down!"

ﻢﺍﺭ

Maharajji was never in bondage to anything. He wouldn't follow suggestions and would do the unexpected. If I asked to stay longer, for example, he would get up and go.

ﻢﺍﺭ

Maharajji would make predictions or say something of personal import in an off-hand manner, in the middle of a political discussion. Often his predictions wouldn't come true. If you wanted a specific prediction from Maharajji, he would often be vague, and he'd never give an explanation for his predictions.

ﻢﺍﺭ

Anything you can say about him—you can also say the opposite.

ﻢﺍﺭ

One time in Vrindaban Maharajji had called us all over, and I was at the front of the pack as we ran across. Entering the room ahead of everyone else, I felt as if I'd caught him unawares. He saw me and got embarrassed. It was as if he'd been caught doing something he shouldn't have—as if he were in the cookie jar! He was looking so guilty, and I was trying to figure out what it was I had caught him doing. Finally I just gave up; he must have been pulling another of his tricks.

ᚯ

Once some devotees were with Maharajji at the Ganga, and they proposed to Maharajji that he bathe there. He protested, but they urged him and finally succeeded in lowering him into the water from their boat. Maharajji at first acted like he was drowning, then suddenly he began to swim around the boat. Later, in recounting the incident, Maharajji told everyone that they had tried to drown him.

ᚯ

Once in the middle of the night at the ashram we were awakened by shouts and the sounds of footsteps. People were running to and fro and lights were going on all over the place. We stuck our heads out the door to discover that Maharajji was up. He wanted rotis. Then he screamed, "There's a snake in the Mothers' room!" And when they went to check it out, what they found there was a rope!

ᚯ

At Kainchi he had this simple little room, which we used to call his "office." There was a window with shutters on the inside that he could open, where he'd often sit, looking out and giving darshan. Sometimes he would jump around in that room like a monkey in a cage or press his face to the bars. At other times someone would come to the window to see him and he'd just slam the shutters closed.

ᚯ

He'd start off a conversation saying one thing, and then by the end of the conversation he'd be making the opposite point. He once told one Western devotee about smoking dope. He said to him, "You like smoking charas

*[hashish]? That's good; Shiva smokes charas. That means you like Shiva."
We were all really thrilled to hear this, but then he started to turn it around,
saying, "What's better that you do, smoke charas or eat food?" About five
minutes later he said, "Don't smoke!"*

भगवान्

*Once he said, "Oh, it's very nice and peaceful here in Kainchi. When you
come here you can really get peace. Shanti milta-hai [Peace is found]."
Then a few weeks later some truck went by on the road and he said, "Oh, this
Kainchi, so noisy—no peace here, ashanti." He'd gone from shanti to ashanti
(not peaceful) in the same place.*

भगवान्

*It was sometimes very hard to figure out what Maharajji was saying. Often
he'd repeat the same word about five times. One of his favorite things was
saying the same thought over and over again, just rewording it different ways,
drilling it into your head. If it was something about someone getting married,
for example, he'd say, "You got married, didn't you? No, you didn't. Did
you? You did." He'd go on like that, back and forth. It was the same way
he'd play with things: He'd pick up something, turn it over, flip it back over,
then flip it over again. He'd do the same thing with words—he'd take a
sentence and turn it around (and your head with it).*

भगवान्

*One morning, Maharajji greeted his devotees with complaints of a very sore
knee. Some devotees took him seriously and they suggested various cures.
Others took the complaint lightly and told Maharajji to cure himself since he
was the cause of his complaints. Nevertheless, oils and balms and compresses
were applied to the area of pain, all to no avail. Maharajji insisted that these
remedies wouldn't work, and what was needed was a certain medicine he'd once
seen in Dada's home. He called it the "moustache-man medicine," and twirled
his moustache to indicate it. He said it was the only medicine that would work.
All this meant nothing to this devotee, who couldn't recall any moustache-
related medicine in his home. Later in the day the devotee went to the bazaar*

to buy supplies for the ashram. While in the pharmacy he noticed a piture of a moustachioed man on a small box containing Sloan's Balm, a heat-producing medicine. He purchased it and gave it to Maharajji. Maharajji shouted, "That's it! The moustache medicine! Put it on!" Moments after the balm was rubbed onto his knee, Maharajji announced that the pain had vanished and that now he was fine.

ॐ

Janaki and Draupadi were sitting before Maharajji, and Maharajji turned to Janaki and asked, "Who do I like better, you or Draupadi?"

Janaki said sweetly, "Why, Maharajji, you love us all the same."

Maharajji replied, "Nahin [No]! I like Draupadi better!" which of course upset her a great deal. She got up and walked out, heading for the Vrindaban bazaar, in order to run away! What kind of guru has preferences? While she was in the bazaar she realized that she couldn't run away, after all. Wanting to do something nice for someone, she bought a little brass murti of Hanuman and returned to the temple and put it in her room.

Immediately afterward Maharajji caught her and asked her, "Where have you been? What have you been doing? What did you buy?" She told him about the little murti. He told her to bring it to him, and when she did he handled it a while and looked it over and then told her to give it to me! I don't know if she had meant it for me or if Maharajji initiated that. The very day after I'd privately wished for a little Hanuman murti, I was given this one.

ॐ

I'd be alone with Maharajji in his room and I'd want everybody to share this experience, so I'd say, "Maharajji, they'd really love to come in."

He'd say, "Should I let them in?"

I'd say, "Yes. Let them in."

He'd say, "Go bring them in." Sometimes he'd say, "Nahin! You just be here." Or he'd say something about all of them being badmash (rascals). I'd argue with him that they were not all badmash, that some of them were confused, just like me. He'd say that that was true, then add, "Nahin, they're all badmash."

ॐ

At the time of the big havan, the fire ceremony, many people said they were going to fast, but after two days they ended up not fasting. And all of those who said they weren't going to fast, ended up fasting.

जप

One time in Allahabad a Sikh family had arranged to feed all of the satsang at their home and entertain us for the afternoon. I wanted to stay behind with Maharajji, so I went and hid up on the roof where nobody ever went.
Everyone was rounded up to leave for the outing, and after they were all gone, I was really afraid. "Oh, what's Maharajji going to do when he finds I'm still here?" I thought. I asked Didi (Dada's wife) what Maharajji would do when he found this out.
She said, "Oh, you better talk to Dada."
So I went to Dada: "Dada! I don't know what Maharajji's going to do."
He replied, "Who does?"

God Does Everything

IN THE TRADITION of the great yogis of India, Maharajji's powers extended far beyond the realm of knowing the minds of others. A profusion of miracles poured out of him, and though he threw dust in our eyes with denials and confusion, we were still allowed to sense this extraordinary process. But as astonishing and dramatic as such phenomena were, they were not, in the eyes of the close devotees of Maharajji, the essence of the matter. Maharajji himself was the miracle. Just being around him made the commonplace seem miraculous, and, conversely, the miraculous came to seem quite ordinary. Yet when devotees gather, it is still the miracle stories that come most readily to their lips. Perhaps this is because such stories are "tellable," while the ocean of love, the tenderness, and the healing compassion with which Maharajji—like Christ—worked his true wonders upon us, these are ineffable.

What were these miraculous powers about? Perhaps they served the function that the great saint Shirdi Sai Baba, who used miracles in an outrageous fashion, attributed to them: "I give them what they want, so they will want what I give." All the miracles concern the physical universe, the world, the material plane, but the essence of the business that we have with such beings as Maharajji is of the spirit—which is far beyond such miracles. Miracles are only the unexpected; and in the spirit there is no expected—so there is no unexpected.

This is how Maharajji became known as Neem Karoli Baba, which means the sadhu from Neem Karoli (or Neeb Karori). This was many years ago, perhaps when Maharajji was in his late twenties or early thirties.

For several days, no one had given him any food and hunger drove him to board a train for the nearest city. When the conductor discovered Maharajji seated in the first-class coach without a ticket, he pulled the emergency brake and the train ground to a halt. After some verbal debate, Maharajji was unceremoniously put off the train. The train had stopped near the village of Neeb Karori where Maharajji had been living.

Maharajji sat down under the shade of a tree while the conductor blew his whistle and the engineer opened the throttle. But the train didn't move. For some time the train sat there while every attempt was made to get it to move. Another engine was called in to push it, but all to no avail. A local magistrate with one arm who knew of Maharajji suggested to the officials that they coax that young sadhu back onto the train. Initially the officials were appalled by such superstition, but after many frustrating attempts to move the train they decided to give it a try. Many passengers and railway officials approached Maharajji, carrying with them food and sweets as offerings to him. They requested that he board the train. He agreed on two conditions: (1) the railway officials must promise to have a station built for the village of Neeb Karori (at the time the villagers had to walk many miles to the nearest station), and (2) the railroad must henceforth treat sadhus better. The officials promised to do whatever was in their power, and Maharajji finally reboarded the train. Then they asked Maharajji to start the train. He got very abusive and said, "What, is it up to me to start trains?" The engineer started the train, the train traveled a few yards, and then the engineer stopped it and said, "Unless the sadhu orders me, I will not go forward." Maharajji said, "Let him go." And they proceeded.

Maharajji said that the officials kept their word, and soon afterward a train station was built at Neeb Karori and sadhus received more respect.

राम

Whenever Maharajji left Allahabad to go to Vrindaban there was always such a procession—sometimes as many as eighteen rickshaws full of people going to the train station! One time we were all lined up and the procession began. I directed the drivers to go the shortest route, but Maharajji intervened and insisted they go the long route. Many devotees were gathered along that route, all of them hoping for one glimpse of darshan as he was leaving. These last darshans delayed Maharajji, and Siddhi Ma and the Mothers with whom he was to travel were all on the train.

It was my pleasure in those days to attend to such matters as reservations, so I was busy seating the Ma's and seeing to their needs. Maharajji was still outside of the station with the devotees when the engineer and the conductor signaled for the train to start. I thought, "Oh, my God. What will happen? I myself will stay on the train with the Mothers. I can't let them go on alone." But for a full four minutes the engineer struggled with the train but couldn't make it budge. Strolling slowly with his devotees, Maharajji came onto the platform. As he boarded the train, he shouted at me in English, "Get out!" As soon as Maharajji took his seat the train began to pull away.

卐

One time Maharajji asked me to make reservations for two first-class, air-conditioned places on the train leaving that very day! All the officials told me it was completely booked from Calcutta to Kalka (the east to west coast of India). Still, to be prepared, I bought two unreserved tickets. I was sure that I was wasting our time and we'd have to cash them in. Maharajji walked into the station, walked slowly along the platform, and stopped, stolid, at one spot. When the train pulled in, a first-class, air-conditioned car was stopped directly in front of Maharajji. I had watched how he chose that very spot to stand in, so I asked the conductor, who happened to be standing right there, for two berths in that car, and he said, "What! Are you crazy? This train is full from Calcutta to Kalka!"

At that moment I lost my assurance and looked over to Maharajji. He merely raised one finger and said quietly, "Attendant."

So I went over to the car attendant and asked again for two berths, and he said, "Yes, yes, there is room for you. You see, a party who was reserved clear through had to get off at Mogul Serai to attend to unexpected business. There are two berths vacant in this car." It was the car directly in front of Maharajji.

卐

One day, Maharajji and his driver were going from Bareilly to Kainchi. They arrived at Kainchi and, a little later, others arrived and said, "You can't have come that way. The road has been washed out for four days and there has been no traffic, not even trucks." The road continued to be impassable for two more days.

ॐ

Maharajji was going to Kashmir in a car, when the clutch started to slip. We were in a small village with no repair facility and the driver was afraid to go on because of the mountainous road. A supposed mechanic was found, but the more he tried, the worse the clutch got, until it wasn't working at all. I asked Maharajji what to do and he said to stop a truck and have the truck tow the car. All the trucks, however, were going in the opposite direction. I reported this to Maharajji, who replied, "Oh, these Brahmins are so stingy, they won't put up enough money to hire a truck to pull the car." (I had a thousand rupees to put up, which was enough.) Finally I got a bus that would pull the car. I bought a rope and we were just leaving when a bus came from the other direction warning that there was a bus check-stop ahead, so that the bus shouldn't try towing the car. It was dark by now, and there were no hotels, so I went to Maharajji and said, "Here are the choices: We can sit in the car all night long like this with no blankets; we can get a truck to tow us back; or we can go on (this last choice implying that we would have to depend on Maharajji's powers, since the clutch was now gone).

Maharajji said, "Let's go on."

All the way to Srinagar there was no occasion to stop or use the clutch, and we never even needed gas. This of course was impossible by normal means.

ॐ

At a mela, Maharajji kept telling people that the Ganga (Ganges River) was not really water but milk. One day Maharajji and several others were out on the river in a boat, and the devotees were eager to experience the truth of Maharajji's words. They said nothing, however. Maharajji told them to get a lota (water pot) of Ganga water and cover it. When he poured it into glasses for them, it was the sweetest milk. Since there were other devotees back at the camp, one of the people in the boat thought he'd take some back for them, but Maharajji grabbed the devotee's glass and threw it angrily into the Ganga.

ॐ

Maharajji once strengthened the faith of an Indian sadhu, who also was called Ram Das, by demonstrating his powers for him. Maharajji said, "Look here, Ram Das, I'm disappearing, see?" He took a small stone and struck it against his body. Ram Das couldn't see Maharajji any more. Then Maharajji said, "Now, see. I am reappearing," and Ram Das could again see him there. Maharajji repeated this three or four times.

ॐ

Once a party of fifty or sixty Congress politicians were going to see Maharajji. He was staying at Hanuman Ghar. From there the road could be seen for a long way, so he knew they were coming. Maharajji suddenly got up and went down the hillside. Accompanied by an Indian sadhu, Ram Das, he walked to a small Devi temple. When the party arrived they inquired about Maharajji's whereabouts. They were directed down the path. Maharajji and Ram Das had sat down in front of the temple. The Congressmen also came to the small temple, and though they stood in open land about six feet away, they couldn't see him or Ram Das. The men were standing practically in front of them, saying to themselves, "Where is Neem Karoli Baba?" Maharajji had become invisible and he had made Ram Das invisible.

Now Ram Das was habituated to hashish and had the cough that naturally accompanies this. He had a spasm and wanted to cough. He couldn't stop it, but he feared that if he coughed these people would hear and naturally guess that Maharajji was there. Maharajji said, "Don't mind. Cough as much as you like," so Ram Das coughed loudly and got relief. But these men heard neither the talking nor Ram Das's coughing. The Congressmen gave up their search and went away, and only then did Maharajji reappear.

ॐ

During a journey a horse started acting up, endangering its riders. Maharajji went up to the horse and spoke to it: "Look here, brother. Let them get down now. Let them down. Do you understand?" The horse immediately became quiet. The devotees stepped down and the journey was continued on foot.

ॐ

An army colonel approached the gate of the army camp and found Maharajji lying on the ground directly in front of the gate. When ordered to move, Maharajji replied that it was God's land and he was with the CID (Central Intelligence Department). The colonel became outraged and told the guards to move Maharajji and jail him in the army stockade. Some hours later the colonel, after having been out, once again approached the gate. Again he found

Maharajji lying before the gate. The colonel started to yell at the guards for failing to carry out his orders, but they assured him that they had done as he had directed. A check of the stockade revealed that Maharajji was still there. After that the colonel became a devotee.

Maharajji and some devotees spent the night in a dharmasalla on the way to Badrinath. Maharajji sent the entire group out of his room and forbade them to enter during the night. They had seen a big cobra on Maharajji's bed. In the morning Maharajji came out with the cobra and shooed it away. Sometime later, in Kainchi, Maharajji was told that a cobra was in the ashram. He made a hue and cry—"Cobra is here, cobra is here!"

A devotee remarked to him, "What is this? So much concern for a cobra now. What happened when you slept the whole night with a cobra? Now you're making such a commotion!"

"You wicked person! Go away!" Maharajji replied.

Maharajji was in Benares with the police superintendent, a devotee. They were going over to a sadhu camp on an island in the middle of the Ganga, and the superintendent said, "We'll take a boat." (In Benares, the Ganga is over a mile across.)

Maharajji countered, "No, we'll go in the water."

The superintendent couldn't swim and protested, "Maharajji, it's over our heads!"

Maharajji replied, "Just put your hand on my shoulder." So they waded into the river, and the next thing the superintendent knew, they were on the island. They returned the same way.

At our house, after the third or fourth day following Maharajji's visit, my wife heard, "Keep some water for me in the night," coming from near the picture of Maharajji. One night she forgot, but later she awoke very thirsty and then remembered to put some water by the picture. In the morning the glass, which she had covered, was nearly empty.

ॐ

There was a party going to Vasudhara (near Badrinath), where the Ganga starts, but one Ma was sick so the group wouldn't take her. As the party left to go, the Ma was bewailing her fate, and Maharajji came and said, "You want to see Vasudhara." He touched her hand and said, "Now walk out on the porch." She did so and what she saw was Vasudhara. She was in ecstasy. It turned out later that the party couldn't reach Vasudhara because of a roadblock. When they returned she told them that she had been there, but of course they didn't believe her. She described it in detail, and an old guide who had been there before corroborated her description.

ॐ

Word reached Maharajji from the pujari (priest) in Kanpur that the new murti, not yet consecrated, had been broken. Maharajji and some of us immediately set out for Kanpur, driving all night. I felt that by this intensity Maharajji was teaching the discipline of sticking to something: There was to be no sleep until Ram's work was done. I tried to slow Maharajji down, however, by quoting the proverb, "Don't travel at night and don't be idle at noon."

Maharajji said, "The same principle doesn't apply in every situation." When we arrived we found that the murti was no longer broken. Then Maharajji told a story of the saint, Ramakrishna, in which the Durga (an aspect of the Divine Mother) murti had been broken and Ramakrishna did puja to it and sang to it, and soon it was all fixed.

ॐ

A man was trying unsuccessfully to dig a well on his property and finally sent his son to Maharajji for help. Maharajji came to the farm, urinated, and left, saying, "Tell your father to try again." Indeed, a well was found, which is still gushing today.

ॐ

At a certain mela a flood destroyed a bridge which kept collapsing every time they tried to rebuild it. The organizer of the mela came to Maharajji for help and Maharajji said he would bless the bridge, but the man insisted that Maharajji come to the site of the bridge itself. Maharajji stood there for a while and the flood waters began to recede. Soon the bridge was reconstructed and the mela turned out to be one of the most peaceful ever.

॥ᵑ॥

People often gave Maharajji blankets. One time when he was through with a blanket it suddenly became much smaller, and he said, "Why are you giving me these blankets that are too small?"

॥ᵑ॥

Maharajji and a devotee had settled in for a journey in the first-class compartment of a train. The devotee felt it would be safer if Maharajji held the tickets until the conductor came, so he gave them to Maharajji. Maharajji looked at them and said, "What is this for?" and threw them out of the window of the moving train. The devotee was shocked but said nothing. As Maharajji continued his conversation, the devotee was worrying about the tickets and the conductor. Finally the conductor knocked on the door and asked to see their tickets. The devotee hesitated a moment and then told Maharajji that the conductor wanted to see the tickets. Maharajji reached out toward the window and then handed the tickets to the devotee. He laughed and said, "Is this what you were worried about?"

॥ᵑ॥

In 1958, I was acting as the leader of the "Landless People" movement. I was arrested and charged with four counts (1) inciting a riot, (2) trespassing, (3) attempted murder, and (4) obstructing a government servant from discharging his duties. I was assured by Maharajji not to worry, that it would turn out all right; but in 1964 I was convicted and sentenced to four years' imprisonment. I immediately appealed the decision.

I was not worried, but my relatives were quite upset and insisted I again go to Maharajji about the case. Maharajji assured me once more that all would turn out okay and added that when a particular judge, whom he named, was in office, then the decision would be reversed. (The name given was not that of the present judge.) The present judge was, in fact, soon transferred, but the replacement was also not the one Maharajji foretold. The case was being argued and was to be completed by the end of a particular day. I thought to myself, "How could this be?" It was a cold, drizzly day and the sun had set and there were still several hours of arguing left, so the judge postponed the case until the next day. On that day one very important paper was inexplicably missing without a trace, so that the case could not be finished. The judge ordered a further postponement until the paper could be reconstructed, and the reconstruction took three years. By that time, now 1968, the judge whom Maharajji had named had been put in that office. The case was dropped under his decision.

गम

I was visiting a saint in the south of India who was known for manifesting many things. As I was getting ready to leave he said to me, "Do you want something, Ram Dass?"

"No, Babaji, I don't want anything."

"Here," he said and held out his hand palm-upward and started to move it in a slow circular motion. I was still sitting at his feet so that my eyes were close to his hand, and I watched like a hawk for the least trickery, careful not to blink. But much to my amazement there appeared to be a bluish light on his hand, which turned into a medallion. The whole business was confusing to me: Why did he do this?

I later heard that Maharajji said of such miracles: "There are those siddhis *(powers), but they shouldn't be used much. They reduce spirit to magic." And he said of such saints: "Let them play. Some saints of the south are very much after miracles." (R.D.)*

गम

Once in Vrindaban before Guru Purnima Day (a day honoring the guru), Maharajji was feeding us by hand. One by one he would feed us each a pera. I tried to feed him one, too. Of course he didn't eat sugar, but I was insisting, with the thought that this was also prasad. "You must eat it, please eat it." So he pretended to eat it.

But Naima caught him: "You didn't eat it, Maharajji." He looked guilty, as if to say, "Oh, you caught me." There it was in his hand. He'd palmed it. That precipitated wonderful play, as he went into his whole magician act:

"Which hand is it in? Ha! You're wrong, it's in this hand." I don't think he was even using his powers for this game. He really was palming it, hiding it in his blanket, and using sleight of hand—all tricks that any magician can do. But he was saying, "See! See! I'm like Sai Baba. I can make it appear; I can make it disappear. I can do anything. Magic! It's magic!"

टम

We were in a car with Maharajji in Bombay. He was directing us to drive through small streets, until finally we came to a house. A Ma ran out and touched Maharajji's feet. It so happened that one of my colleagues had been urging me to ask Maharajji about the Satya Sai Baba miracles and Maharajji had been ignoring the question. Now, some time later in this house, Maharajji said, "Mother, they think manifesting things is so great. Give us some murtis." And in her hand suddenly there were these little murtis of Krishna. Siddhi Ma wrapped two of them in her sari, and when she got home she discovered three of them there.

टम

About the miracle babas Maharajji would say, "What is this? This is all foolishness." He could do miracles, but the greatest miracle was that he could turn one's heart and mind toward God, as he did for me.

I HAVE NO POWERS. I DON'T KNOW ANYTHING.

Maharajji was actually the biggest saint. He had done all the yogic austerities. There are saints in India, very aged ones, who almost never give darshan to people. Except for the few to whom they are kind, these saints cannot be seen. Sometimes they take the shape of a tiger or a monkey or a beggar. You can only have darshan if they want to give it to you, not otherwise. The true devotees of God never wear saffron, carry malas (prayer beads), or put on sandalwood. You can't know them unless they want it, and then you can only know them as much as they allow.

MA, WHAT AM I TO DO—THERE IS NO EYE
THAT CAN FOLLOW ME. NO ONE KNOWS ME,
NO ONE UNDERSTANDS ME. WHAT AM I TO
DO? [SAID FOUR DAYS BEFORE HE LEFT HIS BODY]

THERE WAS still another group of devotees, many of them among the longest-term associates, who didn't conjecture about Maharajji's identity at all.

You can't try to understand Maharajji. You can only put him on as you would a pair of shoes or a piece of clothing and feel him.

तेम

I asked a devotee, "Wasn't your wife surprised when you didn't stop and talk to her?"
"No, never. When we are with Maharajji, we never think rationally about things. She just knew I was with Maharajji."

तेम

It is extremely difficult to catch hold of him.

तेम

I know nothing about such things. I only know that he is my baba.

ALTHOUGH MIRACLES were commonplace around Maharajji, they were rarely discussed during his lifetime. The devotees knew, in no uncertain terms, that he did not like these things talked about. When various devotees would sit around and discuss his miracles, Maharajji would call them over and berate them and say, "You are all talking lies!"

Maharajji said that God loves everything and he (Maharajji) does nothing, and if people wrote about him, millions of people would come to bother him, drawn only by rumors of miracles.

In 1963 a man collected stories about Maharajji. Maharajji said, "You want to bring disgrace? Burn them!" He burned them.

Another devotee wrote an article, and Maharajji tore up the manuscript.

ॐ

Someone asked Maharajji if he'd allow some pictures to be taken. Maharajji said no and expressed his disapproval. The man pressed Maharajji until finally he ceased to resist. The man snapped three or four photos. When the roll of film was developed, these three or four frames were completely blank.

If you happened to see him perform some miracle, such as producing puris, he would tell you not to tell anyone. "I tell you, it will be bad for you. Don't tell anyone."

ॐ

One time the car in which Maharajji was riding ran out of gas in a place where there was none to be had nearby. Maharajji instructed the driver to put water in the tank and continue. Then he firmly warned the driver never to tell of this incident for as long as Maharajji was alive. Maharajji said that if the man told, he would contract leprosy! It was some three years after Maharajji left his body that the man first told this story.

YOU SHOULD NOT TALK ABOUT YOUR WEALTH, WIFE, OR SADHANA OR THEY WILL GO AWAY.

MAHARAJJI'S STRATEGY obviously worked, for he was known to those he chose to be known to, yet unknown to the population at large. As an example, the *Illustrated Weekly of India* did an entire issue concerning Indian saints, past and present. Hundreds were listed, yet in the entire magazine he was not even mentioned. Perhaps that was the greatest sign of his power.

When the Westerners started to come to Maharajji, he changed. He began to allow photographs to be taken and even gave his blessings for a book, *Be Here Now,* which allowed millions of seekers in the Western world to hear of Maharajji and his powers. Why he changed is not known. Perhaps he was preparing his legacy.

Apparently Maharajji did not transmit to his devotees any of the powers that he manifested. Perhaps he felt similar to Shirdi Sai Baba, who said, "I don't give them powers because I don't want them to lose their way." Rather than any siddhis or yogic powers, Maharajji gave us more basic things: faith, loving hearts, and an acceptance of the reality of the Divine. At the same time, he recognized that some of the devotees had desire for such powers, and he enjoyed playing with those people.

In 1967 Maharajji asked me, "You want to fly?" I had a pilot's license at the time, and though I knew that this wasn't what he meant, I said somewhat facetiously, "I already can fly, Maharajji."

Maharajji ignored my response and said, "You want to fly. You'll fly."

It was not until 1972, over four years later, while working with a mantra under the direction of a swami, that I experienced astral flying. (R.D.)

ॐ

One of the first things he said to me in 1967 was, "You know Gandhi?"

"I know of him, Maharajji."

"You should be like him."

Just by saying that, he started in me a train of righteous power fantasies that went on for years. Only recently have I come to see Gandhi in terms of compassion rather than power. Maharajji's statement made me do much work on myself.

To add a bit more fuel to the fire of these attachments of mine, one day Maharajji asked, "Did you have tea at Nixon's house?" I was puzzled, for the question was without a context. But then I remembered that the Englishman who had settled in Almora many years before, who was known as Krishna Prem and was considered by many Indians to be a saint, had originally been named Nixon. I asked Maharajji if it was this Nixon to whom he referred.

"No, the one with the big white house in America. The one with the house bigger than Muktananda's."

There was no mistaking it now; he meant the president. "No, I never did." Then thinking maybe there was a confusion of generations, I added, helpfully, "But my father has."

"Weren't you in Mr. Nixon's house and he gave you tea and was very nice to you?"

"No."

"Oh." Nothing more. Just another little suggestion that perhaps I was to play in the halls of worldly power.

And another day he spoke again about the presidency. This time he said, "You know, Lincoln was a very good president."

"Yes?"

"Yes. He was a good president because he knew Christ was the real president. He was only acting president."

"Oh."

"Yes, he was very good. He helped the poor and suffering. He never forgot Christ."

"Ah!"

Then he asked, "Did you know Lincoln?" There was an embarrassed silence, for everyone present knew of that "impossibility." Then Dada told Maharajji that I couldn't have, since Lincoln died in 1865. It was explained as if to a child. But all of us knew that Maharajji never said things idly. (R.D.)

पू

The head of the state police of Uttar Pradesh, the largest state in India, had come for darshan and was sitting at Maharajji's feet and rubbing his legs with obvious devotion. I was called to join them, and Maharajji introduced him to me and asked me whether the police in America were like the police in India. As I looked at this superintendent of state police rubbing Maharajji's legs I could only laugh at the comparison. I said that the police in America had great power and often forgot they were the servants of the people. And I added that it would be unlikely for the head of any state police to kneel and rub the feet of a holy man. Maharajji then introduced me to the policeman, saying, "This is Ram Dass. He is going to bring the police of America to God." I had to laugh. Now he was implying future powers even greater than my fantasies.

It was also around this time that Maharajji started calling me Samarth Guru Ram Dass. In the past he had called me by one name or another (e.g., "Isha"—Jesus—or Kabir), each for a few weeks. Each time a new name appeared, albeit briefly, I would make inquiries as to the nature of the person who had become my namesake and would try it on for size. Jesus I already knew about. Kabir was a great saint, a very poor weaver who preached the unity of all religions and was legendary for his outspoken beliefs in God. His poetry was already much revered in my heart. At first it seemed that Samarth Guru Ram Das must refer to the Sikh Guru Ram Das, but then I found a book that described a Samarth Guru Ram Das, who was guru to King Sivajji in the 1600s and had constructed many Hanuman temples. The name Samarth meant "all-powerful" and there are many stories of his miraculous powers. He lived in a mud hut next to the king's palace. The king was highly regarded for his concern for his subjects and for his generous feeding of the poor, but apparently now and then his ego got the best of him. When this happened the guru would do things like splitting a rock in which there were many tiny bugs and asking the king, Who was feeding these bugs? This realization of the triviality of his own efforts would again humble the king.

I liked this name, and while I wanted all the powers Maharajji seemed to be alluding to, I knew that if he gave me those powers I would indeed get lost in them. Now and then, however, Maharajji would set me up for an experience that, by allowing me to help him, showed me that the true powers poured forth when one realized, "I can do nothing; God does everything."

On one occasion Maharajji said to me, "Hari Dass is in America. You keep him there for five years."

I knew that Hari Dass had only a three-month visa and that to get a permanent visa—that is, to become a registered alien in the United States—is no easy matter. So I said to Maharajji, "I can't do that. I have no political power in the United States."

But Maharajji would not hear my reply. He just repeated, "You keep Hari Dass in America for five years. I kept Bhagavan Das here for seven years." The implications of this made me laugh. Here was Maharajji, who had all kinds of powers, making this absurd comparison. My power within the United States government was absolutely zero, so again I protested. But he was equally adamant, so I said that I would certainly work on it.

A few days prior to that conversation, a Westerner from Los Angeles, whom I had never met before, came to Nainital to see me. I explained to him that my guru was nearby and took him to see Maharajji, who gave him the name Badrinath Das. The fellow was very taken with Maharajji and genuinely appreciative that I had arranged the meeting. On his last day in Nainital, which was the day after the Hari Dass conversation with Maharajji, Badrinath Das thanked me again and asked me if there was anything he could do for me in the States. I asked him, "For instance, what?" and he told me that he was a successful lawyer in Los Angeles. At the moment I could not think of any friends who were in trouble, but I thanked him for the offer. Then as an afterthought I said, "I have a family full of lawyers, but the only legal thing I need now is to get Hari Dass Baba a long-term visa in America," and I explained to him Maharajji's orders.

Badrinath Das said, "Gee, it's funny you should need that. My brother-in-law happens to be the director of the Western United States Office of Immigration, and we should be able to arrange it with one letter." And so it was done. When Hari Dass came to the immigration department for an *interview, his folder had special VIP stickers on it, and his alien visa was granted with no difficulty.*

Obviously Maharajji had known how it all would happen, but instead of bringing it out with Badrinath Das himself, he let me help him.

But while with one hand Maharajji played with my desires for worldly power, with the other he subtly uprooted them. One day while I was sitting with Maharajji and KK, many CID (Indian Intelligence Agency) men came to have Maharajji's darshan. They were in attendance upon Indira Gandhi, who was visiting nearby. After they left Maharajji said, "What good is all that? A king can only order his men to obey, but a saint can order wild beasts and animals to obey and they would do so also."

Between this belittlement of a worldly king, the Samarth Guru Ram Das stories, and Lincoln's appreciation of who the real president was, Maharajji impressed upon me the very real limits of the worldly power that most humans seek. These teachings have continued to work upon me since that time. (R.D.)

Among the thousands of seekers who came to Maharajji's feet were many men and women of worldly power, either political or economic—even though Maharajji made light of worldly power. Sometimes Maharajji avoided them, and at other times he seemed to go out of his way to help or guide them.

Maharajji was staying at the home of the superintendent of the Agra Central Jail when he unexpectedly got up and left for another place. He told them that a wealthy importer was coming to bother him. A few minutes after Maharajji had left, a limousine drove up and a large man approached the house, laden with prasad.

राम

Maharajji tried to avoid at least two or three governors who wanted to see him. But one of the governors arrived unannounced. Maharajji said, "If he is that keen to see me, how can I stop him?"

राम

Maharajji was involved in politics to the extent that it served his devotees. He would say, "Yes, you'll become governor," or, "You'll become vice-president of India," and so forth.

ꣳ

Once the wife of Vice-President Giri came. Maharajji refused to see her, although he had announced that she was coming before she actually arrived. "Give her prasad," he said.

The governor came along with his son, and though Maharajji was resting they bothered him anyway. When Maharajji spoke with them the governor asked if Giri should contest the election for president.

Later Giri himself came with four other men. Maharajji saw him alone for fifteen minutes. After that Giri left, went back to Delhi, and announced his retirement as vice-president. When asked why, he said, "It is the soul's voice telling me." He then entered the race for president of India.

Before the votes for the presidential election were counted, Maharajji exclaimed, "Giri has won." And he had.

ꣳ

Maharajji never wanted any publicity and he always tried to avoid VIPs. He kept away from devotees who became important. They would often tell me, "He used to visit us often, but now that he has placed us on the throne, he has forsaken us. He won't come any more. I wish he hadn't put us there. At least we would be able to have his darshan."

ꣳ

India's Prime Minister Nehru flew into the Calcutta airport one day en route to Assam. An airport conference was held for the press, attended both by reporters and by government officials. As Nehru spoke, another plane landed nearby and passengers disembarked. A few minutes later, Nehru noticed that his audience had shrunk and some of the people had made their way to the newly arrived plane. Nehru questioned his advisors, the closest of whom was an old devotee of Maharajji. He told Nehru that Baba Neem Karoli was on that plane and the people were rushing to have his darshan. Nehru expressed great surprise and said, "India is fortunate indeed if there exists a saint so great that people will leave their prime minister to see him."

ꣳ

Shortly after the outbreak of the India-China war in 1962 the military commanders of India advised Prime Minister Nehru to order a total evacuation of New Delhi, as a Chinese invasion appeared imminent. Understandably, Nehru was very reluctant to issue this order. During the long history of India, Delhi had been abandoned several times in the face of a military takeover, and on each occasion it foretold the defeat of the country. Nehru's generals, however, advised him to issue the evacuation order within twenty-four hours to avoid catastrophe. Nehru was desperate. He even asked his chief minister, a long-time devotee of Maharajji, to contact Maharajji for advice. The minister told Nehru he had faith that Maharajji knew everything and if Maharajji wanted to give darshan he would come. He said that Maharajji would never fail to answer someone's call if it was sincere. In any case, Maharajji's whereabouts were unknown to the devotee. That same evening, Maharajji telephoned and said to the devotee, Nehru's minister, "Tell him not to worry. Everything will be all right. They've already begun to retreat." The next morning, the top military brass told Nehru that during the night the enemy had retreated through the mountain passes and the fighting had subsided.

ॐ

For a long time Prime Minister Nehru had expressed the desire to have Maharajji's darshan, but Maharajji always managed to avoid seeing him. One day a close friend of Nehru's who was also a devotee of Maharajji appeared to convince Maharajji to meet him. Maharajji said he'd come to the prime minister's residence, but he warned that there should be no ceremony or fanfare on his behalf.

During Nehru's last days, Maharajji used to say, "Nehru is a good man. He worships God internally. He doesn't make much of it."

ॐ

Mujib's brother came. This man did not know if his brother, Mujib, was living or dead. Most people thought he was dead. But Maharajji said, "Don't worry. Your brother will come and he will come like a king." And so he did, to lead the formation of Bangladesh.

ॐ

One day an ordinary man came to see Maharajji, simply in order to have his desire fulfilled: He wanted to be a minister. Maharajji said, "Okay, you will be a minister. Take prasad and go." One day many years later I was alone with Maharajji in the room at Kainchi. For hours we were alone there together and he was deep in some samadhi *(spiritual trance) state, when suddenly he called out a man's name. Fifteen minutes later a car with a flag drove up to Kainchi with some government minister. I told Maharajji, who said to give him prasad and then call him in.*

That man came in and said, "Maharajji, once I met you. You told me that I would become a minister. Now I have become a minister. It is due only to your grace. Before taking the post, I felt I should come here and take the dust of your lotus feet. So I have come here for your darshan. Then I will assume my post."

Only now and then did Maharajji discuss politics at all. Usually he didn't seem to be particularly interested in worldly affairs unless pressed by his devotees. Often his perspective on the issues of the day seemed cosmic and frequently amused.

One day in speaking with a Western devotee, Maharajji inquired as to whether the scientists were now planning to send a rocket ship to Mars. When the devotee told him yes, they were, Maharajji laughed and laughed.

राम

A politician said to Maharajji of his own work, "We are doing so much for the people."

Maharajji replied, "Where is your green revolution?" referring to the drought. "You think you can do everything. You can do nothing. Only God can do."

राम

Maharajji, though he expressed favor for India's independence, said, "The British were good at heart."

राम

Twenty-five years ago a few of us were sitting with Maharajji, and he said about the Pakistan-India partition, "You will see, one part of Pakistan will be with India."

जय

In 1962, during the India-China war, I told Maharajji, "Chinese forces have entered Assam. Our forces have acted like spectators. If they continue not to fight, the Chinese will come to the plains."

Maharajji said, "Nothing will happen. China will retreat. India is a place of rishis (sages) and self-sacrifice. Communism can't come."

"But, Maharajji," I continued, "why have the Chinese forces come?"

"Just to awaken you," he replied.

जय

They were speaking of a possible Communist takeover and Maharajji said, "No! No, Communism can't come here. All the people are religious-minded and devout. Communism comes only to those countries where there is no faith in God. In countries where there is religion and it is being observed, no Communism can come."

> *INDIA IS A GOLDEN BIRD. IT IS*
> *A COUNTRY OF RISHIS AND SAINTS.*

> *CHANGE IS THE WAY OF THE WORLD,*
> *AND IF IN THE KALI YUGA [DARK AGE] IT HAS*
> *TO GO THIS WAY, LET IT GO. UNLESS*
> *YOU ARE THE LORD, YOU CAN'T STOP*
> *IT ANYWAY, SO WHY BERATE IT?*

MAHARAJJI AS GOD

ALTHOUGH MAHARAJJI protested that only God could do, that he could do nothing, many of the devotees saw in him an identity with God.

There are so many classes of saints and sadhus. Maharajji was the saint of a different nature, which is called advait vad: *There is only God, I myself am God and all things are my own heart and soul and God is present everywhere.*

Maharajji was a follower of advait vad. He saw his own soul in everybody. For him it was all One.

ॐ

Maharajji was like Krishna: Sometimes he was like God and sometimes he was like an ordinary person.

ॐ

Outwardly he is a man, but he is not a man. He used to talk here but he was somewhere else. He can cause his atma *(spirit) to enter into any person at any time to get his work done. His body was burned and can't return, but his atma can come in any form. In a dream he told me, "You can have my darshan but not in this form!"*

ॐ

He was so much a part of our lives that we didn't realize when we were with him the extent of his powers. He veiled his greatness. We never collected anecdotes because we thought he would go on forever.

ॐ

A very learned sadhu came to visit KB at his home. For hours every day the two discussed philosophy. The sadhu said that the universe is still ruled by sages, celestial beings who form a hierarchy ruled by the Supreme King. He said that the earthly play and the earthly rulers were under the control of these eternal sages. He proceeded to describe the Supreme King and his behavior. KB was shocked. The sadhu had described Maharajji perfectly. Sometime later Maharajji came to KB's home, and upon seeing the sadhu's photograph on the wall, Maharajji became furious. "How did you get that photo? Where did you meet that man?" he shouted. "You wretch! You talk too much and you force other people to talk." Maharajji left, leaving KB more curious than ever. Some years later, KB spoke with Maharajji about dharma *(spiritual way of life) and rulers, ever keeping in mind the mysterious revelation of the sadhu. Referring to King Janak, the mythical sage-king of ancient India, he asked*

Maharajji whether Janak was the last of such enlightened rulers in the world. Maharajji replied, "No, no! There is still such a king of the world today. There's a king of the whole universe, greater than Janak."

卐

A sadhu in Bombay gives descriptions of the saints who are in Siddha Loka *(highest spiritual plane) and says that Maharajji is sitting naked upon a white stone in the snow above us all.*

> ASK GOD OR HANUMAN. I'M JUST
> AN ORDINARY BEING. I CAN DO
> NOTHING.

One summer evening we were sitting around Maharajji, who was lying on his back, seeming very far away and blissful. I was holding his right hand and quietly began to study the lines on it. Maharajji roused a little and in a faraway voice asked me what it was I was seeing in his palm. I told him, "Maharajji, it says in your palm that you will have God's darshan." Like a small child with an air of delighted secrecy, he whispered to a nearby devotee, "Oh, they have found out!"

> I AM THE FATHER OF THE WORLD.
> THE WHOLE WORLD IS MY CHILD.

Brahmachari Maharaj was a great saint, highly revered in the Kumoan Hills. When he and Maharajji met, Brahmachari Maharaj did dunda pranam. It was a hot day, and Brahmachari Maharaj sent Tewari to get water for making a lassi *(a drink of churned yogurt, water & sugar). Brahmachari Maharaj drank water only from a distant spring, so Tewari was some time in getting the water. When he returned, Brahmachari Maharaj berated him: "You have no insight. You don't understand. This is no ordinary saint. Maharajji could drink tap water. It doesn't matter for him."*

卐

Once Maharajji arrived in Lucknow and met Shri Brahmachari Maharaj. After a brief greeting they entered an inner room and bolted the door. When fifteen or twenty minutes had passed the door opened and Shri Brahmachari

Maharaj came out, his face shining. He stood silently, smiling. Maharajji could be seen inside the room in a peculiar mudra—his entire body appeared like a round, soft body. He came out almost at once, and his body appeared to be very reddish in color. For a few silent moments the two saints stood together, then Maharajji left.

॰ॱਪ

When Gandhi was shot and all were crying, Brahmachari Maharaj asked, "Why is everyone crying?" When he was told, he said, "There is only one being in India who could bring him back to life and that is Neem Karoli Baba."

॰ॱਪ

Maharajji fed puris to a visiting swami from Sivananda ashram and told him to sit in the cave behind the temple. The swami, however, felt very attracted to Maharajji and soon returned to him. Maharajji then sent him to sit under the big tree, a position from which he could watch Maharajji. In front of his eyes, the Kainchi scene transformed into the Sivananda ashram in Rishikesh and Maharajji became Sivananda. Then Maharajji/Sivananda walked up to the swami and said, "Do you think there is any difference between us? Are we not the same?"

The swami said, "You are there in that form, too. You are really only he. You are deluding me in this form." Maharajji said nothing in reply. He only smiled.

I AM EVERYBODY'S GURU.

I have yet to find another man at this stage. One can go up quite all right, but it is very difficult to reach the highest realization and come back to the physical plane. Maharajji seemed to be on all planes at once. That is the highest state.

॰ॱਪ

I treated him as an ordinary sadhu until I realized who he was.

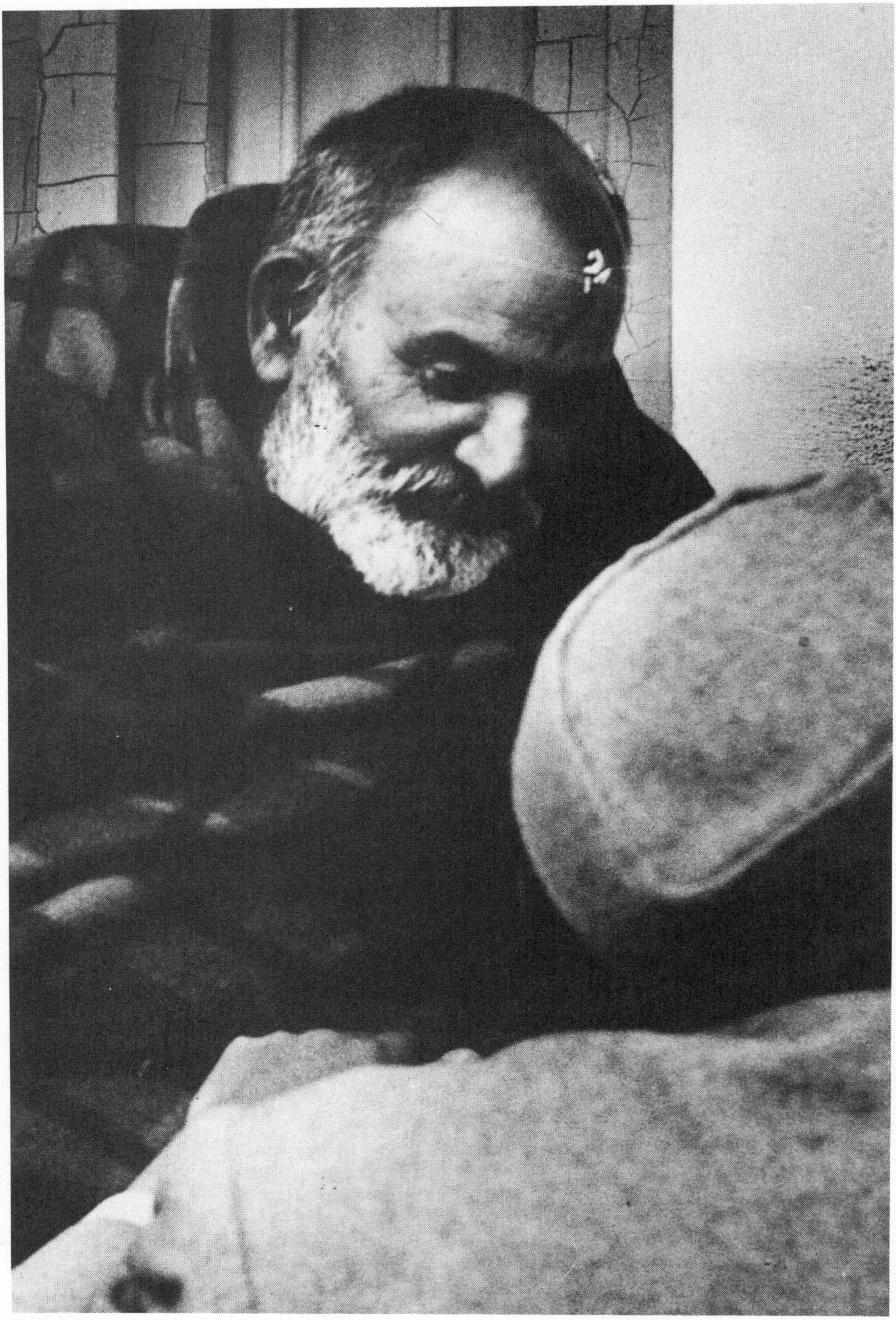

Rameshwar Das

The Stick That Heals

MAHARAJJI OFTEN UTILIZED his awesome powers to spread an umbrella of protection over his devotees. Nowhere was this more apparent or breathtaking than when it involved the healing of a devotee's illness. For some devotees the healing took place with a touch or a glance or a word; for others he prescribed medicines. Some stories reflect just how unusual these medicines were. To other devotees who came to him with illnesses, he implied that he could do nothing and sent them to doctors or to special temples to be cured. But when the situation demanded it, and the devotee's faith was strong, Maharajji seemed to effect cures at great distances, via telephone or even in dreams. When confronted with his miraculous healing powers, Maharajji denied all. All he would say at these times was "Sub Ishwar hai. [It's all God]."

After one of Maharajji's long-time devotees had a serious operation, Maharajji remained in her house for nine days. Someone asked him why he was staying so long when usually he never stayed more than few days in any one place. Maharajji replied, "Why do you ask? You're not the one who has to feed me. Why are you worried?" On the seventh night the woman had a relapse. The doctors treated her with sleeping pills, saying that she should rest, but all to no avail. She could not sleep. Her husband informed Maharajji, who said, "Don't worry, I'm coming." Finally, several hours later, he went to her room where he rebuked her soundly for not going to sleep as the doctors had ordered. Then, lifting his right leg, he touched his big toe to her forehead and within seconds she fell into a deep sleep. When she awoke she was well.

राम

A devotee was admitted to the hospital for an operation. The doctors said that he was dying of cancer and that an operation was his only chance of survival. His family went to get Maharajji's blessings. Maharajji said, "Go ahead with the operation. He can't have cancer. He'll be all right after the operation." For two or three days the man was near death. Maharajji sent some prasad to him with a Mother, who stayed at his bedside for two days. The operation was performed and no cancer was found. Cancer had shown up on the tests, but by the time of the operation it had disappeared.

राम

Once a Harvard professor and his wife came to visit Maharajji. The wife was an artist and she sketched a likeness of Maharajji as she sat before him. That night she became violently ill, shaking with fever and coughing blood. This was extremely unusual, as she was a very healthy woman. It was also unfortunate because they were on a tight schedule and had planned to leave that day for Delhi. When word of her illness was taken to Maharajji, he replied, "She will go to Delhi today." But the doctor came and said she would have to be transported to better lodgings and that it would be at least a week before she could travel. They bundled her up to take her to better lodgings and passed by the temple en route, so they stopped the car. Everyone went in to pay their respects to Maharajji, including the sick woman. The closer she got to him, the better she felt—and when she was directly in front of him, she felt completely well. He was beaming at her. She took out her sketch of him and he wrote राम, राम, राम *(Ram, Ram, Ram) all around the edge of the drawing.*

राम

The daughter of the police inspector of Rampur was dying of typhoid, and the only treatment they had in those days was to take away all food. They hadn't fed her for about forty days, so she was on the very edge of death. A letter came from Rampur to Nainital asking Maharajji to come and give darshan to the girl. Actually, the day before the letter arrived, Maharajji had said, "Come, we have to go to Rampur." They went. In the bedroom he said, "They are starving my daughter. What's going on! I'm very hungry. Make me food." Then he ate and said to the girl, "They are starving you. Here, eat this chapatti. Get up and eat this." She managed to get up and eat a bit of it. Then he said, "I'm tired. I have to rest. You sit in the chair and I'll sleep on the bed," The girl did as he instructed. For about an hour he was completely silent, apparently asleep. Then he got up and left, and she recovered.

One of the Ma's was having back trouble during a pilgrimage. She had a dream of Maharajji and vibhuti *(ash from sacred fires, commonly used for healing), but she was rubbing it on his back, which was hurting him. The next day another Ma said, "We have some vibhuti from Maharajji. Let us rub it on your back." They did, and she improved and continued the pilgrimage.*

There was one woman who was pregnant, but all the doctors told her that it was an irregular pregnancy and that she would not be able to carry it to term. Then she had Maharajji's darshan. He just looked at her and said, "Thik ho jaega [It will be all right]." She carried the baby full term and gave a normal delivery to a perfectly normal child.

When R's daughter was only one year old, she tumbled out the window of their home—a thirty-foot fall. She was unhurt, and the next day, having received word that Maharajji had come to Kainchi, they took her to him. Maharajji said she would be okay. When this same little girl was two, she again tumbled thirty feet—out of another window in their home. This time, also, she was unhurt and again Maharajji had just come to Kainchi, so instead of taking her to a doctor they took her to Maharajji, who casually said that she'd be okay. This same incident was repeated a third time when she was three. This time the girl herself remembers. She said, "I remember the falling. I felt as if I were floating down." This time when they took her to Maharajji, he said to her parents, "I won't let her die."

A devotee's son was very sick and he asked his mother to give him some vibhuti from Maharajji. Then he fell asleep and dreamed that he kept trying to dive into a lake and Maharajji kept pulling him out. When he awoke the illness had passed the point of crisis.

My wife had paralysis of her eye and mouth, and it became so bad that she wanted to commit suicide, but she was very young.

We slept in two cots. One night we both saw Maharajji at the same time, 3:30 A.M. My wife asked me to get up and arrange tea for Maharajji. I got up but there was no one there. Neither of us could sleep, so we had tea ourselves. Suddenly I looked at my wife and saw that her face was again moving and her eye was blinking. The doctor later said, "This is impossible. God has done it."

Several days later Majarajji came at 6:00 A.M. and asked, "What happened to your wife?" All her luster had returned. We have seven children now.

My mother had a dream in which a sadhu was wounded in the head and she put something in his mouth that Maharajji had given her. She awoke upset at such a strange dream. Hari Dass came to our house the next day to get food for people at the temple. The food was not ready, so Hari Dass was told to wait. He went down to the bathroom and then passed out on the stairs coming up, hitting his head which bled badly. My father arrived and, finding Hari Dass on the stairs, called my mother and together they brought him up to a bed. He was unconscious and there seemed little hope, but my mother remembered her dream and got some vibhuti that she had obtained from Maharajji. She placed it in Hari Dass's mouth and he got up within half an hour.

ॐ

R's wife was dying and she needed surgery. None of her special blood type was available, even in Bombay. She went into surgery saying Maharajji's name, and to the surgeon's surprise it was almost a totally bloodless operation. She later said that she had experienced going to a plane of consciousness where Maharajji had said, "Take her away. She'll stay there."

ॐ

Dada's nephew was dying of smallpox and apparently the last moment had come, for the body had been moved from the bed to the floor. It was suggested that a drop of water from the Ganga, with which Maharajji's feet had been washed, be placed in the boy's throat. When this was done the boy sat up, and by the next day the smallpox was gone.

At that same time, many miles away in the hills where Siddhi Ma was with Maharajji, suddenly Maharajji developed these spots all over his body. Since smallpox was not frequently seen in the hills, the hill people were not familiar with what it looked like. They got lotion and treated it as an allergy. By the next day the spots were gone and Maharajji said, "That was wonderful lotion. What could those spots have been? I must have been allergic to something." Only much later was it ascertained that the boy's cure and Maharajji's "allergy" coincided.

ॐ

Maharajji was giving darshan in a small room of the ashram, when a disturbed-looking man came in. Maharajji at once started screaming at him and held out his hand toward him. The fellow mumbled and shook his head, but Maharajji kept demanding something from him. Finally the man reached into his shirt pocket and pulled out a tiny bird with a stick through its chest. It looked quite dead. Maharajji took the bird, still yelling at the crazy man, and pulled the stick out of the bird's body. He then gave the bird to the pujari, saying, "Take it out and give it water." As the pujari took it and headed out the door, the bird flew out of his hand and away.

ﬨﬤ

One evening in Agra Maharajji came to our house. He began to walk up and down the verandah, this way and that, again and again. It appeared to us that he was taking on someone's pain. After a few hours he sat in a chair and asked for some hot tea. The phone rang. Devotees from Lucknow were trying to locate Maharajji. They said to tell Maharajji that there had been a two-and-a-half-hour operation on one of his devotees, a poor seventy-six-year-old woman from the hills, and that it had been successful. In his way Maharajji had been with her throughout the operation. He appeared upset all during this time. When the call came he expressed great relief.

ﬨﬤ

My wife had known Maharajji since her childhood and her whole family had been devotees for a long time. I did not meet him, however, until 1962, when I had an operation on my lungs. I was in critical condition. My wife spoke to me then about Maharajji and I was remembering all that I'd previously heard about him and was praying to meet him before my death. On that same day Maharajji came to our home, approached my bed, and blessed me. From that day my health began to improve, and the illness has never returned. During every visit thereafter Maharajji told me that my health would be fine.

ﬨﬤ

Yudisthra had brought Maharajji to Bhumiadhar in a car. Yudisthra went to take a bath in the waterfall. He came running back and told Maharajji that he had been bitten by a snake, then he fell down unconscious. His hand had become blue black. Maharajji told Brahmachari Baba to spread a blanket and put Yudisthra on it. Then Maharajji told him to get a glass of water, which Maharajji then held in his hand under his blanket. Maharajji was shouting, "He has been bitten! What will happen?" The man remained unconscious.

After a few minutes Maharajji gave Brahmachari Baba the water and told him to rub it over the place where the snake had bitten the man. As soon as he started to apply the water, Yudisthra regained consciousness. In another hour, he was well again.

ट्रम

Once when I was a child I was very, very sick with a high fever. My mother telephoned Maharajji and he came right away. He just laid his hand on my head and the fever left me.

ट्रम

In 1964 I suffered a heart attack. My wife was very worried, but I felt a calm assurance in my soul from Maharajji that I would not die.

ट्रम

Early one morning, five young men came to Kainchi. They waited nervously for Maharajji to make his appearance. As soon as he emerged from his room he questioned them. They answered that they were Moslems from a nearby city. Their close relative was dying and had asked them to go and request Maharajji's blessing. Maharajji asked his attendants for some water, which was handed to him in a plastic cup. He raised it to his lips, whispering something, then he blew into the water and gave it to the boys. He told them to return at once to the sick man and to make him drink it. "Thik ho jaega [He'll be all right]."

ट्रम

At the home of some devotees in Lucknow Maharajji was giving darshan to a large crowd. Outside Maharajji's room a sadhu recited the Gita in a loud, punditlike voice while the man of the house cared for his sick cat nearby. Maharajji shouted to his devotee, "What are you doing with that cat?" The devotee explained that since the cat was extremely ill he was warming it in the sun, and, further, he thought of taking it to the vet. "It's a fact of nature,"

Maharajji said, "that cats don't usually need doctors. She's the property of Mother Nature; she'll be all right." He took a small sweet, saying, "Give her this." Although the cat was so ill that it wouldn't even drink milk, it ate the sweet without hesitation. A minute later it leaped up and jumped on the sadhu, interrupting his recital. Then it bounded away. When the devotee came back into the room, Maharajji said, "Your cat is all right now? Animals cure themselves. When they're sick, they won't eat food. They'll find herbs and eat them."

In Lucknow a woman suffering from high blood pressure called her husband at the office and said she was feeling giddy and asked him to come home, as she couldn't reach a doctor. When he got there, she was still unable to reach a doctor. They were wondering what to do when the telephone rang and it was Maharajji calling from Agra. He said, "You are worried about your wife's high blood pressure? Don't worry. Nothing is wrong with her. Give her a glass of water."

One morning at 4:00 A.M. when Maharajji was staying at my house, he said, "Come on, let's go."
I said, "Maharajji, I'll get my car and take you."
But he said, "No, I will walk."
So I got my sandals. Maharajji went barefoot. I didn't know where we were going, but I always entrusted myself to Maharajji because, even if he said he didn't know where a place was, he knew. Often Maharajji would ask, "Do you know where such-and-such is?" I'd say no and then he'd take us there. So I surrendered myself to him.
We went into a slum. Maharajji came to a shack with only a windowlike door, which he pushed open and looked inside. There, a young boy of about twelve was lying on a cot, very sick. Maharajji said to the boy, "Get up, you aren't sick." As soon as the boy was able to get up and lean against the wall, Maharajji lay down on the bed. At this point, the old, blind grandmother who was taking care of the boy awakened and asked, "Who is there?"
I answered, "A mahatma [great soul] has come."

Maharajji asked her, "Has he been feverish with chills for two weeks?"
She said yes.
The boy probably had typhoid fever. Then the Ma was uncomfortable
because she had nothing to offer Maharajji. Maharajji saw this and spied an
old can with water in it.
"Ma, have you got some pani *(water)? I'm very thirsty."*
She was happy to have the opportunity at least to give water. He drank
deeply and then offered the container to me, but he knew I would never drink
from it, and I said no. We left then, and the boy recovered.

राम

Ram Dass gave a talk in Ohio in 1972 or 1973. A boy who attended the
lecture that night got on the first plane the next morning, flew from Cleveland,
Ohio, to New York, to London, to New Delhi, where he got in a taxi and
rode up to Kainchi. Less than thirty-six hours earlier he had heard Ram Dass
talking about Maharajji. He walked into the ashram. He had taken off his
shirt, since it was so hot, and I could see that on his chest he had a bad rash. I
welcomed him and asked him where he had come from, and he told me his
story. Then I asked him why he hadn't treated his rash. He explained that all
the medical authorities had told him it was incurable; he'd tried injections and
salves, and nothing had worked.
I said that that was silly—it was just tinia corpus, which is really very easy
to cure. I said that, in fact, Dwarka was going to Nainital and he could get the
sulphur tar to cure it and could bring it back that night. Then in a few days
the rash would be gone. And he said to me, "I heard Ram Dass just two days
ago. And now I've met Doctor America (Maharajji's nickname for me) and
I'm here in Maharajji's ashram. Anything you say!" His eyes were as big as
saucers.
Dwarka brought back the sulphur tar. I showed the boy how to use it and
told him the rash would be cured in just a few days. He agreed to use it and
said he was on his way to Badrinath that day for a week. And he went off to
the chai stall.
I got to thinking that it had been a long time since I'd practiced medicine and
I was a bit rusty. I went to where I was staying and checked my medical books
about this disease that I had just diagnosed. I realized that I had diagnosed the
wrong disease. The treatment I had given him was absolutely useless, so I
raced down to the chai stall, just in time to see him get on the bus and be gone.

I felt very bad. By misdiagnosing his disease, not only had I failed as Maharajji's representative, but I'd sent the boy off with a useless medicine—and when he came back, he was going to think that all the people around Maharajji were fools and incompetents. The week that he was gone was just awful for me. I had done something terrible.

After a week passed he came back. I saw him from across the ashram and ran out to him and said, "I'm sorry!"

He said, "Sorry? Look!" He opened his shirt and his chest was completely healed. Not even a scar. It was all gone. I didn't understand, but I knew it wasn't the medicine that I had given him.

I went to the window of Maharajji's room we called the "office," and I said, "Maharajji, thank you. You cured him."

He said, "Sub Ishwar hai [It's all God]."

ॐ

A woman devotee was sick from eating too many pickles. She loved them but had a bad stomach and couldn't digest them, so when she'd eaten mango chutney, the next morning her stomach was bad. Her husband told Maharajji that his wife was sick, so Maharajji came running with something wrapped in a piece of paper. We all thought that he had brought some secret herb or ancient remedy. Maharajji opened up the packet and handed the contents to her husband: a cellophane-wrapped tablet of Gelusil!

ॐ

I had discovered that I had diabetes and wasn't supposed to eat anything spicy, starchy, greasy, or sweet. Right after that, I went to Kainchi for the first time and was served a big plate of puris cooked in grease, some halva, and some spicy potatoes—all precisely the things I shouldn't eat. The doctor had told me that if I ate such things I could get very very ill. I thought about what the doctor said and looked over at Maharajji, who was twinkling. I was trying to decide whether to have faith in the doctor or faith in Maharajji. (At that time I didn't even know if he was my guru.) It was my first day "on the job" as Maharajji's devotee.

I finally decided to eat the food. In fact, I was so hungry I ate two big plates of it. Every day thereafter, I would come and stuff myself. After a few weeks, I went to Nainital and had my blood-sugar level tested. It was down to borderline low. The doctor said, "I don't understand how this could have gotten so low so quickly. This doesn't make sense."

I said, "Well, I think I know what happened."

भगवान्

My mother was ill. Many doctors had seen her and had said she was septic and must go to the hospital. My mother, who is very orthodox, did not want to go. I wrote to Maharajji and he asked me to take her to a homeopath whose name he gave me. My mother was cured. However, the old homeopath, who had never met Maharajji, said, "So many are sent to me by this Maharajji and no matter what medicine I give them, they are cured, even when the disease is chronic. I don't know how it is done!"

भगवान्

One time while I was staying at Kainchi, my wife came for Maharajji's darshan, though I didn't know she had come. In those days she was feeling great pain in her heart. Whenever she would go up or down the stairs, her heart would start palpitating. She would come to me, weeping, thinking she was about to die. But, putting my faith in Maharajji's power, I had no worries about her and never spoke of this to Maharajji.

This day, she came to Maharajji herself and told him. Immediately Maharajji called out, "Where is he? Call him!" I came, and he said, "What? She is ill and you don't care?" He went on talking like this. I didn't reply because I knew that whatever you are thinking, he knows and he replies to your thoughts as if you had spoken them. You think and he talks.

I was thinking, "Why should I do anything—it is all in his hands."

He replied out loud, "No! There is a doctor—go to Agra. He is a heart specialist. He is a great disciple." Then Maharajji turned to one of the Ma's standing by and said, "Tell him how I sent your relative to him. This doctor is a great saint."

She said, "When I showed the doctor the letter that Maharajji had sent us, he came running to treat my relative at the house."

Maharajji said, "And what happened?"

"Well, in only two or three days she was all right."

"Just see! Just see!" Maharajji exclaimed to me. "He is my great disciple. You go! Tomorrow, you leave this place. Jao! Go! If you need money, I will give it to you. You must go!"

I didn't say anything. I just thought in my heart, "Well, Maharajji, you are so great. I have no need of going there. You are God. You can cure her."

He immediately replied to my thoughts, "No, no, you must go! Badmash! This is my order!" I kept mum. He said, "Don't you know? The doctor is a great saint. The moment she has his darshan she will be all right. You see his grace, you go to him, there will be no need of medicine. You see him. She will be all right. You go! Tomorrow you will have to go! Don't deny it!" I had been thinking that I would not go. "What? You don't obey my orders? Obey my orders! You are very wicked. You have to go."

Well, I was thinking, it is a great trouble to me—but he says I have to go, and so I must go. The next day, I thought he would direct me to go, but he didn't say anything about it. He said, "Well, come here, sit beside me. How many people are coming to the temple? Give them prasad, give them whatever they need." But he didn't say anything about going to Agra. From that day, even till now—eight years—my wife has had no pain.

IN HIS EARLIER years, in some of the villages on the plains of India, Maharajji became well-known for his curing of insane people. In those days many such people would be brought in chains to Maharajji to be helped. In the later years he would do much less of this and often had such people taken to a temple known as Bala Ji Hanuman—yet still, with a word or a glance or a pointing of the finger, he could straighten that which in the mind was crooked.

An Indian man had brought his widowed mother who had been emotionally and physically destitute since her husband's death. She had been a devotee of Maharajji for many years but it seemed she saw him only rarely, so her son brought her to Maharajji hoping that this would help her. When Maharajji came out, I was troubled to see that the man and his mother were standing way in the back and that all the area near Maharajji was taken up by the young Westerners.

I got up the nerve to be a busybody and ask people to move aside so that these people could come forward. People did move, instantly. Then Maharajji took the widow into the small room, where she stayed with him for some time. She came out a different person, really radiant. I was impressed by that, and her son and granddaughter were very moved, too.

One of the Westerners became quite manic. He stopped sleeping and began walking through the town naked, stealing things, and acting irrational in many ways. Finally he took off in a taxi, with only a shawl wrapped around himself, to go see Maharajji at a temple some two hundred miles distant. When he arrived he entered the temple and walked toward Maharajji. As he approached, Maharajji held up his index finger, and the man later reported that immediately it felt as if all the incredible high energy with which his body had been charged for days, giving him the feeling that he had supernatural powers, was drained out of him instantaneously. He recalls being angry with Maharajji for taking this energy from him.

ॐ

Many years ago in Neeb Karori village, crazy men were sometimes brought to Maharajji, bound in chains. Maharajji used to say, "Free them and keep them near Hanumanji." He would take a small bamboo stick and proceed to hit them on their heads. Then he would ask, "Are you all right?" They would say, "Yes." Then Maharajji would ask them to do some work, saying something like, "Bring a stick of rambans [cactus plant]." When they would bring it, he'd say, "Now it's all right." They were allowed to stay for a day or two and then he would ask the people who brought them to take them back home.

ॐ

Many years ago, a Mohammedan lived behind the place where Maharajji was staying. They loved each other very much. One day, two crazy men were brought there and Maharajji said to the Mohammedan, "You make one of them all right and I will make the other one all right." The one who was with Maharajji became all right within a short time, but the Moslem took some time and his man was still not all right. The devotees were sitting there watching. Maharajji called the other crazy man over to him and hit him gently on his head, and then he too was perfectly all right. But Maharajji said, "Oh, the Mohammedan did it first."

ॐ

I was with Maharajji when he went to the sanitarium to visit the principal's younger brother, who had gone insane. He was brought into the room in chains and his unfocused eyes were rolling around in his head. Maharajji stood in front of him talking to him. Suddenly the man fell to the ground at Maharajji's feet and was perfectly sane. The man was able to answer all questions. Later he was released, although it wasn't to be his last bout with mental illness.

॥ॐ॥

Once a Western devotee stood before Maharajji in a rage of defiance. He was drug-intoxicated and came to believe that he himself was Jesus Christ and that Maharajji needed to repent. Before many other devotees there, this fellow shouted his defiance. Maharajji silently engaged the fellow's gaze for a few moments, with a look of openness and compassion. The man still continued his tirade, so Maharajji nodded his head and then told some devotees to throw him out. Even after he was outside, Maharajji sent more devotees out to be sure that he had gotten on the bus and left town. (Later, when asked how he had felt during this time, the man said he felt engulfed with Maharajji's love and was expecially touched that he would send people out to help him board the bus.)

MAHARAJJI DID NOT heal all who came to him with illness or who prayed to be healed. Why some were healed and others were not was known only to him. Sometimes he would apparently lessen the illness but leave the individual with some of the suffering. His comments at these times suggest that Maharajji's healing acts were intimately related to the karma of the individual—that often it was necessary for the person to suffer part or perhaps all of the pain of the illness. While most people do not want to suffer, Maharajji now and then reminded his devotees that suffering brings us closer to God.

When my daughter was born she was very sickly. I took her to an allopath and to an ayurved (doctor of herbal medicine), but no one could help. I took her to an astrologer, who said, "She has three planets indicating death. If she lives past two-and-a-half, then bring her to me for her chart. Now it is useless." Then I brought her to Maharajji and asked his help. Maharajji just bent his head down on his arm and hid his face for some time. For about five minutes he concentrated. Then he picked up his head and said, "Don't worry, she'll be all right." After that darshan, my daughter caught pneumonia—again and again—but she lived. She is now six years old. I don't worry about her. What comes now is karma and we must deal with it.

ॐ

One of Maharajji's devotees was seriously poisoned. He was suffering gravely and no one expected him to survive. Maharajji said, "You have to be satisfied with that little bit of suffering. You have to take on some of it." In other words, his suffering would have been worse but for Maharajji's grace. But indeed he survived.

ॐ

My elder sister has always been very sickly, with various maladies. Maharajji told her that it couldn't be helped—that she must somehow work off past samskaras (karma). *He told her to keep her mind always in devotional thoughts or she would lose everything.*

ॐ

Maharajji asked an Indian girl four times, "Do you like sorrow or joy?" Each time the girl answered, "I've never known joy, Maharajji, only sorrow." Finally, Maharajji said, "I love sorrow. It brings me closer to God."

ॐ

I got a very bad arthritic pain for the first time on a Saturday. By Sunday, after Maharajji had departed for Agra, the pain had stopped. In the winter it came back again very intensely, but I didn't do anything for it. I want to keep the pain to remind me of that day. It was the last darshan I had of Maharajji.

YOU GET WISDOM FROM SUFFERING. YOU ARE ALONE WITH GOD WHEN YOU ARE SICK, IN THE CREMATION GROUND OR HOSPITAL. YOU CALL ON GOD WHEN YOU SUFFER.

Again, for reasons known only to Maharajji, sometimes he would seem to bargain with death and push it away from one of his devotees, while at other times he would not intercede and the devotee would die. Because Maharajji knew the time of each person's death, but hated to be the bearer of bad news, he would often be absent at the time when one of his devotees must die. In some cases, when pressed, he gave a subtle clue, but often it was merely his absence that was the clue for the devotees who had come to know his ways.

Once a neighbor lady came to my wife and said she was going for the darshan of another local baba. She asked my wife to accompany her, so my wife went along. The neighbor showed her hand to the baba, as he was considered an expert in palmistry, astrology, and such things. But the baba said, "I don't want to see your hand; I want to see her [my wife's] hand." She didn't want to show it, but he insisted and he told her that she would die in six months. My wife told this to Maharajji, who immediately exclaimed, "Sub gulat [It's all wrong]! Why did that baba say that? Will you not die? A time will not come when you will die? Everybody will die! Why didn't you say to him, 'What—will you not die? Are you immortal?' He will also die. Everybody will die. Why does he say such things? It's very bad that he says such things. Wicked!" Then Maharajji narrated another story about a saint. I was there to hear it.

"Well, there was a saint. A woman came to see him. Her husband had just died. She bowed to his lotus feet, and he gave her his blessing and told her that she would have five sons. She said, 'But Maharaj, I have come to you because my husband has just died. How will I have five sons?' The saint replied, 'I have told you that you will have five sons and I will keep my word.' And her husband came back to life." Then Maharajji said, "And I will do the same thing. Since I have given my word, I will complete it. You will not die. You will live for seventy-five years. Don't be worried." That was eight years ago. She is still alive.

राम

Maharajji was walking by a place where a palm reader was working. And the palm reader, in reading the palm of one of Maharajji's devotees, said that he would die in three days. The devotee was of course very upset. But Maharajji said, "He's so smart. But what that fool doesn't realize is that it is he who is going to die in three days." And he did.

I was in a boat with Maharajji and he told me to jump in the water. I was afraid and said, "Maharajji, I can't swim. I'll drown."

Maharajji pointed to a high bridge and said, "If the right time has not come, you could jump from that bridge and not die." As he said that I felt great faith and jumped in, and it was only up to my waist.

There was a peddlar who lived in Ram Ghar. He became very ill and the worried family took him to a local baba for help. This baba said the man would die very soon but that he did have some medicine that might save him. The family then also consulted Maharajji, telling him of the first baba's verdict. Maharajji responded quickly, "Nonsense! He will live to be in his eighties. That wicked baba just wants to scare you so he can sell you his medicine."

The husband of a sick woman went to Maharajji, and Maharajji made a stick in a certain way and gave it to the man with instructions to put it under his wife's pillow. He did this and soon she got better, but when they looked for the stick it was missing. The husband, who was now greedy to have the stick, went to Maharajji and told him the stick was missing. Maharajji said, "You have your wife. What do you want with a stick?" Later the mother of another man became ill, so the man went to Maharajji and said, "You gave so-and-so a stick to heal his wife. Will you give me a stick to heal my mother?" Maharajji said, "She was a young girl and I saved her. Your mother is an old woman and she'll die." And she did.

My father had a series of operations, and before and after each one Maharajji visited him. The last time he became ill, however, Maharajji didn't come. We knew that his life would soon be over. Maharajji came after his death.

The same thing happened to my mother. When my mother became ill, Maharajji came to Kanpur but didn't visit our house, though he would always visit us when he was in town. She died. Two days later, Maharajji came to the house and went to the prayer room where a photo of my mother was kept. Maharajji started weeping like a five-year-old child. Weeping, weeping, weeping.

ॐ

After Maharajji's death something happened that brought me to him. My young brother-in-law, dying of cancer, was down at the cancer research institute in Bombay, away from us all. The doctors wired us that he would die that very day, that he was in the absolute, final stage of cancer. We were all very sad. I went to Jaunapur (Maharajji's new temple in New Delhi), thinking that if Maharajji is really as great a saint as they say, he could help us. Out of the merit of his own tapasya (austerities) he could help us. So I went and prayed for three things: First, I prayed that my brother-in-law's life be extended for two more months. I wouldn't ask for a cure (what is ordained must be; a ravaged body must die), but an extension could be granted. Second, I asked that he die here, surrounded by his family. Third, I asked that he have a peaceful death.

Next we heard from Bombay, and they said he'd had a remission and was released from their care. He flew immediately to Delhi to join us. Here, the doctors examined him and declared him fit enough to return to work! Well, this remission lasted for two months and one day, until he got sick again and died peacefully, surrounded by all of us. Why did he get that one more day? He went to Maharajji's temple on the last day of the two months and received prasad. That prasad saved him. He couldn't die on the same day as receiving prasad.

ॐ

When it came time for my father to die, Maharajji said to him, "Ask me for anything."

Father said, "I want nothing. I've lived my life. Now I want to die by the Ganges at Kashi [Benares]."

Maharajji said to him privately, "You must live one more year. You will die by the Ganges but not at Kashi."

One year later, at Dharagan on the Ganges where I had a new house, my father said, "You have a house in Dharagan, but you don't know how unfortunate it is for you." That was when he visited in July. He died there in November.

ᛁ‍‍‍

In 1951 my father, the district magistrate, was ill and in great pain. He'd had a ninety-nine-degree temperature for thirty days. Four days before he died, Maharajji came and brought him four roses. To my father he said, "You'll be okay." To me he said, "The body has to finish."

ALTHOUGH ALL these incidents concern Maharajji's devotees, his healing energies extended far beyond them. In the following story about Subrahmanyum—Dr. Larry Brilliant, a Western physician who was brought to Maharajji by his wife, Girija—we catch a glimpse of how Maharajji worked indirectly. In this case he worked through Subrahmanyum and the World Health Organization of the United Nations to speed the eradication of smallpox.

The first thing he said to us as we walked in and sat down was, "Doctor—Doctor America! How much money do you have?"
I said, "Oh, Maharajji, I have five hundred dollars."
"No, no, no, really—how much money do you have?" I insisted that this was all I had. He said, "Yes, yes, yes, that's in India. But how much money do you have in America?"
I thought about it, and I confess to being a bit concerned that this was an appeal from him for money for some temple, and I said, "I have only five hundred dollars back in America," which was true. Then I hastened to add, "But I also have a very big debt from medical school. I had to borrow a lot of money to go through medical school, and even though I have a thousand dollars, I owe a lot more than that."
He said, "What? You have no money? You are no doctor!" It sounded exactly like something my mother would say. He looked at me and laughed and laughed: "You are no doctor. You are no doctor, you are no doctor, U N O doctor, U N O doctor . . ." I didn't understand what he was saying. Then he said, "You are going to give vaccinations; you will go to the villages and give vaccinations."
"You want me to give a shot to someone here?" I asked. I didn't understand

what he was instructing me to do. Everybody else understood except me. Finally he looked at me and said, "Doctor America—UNO doctor. United Nations Organization doctor. You will work for the United Nations. You are going to go to villages and give vaccinations."

In fact, I had made a very casual inquiry of some acquaintances who worked for WHO, the World Health Organization, but they replied that WHO was not hiring anyone at all. Meanwhile, over the next few weeks Maharajji was always asking me, "Did you get your job?"

I'd always say, "No, Maharajji," and quickly drop the subject.

One day Maharajji said to me, "Go to WHO. You'll get your job." So I went to the WHO offices in New Delhi and saw the man to whom I had originally spoken. He was very friendly but pointed out that WHO had no openings, and, in any case, they only hired expert consultants from medical schools and institutions outside India. Then he said, "But there is one program. If they could ever do anything, it would be really nice, but it's doubtful they will be able to achieve their goal, because it's so difficult. It's the smallpox program. The Indian government right now is adamantly against expanding the WHO program to fight smallpox. They have other problems, such as malaria and family planning. Smallpox is not their highest priority. But I'll take you to see the French doctor, Nicole Grasset, who directs that program."

We made an appointment to see her and then I returned to the home of two of Maharajji's devotees, the Barmans, and borrowed Barman's suit and bought a terrible tie. I tied my hair into a pony tail and hid it under a white shirt. My costume was bizarre and ill-fitting and Nicole realized at once that I was just another hippie. She said, "I'm sorry. We really don't have a job. But it's awfully nice to meet you."

So I went back to Maharajji and he again asked, "Did you get your job?" I said, "No, Maharajji. Let's just cut this out."

Two more weeks passed, and Maharajji looked at me and said, "Go back to WHO."

I took the bus-train–bus-rickshaw trip back to WHO. Once more I talked to my acquaintance, Ned, and this time I filled out a different type of form, typed it a bit more properly, and sent it in and spoke with Nicole on the phone. Of course there was no job there.

The next week Maharajji asked if I got my job and then asked me to call Nicole. It was getting embarrassing. This time I called her from Vrindaban. Again she told me there was no expansion of the smallpox program, no possibility of hiring American doctors—but she thanked me for continued interest in the work.

Sometime later Maharajji suddenly called me and said, "Immediately! Go to WHO."

I took a train and went immediately to WHO. When I walked in the door there was another man there. He said to me, "What are you doing here?"

I gave my usual line, "I've come to WHO to work for the smallpox program. My guru told me I would work for WHO."

I went up to Ned's office again and telephoned Nicole. She said there was still no expansion of the smallpox program, but that something had happened that day: the chief of the global smallpox program had come from Geneva. She suggested I come to meet him. I went to meet him and of course he was that man in the doorway whom I had just told I would be working for WHO—and it was his program I was going to work for. He interviewed me and wrote a "note for the record": "This young man seems to like foreign cultures and will probably do very good international work someday. However, he has no experience in public health, no training past internship, and I wish him good luck in the future. We have no job for him." What he said to me was that WHO could not hire me for several reasons: First, I had no public health training. I had never even seen a case of smallpox. Second, because of political tensions, the Indian government preferred at that time not to have Americans working in India. Third, they had not yet really geared up the program for smallpox eradication in India. Smallpox had been eradicated in all but four countries, but the strategy was to work on the other three first and then come to India.

That was it. He added that there was a smallpox program in Pakistan, and if that interested me, I had best give it some more thought.

I paused and sheepishly said, "I'm going to have to ask my guru."

I went back to Maharajji. When he asked if I got the job, I said, "No, but there's a possibility of a job in Pakistan."

He yelled back, "No! I said India!" So I telephoned back to WHO and told Nicole my guru insisted I work for WHO in India.

That must have amused her, but she was polite as usual and thanked me for calling.

After two months of this, Girija and I were exhausted and frustrated. We decided to take a vacation from it all in Kashmir. As we were leaving the ashram, I called Nicole at WHO and told her our plans. "If by any chance a job comes through," I said, "please call me in Srinagar."

"You know," she said, "a very strange thing just happened. I suddenly had this inspiration. I don't know—maybe it's your guru or something like that, but can you write?"

"Yes," I said. I'd edited some medical journals.

"Well, you know we can't really hire you as a smallpox doctor, but if you're really that determined to work for WHO, maybe I could hire you as an administrative assistant."

"Look, anything. Maharajji said I'm going to work for you and I'm going to go to villages and give injections. He's never been wrong."

She changed my application from that of a doctor to that of an administrative assistant and sent a telegram to D. A. Henderson, the program chief in Geneva, Switzerland: "I'm going to hire Brilliant." She suddenly really wanted to hire me and put the application through. Still WHO had not created a post in her unit.

After our vacation in Kashmir we returned to Kainchi and Maharajji's first smiling question: "Did you get your job yet?"

"No, Maharajji. It's really very complicated." Again he had me go back to Delhi. It was ten times now that I'd gone back and forth, like a yo-yo, each time putting on Barman's suit and that awful tie.

When I got to WHO I found that my application as an administrative assistant had been approved, but that I would still have to pass a security clearance. Every American working for WHO must have one. When I got that piece of paper for a security clearance I knew this was the end of the game. There seemed no chance in the world that I could get a security clearance. We had been part of the left-wing antiwar movement in the States; I'd been a leader of a radical organization, the Medical Committee for Human Rights. There was absolutely no chance for a security clearance.

I came back to Kainchi feeling terrible. I explained all this to Maharajji and said that there may have been a lot of stumbling blocks up till now, but this was the last straw.

Maharajji said, "Oh. Who is the person who is supposed to give you this job?" I couldn't remember precisely who, but I mentioned that Henderson was the boss. Maharajji pretended to be a real fakir (sadhu). He sat up straight and put his blanketed arm up before his face and asked, "How do you spell his name?" I started spelling it. "Wait," he said. And then he began repeating the letters slowly in a deep voice. He peeked out at me through his fingers, which were covering his face, laughing all the time. He continued spelling the name and he pretended to go into a trance, always peeking at me to be sure I was watching and properly impressed, but giggling as he did so.

At the same time, in Geneva, Dr. Henderson was attending a cocktail party at the American Embassy. The American ambassador and the surgeon general were there. The surgeon general asked Henderson how the smallpox eradication program was going. "Great," said Henderson. "We have thirty-four countries cleared and only four are left."

"Are all the countries helping you?" asked the surgeon general.

"Yes. Russia's given us vaccine. Sweden's given us a lot of money. All the countries are helping."

The surgeon general asked, "What about America? What are we giving you?"

"Well," said Henderson, an expert in getting support for his program, "not so much."

"What do you need?"

Henderson replied, "I don't know how I got into this, and I don't know why we're doing it, but we want to hire this young American doctor who has been living in an ashram in India. We've never done anything like that before. And the kid can't get a security clearance."

The surgeon general of the United States said, "Security clearance? What does he need that for?"

Henderson replied, "Every American, in order to work for the United Nations, has to have a security clearance."

The surgeon general said, "I didn't know that. Who gives him the clearance?"

Henderson said, "You do."

"I do? Give me a napkin and tell me what the kid's name is." He took a cocktail napkin and wrote, "Brilliant—okay to start work." He gave the napkin to Henderson, who telegraphed WHO in New Delhi that I'd been cleared to work.

The next morning Maharajji called us into his "office." He was being too nice. Laughing and smiling, he had tea and jelebees brought in, and he hugged us. We were rubbing his feet. It was so blissful. Then suddenly Maharajji said, "Okay. Time for you to go."

We thought he meant to leave the ashram.

We stood up and pranammed and then walked out and around the corner, and just as we approached the gate to the ashram the postman came with a telegram from New Delhi: "We have been notified today that you have received a US security clearance. Come immediately to WHO–New Delhi to begin work."

So I went to WHO and began work as an administrative assistant. During the week I worked in Delhi, and on the weekends we came to the ashram to be with Maharajji. I remember one darshan in the back at Kainchi, where we talked for three hours about smallpox. It was the most horrid disease I had ever seen. He told me everything about it: where it was located in India, where the bad epidemics were, what the seasons were, what the transmission cycle was, what places we would have trouble with—everything about the epidemiology.

He knew much more than I knew, even after I'd worked with WHO for about three months. I asked him, "Will smallpox be eradicated?" I remember his answer because I wrote it down: "Smallpox will be eradicated. This is God's gift to mankind because of the hard work of dedicated medical scientists."

At the WHO office I was occasionally assigned to write up the operational plans, since my native language was English. Maharajji would help to organize the whole plan. Because my source of information about conditions in India was, well, so direct, shall we say—and because Maharajji's advice was so good—I began to get more and more responsibility. Still, after about a month of this I was not feeling that Maharajji's prediction had come true, because I still wasn't going to the villages to give vaccinations. There was as yet no such program.

The project slowly moved to the point where we were about to go into the field. September was to be the first month. Some of the staff would go into the field, but not me, of course, since I was just an administrative assistant. I was to stay in New Delhi and mind the shop. However, it so happened that two of the Russian doctors who were to be assigned to an area where Maharajji had lived for a long period were held up by Soviet government formalities. There was this blank spot on the map—and there was just nobody except me who could be sent there.

I was sent out of the office and into the villages. The jeep that Girija and I drove had a big picture of Maharajji on the dashboard. Often when we went into a civil surgeon's office and told him about the importance of a serious smallpox program, he would say, "Yes, yes, thank you for coming. Now please leave. I've got so many other problems." Then, because of Indian courtesy, he might walk us out to our jeep—and he'd see Maharajji's picture on the dashboard and ask us why we had it there. "Oh," I'd say, "he's my guru. He told me to go work for the United Nations. He told me smallpox would be eradicated. He told me this is God's gift to mankind through the hard work of dedicated medical scientists." And then the civil surgeon might say, "Oh, please come back into my office. Take tea! Since smallpox is going to be eradicated, how shall we get organized?" It kept happening like that.

Every time—simply because Maharajji had said smallpox would be eradicated, and because all the Indian officials had heard that anything he said came true—they took our work seriously and put other things aside to help us.

Often, skeptical WHO or Indian officials said to me, "Look, you understand India. You may eradicate smallpox everywhere else, but you know India will never eradicate smallpox. It's just not possible." But when they heard what Maharajji had said, the Indian officials would often completely change their opinions.

Soon we were assigned to areas that were selected because of the negative attitudes of the local doctors. We talked about Maharajji's prediction. Some of the officials remembered when the Chinese invaded India in 1962 and Maharajji had said the Chinese troops would go back to China by themselves. And so these doctors would change their attitudes and motivate their people to do tremendous work, and soon smallpox would be beaten in their area. The effect of this was that, although I knew very little about smallpox or the UN system, every time I was sent to a difficult area, through Maharajji's grace smallpox would disappear.

WHO kept sending me to strange and remote places. I thought perhaps it was just in Uttar Pradesh that I had such luck, but in January 1974 they sent me to a remote part of Madhya Pradesh, to a place that just happened to be part of the Shahdol District—Amarkantak!—Maharajji's old sadhu stomping grounds, which at that time was experiencing the worst epidemic in India. Nearly everyone in the district had known Maharajji, and when they learned that he had said smallpox would be eradicated, they cooperated and, despite their earlier skepticism, mounted a tremendous campaign in the remote hills. The epidemic was over!

People within WHO began to ask me about Maharajji. Nicole, my boss, really opened up to Maharajji in a beautiful way. First of all, she did think Maharajji had somehow influenced her to hire me. Second, since she always asked everyone's advice before making difficult decisions, she got in the habit of asking us, when we'd go to see Maharajji over the weekends, what he would advise about specific problems in the eradication program. He would send his advice back through us. His answers were full of wisdom on every level, practical as well as spiritual. Many smallpox workers began to respect him. Members of the smallpox staff had a quality about them that was different from any other group I met in the UN program: they were very inspired. We talked freely about Maharajji, as they were all devout individuals.

It took only two years of intense effort to conquer smallpox in all of India. When we started in 1974 there were 180,000 cases with 30,000 deaths in only one year. A total of 400 epidemiologists from 30 different countries and 100,000 Indian workers worked in a frenzy of compassion and commitment. Everyone in India had said it could never be done— even many WHO officials—but Maharajji said it could be done. He said it was God's gift to mankind, and it was.

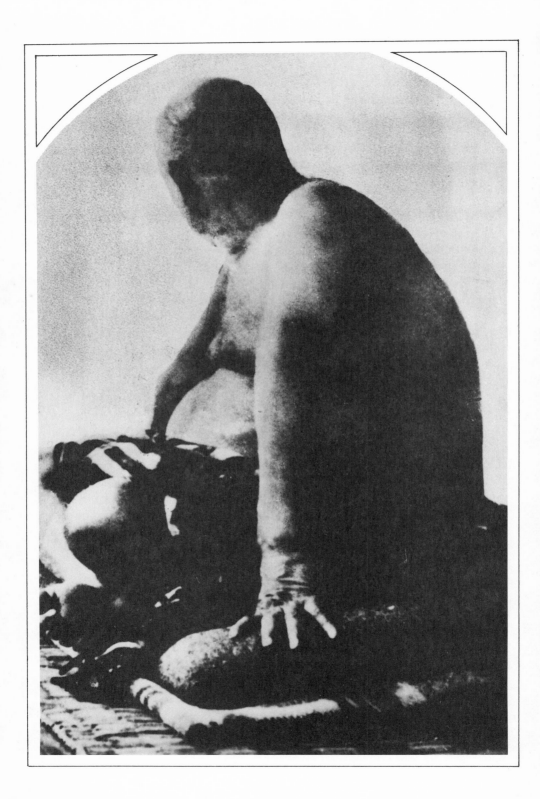

Embodied Spirit

PERHAPS NOTHING concerning Maharajji is more mind-stretching than the manner in which he related to the physical universe, especially to his own body. Although at first glance his seemed like an ordinary human body—and he seemed to go out of his way to prove that it was—there was ample evidence not only that it was not ordinary but, indeed, extraordinary beyond comprehension.

Perhaps most subtle was the attractiveness of his body. Although a passerby might have described him as a short, rotund, elderly gentleman, another look and such a description would have become irrelevant. There was a quality to Maharajji's body that made it compellingly attractive to us devotees. Most of us could be fulfilled hour after hour just by gazing at this form.

When I think of him now I remember his hands—not just holding his hands but watching the way they moved. His fingers were very flexible yet full of strength. When he was not using his hands they were completely relaxed and open, completely flat. The tips of his fingers had an unusual shape. More than his face, I remember his hands.

ꠣ

He was spontaneity itself. He would assume amazing postures. He flowed like the Akash. He seemed totally fluid. His flesh had an amazing quality to it; it had a glow and a softness that was unusual, like a baby's skin.

ꠣ

Sometimes the beauty of his body was so startlingly radiant it took your breath away. In the July heat of Vrindaban before Guru Purnima Day, he came out wearing only a white dhoti, and all I could think of was the description of Hanuman in the Ramayana: "A body shining as a mountain of gold . . ."

ꠣ

I always expected to see him wrapped in his blanket. One day I came around the corner into the room and there he was, with only a sheet around his waist and legs. It was one of the most shocking things I had seen in my life, though it wasn't frightening. I don't know why. I'd seen photographs, but I wasn't prepared for seeing the vastness of who he was.

Another time I saw him sitting outside on the tucket with just a sheet around his waist. This time he seemed to me to be like an infant. Here was this massive being who looked like a delightful little baby, wrapped in his diapers and playing.

ꠣ

My mother and aunt snuck into Maharajji's room when he was out taking a bath. They caressed his blanket and put it to their faces. Afterward they could only talk about how it smelled like a baby's blanket.

ꠣ

At times he seemed fat and at other times thin; sometimes tall and sometimes small; now heavy and then again light. And his joints didn't function like ordinary joints.

Not only did he outrageously manipulate his own body, the one with which we were familiar, but he apparently took on other bodies at will.

Once I was alone in the night with Maharajji. We were in Vrindaban. He said to me, "Okay, you take me for a walk."

Maharajji has such a massive body, and I said, "Maharajji, how can I take you for a walk?"

But he insisted. I put out my hand, palm-up, and he put his force full-weight on my palm. I said, "Maharajji, you are too heavy."

He said, "Is it so? Then you put me somewhere."

So I found him a place to sit for a while. Then he said, "Now, you take me again." And this time, I found he was very light. Much lighter than a baby.

From that day onward, the feeling that he is walking beside me is still there.

ॐ

When he would appear in a village in his earlier years, he would often just play with the children, showing them incredible feats with his body. Every joint seemed as if it were not interconnected. I would never have believed it. Twenty of us were present when, to entertain the children, he brought his arms over his head from back to front without unclasping his hands.

ॐ

Once a famous orthopedist was visiting Maharajji. Maharajji showed him the way the right joint of his right arm could move in a very unusual way. The doctor examined it carefully, for he had never seen such a thing. Then he said, "Well, as a child you must have broken the joint and it never healed."

"Oh," said Maharajji, as if impressed. "Well, what about this one?" And then he did the same thing with the other arm.

ॐ

When they wanted to make the murti of Maharajii after he left his body, they came to me asking for some photo of him—the best one for a murti. I told them that I had known Babaji for so many years and had many hundreds of photos, no two alike. And Babaji himself—sometimes he was short, sometimes very fat, sometimes quite slim. I have never been able to know which was the real Baba. You could give him any form you liked, but he could not be captured. He was like the air.

॥ॐ॥

The teenage daughter of a devotee sometimes stayed at the temple overnight. She watched Maharajji frequently and finally said to him, "Maharajji, during the day when all the people are around you seem so helpless and old. But at night, once the gates are closed, you are running about. How come?" Maharajji laughed.

॥ॐ॥

Mrs. Soni once visited Maharajji and he was not looking well. "Maharajji, you are not looking well at all," she said.
"Aren't I, Ma?" And then he did something with his body and he suddenly looked radiant. "How do I look now, Ma?"
"You look much better, Maharajji."

॥ॐ॥

A family was at the temple with their old grandfather. When they came before Maharajji he pointed at the grandfather and said, "We've met before." But the grandfather said he didn't think so. He was quite sure they had never met, but Maharajji was insistent. Finally Maharajji closed his eyes for a moment and then said, "Don't you remember? You carried my sleeping roll at the railway station."
At first the grandfather just thought Maharajji had mistaken him for someone else. But then he remembered that when he was eleven or twelve he had been on a bicycle trip with some schoolmates. His bicycle had broken down and his companions had gone on without him. He needed a few rupees to get the bicycle repaired but had none, so he went to the railway station, thinking that perhaps he could make believe he was a porter and carry someone's bag.
The problem was that he was very small, so the bag would have to be very light. He stood near the first-class carriages. Suddenly a man got off the train. He was wearing a suit and shiny shoes and a derby hat. He had a blanket roll, which he entrusted the boy to carry to a home at the edge of town. The roll was very light, but when they arrived the man gave the boy five rupees (much

more than the job was worth) and told him that he could come back and visit
the next day if he liked. But the boy took the money, got his bicycle repaired,
and went on his way. He never went back.

गुरु

Once a beggar boy came to our hotel. We gave him some food but the boy
wouldn't leave. Finally he asked for a toy and we turned him out. Later,
Maharajji said, "I came to your hotel but you turned me out."

गुरु

There were two sisters who revered Maharajji very highly. One of them
went into the toilet and came out in an ecstatic state, saying, "I just had
darshan of Maharajji in the bathroom!" This was at a home far from where
Maharajji was at the time. The other sister rushed into the bathroom and what
she found there was a huge cobra.

गुरु

Once when CS was washing Maharajji, he was thinking about
Gorakhnath, who had no real body but would manifest different bodies. CS,
meanwhile, was soaping and washing Maharajji and kidding with him, but
this was in his mind as he was doing so. As he went to tie the dhoti on
Maharajji, he experienced that there was nothing within it. And at the moment
he had this thought, Maharajji turned and yelled at him, "Get out, get out,
I'll tie my own dhoti."

THE EXTRAORDINARY postures into which Maharajji placed his body
were no more random than anything else he did. Some of his older devotees got quite proficient in reading Maharajji's body language, for
many of the positions were actual *mudras* (statements in form) that gave
blessings, activated certain powers, or brought about certain changes in
the environment.

Siddhi Ma was holding a picture of Maharajji in which he is lying on his
side, a classic pretzel, with one hand on top of his head. She said that this
mudra of hand on top of head means: "Don't worry about anything. I've got
everything under control."

SOMETIMES HIS devotees apparently pulled upon him from two places that were quite distant from one another. At such times, rather than disappoint anyone Maharajji would demonstrate one of his neatest talents—that of appearing in two places at once.

Once Maharajji went to a barber to have his beard shaved. As the barber was working, he told Maharajji that his son had run away some time ago and that he did not know where he was. He was missing him terribly and worried about him. Maharajji's face was only half shaved, the other half still lathered up, but Maharajji insisted that he must go out just then and urinate. He returned shortly, the shave was finished, and Maharajji left. The next day, the barber's son returned to his father with a strange story. He had been living in a town over one hundred miles away, and the day before, this fat man, whose beard was only half shaved, had come running up to him in the hotel in which he worked. He had given him money and insisted that he return at once to his father, by train that same night.

ॐ

While staying at a devotee's house Maharajji asked to be locked in the room. The windows were barred and the door locked from outside. (Rooms in Indian homes often have heavy bars on the windows to keep the wild monkeys from coming in. They also have independent slide bolts on both the inside and outside of the door. Thus, if they are locked from the outside, they cannot be opened from within.) A short while later a devotee arrived, asking where Maharajji was going. The host said, "What? He's locked in the room."

"That's impossible. I just saw him on a rickshaw going toward another area."

My sister, at that time, received Maharajji at her door. "I want khichri. I'm not feeling good so I'll only eat khichri," he said.

Meanwhile, at the host's house, they opened the door and found the room empty, but none of the bars had been tampered with, so they locked the room again. After about an hour, they heard some sounds from inside the room. They opened the door and this time found Maharajji inside.

ॐ

Maharajji appeared at 3:00 A.M. in the room of an old woman in her locked house and said, "Why are you bothering me, Ma?" She had been praying to him at that time.

जय

Devotees had just completed the building of a new Hanuman temple for Maharajji in Panki, near Kanpur, and the time for the official opening ceremony was near. Maharajji was staying in Allahabad and had told everybody that he wouldn't personally attend the function. On the morning of the opening of the temple, Maharajji went into his room in Allahabad and asked to be left alone for a few hours. He was locked in from the outside. The next day some devotees arrived in Allahabad to give out some of the prasad from the puja in Panki. They gave some to Maharajji's host and they described the colorful puja and bhandara. They said that everything had gone off perfectly; Maharajji even came, despite his having told everyone in advance that he wouldn't.

"That's impossible!" said the host. "Maharajji was here in Allahabad the whole time."

"Well, he was also in Panki. He was at the temple from eleven to twelve o'clock," they replied.

IF YOUR KUNDALINI [SPINAL ENERGY] AWAKENS, YOU CAN GO TO AMERICA WITHOUT A PLANE

While visiting in Kanpur, a Nainital devotee had Maharajji's darshan. As he was leaving, Maharajji gave him a message to deliver to the temple upon his return to Nainital. The message was that they should expect Maharajji within a fortnight. When he got to Nainital the next day, the devotee went straight to the temple before going to his home. He wondered why so many people had come to the temple when Maharajji was away. He overheard them say that Maharajji was inside one of the rooms.

"I can't believe it," he said. "I just saw him yesterday in Kanpur. It's impossible."

"No, Baba has been here for fifteen days," they told him.

"But I've brought a message from him in Kanpur. He says that he won't be here for two weeks." The devotee approached Maharajji's room. "Babaji, what is this?" he asked.

"Hap! Get out! Go away! Don't tell anyone anything. You're telling lies!" Maharajji shouted at him.

जय

A devotee of Maharajji lived in Agra and hadn't had Maharajji's darshan for a few years. Upon hearing that Maharajji had come to New Delhi, the man talked with Maharajji over the phone.

"Why haven't you come to Agra? You haven't given me your darshan in so long. May I come to Delhi?"

Maharajji replied, "No. Don't come here. I'll come to Agra."

"When?"

"Soon."

The man couldn't accept Maharajji's word so he begged for permission to go to Delhi, but Maharajji insisted that he would visit the man in Agra. The devotee then hung up the phone, and as he turned toward the door he saw Maharajji standing there. The devotee fell at Maharajji's feet. Maharajji talked with him for three or four minutes then left to return to Delhi. The man again phoned the hosts in Delhi and they said that Maharajji had just gone to the bathroom a few minutes before. Then immediately afterward they said, "Oh, here he is now."

ᜒᜈᜒ

Once at Neeb Karori a man wanted to travel with Maharajji to Vrindaban, and Maharajji didn't want to go. Maharajji said, "Lock me in this room. I have work to do." When the man returned from Vrindaban, he reported that he and Maharajji had had a wonderful time together. But when the room was opened, Maharajji was still within.

ᜒᜈᜒ

A devotee who was attending Maharajji was once thinking of how Maharajji could be in more than one place at a time. Three times Maharajji said to him, "You go out and see what's going on in the other rooms." Finally the devotee went out into the hall. There were six rooms in the house and he saw Maharajji coming out of every one of them.

ᜒᜈᜒ

A devotee had to leave the Hanuman temple at Nainital, where Maharajji was staying, to go to the plains on business. As he left he was sad, thinking that Maharajji might not be at the temple when he returned and that it would

*be a long time before he'd be with him again. He was on a train that had
stopped to take on water at a small station. Someone came to him and said,
"Look over there. There's Neem Karoli Baba." The devotee thought, "This
is strange. I left him in Nainital." He went to the other end of the platform
and found Maharajji sitting there surrounded by devotees, behaving as usual.
The men talked with Maharajji and also with the other devotees, and after a
while Maharajji said, "Go back to your train. Otherwise you'll be left behind.
It's about to start."*

*After finishing his business, the devotee returned to Nainital and found
Maharajji still there. Maharajji hadn't left the temple the entire time.*

*My mother once saw Maharajji in two places at once. She was in
Bhumiadhar walking toward him when suddenly she saw another Maharajji,
the same as the first. One was sitting on the roadside, the other in the forest. A
few moments later, one form disappeared, and she spoke to the "remaining"
form of Maharajji.*

*On January 14, 1965, in the clothes closet of the darshan room in Dada and
Didi's home, some footprints appeared on the wall, which they interpret to be
Maharajji's and celebrate yearly with a bhandara. When they confronted
Maharajji about the footprints, he said, "I came, but Didi caught sight of me."*

*Once Maharajji was resting, and the Ma's sitting in the room had the
sensation that Maharajji was not there. When they felt his energy return, they
asked him where he had gone. He laughed, and when they said he could go to
America without a plane, he upbraided them and laughed again.*

*Once I was having lunch in America with a Nobel Prize winning physicist.
He asked me about Maharajji and I proceeded to share a number of stories with*

*him. He found it all fascinating and could allow for the truth of all of it, until
I got to the stories of how Maharajji could appear in two places
simultaneously. To this the physicist replied, "That's impossible. The basis of
physics is that something cannot be in two places at once."*

"But you see," I said, "Maharajji did it anyway." (R.D.)

THERE HAVE BEEN no explanations from Maharajji himself about the
play of his body. However, this story suggests another reality in which,
at least to Maharajji, it made perfect sense.

*Once when we were in the mountains during a very cold spell, Maharajji
put on nine sweaters. Later, at bedtime, he said, "You people think I do this
for worldly reasons. Don't be silly," and he took off all the sweaters and the
blanket and slept all night with nothing on.*

ONCE YOU CAN allow for these phenomena that Maharajji manifested
with his body, it is difficult to return to your concept of him as an ordinary mortal. But he put up a good fight to convince us of just that. He
demonstrated some vanity, illness, aging (though the stories below
suggest some confusion on that), and, ultimately, death. But for the
devotees, all of this was just more of his play.

*When Maharajji visited us on one occasion, he noticed a picture of himself in
which he is laughing and in which his beard is quite long. He began abusing
me, asking me why I hadn't told him his beard had grown so much. Why
hadn't I had him cut it? "Now," he said, "it has ruined the whole picture!"*

जय

*During an evening darshan in Kainchi Maharajji had been in the back with
the Ma's, who had just finished doing puja to him. He came out and sat on
the tucket. He looked perfect: the most handsome, regal being. He had just
been shaved and had a perfectly centered, round yellow tilak (marking of
religious significance) on his forehead. He sat down like a king and we sat
before him in silence for a long time. He seemed to be saying, "I'm so good-
looking!"*

जय

In an elevator in Bombay Maharajji looked at himself in a mirror and smoothed his moustache.

ॐ

About two weeks after we got to Kainchi Maharajji said, "Doctor, I have a headache," so I ran to the back rooms where I had my medical supplies and pulled out aspirin with codeine. I was thinking, "Now, really, do I want to give this man codeine?" He was, after all, an old man, and I didn't know what his response would be. As I was fumbling with my vials, Maharajji sent me a message that he didn't want a pill; he wanted an ointment. At the time I really wasn't very big on ointments, and all I had was pills, so I had to tell him that I didn't have any ointments.

Chaitanya came to the rescue, though, with some Essential Balm, a Chinese ointment that comes in a small, tightly sealed red container. Being very happy that a Western doctor had managed to get some balm for this poor old man who had a headache, I raced back to Maharajji, tripping over the devotees sitting in front of him, lunged over to him, and handed him the little container. And he said, "Oh, doctor! Your medicine is so good! This is wonderful! This is exactly the medicine I wanted!" He looked at it and tried unsuccessfully to open it. (He didn't have that much patience with these kinds of things.)

Then, putting the closed container on top of his head, he said, "Doctor! This medicine is so good. It's wonderful. It's taken away my headache completely. Oh, doctor, you're such a wonderful doctor! You're so good. Your medicine is wonderful. Everything is perfect. My headache is completely gone."

ॐ

One day Maharajji complained that he had a cold and needed socks and medicine. KK laughed and said, "Oh, Maharajji, there is nothing wrong with you. Why do you try to fool simple people like us?" Like a child, Maharajji laughed as if he had been caught at a trick, and soon he was better.

ॐ

In Vrindaban Maharajji was really sick. He'd been taking heart medicine for two years, because he'd had several heart attacks. Sometimes when he was sick he would call for me, and one such day we entered to find him sitting on his tucket. In front of him on the tucket was the largest handkerchief I've ever

seen, with which he kept blowing his nose. He was a very funny caricature of
a man with a bad cold.

He said, "Oh, doctor. I'm terribly sick. Won't you give me some
medicine?" I said, "Yes, Maharajji," and I asked him about his symptoms. I
decided he had a cold, so I ran out to the bazaar and brought back, in three
separate packages, homeopathic medicine, ayurvedic medicine, and Western
medicine. I pointed out each one to Maharajji: "Here's the homeopathic
medicine. Here's the ayurvedic medicine. And here's the Western medicine."
(The latter was Vitamin C, aspirin, and Dristan.)

He threw aside the homeopathic and ayurvedic medicines and said, "This is
the medicine I want." And he gobbled up the Vitamin C, the aspirin, and the
Dristan.

Very often he'd say to me, "You know, Western medicine is very good."
And he'd call me Doctor America.

हरि

A doctor who had met Maharajji at least twenty-five years earlier came to
visit the baba. After fifteen minutes, Maharajji said, "I have a pain, doctor.
Will you massage my leg?" The doctor began massaging, using oil, and then
said, "I've seen many old people and they stiffen, but there is no change in
your nerves. In fact, your body seems younger than when I knew you in
1942."

Maharajji said, "Go! These doctors are fools. After all, one is born, he has
to die. A saint told him about nerves. What does he know about nerves?" And
Maharajji sent the doctor away.

हरि

A woman once told Maharajji, "My relative's wedding is approaching.
Maharajji, you'll have to attend."

Maharajji said, "I'll go to it," and he did—but not in his usual shape. He
told her at the wedding that he was very hungry, and when she asked what
he'd like to eat he replied, "Khir, khir, nothing else. Bring khir." She brought
khir and when she went to bring some more, he disappeared. Sometime
afterward, when she again met Maharajji, she rebuked him for not attending
the wedding.

He shouted, "No, no! You fed me khir yourself. But you didn't bring me
khir a second time, so I ran away. I had you there!"

*THE GREAT SADHUS DON'T HAVE A HUMAN BODY.
THEY ARE OMNIPRESENT. IF A SAINT CHANGES
FORM, HE DOESN'T NECESSARILY HAVE TO
TAKE ON A HUMAN BODY. THE SOUL IS THE
SMALL FORM AND THE HUMAN BODY IS
THE HUGE FORM.*

*At Neeb Karori, a Ma came to clean out the underground cave in which
Maharajji spent much time in seclusion in those days. As she entered,
Maharajji was sitting there with snakes wrapped around him. She told him she
would not come in if the snakes were there, and she ran out of the cave. He
called out to her not to worry, and as he stood up the snakes disappeared into
his body.*

ﭏﭏ

*Once when we were in the forest in the dead of night, I said to him, "Show
me God."*
*He said, "Just rub my belly." I got tired because it kept growing bigger and
bigger, until it seemed like a mountain. He was snoring and the snore sounded
like a tiger. It was just play, but if you were testing him he wouldn't show
you anything.*

ﭏﭏ

*Sometimes when Maharajji lay on the tucket it was too small; at other times
he was like a shadow, or a very small child under the blanket.*

ﭏﭏ

When you walked with him he was sometimes huge and sometimes little.

ﭏﭏ

*Before there were buildings at Bhumiadhar, there was just a little outhouse.
Maharajji once needed to go to the bathroom, so Siddhi Ma obtained water in a*

lota from a nearby house and waited outside. When Maharajji came out she saw his huge form and felt literally the size of a fly in relation to him.

†ᵐ

A devotee once told me that Maharajji always became very small whenever he stood before the Hanuman murti in Vrindaban. Of course, I then desired to see this phenomenon but said nothing of it to anyone. One day, just after lunch, when Maharajji usually rested in his room, I was standing alone before the murti. To my great delight, Maharajji arrived at the temple to take Hanuman's darshan. We were both leaning against the rail and he caught my attention with an intense stare, and as I looked at him he became smaller and smaller—each form fading out as a smaller form appeared. It looked very ethereal.

†ᵐ

Maharajji once said, "I am coming to America."
The Westerners asked, "In our hearts?"
"Nay," he replied, "In a body. Will you take me to America? Where will I stay?"
Once as Maharajji was leaving my house I was afraid he'd fall (he was an old man), so I caught his arm. He took my hand and pressed with such force (yet without showing any sign of exertion) that I was about to fall down. Then I realized he was not an "old man."

†ᵐ

In 1962 an old woman came for darshan of Maharajji. When she saw him she exclaimed, "How can Neem Karoli Baba be alive? He must have died a long time ago! My father was a devotee of Neem Karoli Baba, and my father said he knew Baba for forty years before that. I am seventy-three now; I last saw Baba when I was seven and he didn't look any different from the way he looks now." Maharajji upbraided her and wouldn't let others speak with her after that.

†ᵐ

Maharajji once said, "I used to come here to see that fakir who rides on a horse, that Gorashin Baba." (Gorashin Baba lived some three hundred years ago.)

तेरम

Once in Lucknow an eighty-year-old Moslem arrived, who said he had known Maharajji as an adult since he himself was ten or fifteen years of age. Maharajji said, "Don't believe him!" Another man of over eighty years said he knew Maharajji almost seventy years before, when the man was twenty years old, and that Maharajji had given him his blessing to take his first job.

तेरम

Several people were once discussing a saint who had lived some five hundred years earlier. Maharajji said, "Oh, I knew him."

तेरम

In 1961 Maharajji made a pilgrimage to Chitrakut with several devotees. While there, he stood on the banks of a river and kept shouting across it for a certain Gopal, a shepherd. Over and over he would call for him. No one knew of such a man, but Maharajji said that Gopal was a friend of his who would bring him many things. After much inquiry, it was discovered that four generations back there had been such a person who was devoted to such a guru. Gopal's grandson was eventually found, and he was a very old man.

तेरम

To one old woman who was confused by seeing Maharajji unchanged after so many years, he said, "Ma, I was dead. I have been reborn in the hills."

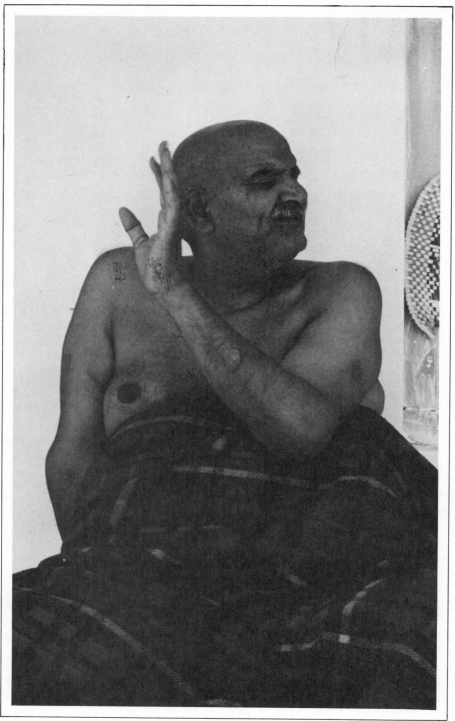

Maharajji's Teachings:
About Attachment

MAHARAJJI GAVE NO formal teachings. Yet his every manifestation—every word, glance, gesture, movement—taught those of us who were open to him in ways that often bypassed our intellect and were heard directly by our hearts.

Many topics came up in Maharajji's dealings with his devotees: truth; money and poverty; anger; drugs; sex, family, and marriage; pilgrimages, rituals, saints, and sadhana; service and surrender; and, of course, love. In Maharajji's infiniteness we found messages about all these matters—messages to guide us, not always without confusion, on our journey back home to God.

Because Maharajji, in his mirrorlike way, responded from moment to moment to those around him and to their unique karmic predicaments, someone seeking a general teaching about a topic through a collection of his utterances and the stories about him would undoubtedly be confused. At one moment he would say one thing and a moment later the reverse.

But each person was on a different stage of the journey and thus needed a different teaching. And in this river of contradiction that flowed from him, in these teachings that are no teachings, there is more profound guidance than a simplistic "do this" and "do that." There is the continuous reminder of the existence of the spirit—and that what appears to us in this world is not as it seems.

To see, to hear, even to know about such a being who is "in the world but not of the world" is more than teaching; it is grace.

Maharajji was talking in a room with only a few people, and to one man the talk appeared meaningless. He said, "Babaji, you should give instructions and lessons to people." Maharajji didn't answer. "Sometimes," the man went on, "give us answers and teach us something." Again Maharajji didn't answer him. The man repeated his statement a third time.

Obviously irritated, Maharajji shouted, "What are the instructions? What is this? What are the lessons? This is all foolishness! Lessons!" Turning to the men standing there—one was a goldsmith, one a shopkeeper, one a clerk, and one a teacher—Maharajji asked each how he would pass the following day. Each man gave a similar reply, saying that he would go to work as usual, would pass the day in his habitual manner. Maharajji said, "So many people are here and they'll all do what they have to do tomorrow and they have all preplanned it. What's the use of giving a particular teaching? You'll do what you want. So what are teachings? There is no use forcing anything on anybody. No matter what I say, you'll still do what you want to do. Yet you want me to dictate something. These teachings have got no meaning. There is no use in teaching people. It is the Almighty who teaches everybody—they all come well taught. There is one Supreme Teacher and he has taught everybody. Teachings are nothing. One who poses as a teacher does so only to satisfy his own ego."

राम

In 1970 or 1971, K complained, "Maharajji, I have been with you all this time and I haven't learned anything."

Maharajji replied, "All right, I'll tell you." But he always avoided telling him.

राम

Once a Mother came to Maharajji and said, "Maharajji, you always talk about worldly things—how many children, how much education, which job, how much money. Why don't you teach us about Brahm [the Formless]?"

Maharajji said, "Okay, I'll teach you." The Mother went off to do her work at Kainchi, and when it was time for the last bus to Nainital she was making her pranams and was going to the bus. Maharajji asked her, "Now you are going?"

She said, "Yes, I have to attend to my family, prepare meals and all."

Maharajji said, "Listen, don't go just now. I'll teach you about Brahm. You sit here." She insisted she had to go home and look after her family. He said, "No, no. I'll teach you about Brahm. You sit here. Don't go home today."

"How is it possible? I must go."

"But first you wanted Brahm, and now you ask how it is possible?"

After she left, he said to me, "Look at her. First she was talking about Brahm and now she is thinking about home. One person cannot do two things at one time. Brahm is not a thing, a toy that you can play with. You have to sacrifice something."

Maharajji always allowed people to do what they wanted, and would seldom tell anyone not to smoke or drink. He never lectured a person but would arrange the circumstances whereby he or she would want to give up a habit.

When asked about the process of devotees giving up their desires, Maharajji would say, "When the time is right."

In compassion for the smoking habit of one devotee, Maharajji would stop the car while they were traveling on the pretext of needing a drink or to urinate, thus letting the devotee have time to smoke.

M had a betel (leaf chewed for digestive purposes) habit but would chew only the finest quality. Once, when I was going to Nainital, M gave me two rupees for betel, and Maharajji found out about it. The next morning a lady brought betel for prasad to Maharajji (not a frequent occurrence). "What's this?" Maharajji asked. "Oh, betel. M! Here is your betel!" And every day during M's stay at Kainchi, a different person would bring fresh betel as prasad. Maharajji had never ordered it, but in its natural course it was brought.

On M's final day he went into Maharajji's room and found him waving a flower, which M thought Maharajji would give him for his wife. M invited Maharajji to come to his home on the plains, and Maharajji said he'd come in November and bring all the Westerners. "Where will they stay?" asked Maharajji. "How will you arrange for their food?" And M replied, "They'll cook their own." With tears in his eyes, Maharajji sent M away, without giving him the flower or the now-customary betel. A few moments

*later, someone came in the room with sweet betel. Maharajji called M back:
"M, here's your betel for your journey." Then Maharajji gave him sweets,
fruit, and the flower for his wife as well.*

ﬁﬃ

*Regarding one devotee's habit of drinking liquor, Maharajji commented,
"What friends do is all right."*

ﬁﬃ

*One day in Vrindaban, Dada was so busy serving that he could not find a
moment free to sneak a smoke. Maharajji turned to him and said, "You go and
take your two minutes and finish," and made as if he were smoking.*

ﬁﬃ

*Maharajji said of people who had bad habits, such as smoking, drinking, or
even eating fish, eggs, or meat, "They have their habits. They enjoy them.
Why should I stop them?"*

NONATTACHMENT FOR sense-objects is liberation; love for sense-objects
is bondage. Such verily is knowledge. Now do as you please." This
quotation from an ancient Hindu text, the Ashtavakra Gita (XV:3), most
succinctly conveys Maharajji's teachings about attachment. He showed
in his own life that what pleased him was to have nothing to be attached
to and thus be free to be with God. In his earlier years he had wandered
about wearing only one cloth, carrying a piece of broken clay pot that
served both as a water pot and an eating dish. In later years he still wore
only a simple dhoti, but with a blanket, and now and then an undershirt
or sweater or socks in the freezing mountain nights. The rooms in which
he stayed were a stark reminder of nonattachment. There was only the
tucket and a water pot. Nothing else.

He reminded us to be unattached to things, to people, to our work,
and even to righteousness. Some he goaded to more and more renunciation, while others he counseled to be patient and gentle in the process of
becoming free.

MAHARAJJI QUOTED: "Aye thei Hari bhajan koo, oothan lage kapas [I
had come to realize God and sing his praises, but as soon as I came out
of the womb I began collecting cotton fruit (the fruit that when ripe and
good-looking distintegrates at the touch)]."

ATTACHMENT IS THE STRONGEST BLOCK
TO REALIZATION.

IF YOU DESIRE A MANGO AT THE MOMENT
OF DEATH, YOU'LL BE BORN AN INSECT.
IF YOU EVEN DESIRE THE NEXT BREATH,
YOU WILL TAKE BIRTH AGAIN.

HE QUOTED, "IF THE CLAY IN A POT IS
UNBAKED, THEN WHEN THE POT BREAKS, THE
CLAY IS REUSED. BUT IF THE POT IS BAKED,
THEN WHEN IT BREAKS, IT IS THROWN AWAY."

LUST, GREED, ANGER, ATTACHMENT–
THESE ARE ALL PATHS TO HELL.

IF YOU DO NOT MAKE IT EMPTY,
HOW WILL YOU FILL IT UP AGAIN?

IF YOU WANT TO SEE GOD, KILL DESIRES.
DESIRES ARE IN THE MIND. WHEN YOU
HAVE A DESIRE FOR SOMETHING, DON'T
ACT ON IT AND IT WILL GO AWAY. IF
YOU DESIRE TO DRINK THIS CUP OF TEA,
DON'T, AND THE DESIRE FOR IT WILL
FALL AWAY.

SAINTS AND BIRDS DON'T COLLECT. SAINTS
GIVE AWAY WHAT THEY HAVE.

HE CHIDED: "THIS WORLD IS ALL ATTACHMENT.
YET YOU GET WORRIED BECAUSE YOU ARE
ATTACHED."

Maharajji said to Dada, who was the head of a family of devotees, "You have become entirely mine. What is family to you? You are a fakir. You need only two chapattis a day and those I will give you. What is attachment for the saints and mahatmas?" The family became upset at this, but Maharajji said that if Dada realized the truth of what he said, then there was no need for him to leave them.

ॐ

Maharajji said to a devotee, "Why are you attached to this cat? I keep telling you to give up all attachments and still you are attaching yourself to a cat!"

MARRIAGE IS MORE ATTACHMENT. YOU NEED MORE DEVOTION AND DISCIPLINE TO HAVE UNION WITH GOD WHEN YOU ARE MARRIED.

I was sometimes busy tending to the orchard. One day Maharajji said, "Well, that orchard belongs to me. You work like a manager. It is my property. A manager has no attachment. The moment he is turned out from a place, he will just go. So you live like a manager."

ॐ

Maharajji told me the following story: "Samarth Guru Ram Das was the guru to the king and lived in a small mud hut next to the palace. One day the king came out of the palace and did obeisance to the guru. Then the king handed him a scroll in which he had bequeathed all his kingdom to the guru. The guru took the scroll, read it, accepted it, and then said to the king, "Now you run it for me!" (R.D.)

ॐ

Maharajji asked one old devotee with a big pocket watch why he was so attached to it. The devotee threw the watch against a stone and broke it.

ॐ

Once a sadhu offered me some land that he had, so that I could have an ashram for fellow Westerners. I asked Maharajji about it. He said, "He wants to give you his attachment. It's not a pure gift. If it were pure he'd just give it to you instead of talking about it." (R.D.)

He kept admonishing me: "Ram Dass, give up attachments." I often tried to put the onus on him by replying, "It's all your grace." But he was reminding me that I had to make the effort, for he just kept repeating, "Give up attachments. You should have no ashrams. No attachments of any kind." (R.D.)

Once Maharajji was reiterating to me for the hundredth time that I should give up attachments. I told him that another teacher had told me the same thing. "Does he have desires?" asked Maharajji.
"Yes, I think he still does," I replied.
"Then how can he free you of desire?" (R.D.)

Kali Babu told Maharajji of a utensil made of various metals that was good for keeping water and was supposed to make you healthy. Maharajji hounded him until he finally had such a utensil made. Maharajji used it all day, drinking water. Then he told Kali Babu to lock it up overnight and that he would use it again the next day. Suddenly Maharajji said, "What? Am I getting attached? Give it away."

One devotee said, "Was he involved with worldly matters? I don't think he had attachment for anything or anybody. He was just a mirror of your attachments."

> *I AM IN THE WORLD BUT NOT CONCERNED*
> *WITH THE WORLD. I AM GOING THROUGH*
> *THE MARKETPLACE, BUT NOT AS A PURCHASER.*
> —*MAHARAJJI QUOTING KABIR*

Maharajji was totally unattached. From the moment he left Hanuman Garh temple he never repeated its name; from the moment he left Kainchi temple he never turned to look back. "When I have left, I've left," he used to say.

TEMPLES ARE BUT PILES OF STONES.
ATTACHMENT HOLDS YOU BACK.

I DON'T WANT ANYTHING. I EXIST
ONLY TO SERVE OTHERS.

I had purchased a mohair blanket for Maharajji in Australia and was very excited about giving it to him. When the day for the presentation came, a group of us were ushered into the small room we humorously called his "office" and we knelt before him. Somewhat pridefully I placed the blanket on the tucket next to him, and we all waited for whatever lila would follow. It would be fun to watch him put it on and maybe he'd give us his old blanket, or . . . There were a thousand maybes. But none of our speculations prepared us for his actions. First he ignored the blanket, then reached down and with three fingers picked it up as if it were a dead animal. He brought the blanket across in front of him and gave it to a woman in our group who had come to meet Maharajji for the first time. Then he turned to me and said, "Was that the right thing to do?" We were all stunned.

It took me a moment to reorient, to appreciate what he had just done. Then I said, "Perfect." (R.D.)

ॐ

One devotee said that Maharajji did not need anything and didn't like to receive gifts.

ॐ

Two long-time devotees were told that they would be able to find Maharajji at a certain temple on the banks of the Ganga, so they went there immediately and found him. He acted as if he'd never seen them before. A few minutes later Maharajji suddenly got up and said, "Let's go! Let's go!" The three of them ran until they found a tonga *(horse carriage), which they boarded and continued on their way. While they were riding along, the two devotees asked*

Maharajji why he had run off so quickly. "Don't you know?" he replied. "That rich lady is coming to see me. She has an English blanket that she wants to give me, but I don't want it." Just then a limousine passed them by, going in the opposite direction. Maharajji laughed and said, "Look! There she goes now!"

॥ॐ॥

As a special gift for a holiday, a devotee worked long and hard making very beautiful garlands out of silks and satins, made to resemble flowers and leaves. When he presented them to Maharajji he tried to slip one garland over his head but Maharajji adamantly refused to allow this. He said, "Take these away. They were made for the world to admire."

॥ॐ॥

One devotee observed that it was not what you gave Maharajji but the spirit with which you gave it. He could delight for a long time in something so simple as a leaf, if you gave it to him from your heart.

॥ॐ॥

Late one night Maharajji gave me this big Kashmiri apple. I had missed supper for some reason that night and I was hungry. As I was walking up the trail I thought about eating the apple. Apples are juicy and clean, and anything clean in India is important. I also thought about how there are no stones in an apple (something you can appreciate after you have eaten rice with stones in it). Just the fact that something can be born without a stone in it—there's a nice quality to it, kind of friendly.

When I finally reached the kuti the desire had become manifest, something really tangible. We tend to think that a desire is somehow much subtler than a table, but at that time it struck me that desire was the most real thing in my universe. Suddenly I understood about the process of bringing what's called prasad, or a gift, to a saint. In the Gita it is said that if you offer only a flower in the heart of devotion it's like the purest gift you can give. At that moment I wanted to offer the desire as my prasad.

I saved the apple, and the next day, because I came to the temple earlier than most people, I put my apple on the tucket. In the course of the morning, before Maharajji came out, many people arrived and soon the apple was buried under other fruit, flowers, sweets, and so forth. But I kept my eye on the apple. About a half hour later Maharajji came out, shuffled through all these offerings, pulled out my apple, and flipped it to me.

Once I was feeling damned frustrated and I told Maharajji that I didn't want to remain in the world, that I just wanted to be a sanyasi (renunciate). "You can't be a sanyasi just now. Look at these people here," Maharajji said, indicating the Westerners sitting all around. "These devotees here have enjoyed the material life up to the limit—and you haven't yet. If you became a sanyasi now it will be very difficult for you. You should first taste these things, and then you can leave them."

I was just saying to Maharajji that this maya (worldly illusion) is very difficult to transcend. My father was a devoted bhakta all his life and still he would worry about the health and welfare of his children. So I said to Maharajji, "This maya is very hard to overcome."
    Maharajji said four things to me: "Maya? Kya hai? Kahan hai? Nahin hai [Maya? What is it? Where is it? It is not]!" That was all. Such a peculiar day that was.

IT DOESN'T MATTER IF YOU ARE MARRIED OR NOT, IT ONLY MATTERS HOW MUCH YOU LOVE GOD.

Maharajji would sit out in the back in his chair, looking up at the hills, saying, "Look at those trees on that mountain. Who waters them? Who takes care of them? Those are the assurance that God exists for people. Those are what people can look to, to know about God."

Maharajji had no inhibitions. He would sit sweating in the dirt. "It's Mother Earth I'm sitting on and I'm made of earth," he would say. "Every land is God's."

*IT'S BETTER TO SEE GOD IN EVERYTHING
THAN TO TRY TO FIGURE IT OUT.*

*IF YOU HAVE A TOOTHACHE, YOU DO WHAT
YOU DO, BUT THE MIND REMAINS ON
THE TOOTH.*

*A devotee asked, "How can I be unattached if I have a baby?" and
Maharajji replied: "Just have faith in God and remember God and it will
happen gradually and you will be living unattached like the lotus flower."*

*IF YOU ARE FREE OF ATTACHMENT, YOU
WILL LEAD A SIMPLE LIFE IN A SIMPLE
ENVIRONMENT.*

*Once Maharajji called a young Western devotee into the room with a local
sadhu. The girl was dressed in a nice sari and was wearing jewelry, the sadhu,
in typical sadhu dress. Maharajji pointed to the Westerner and said, "She's a
sadhu."*

The sadhu objected: "How can she be a sadhu? See how she is dressed."

*Maharajji rebuked him and said, "She doesn't care for any of these things.
It doesn't matter to her whether she wears silk or rags. She will even wear
diamonds. She is not attached to these things. She has no lust, greed, anger, or
attachment. She will wander about all her life. She has no home in the
universe."*

Then he sent the girl out of the room.

*GOD WILL GIVE YOU EVERYTHING YOU
NEED FOR YOUR SPIRITUAL DEVELOPMENT.
HOLD ON TO NOTHING.*

*LOVE THE POOR. SERVE THEM. GIVE
EVERYTHING TO THE POOR, EVEN YOUR
CLOTHING. GIVE IT ALL AWAY. JESUS
GAVE AWAY ALL, INCLUDING HIS BODY.*

About Truth

IN TRYING TO understand Maharajji's teachings about truth, one would have to decide whether what Maharajji did or what he said was the more accurate reflection of those teachings. On the one hand, he was continually instructing devotees to tell the truth, no matter what the cost.

> *TOTAL TRUTH IS NECESSARY.*
> *YOU MUST LIVE BY WHAT*
> *YOU SAY.*

TRUTH IS THE MOST DIFFICULT
TAPASYA. MEN WILL
HATE YOU FOR TELLING THE TRUTH.
THEY WILL CALL YOU NAMES. THEY
MAY EVEN KILL YOU, BUT YOU MUST
TELL THE TRUTH. IF YOU LIVE IN
TRUTH, GOD WILL ALWAYS STAND
WITH YOU.

> *CHRIST DIED FOR TRUTH.*

WHEN ASKED HOW THE HEART
COULD BE PURIFIED, HE SAID,
"ALWAYS SPEAK THE TRUTH."

A man came to Maharajji, and Maharajji asked him for some money for bricks for an ashram. The man said he had no possessions and went away. Later he came rushing to Maharajji, saying his shop was burning and that he would be ruined.
"I thought you said you had no possessions!"
"Oh, I was lying . . ."
"You are lying now. Your shop is not burning."
The man went away and returned to his store—and found that only one bag of chili was smoking.

I had given the first copy of Be Here Now *to Maharajji when it arrived. He had asked one of his devotees to put it inside his room, and I had heard nothing more about it. Five months later I was called from the back of the temple. When I arrived at Maharajji's tucket he was holding the book. His first comment was, "You are printing lies."*
"I didn't realize that, Maharajji. Everything in the book I thought was true."
"No, there are lies," he said accusingly.
"That's terrible," I said. But I was confused because I wasn't sure whether he was serious, so I asked, "What lies, Maharajji?"
"You say here that Hari Dass built the temples."
"Well, I thought that he did."
At that point Maharajji beckoned to an Indian man who was sitting nearby and asked him, "What did you have to do with the temples?"
"I built them, Maharajji." Maharajji looked at me as if this proved that I had lied.
Then Maharajji said, "And you said Hari Dass went into the jungle at eight years of age." Again he called another man forward, who ascertained that Hari Dass had worked as a clerk in the forestry department for some years.
All I could lamely say was, "Well, someone had told me that he went into the jungle when he was eight years old."
Again and again Maharajji confronted me with things I had said that were not true.

Finally Maharajji said, "You believe everything people tell you. You are a simple person. Most Westerners would have checked. What will you do about these untruths?"

My mind spun. What could I do about it? The first printing of thirty thousand was already in the stores and certainly couldn't be called back, but Steve Durkee had written that they were about to print another thirty thousand. So I said, "Well, I could write and have the lies deleted for the next printing."

"Fine. You do that. It will hurt you if you are connected with lies." And with that he turned to other matters. I surveyed the damage in the book and prepared a letter for Steve at the Lama Foundation in New Mexico where the book was published. It would only be necessary to delete two entire paragraphs. Although the changes seemed of minor importance, I considered Be Here Now *to be Maharajji's book, and if Maharajji wanted it changed, it had to be changed.*

About two weeks later I received the reply from Steve, who said that the changes couldn't be made in the next printing. When he received my letter at Lama, which is up in the mountains north of Taos, he had just returned from visiting the printer in Albuquerque. On that visit he had arranged for the reprinting, and the printer, as a favor, was going to rush the job and put it on the press the next day. The press would print, cut, and assemble the entire book in one continuous process. Steve had then done other business for two days on the way back to Lama, and though he hadn't spoken to the printer (because there are no phones at Lama), he was sure that the job had been done. But he assured me that the changes would be made in the following printing, which would probably occur in three or four months.

With the letter in my jhola (shoulder bag) I took an early morning bus to Kainchi. As I entered the temple, Maharajji yelled, "What does the letter say?" It always struck me as humorous when he did that, for if he knew there was a letter he obviously knew what it said. He just wanted me to tell him. So I reported, and when I had finished he said, "Do it now." I repeated the explanation patiently about the Web press and that the changes couldn't be made for these thirty thousand copies. And he repeated, "Do it now." I explained that it would mean throwing out all thirty thousand books and a loss of at least ten thousand dollars. Maharajji's retort was, "Money and truth have nothing to do with one another. Do it now. When you printed it first you thought it was true, but once you know it isn't you can't print lies. It will hurt you."

Well, if Maharajji wanted it changed now, then that's the way it would be. It would mean the loss to Lama of all the profits, and they weren't going to be overjoyed about that; but, after all, the entire sum of money came from

Maharajji anyway. Although it was not yet 9:00 A.M., Maharajji sent me from
the temple, telling me again to "Do it now."

I thumbed a ride back to Nainital and cabled Steve with the new
instructions. About a week later I received the reply from Steve. He reported
that the strangest thing had happened. When he had gone to the post office, my
cable was there, and in the same mail was a letter from the printer. It seems
that immediately after Steve had left, he had proceeded as promised to put the
plates for reprinting the book on the press. But the printer found one plate of
one page—a full-page photograph of Maharajji— missing. So he went to the
files, thinking he would get the original and make a new plate, and much to
his surprise he found that the original of that page was also missing. Not
knowing what to do, the printer pulled the job off the press and was holding it
for further instructions. So, Steve concluded, it took only a phone call to
change the two paragraphs, not ten thousand dollars as I had feared. I rushed
back to Maharajji with the news, but that day and the next he never gave me
a chance to speak. (R.D.)

तुम

When Dada's sister-in-law was visiting, Maharajji called me up to his
tucket in her presence, pointed at this woman, and asked me if I "remembered"
her. In truth I did not, but it seemed like something of a faux pas not to
remember, so I smiled knowingly as though I did. Maharajji smiled as though
he accepted this and said, "Yes, she is Dada's sister-in-law."

Then that insidious "cleverness" took over and I reasoned to myself that if
she was Dada's sister-in-law I had probably met her in Allahabad where Dada
lived, so I said, "Oh, yes, we were together in Allahabad."

To which she said, "No, we never met in Allahabad. We met here in
Kainchi last spring." I was caught red-minded. Maharajji turned to me and
held up that finger which, in this case, clearly meant "Caught you! Watch it!"
(R.D.)

तुम

In Allahabad, Maharajji caught me in what we in the West call "a little
white lie." We were gathered around him, and in the group was an important
official of the state supreme court. For the first time in all the years I had been
with Maharajji, I heard him telling the official what an important person I
was in the United States, that I was a professor and wrote books. All of that
seemed so irrelevant when I was around him, and it sounded strange to hear
him plugging my Western social-power virtues. When he stopped, the supreme

court official said to me, "I am honored to meet you. Perhaps you would like to visit the supreme court."

The dual fact that I came from a family of lawyers and that I was in India in order to immerse myself in the spirit, made the entire prospect of such a visit unappealing to me. And yet, he was an important person and I couldn't just say what I had been thinking. So I said, rather ambiguously, "That would be very nice."

At that, the official said, "Would tomorrow at 10:00 A.M. be convenient?"

I was trapped, and I could think of only one way of escape. I said, "We'll have to ask my guru. It's up to him."

So the official asked Maharajji, and he answered, "If Ram Dass says it would be nice, he should go." And then he looked at me in a way that could only be interpreted as, "Got you again."

The story of the next day's events shows that even simple people like me do learn. I visited the court with this gentleman, and in the course of the visit we stopped in the chambers of the law review, where the lawyers all hang out. It was at the time of Nixon's dramatic approaches to China. When all these lawyers saw an American with this important official they surrounded me and questioned me about Nixon's China policy, which was of considerable concern to India. I gave as erudite an answer as my reading of the situation would allow. That evening when I was once again at darshan with Maharajji, another dignified-looking gentleman, who turned out to be the leading lawyer in the city, took me aside and asked if I would be willing to address the Rotary Club and the Bar Association. I got a sinking feeling that if I didn't watch my step I would be on the creamed vegetable circuit of India. And remembering the entrapment of the day before, I said, "I'd prefer not to speak before either of these groups, but of course I will do whatever Maharajji says."

So the lawyer pleaded his case before Maharajji, and Maharajji seemed delighted at the invitations. He kept repeating them to all who would listen as if to imply that such invitations were a major coup, a great breakthrough, and very important. I began to feel betrayed by Maharajji. Then Maharajji turned to me and asked, "What are you going to speak about?"

I thought quickly and grasped at the only association that came to mind: "I'll talk about law and the dharma."

"Aha!" said Maharajji, "and will you talk about Christ?"

"Of course."

"And Hanuman?"

"Certainly."

"And me?"

"Absolutely."

By this time the lawyer was looking a little green about the gills, and he

interjected, "Well, we thought he might talk about Nixon's China policy,
Maharajji."
   Maharajji looked shocked. "Oh, no! Ram Dass could not do that. He can
only speak about God."
   The lawer then backed off, saying, "Well, that wouldn't be quite
appropriate. Perhaps I can gather a few lawyers at my home to talk about
God." Needless to say, he never did. I had learned my lesson. Maharajji
would back me up when I spoke the truth, no matter how difficult it might be.
(R.D.)

IN CONTRADICTION TO all of these teachings, however, Maharajji
frequently lied. Because of this, when Maharajji predicted something no
one knew whether it would actually happen. Although his lying was
pointed out by those in the local communities who did not like him (and
there were a number, because he was so outspoken), such inconsistencies
made no difference for the devotees. For us, perhaps the lesson was that
a free being has his or her own rules; but until you are free, you'd best
tell the truth.

   Maharajji would usually agree to any request from a devotee. People
frequently invited him to come and bless their homes and to partake of the food
prepared by the family. He would inevitably agree to all these requests, yet
more often than not he wouldn't go.

ूँ

   When questioned by one of his devotees about his habit of making and
breaking promises, Maharajji replied, "I'm just a big liar!"

ूँ

   A devotee asked Maharajji why he always told nice things to people, or
predicted a bright future, when in fact he knew that the opposite would
happen. Maharajji replied, "Do you expect me to tell people that their loved
ones will die? How can I do that? All right, since you advise me, from now on
I'll answer people frankly." A while later, a woman came for his blessing that
her husband get well. Maharajji shouted at her, "Mother, why have you come
here? Your husband is at home in bed dying and in a coma. He can't be saved.
You should go!" Shocked and hurt, the woman left. Maharajji was equally
blunt with a few more people. Then he asked the devotee, "How can you
expect me to be blunt with people? How can I hurt their feelings?"

Maharajji would lie to someone so as not to hurt their feelings; but then he would tell the truth in some other way. When K asked about his sick mother, Maharajji said, "Who will feed you if she is not here? She will be around for a long time." But then Maharajji called a specialist from Agra and had her examined.

The specialist said, "This woman cannot survive more than twenty-eight days."

This surprised the doctor because he had never used that number, saying, rather, a month or two. On the morning of the twenty-ninth day she died. K felt that Maharajji brought the specialist as a hint. Saints give clear hints, but we can't always understand them.

Maharajji would say something and later, if he contradicted himself and the contradiction was pointed out, he would say, "I didn't say that."

I wrote for Maharajji's blessing just before I was to take an exam. "Will I pass?" I asked him. But there was no reply. I failed. Heavy with the weight of my first failure, I ran to Kainchi and found Maharajji smiling. I told him that I had sent many letters and he hadn't answered.

He replied, "You wanted to know. I can't speak a lie, and the fact was very bitter."

"Shall I appear for the exam again?" I asked.

He replied, "Yes, this time nobody will stop you."

I passed.

Once two men came for darshan. As they stood before Maharajji, telling him all sorts of glorious things about themselves, he grew increasingly more impatient. When they reached a stopping point, Maharajji gruffly sent them away. As they were walking away, he turned to us and said, "They stand there telling me lies—they were trying to fool me! Don't they know that it is I who am fooling the whole world?"

About Money

"KANCHAN [GOLD]," Maharajji would say and shake his finger. That and sexual desire were the two main obstacles to realizing God. Again and again Maharajji warned about these fatal attractions, these clingings; but how few of us could hear him. He referred to the Western devotees as kings. Most of us had come from comfortable economic backgrounds and so we knew that financial security would not in itself bring liberation from suffering. To know such a thing was a great step forward on the path. Many of the Indian devotees had known only financial hardship and deprivation, and for those people it was often hard to hear that

worldly security was not one and the same as freedom. Yet there were some devotees who, though they had never tasted of material security, seemed to have no concern with such matters. It was as if they were truly born for God.

To each person Maharajji reacted in a different way about money. To those for whom the attachment to gold was not the primary obstacle, he never mentioned the subject. With others he talked about money all the time, awakening in the devotee both paranoia and greed, rooting out, perhaps, the sticky karma of that particular attachment. Most frequently

Maharajji seemed to be suggesting that people keep as much as they needed to maintain their responsibilities to body, to family, and to community, and distribute the rest to the poor. He kept reminding us that if we did that and trusted in God, all would be taken care of.

Sometimes he gave us a rupee or two, which seemed at the time like he was giving us a boon of future financial security. Some of the devotees held on to those rupees and have never since known financial need. Others gave the rupees away immediately to the first begger they met; those devotees have not known need, either. Such a boon is known as the "blessing of *Lakshmi* [the goddess of wealth]." Such a blessing was clearly Maharajji's to bestow.

In 1969 I wrote to KK, asking if I could send some money to Maharajji. The answer from Maharajji, delivered to me in a letter from KK, read: "We do not require any money. India is a bird of gold. We have learned 'giving' not 'taking.' We cannot attain God as long as we have got attachments for these two: (1) gold (wealth) (in Hindi, 'Kanchan'), and (2) women (in Hindi, 'Kamini'). No two swords can be put into one sheath; the more we sacrifice (tyaga), *the more we gain. . . ."*

> IF YOU HAVE ENOUGH FAITH
> YOU CAN GIVE UP MONEY AND
> POSSESSIONS. GOD WILL GIVE
> YOU EVERYTHING YOU NEED FOR
> YOUR SPIRITUAL DEVELOPMENT.

A tiny, gnarled old woman came for Maharajji's darshan. She was, I think, from one of the local farms. Tottering up onto the porch, she touched Maharajji's feet with her head and sat down. Then with much difficulty she unknotted the end of her sari and took from it some crumpled rupee notes and pushed them across the tucket toward Maharajji. I had never seen anyone give Maharajji money and I watched with some discomfort, for this woman was obviously as poor as the proverbial church mouse. Maharajji pushed the money back at her and indicated that she was to take it back. With no expression she reached for the money and started to put it back into her sari. The full meaning of the situation escaped me, for I understood too little of the culture to appreciate what was happening.

But then Maharajji seemed to have a second thought and demanded the money back from the Ma. Again with arthritic hands she untied the corner of the sari and handed him the bills. There were two one-rupee notes and one two-rupee note (four rupees are worth about forty US cents). Maharajji took them from her and immediately handed them to me. I didn't know what to do. Here I was a "rich Westerner" (in India even poor Westerners are "rich Westerners" because of the relative values of the economies), with a private car (a rare luxury in India) and traveler's checks. I just couldn't accept this money. But when I tried to hand it back to the woman, Maharajji refused to allow it. I was told to keep it.

That night I put the four rupees on my puja table and reflected on them for a long time, but no great clarity was forthcoming. Later, one Indian devotee told me that I should hold onto the money, that if I did I would never want.

During that period an old Sikh couple had taken to visiting me at the hotel. They ran a tiny dried fruit store and were obviously very poor. Yet each time they came they brought me offerings of dried fruit, kneeled at my feet, and told me in great detail of their hardships in life. Why they had taken it into their heads that I could help them, spiritually or materially, I have no idea, but they kept coming. Then one day they told me that due to illness they must leave this region and move to the plains, where their financial predicament was going to be, if anything, more precarious. I felt that I wanted to give them something for their journey, but nothing came immediately to mind. Then I thought of the four rupees. I got one of the rupees and explained to them how it had come to me and that if they held on to it, everything would be all right with them. They left Nainital and I have not heard from them since. I still have three of the rupees. And thus far I've always had more than enough money. (R.D.)

जय

DS said that he had always kept all the money Maharajji gave him, which amounted at one time to over two hundred rupees. Then somehow it was all stolen from his home. After that, whenever Maharajji gave him money it would be with the added admonition not to lose it. DS took out an envelope from a hiding place in his home and showed it to me. Inside was a small packet of rupee notes—tens, fives, twos, and ones—all of them stapled together many times over.

जय

Maharajji pulled two rupees out from underneath his blanket and stuck them in my hand. He said something I couldn't hear when he put them in my hand. I didn't have them very long. I gave one to the Tibetan mandir (temple) *in Manali, and the other I gave to a beggar.*

ॐ

I don't know where he would get it, but he used to give me money. One time he was about to give me a great deal of money when I asked why, since I was earning enough, and he was a sadhu. If he gave me this surplus, then I might take it to go to the movies or go drinking. "Would you like that?" I asked him.

"No," he said, and so he didn't give me the money.

ॐ

Once he gave me five rupees, and my sister thirty, which he said to keep with us. She kept the money but I gave mine away. I told him I would not keep these things.

ॐ

Once, shortly before he disappeared, he gave me a hundred-rupee note. I told him I didn't want it, but he said I should keep it; and when I again refused, he said, "Okay, then I'll keep it." I don't know how it happened, but after I left I found the one hundred-rupee note in my pocket.

ॐ

During Swami N's first darshan, Maharajji gave him ten one-rupee notes and told him to keep them as prasad. Swami kept the money in his purse, and from that day he has never been without sufficient money. His purse always has more than enough.

ॐ

He gave me the two rupees. That was the only time he gave me anything apart from the laddus and prasad. I remember the two rupees distinctly, being astonished and worried because I didn't know what to do with them. "What am I going to do now?" I thought. "What's this money for?"

जय

One day this man came to my house to have the darshan of a sadhu staying there. He spotted the photo of Maharajji that I keep there and said, "I know him. I know him," and began to relate the story of his darshan with Maharajji.

He had been a young boy and very bitter at the world. One day he had gone to an old Shiva temple, and there in the compound Maharajji was sleeping. (The man gave an accurate description of Maharajji—lying on the ground, wearing only a dhoti, and covered with a plaid blanket.) Maharajji had sat up and at once commanded the boy to bring some milk for him. The boy became angry at this baba for treating him like this. Maharajji pulled thirty rupees from under his blanket and told him to buy the milk with it. The boy ran out with the money and came back with half a kilo or so of milk. He pocketed the change and Maharajji never asked for it. He left with the money, which was much needed by his family. Maharajji knew better than to ask if he needed money or to give him a gift. The boy was too proud, so Maharajji tricked him into taking the money.

जय

One time when we were all living in Kainchi Valley, Balaram asked Maharajji if we should request money from anyone to fix up the house. Maharajji said yes, that we should write to Harinam. I wrote the letter on an aerogram, which we showed to Maharajji before sending. Balaram folded it up, sealed it, and mailed it, and when Harinam replied, he said he'd send money—and that he thought it had been nice of us to enclose the two-rupee note, but why had we put it there? We had not put any two-rupee note in that letter, and as far as I know, Maharajji never mentioned it. This was one of the little money tricks he liked to play.

*MONEY IS NEVER A PROBLEM. THE DIFFICULTY IS IN THE
CORRECT USE OF IT. LAKHS AND CRORES [LARGE
AMOUNTS] OF RUPEES WOULD COME EASILY IF THEY
WERE GOING TO BE PUT TO WISE USE.*

*Recently I was confronted with the problem of which medium to use for the
construction of the meditation hall at Maharajji's temple near Delhi. On the
way there one day I met two men who introduced themselves as architects. I
became interested, so I asked what sort of work they were doing. They replied
that they were designing a five-star hotel in Patna. This told me that they must
be good, so I asked them to stop for ten minutes at the temple to give me their
advice on my problem. When they saw the temple and the pictures of
Maharajji one man exclaimed, "So this is where the ashram is! I know him.
He is the cause of my life!" I asked him to explain what he meant.*

*He said that when he was young, his family had taken him to see
Maharajji. Maharajji had turned to him and asked, "What's the problem?
What do you want?" and the boy had answered, "Money."*

*Maharajji then pulled a ten-rupee note out from under his blanket. Everyone
laughed at the incident and after a while they all left. The boy's family then
suggested that they all go to the movies with the prasad money, but he refused
to part with it and has kept it to this day. Money has come to him whenever
he needs it. If he has needed ten thousand rupees by evening time, it has been
put into his hands by the afternoon—all this from the faith derived from only
one or two darshans.*

*The architect volunteered to help design the meditation building free of
charge, in thanks to Maharajji.*

राम

*Once when V was to return home, he found that he was a little short of
money, so he made arrangements to borrow two hundred rupees and then went
to Kainchi to pay his respects to Maharajji before leaving. Maharajji blessed
him and sent him out. Then he called V back and said, "You've changed your
program. You're not going to Lucknow. You're out of money. You are short
two hundred rupees." Maharajji called for the pujari who had the keys to the
temple box, but the pujari was at the bazaar, along with the keys. Maharajji
sent V to go and pray to Hanuman, then immediately called him back.*

Maharajji reached inside his blanket and pulled out two hundred rupees. V asked how he got the money, and Maharajji said that when V went out to see Hanuman, someone came into the room and gave it to him.

तृष्

When I was young I had no money with me, but Maharajji kept insisting I had plenty. My father and I were in the vegetable business, and every time I would bring vegetables, the full price was never paid. What Maharajji gave me I accepted, but I just didn't tell my father because he would be angry. But I never could be sure how accounts balanced. Once I even said, "Maharajji, this is very little money that is coming for the food I brought."

Maharajji said, "It's all right. Take it." Another time he said, "You shall have a house." And later, "Give it all away." Now I have a house and two shops. I'm a rich man, due to Maharajji.

तृष्

KK had prepared a pattal *(leaf plate) of sliced fruit for him, and as he was talking to Maharajji, he held out the fruit and Maharajji would eat a little bit. Maharajji called me over from where we Westerners were sitting. "Bring that Peter over here," he said. (This before he'd given me my name.) He said, "What would you give me?"*

I said, "Baba, I'd give you everything I have." This had something to do with his previous conversation, when he'd called me over to make a point in the conversation he was having with these Indians.

He turned to the Indians to say something like, "Do you see this? Did you hear that?" Then he scooped up the apples from the pattal that KK was holding, and with his hands he lowered them into my hands and said, "With these apples, I'm going to give you many dollars." He said "dollars" in English. (The Indians later said to me, "Do you know what he said? Do you know the blessing you just got?!")

I answered him, saying, "Maharajji, what kind of wealth? All I want is spiritual wealth."

And he said, "Nahin! Bohut dollar [No, that's not what I mean]! Jao."

You can see how that blessing is not inappropriate to my becoming a doctor, since everyone thinks that doctors get a lot of money. If I do become wealthy as

Maharajji said, what I would like to do is start some businesses that would employ a lot of the satsang (fellow devotees).

MONEY IS AN OBSTACLE. ONE IN COMMUNION WITH GOD NEEDS NO MONEY.

There was a shopkeeper in Kainchi whose daughter was to get married soon, but he did not have enough money for the wedding. Maharajji told him not to worry; in three days he would get plenty of money. Three days later there was a landslide and the road was blocked, and all cars and trucks had to stop there. Whatever grains and foodstuffs that he had gathered in preparation for the marriage ceremony were consumed by these people, and in this way he got a lot of money.

॥४॥

Maharajji used to stay in Kanpur for a few days at a time. There lived one of the wealthiest men in India, whose whole family were devotees. Maharajji had never come to their home, a palatial mansion, and on one of his visits they insisted he come. He came with a crowd of people. The family did puja and then served a magnificent feast of many rare delicacies. They tried to instruct Maharajji as to what to eat first, followed by this, then that. Maharajji put everything—sweets, curries, fruits, vegetables—into one bowl, mixed them together, and ate. When he was finished he took the wealthy man's driver, of whom he was very fond (who had also driven him to Amarkantak, a trip of many days), and drove away. Maharajji said to him, "Now let's go to your house."

The driver, who lived in a slum hut in a very poor section of Kanpur, couldn't believe Maharajji, but he was insistent. Upon reaching there, Maharajji said, "I'm hungry. Bring me food." Being very poor, they had nothing in the house. The family had already eaten and preparing rotis would take time. Maharajji said, "No, there's gur [crude brown sugar] in that jar. Bring it to me!" They went and found the gur and Maharajji relished it.

I once complained that Maharajji only visited the rich; then he took me to live for several days with the cobbler in a poor small room. Although we were very cramped, Maharajji was happy.

श्री राम

He seemed to be happiest among the poor people. With them he would get a soft, happy quality in his face.

श्री राम

Maharajji said to a complaining devotee, "You don't have money in your destiny, so what can I do?"

श्री राम

A rich man who had come for darshan was asking Maharajji to give him his blessings in order that he get wealthy. This is what Maharajji said: "Look, you're already stinking rich. I'm not going to give you any blessings that you get rich." This man wanted blessings to be as rich as Tata (one of the richest men in India).

Maharajji started to tell the story of Birla (another very wealthy Indian). Birla had been an ordinary guy who also had gone to his guru and asked to be made the richest man in India. His guru had told Birla to wait and serve, so Birla started serving his guru—cleaning the shit, washing the dhotis, this and that. Years and years passed but still his guru made no mention of giving him the blessing of bottomless wealth. For ten years Birla had faithfully served his guru, never again mentioning his desire.

One day the guru called Birla in and said, "Okay. Here it is," and he took a lota and urinated in it. "Take this lota of piss. Cover it and get on the train to Calcutta. When you get to Calcutta, get off the train. When you get off the train, drink the piss. This is the blessing."

So Birla faithfully obeyed. When he got to Calcutta, he drank the urine, which by that time had miraculously transformed itself into nectar, so I presume he didn't have to gag. One thing led to another, and he became the richest man in India.

After hearing this story, the rich man said, "Maharajji, Maharajji! Let me drink your piss!"

"Nay, nay, nay, nay. I won't give you any piss."

"Anything, anything! Give me your piss!"

And Maharajji said, "Oh, no. I won't bless you for wealth. I will only bless your grandsons. I won't bless you. You've already got enough."

"Okay, okay. Do it. Do it. Anything."

This went on until Maharajji finally relented and said, "I won't give you any urine—I'll give you a piece of roti." Maharajji then asked us, "Has anybody got any roti? Anybody got any roti?" I had earlier gotten a little piece of roti; I had taken a bite out of it and kept the rest in my hand. I gave my half-eaten piece to Maharajji, who blessed it and gave it to the rich man.

He exclaimed, "Oh, this is the greatest thing." He was delighted.

Then Maharajji went on to something else, and while he was talking, another devotee turned to the rich man and told him the bread was juth *(unclean, impure, filthy, contaminated) because I had eaten some of it. All of this going on behind Maharajji's back. The rich man gave the roti back to me—roti blessed with millionairehood! I ate it!*

राम

Maharajji always told me to spend my money: "Spend it. Don't save it. Keep the money flowing. Give it to the needy. Spend it."

राम

When I first met Maharajji I was out of money, and my plane ticket back to the West was to expire within a week. But believing that "Clinging to money is a lack of faith in God," I stayed on. Nearly two years passed, during which time all was provided for me, but I never actually had any money. Then I found out that I had inherited a thousand dollars. I immediately offered it all to Maharajji in my heart and had the money sent to India. As I was leaving for Delhi to pick it up, I asked what I could bring Maharajji. He asked for twenty brooms and several tins of milk powder, and as I was walking out the door he called me back in and asked me to bring him a blanket. The blanket was the first thing I bought with the money.

When I returned to Kainchi, every day Maharajji would ask me for some

amount of money or other, as would the Westerners. I would always give. It
was not my money. Then, when it was nearly gone, all but one twenty-dollar
traveler's check, Maharajji told me not to cash it. About a week later he sent
me to Nepal and asked me to stay there for four months.

Of course I now had no money. He asked a few people to give me
money—altogether maybe five hundred rupees—and sent me off. In Nepal,
while traveling with a companion, I lost all my rupees. We knew it was
Maharajji's doing, and as we walked back to the hostel a small boy came
beaming up to us, asking if everything was all right, just the way Maharajji
does. We both felt it was he. At the hostel I rediscovered the twenty dollars,
and with that we returned to Kathmandu. It was in Kathmandu that we
learned Maharajji had left his body.

MONEY SHOULD BE USED
TO HELP OTHERS.

During the summer in Kausani, one of the Western devotees told me that he
wanted to give some money to Maharajji. He had earned and inherited quite a
bit of money and had been very generous in a quiet way, helping out various
members of the satsang who had used up their own funds. He asked me how
much I thought he ought to give to Maharajji.

"Why don't you give all your money to Maharajji?" I suggested. "Since
you say that your only concern is that your money be used consciously—and if
Maharajji is your guru you must accept that he is more conscious than you
are—obviously he should decide what to do with your money. If he thinks you
should be responsible for it, he'll give it back to you."

But the devotee didn't see it that way and so he gave Maharajji about two
thousand dollars. Now in our daily visits Maharajji kept querying me as to
what I thought he should do with the money—Did I think it should be
returned to the devotee or not?

Although I didn't understand the implications of any of this, I urged
Maharajji to return the money to the devotee—mainly, I think, because I felt
the gift reflected a lack of faith. The money was returned at that time, but I
don't know what finally happened . . . (R.D.)

राम

I do. The following year, when this devotee was about to leave India, he
wanted to try once again to give the money to Maharajji. In Delhi he changed

*his remaining money into rupees and gave it to me, as I was staying in India.
I agreed to try to give the money once again and, if it was not accepted, to
eventually return it to him in America. I took the rather large bundle of rupees
back up to Kainchi and discussed the matter privately with Dada. Some days
later as the satsang were about to leave for the bus back to Nainital, Dada
announced that I was to remain in Kainchi for the night. This produced quite a
stir, since it seemed that some mysterious special privilege was being
conspicuously bestowed. I was no less mystified than anyone else, as by now I
was used to carrying the bundle of rupees around and had virtually forgotten
them. After evening darshan and supper, when we had all retired to rooms for
the night, Dada appeared, flashlight in hand, to escort me down to the
darkened temple. There, it seemed to me that I heard the soft breathing of
sleeping Hanumanji while I slowly stuffed rupees through the narrow slot of
the donation box.*

राम

*"Serve the poor," Maharajji said.
"Who is poor, Maharajji?"
"Everyone is poor before Christ."*

राम

*It was the mela. Maharajji had a tent there and prasad was being distributed
all the time to all the devotees who came. People were preparing food from
eight in the morning until two or three in the afternoon. The biggest
millionaire in India arrived, and Maharajji immediately yelled, "Go away! I
don't want to see your face! Get out! You go away!"*

*The man said, "Well, Maharajji, I have come with these two bags of flour
for you to give to the poor, in your bhandara. Please accept."*

*Maharajji yelled out, "No! Go away! Don't show me your face. Don't
come here."*

*When that man still didn't go away, Maharajji stood up and went away
himself. Still the man didn't go. He followed Maharajji, saying, "Oh,
Maharajji, give me some teachings. What should I do?"*

*Maharajji replied, "What teachings should I give you? Will you follow me?
If I give you teachings, will you follow me?"*

The man kept mum.

Maharajji said to him, "Whatever wealth you have, you give it to the poor. This is my teaching. Will you follow it?"

GIVE UP MONEY, AND ALL WEALTH IS YOURS.

Again and again Maharajji reiterated that one should not be attached to money, because it just causes trouble. He was fond of telling the story of a man who made much money, whose son became so greedy for the money that he came to his father with a gun demanding some of it. Then the father said, "Take it all."

I had seen again and again in America how much trouble money made in families and what greed and bitterness could exist between a wealthy father and his children—all over money. Although I didn't feel that way toward my father, I wasn't oblivious to the fact that someday, at his death, I would inherit much money. Then one day Maharajji called me to him and asked, "Your father has much money?"

"Yes, Maharajji."

"He is going to leave it to you?"

"A share of it he will leave to me." I thought of the pride my father had in remembering his own earlier financial hardships, due in part to his father's untimely death, and how he had built financial security so that none of his children would ever face what he had faced.

"You are not to accept your inheritance."

I had never even considered that. Knowing that I would not have personal use of this money has affected me much to the good. And since that time my father and I have become much closer. (R.D.)

CLINGING TO MONEY IS A LACK OF FAITH IN GOD.

J's brother was told by Maharajji to give all his money away. He said, "No, Maharajji, what about my family?"

Maharajji said, "You'll have so much more. Give it all to me. Give it to me."

Sometimes Maharajji would send a message to Haldwani asking J's brother to get him railroad tickets, but the brother would hide so he wouldn't have to get the tickets. Finally Maharajji said, "I'm making my grace toward J. You are greedy. Now you'll suffer." At the time, J was poor and all the rest of the brothers were rich. But now J is doing well and the one brother has lost his business and has nothing.

MONEY BRINGS ANXIETIES.

In earlier years Maharajji had spent time wandering with a sadhu. Later the sadhu started to hold on to money and entrusted some to one of his devotees to hold for him. Maharajji came to the devotee and persuaded him to use half the money for his daughter's dowry. When the sadhu heard this he was angry with Maharajji. Then Maharajji is supposed to have said, "You are ruining yourself. Get rid of it all." The sadhu saw that he had indeed gotten caught, and he started a huge fire and burned all his possessions. Maharajji said of him, "He was a good sanyasi."

॥ฯ॒

One day when I was alone with Maharajji and a translator, Maharajji was warning me about money. "Money is all right for a grihastha *(householder) but it is worst for a yogi. Money is your enemy. You should not touch money."*

I asked him if it wasn't all right to keep enough money for one's daily needs. He said that that was all right: "'Keep only as much money as is necessary for your needs and distribute the rest." Well, such an instruction gave me all the latitude I needed, for who defines "needs"?

Soon Maharajji returned to our earlier conversation about my having money. "Money is your enemy. You should not touch it."

"But, Maharajji, isn't it all right to keep enough for daily needs?" But this time he answered, "No! Money should go around a saint, not through him." He had just filled in the loophole.

When I returned to the hotel that night I reflected that these new instructions required some action, at least the beginning of some experiments with money, so I decided to try for a time literally not to touch money. By not having money in my pocket there would be the opportunity, each time I would usually reach into that pocket, to become conscious in the use of money. But on the other hand, I reasoned, I didn't want to become financially dependent on others. The Indians for the most part could not afford it and neither could most of the Westerners. So, as a first experiment, I turned over to one of the Westerners all my money, and he became my "bag man." He would pay bus fares and so forth. While I appreciated that this was not the spirit of Maharajji's instruction, it would at least adhere to the letter of the law, "You should not touch money." Of course, I knew Maharajji meant something more. I'm still learning about it today, seven years later. (R.D.)

A SAINT NEVER ACCEPTS MONEY.

When the engagement of one family's son was settled, they brought sweets to Maharajji. Maharajji said, "I was just remembering you. Good you came. So your son is engaged, and you got money from your in-laws. Uncles and aunts each got a hundred—what about me? How about a hundred?"

I first heard Maharajji's name about ten years ago in Kanpur. They said that he was a very high-class mahatma and that he knew everything. A friend told me of his darshan with Maharajji: "I have seen him. He has some power or some ghost in his hand. This is how he knows everything. It's not a spiritual power but some ghost or something."

There were some influential businessmen who went to Maharajji, and he told them to buy a certain type of goods and sell them. In one day, each of the three men made twenty-five or thirty thousand rupees. They thought that if they stayed near Maharajji, he would let them know how the market was going to behave. They went to him and he asked, "Did you make some money?" Each answered with the amount he had made and then asked Maharajji for further instructions.

Maharajji said to a devotee, "What will be the result if everyone comes for money? These Kanpur industrialists are bad. They'll give me trouble." Then Maharajji said to one, "Okay. You've got thirty thousand rupees. Tomorrow, bring three thousand for me." To another he said, "You bring fifteen hundred." To the third, "You bring twelve hundred." They all agreed but never returned, thinking he was corrupt. Maharajji was not anxious about money, but he wanted to have his life free from those speculators. Of a fourth man, a relative of mine, Maharajji asked that he bring nine hundred rupees. The next day the man returned. Maharajji asked, "Did you bring the money?"

"No, Maharajji, I haven't brought it," he replied.

"Why?"

"Maharajji, I come here to take something, not to give."

"Oh, you come to take, not to give. All right, come on. I don't want money. Let those other people not come." My relative became a devotee.

ॐ

Once the Queen of Nepal came, as her husband was very much devoted to Maharajji. She presented Maharajji with many things, but he said, "No, distribute it among the people." He grabbed me and said of her, "There is big money there. Shall we get some?"

I said, "Yes." We both laughed. Such was his humor. Usually people only report Maharajji as saying that he never touches money.

Maharajji once said, "The money you earn should be straight. What do you want—to bring a bad name to me?"

ॐ

A sadhu who was visiting the temple upbraided Maharajji for having temples and being attached to possessions. He sat on the tucket with Maharajji and was very fierce. Maharajji just listened and kept the devotees who were present quiet. A little later the sadhu brought out a shaligram, *a special stone used in doing puja to Shiva. Maharajji said to the sadhu, "You will give it to me?"*

"But Maharajji, I need it for my puja."

Then, playing into the sadhu's accusation that Maharajji was a materialist, Maharajji said, "You will sell it to me?"

"Oh, no," said the sadhu. But Maharajji finally convinced the sadhu to sell it to him for forty rupees. And the exchange duly took place.

Then Maharajji said, "Give me your money."

The sadhu took out the forty rupees and begrudgingly gave them to Maharajji. But Maharajji said, "No, give me the rest of it." The sadhu brought out several hundred rupees and gave them to Maharajji, protesting all the while that this was all the money he had, so how would he live? Maharajji took the rupee notes and threw them into the brazier that was burning before them. The notes were consumed. The sadhu was very upset and admonished Maharajji for burning the money and protested that now he would starve, and so on.

At this point Maharajji said, "Oh, I didn't realize you were so attached to the money." And with that he took a chimpter *(a set of tongs), reached into*

*the fire, and began pulling new, unburned rupee notes from the fire until he
had returned all the rupees to the sadhu. After that the sadhu did not sit on
Maharajji's tucket any longer—but at his feet.*

ALL THE MONEY IN THE WORLD IS MINE.
EVEN THE MONEY IN AMERICA.

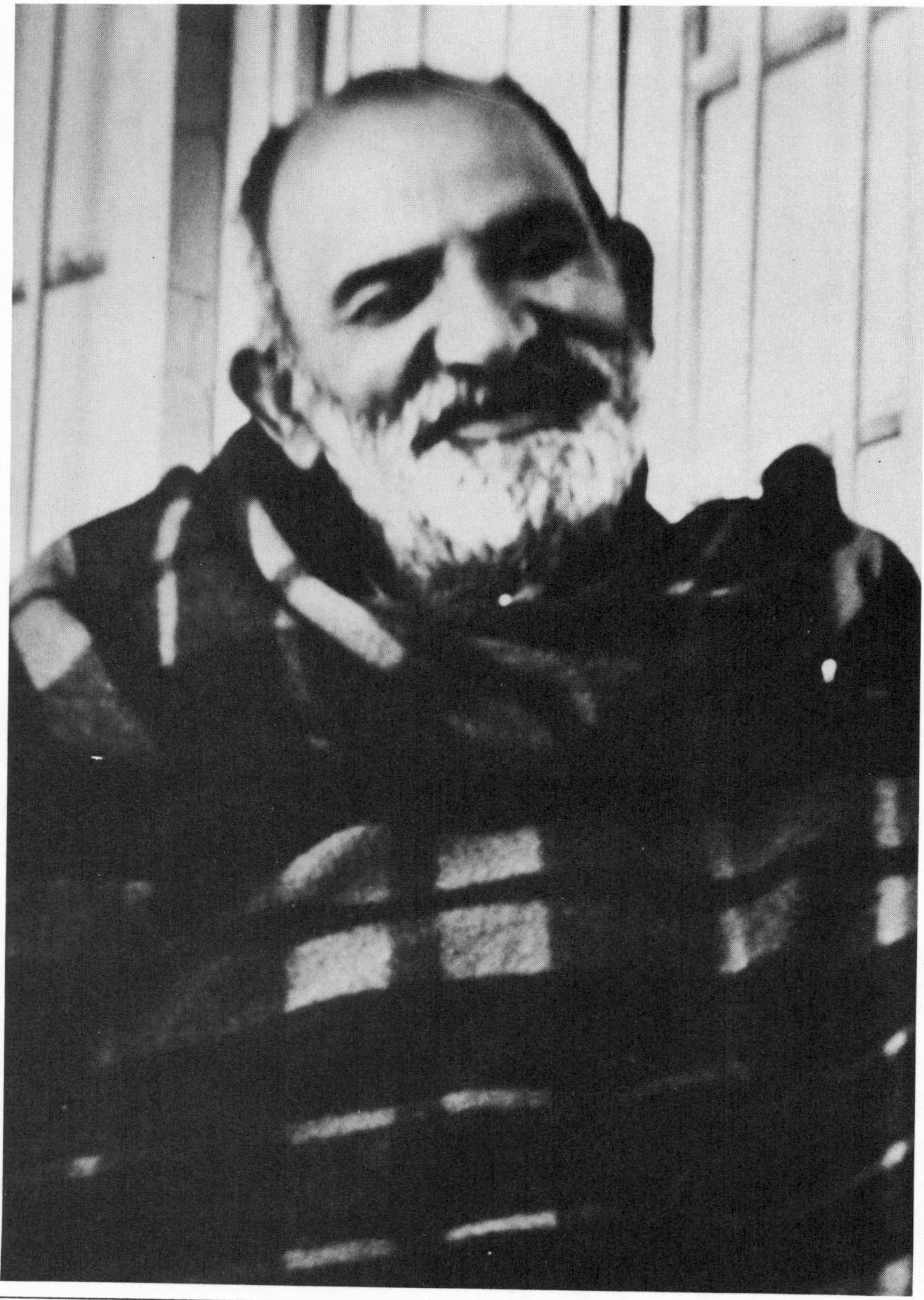

Rameshwar Das

About Drugs

IN INDIA THERE is a long tradition of the use of charas. Smoked in a chillum and mixed with tobacco, charas is used extensively by a large percentage of the millions of wandering sadhus. For those who are followers of the god Shiva, smoking is part of the religious ritual. For others of a devotional bent, it is used to accentuate the emotional fervor of the devotional practices.

In his earlier years, when Maharajji was also a wandering sadhu, he undoubtedly sat in the jungle around many a fire with other sadhus and may or may not have used charas himself. And in his later years, although he himself did not use such things, he was supportive of those who did. In many instances he helped sadhus to obtain charas or arsenic (another substance used, in tiny doses, by sadhus). He took a dim view, however, toward the use of hashish by householders (i.e., those with families), often directing at them a stream of abuse, or at least kidding and constant prodding about the matter. He said that it made them forget their responsibilities. For the Westerners he generally discouraged the use of such drugs as hashish and opium as means for altering consciousness ("Food is the best intoxicant," "love is the best medicine").

However, to some of the Westerners who were genuinely pursuing the renunciate life of the wandering sadhu and who were habituated to smoking hashish for devotional practices, he did not discourage its use.

While charas was a product native to India, LSD was not. Because so many Westerners had experienced the awakening of the spirit through ingesting LSD, it was inevitable that Maharajji and LSD would someday meet. And this meeting produced, over a six-year period, much lila.

Maharajji knew I smoked—he knows everything. But Maharajji never told me to quit this habit, never said it was bad, never said anything about it.

Sometimes other babas and I would be in my room below the temple, smoking chillums. If Maharajji would come by, he would never *come into the room when we were smoking. Sometimes he'd pass by the doorway and mutter loudly to whomever was with him, "Let those sons-of-bitches [literally, "sons-in-law"] be!" and pass on by.*

Maharajji would even obtain charas for me. If a man came to Maharajji for darshan, Maharajji would ask him to hand over to me whatever charas he had. Maharajji filled many people's desires in this way. Whether it was charas, money, sweets—whatever they wanted—Maharajji would be the agent to procure it for them.

Oftentimes at Kainchi, if a sadhu who was a chillum-baba came for darshan, Maharajji would send him to the back of the ashram to smoke with me.

I have seen Maharajji give hashish to people with his own hands.

*WHEN PEOPLE SMOKE HASHISH TOGETHER
THEY FORGET EVERYTHING—FAMILY, DUTY—
AND THEY THINK THAT ANOTHER PERSON IS
THEIR CLOSEST BROTHER.*

*HASHISH IS BAD FOR THE HEALTH. IT GIVES
YOU LUST, ANGER, GREED, AND ATTACHMENT.
IT IS BAD FOR THE HEART AND BREATH.*

*YOU SHOULD SMOKE HASHISH LIKE LORD
SHIVA, ONLY TO BE WITH GOD. SMOKING
HASHISH IS NOT NECESSARY. IT DOES
YOU NO GOOD TO SMOKE. IT ONLY LASTS
A SHORT WHILE AND IT ISN'T GOOD FOR
THE HEART. DEVOTION TO GOD IS AN
ADDICTION THAT LASTS ALL THE TIME.*

In his earlier days, Maharajji frequently visited a certain sadhu at his dhuni
*(open fire) outside the city of Aligarh. This sadhu habitually smoked charas
and* ganja *(marijuana), along with any other intoxicant he could find. One day
he showed Maharajji a new drug that he said gave the most intense and blissful
intoxication. Offering some to Maharajji, he warned that only the smallest
amount was needed, but Maharajji took the whole piece and swallowed it all.
Moments later Maharajji fell unconscious and collapsed. The sadhu knew the
remedy for overdose—four kilos of milk—and when this was brought from the
bazaar he poured it down Maharajji's throat. Maharajji revived and sat up.
Seeing the sadhu seated across from him, Maharajji slugged him in a moment
of fury. "You tried to kill me! He poisoned me! Hap! Wicked person," he
shouted as he ran away.*

जप

*A sadhu named N Baba, who usually lived beyond Bageshwar on the
glacier side, considered Maharajji to be his guru and would sometimes visit
him. Maharajji would offer him a place on his bed, but the sadhu always sat
on the floor. The sadhu ate arsenic to keep out the cold. Five or six years
earlier, the baba had come for a visit and Maharajji asked him, "N, what do*

you eat?" and the sadhu replied that he ate arsenic. Maharajji said, "Let's see." The sadhu took out of his bag enough to kill two people. Maharajji grabbed it and ate the whole thing. Everyone was shocked, but Maharajji only asked for a glass of milk. He showed no effects.

ᴛᴍ

One day Maharajji was walking alone along the Ganges. He encountered some sadhus in their small kutis there. They asked him who he was, where he stayed, what and where he ate. Maharajji explained that he was just a wanderer with no home, that he stayed where he could and ate when food was available. They asked him to come stay with them a while. "Will you feed me?" he asked. They told him of course they would, so he sat with them a while. A sadhu came along and began preparing a chillum for everyone. It was passed around, and when it was offered to Maharajji he became very abusive, calling them bums and fakes and accusing them of trying to ruin him and of ruining themselves. Then he stormed away. Shortly afterward another sadhu came into the kuti and asked them if they hadn't been able to recognize Maharajji. What kind of sadhus were they if they couldn't even recognize a siddha mahatma *(highest saint) who visits them personally. They mumbled, "How could we recognize him, the way he behaved!"*

ᴛᴍ

Some of the Westerners had another kind of drug karma, for they had been involved in smuggling hashish. When Maharajji found this out, he embroiled them in a complex smuggling operation that necessitated their being away from the temple and thus from his presence for long periods of time.

The proceeds from this venture were to be used for charitable purposes. Offering now to God the results of what they had done previously for personal gain was a powerful lesson, which they appreciated. However, they were very unhappy at being banished from the gatherings around Maharajji.

That their guru should be countenancing and even encouraging such activities led them into deep reconsiderations of their own models of good and evil. His involvement also led to a bravado in the operation for they felt that with his protection they could not get caught. However, when it occurred to them that it was not necessarily Maharajji's way to interfere with karma, and that it might be their karma to go to jail, the unique exhilaration was lost. By the time they had finished the project they had had more than enough of these illicit activities.

ᚐᚔᚕ

In 1967 when I first came to India, I brought with me a supply of LSD, hoping to find someone who might understand more about these substances than we did in the West. When I had met Maharajji, after some days the thought had crossed my mind that he would be a perfect person to ask. The next day after having that thought, I was called to him and he asked me immediately, "Do you have a question?"

Of course, being before him was such a powerful experience that I had completely forgotten the question I had had in my mind the night before. So I looked stupid and said, "No, Maharajji, I have no question."

He appeared irritated and said, "Where is the medicine?"

I was confused but Bhagavan Das's suggested, "Maybe he means the LSD." I asked and Maharajji nodded. The bottle of LSD was in the car and I was sent to fetch it.

When I returned I emptied the vial of pills into my hand. In addition to the LSD there were a number of other pills for this and that—diarrhea, fever, a sleeping pill, and so forth. He asked about each of these.

He asked if they gave powers. I didn't understand at the time and thought that by "powers" perhaps he meant physical strength. I said, "No." Later, of course, I came to understand that the word he had used, "siddhis," means psychic powers. Then he held out his hand for the LSD. I put one pill on his palm. Each of these pills was about three hundred micrograms of very pure LSD—a solid dose for an adult. He beckoned for more, so I put a second pill in his hand—six hundred micrograms. Again he beckoned and I added yet another, making the total dosage nine hundred micrograms—certainly not a dose for beginners. Then he threw all the pills into his mouth. My reaction was one of shock mixed with the fascination of a social scientist eager to see what would happen.

He allowed me to stay for an hour—and nothing happened. Nothing whatsoever. He just laughed at me.

The whole thing had happened very fast and unexpectedly. When I returned to the United States in 1968 I told many people about this acid feat. But there had remained in me a gnawing doubt that perhaps he had been putting me on and had thrown the pills over his shoulder or palmed them, because I hadn't actually seen them go into his mouth.

Three years later, when I was back in India, he asked me one day, "Did you give me medicine when you were in India last time?"

"Yes."

"Did I take it?" he asked. (Ah, there was my doubt made manifest!)

"I think you did."

"What happened?"

"Nothing."

"Oh! Jao!" and he sent me off for the evening.

The next morning I was called over to the porch in front of his room, where he sat in the mornings on a tucket. He asked, "Have you got any more of that medicine?"

It just so happened that I was still carrying a small supply of LSD for "just-in-case," and this was obviously it. "Yes."

"Get it," he said. So I did. In the bottle were five pills of three hundred micrograms each. One of the pills was broken. I placed them on my palm and held them out to him. He took the four unbroken pills. Then, one by one, very obviously and very deliberately, he placed each one in his mouth and swallowed it—another unspoken thought of mine now answered.

As soon as he had swallowed the last one, he asked, "Can I take water?"

"Yes."

"Hot or cold?"

"It doesn't matter."

He started yelling for water and drank a cup when it was brought.

Then he asked, "How long will it take to act?"

"Anywhere from twenty minutes to an hour."

He called for an older man, a long-time devotee who had a watch, and Maharajji held the man's wrist, often pulling it up to him to peer at the watch. Then he asked, "Will it make me crazy?"

That seemed so bizarre to me that I could only go along with what seemed to be a gag.

So I said, "Probably."

And then we waited. After some time he pulled the blanket over his face, and when he came out after a moment his eyes were rolling and his mouth was ajar and he looked totally mad. I got upset. What was happening? Had I misjudged his powers? After all, he was an old man (though how old I had no idea), and I had let him take twelve hundred micrograms. Maybe last time he had thrown them away and then he read my mind and was trying to prove to me that he could do it, not realizing how strong the "medicine" really was. Guilt and anxiety poured through me. But when I looked at him again he was perfectly normal and looking at the watch.

At the end of an hour it was obvious that nothing had happened. His reactions had been a total put-on. And then he asked, "Have you got anything stronger?" I didn't. Then he said, "These medicines were used in Kulu Valley long ago. But yogis have lost that knowledge. They were used with fasting. Nobody knows now. To take them with no effect, your mind must be firmly fixed on God. Others would be afraid to take. Many saints would not take this." And he left it at that. (R.D.)

राम

When I asked him if I should take LSD again, he said, "It should not be taken in a hot climate. If you are in a place that is cool and peaceful, and you are alone and your mind is turned toward God, then you may take the yogi medicine. (R.D.)

> ## LSD IS GOOD FOR THE WORLD BUT NOT SPIRITUAL.

LSD ALLOWS YOU TO COME INTO THE ROOM AND PRANAM TO CHRIST, BUT AFTER TWO HOURS YOU MUST LEAVE. THE BEST MEDICINE IS TO LOVE CHRIST.

> ## LSD IS NOT THE TRUE SAMADHI.

Once a Westerner asked me to translate for him. He wanted to ask Maharajji how he could help his friend back in America. The friend was in a very confused state through so many LSD trips. Maharajji said to tell the friend to remember God all the time.

राम

I had brought a picture with me of a boy who had died in America under strange circumstances. In 1968 he had come to see me in New Hampshire and had become one of my first students of yoga. He would come and visit each week and he immediately absorbed everything I shared with him of what I had learned in India. I had eventually wanted to send him to Hari Dass for further training, but he had preferred to go to live in a cave in Arizona to continue his sadhana. I had taught him all I could, but he wrote me letters and checked in every few months during the winter of 1968/69.

I didn't hear from him for a while and later learned that he had died in the cave. His mother had shared with me his final diary entries, which were most unusual. I suspected that the final diary entry had been written while he was under the influence of LSD. The story was that he had been found dead with blood coming out of his nose and that there was blood on the wall. Perhaps he had been doing pranayam *(yogic breathing practice) and had burst a blood vessel. The entries were as follows:*

> *Ramana Maharshi and my guru are both navigating my maha samadhi . . . no worry . . . I am in infinite bliss . . . and will guide you from within . . . write Ram Dass and tell him the good news that I have no longer to undergo sadhana . . . am there. . . . Love, love. . . . I know what is happening, also the guru is with me inside . . . know that I left the body completely identified with Jesus. . . . Jesu está conmigo. Yo estoy en su corazon . . . con guru.*

I had promised his mother that when I was next with Maharajji I would ask him about her son. At the appropriate time I fetched what had been his high-school graduation picture and handed it to Maharajji. He peered at it closely and then said, "He's not in his body."

"That's right, Maharajji."

"He died from taking medicine."

"Aha, I thought so." (This implied to me that he had not indeed entered true samadhi but had probably done pranayam while on LSD.)

But then Maharajji, apparently understanding my doubts, said, "No, it is all right. He will not take rebirth. He finished his work. Now he is one with Christ. He loved you very much. He cried about you." Maharajji was silent for some time and then he added, "You should tell his mother she should not worry. He is with Christ. He is watching over her. He finished his work." (Maharajji had quoted exactly the words of the diary, and he had showed me that under certain circumstances LSD could be the vehicle for returning to God.) Then Maharajji sat silently with eyes closed. The moment was one of great power. (R.D.)

॥ꣳ॥

One morning a number of us who had taken acid decided to break into the
ashram early and get front-row seats, so we all went tramping through the
potato patches, over the stream, and across the wall. We took our morning
baths amid calls of "Sitaram [salutation using the names of Sita, Ram's
consort, and Ram]!" put on our fresh clean clothes, and got our front-row seats
in front of the tucket. We got centered, did our meditations (or whatever else
one does while waiting for Maharajji to come out). We were all lined up,
tripping; I was sitting at one of the short ends of the tucket. All of a sudden
the door burst open—bam—and there was Maharajji in a brand-new
psychedelic blanket that one of the devotees had given him. No one had time to
leap to his feet. He was just suddenly there, twinkling like a star. Everyone
was trying to get up and he just kicked his way through, sat down on the
bench, and ignored us all.

He just sat there, occasionally looking at someone, then he'd continue to look
at the sky. But he went down the line, checking everyone out, sometimes for
no more than an instant. That lasted for about ten minutes. He had come out
early—and when the rest of the ashram realized that he was out, and came
running, he returned immediately to his little room.

॥ꣳ॥

I'd find the scene really indescribable when we were with him while
tripping. The experience of seeing him sitting there, looking and talking, was
as if there were nobody there at all. It was nobody playing a game of being
somebody! That morning [described above by another devotee] was incredibly
blissful; that whole day was like that.

॥ꣳ॥

At the time of that acid trip [see above], D had gotten Maharajji a new
blanket—blue and yellow and red and green. I have a photograph of that

colorful blanket. A lot of people were stoned on acid, sitting around the table waiting for him to come out of his room. He almost leaped up on the table when he came, he had so much energy. Out he came! There he was! He poked some woman right in the front row in the chest and said, "Do you like LSD?" It was the first thing he said. He started laughing, and soon everybody was laughing. Then he got serious. Everybody started crying. It was as if he were pushing our buttons. At one point everybody was crying, and he said, "What's all this crying? I can't stand crying. Stop all this crying!"

ONE DRAMATIC LSD incident profoundly offended the sensibilities of Maharajji's Indian devotees. A young Westerner had taken LSD and had come to the temple with only a shawl wrapped around him. Then, as Maharajji was walking, holding the arms of two devotees, the young man came up behind Maharajji and attempted to embrace him from the rear. As he raised his arms to do this, his shawl covered the heads of the devotees and at the same time revealed the young man's nakedness. This incident, which might have seemed scandalous to an onlooker, was seen quite differently by the young man himself, as is indicated by the following dialogue between himself and another devotee, who had been present at the time of the incident.

S: Well, you know my own experience with your trip that day was watching you grab Maharajji from behind . . .

R: Yeah, I wanted to kiss him. I wanted to hug and kiss him.

S: And Maharajji was laughing. You had covered Dada's face, and whoever else was walking with Maharajji, with your red blanket as you reached over to grab him from behind. You were naked under the blanket. Maharajji was all giggly and twinkling, wagging his head. When he went alone into his room, you went off to pranam to the sweeper . . .

R: He was the lowest guy in the ashram and he was there, on my way out. I was such a nobody I didn't even have a body. And this guy was God! Standing there with a dirty broom, he had nothing—and I had to pranam to him. The sweeper was only about twelve, you'd never notice him. He was always there, but really he was invisible.

S: While that was going on, Maharajji was in his room, locked in there alone but laughing a lot. I happened to be right there at the window.

Maharajji was asking us all, "What happened? Why is he like that? What did he do?" I said, "Maharajji, I don't know." Then Maharajji said, "He ate too many jelebees." Then he started about LSD, asking "Do you take it? Do you take it? Do you take it?" to all of us outside his window. There was one Westerner who said proudly, "Yes, I do."

Then word came back that you had nothing on at all. There was silence for a while. Then, as we were all looking at Maharajji, he leaned right up against the screen of his window, looked straight at an Indian devotee, and said, "Naked!" The shocked devotee put his hands over his crotch and hunched over a bit, exclaiming, "Maharajji!"

You were sitting outside, singing with everyone. Dada looked out and exclaimed, "There he is! It's him!" Maharajji looked and said, "I don't know. I don't think so. I don't think that's him." This went back and forth for quite some time. Dada would say, "I know it's him. I'm sure it's him." Maharajji just would not recognize you. Finally, after about twenty minutes, Maharajji said, "Well, maybe it is him." And then he called you over and told you to leave.

R: Yes. It was translated as "Maharajji says you're wicked, and you must leave right away." I said, "Okay, Maharajji," but I don't see how it could possibly have upset him. I saw him that day as very loving, all the way through. When I was being carried out—I couldn't walk, I had no legs—I was in complete bliss. I felt as if I were being carried by angels. There was so much love all around me that I didn't feel any confusion.

S: About a month later you came back to the ashram for the first time after the acid trip. All dressed up in a dhoti, with a vest, you came and joined the satsang, sitting outside the window, singing.

R: I don't know what he called me, because my Hindi was really poor then. It was something that he always called Dada. Something like badmash but different. He said, "Fool! Jao!" And it blew my mind. I was so hurt. It was like the rejection of the ultimate lover; it was really painful. I staggered out of the ashram, thinking, "He can't do this to me. I'm going to come back a million times." But the incident created in me the desire to change myself. I started feeling guilty for things I'd done when I was two years old. I was so full of remorse at what a badmash I was that I felt a kind of determination to win his love back.

When I finally did get back in, after I went to Lama Govinda, I came back in with Anata. (This was not long before Maharajji died.) Everyone was sitting around and he was giving darshan. I was so afraid that he was going to throw me out, but I appeared very calm. He looked right at me and said, "Did *you come with her?" I said, "Yes." And he said, "You came from Lama Govinda." "Right." Then he said, "How long," and he rolled his eyes back and looked away—and all of a sudden he whirled back and looked right at me and said, "Jao!" And then some guy right behind me jumped up and ran away! I realized that he'd yelled it right over my head. Then he looked at me and laughed! I was forgiven. After that he looked at me several times and just laughed. It was just bliss!*

After this incident Maharajji started saying, "LSD causes one to become naked and dance around." And he called us all together in the back of the Kainchi ashram. We were all sitting around in a big circle; there were perhaps thirty-five Westerners there. Maharajji went around to each person, naming them by name and asking, "Have you ever had LSD?" And everyone said, "Yes, Maharajji." Every person. (There was in fact only one of the group who hadn't had LSD—a Frenchman who had lived in Israel for some time.) Maharajji thought about it for a while. He was just sitting there, meditating on it.

Later that day four young men came to the ashram. They'd just come. Maharajji said, "Doctor!" I went into the office and he said, "Four young men have come. Go to the gate and evict them from the ashram, because they have taken LSD." I went to the gate of the ashram and I said, "Um, hello. Have you guys, by any chance, taken LSD?"

The four of them said, "No, we've never taken LSD."

And I said, "Excuse me. Let me go check." I kept them at the gate and went to see Maharajji. "Maharajji, they've never taken LSD."

He said, "Go kick them out of the ashram. They've taken LSD."

I went back and asked them again. I said, 'Maharajji says you can't come in. You have to leave the ashram. You've taken LSD." They argued very vigorously. They said they'd never taken LSD. I went back to Maharajji and pleaded for them. I said, "Maharajji, all of us have taken a lot of LSD and, really, I've taken quite a bit! We've all had quite a bit of LSD."

And he said, "Those four boys have taken LSD. Go kick them out of the ashram. That's an order!" So I went out and kicked them out of the ashram. They never came back. I don't understand anything about that incident!

KK once had the desire to try LSD but felt it only proper first to ask Maharajji's permission. When he put the question to Maharajji, Maharajji replied, "What? Is something the matter with your mind?"

About Meditation and Service

MEDITATION

Maharajji often spoke about the value of meditation as a spiritual practice—and he himself appeared to be in a meditative state much of the time—yet he made it difficult for most of us to meditate while in his presence. But when we did, the effects were indeed dramatic.

> *WORLDLY PEOPLE GO OUTWARD, BUT YOU MUST GO INWARD LIKE THE TORTOISE, WITHDRAWING WITHIN YOUR SHELL.*

> *MEDITATION IS GOOD. ONE CAN ATTAIN A PURE MIND BY ONE-POINTEDNESS AND DETACHMENT. MEDITATE UPON ONE POINT AND YOU WILL KNOW GOD.*

> *CLEAR THE MIND OF ALL WORLDLY THINGS. IF YOU CAN'T CONTROL YOUR MIND, HOW WILL YOU REALIZE GOD?*

Maharajji would sometimes say, "What do I know? England is so far off."
But sometimes he'd talk of England as if he'd been there. M asked him for a
portion of the power that enabled Maharajji to see as far as England and
farther. Maharajji laughed and said, "No. Gradually and by practice you can
get that. It is not impossible; regular sadhana and putting up with any
difficulty you come across."

M started doing puja and meditation as instructed by Maharajji. Maharajji
had given him a mantra and told him to start any way he wanted; it didn't
matter. After some time, when M and Maharajji were traveling by horse-
drawn carriage, M asked Maharajji about the wandering mind during
meditation: "It won't stand on one point; but many ideas come in. What do I
do?" Then suddenly a small child ran across the road and the driver pulled the
reins to stop the horse just in time to save the child. Maharajji said, "Like
that," pointing to the driver holding the reins. "As the mind will travel here,
there, and all directions, you should always try to pull it to one point. You
should center it with continuous practice, then automatically it will go to the
one point on which you want to meditate. Ultimately, after years, the mind
becomes quiet."

राम

One time he called me into his "office" in Kainchi and had me sit up on the
bed with him. I was under the impression in those days that meditation was
"something," and here I was with the guru. It was, I thought, time to
meditate, to really "tune in." Not with words, but with, well, nonreaction,
Maharajji kept breaking down these false concepts of meditation. Each would
fall away until finally there was nothing left and I was just sitting there,
feeling nothing transcendental, only emptiness. At that point, as soon as I got
it, he jao'ed me.

राम

All the time he was talking to you he was in meditation. You just felt it.

राम

When Maharajji sat with us we could see that he was in a deep state of
samadhi. With a nod of his head he was off to a distant place; another nod,
and he was back again. We always felt this way about him, that he could be

anywhere. This is what we saw; despite the fact that he totally hid himself, we couldn't help but see it.

॥ॐ॥

We were once in the back of the ashram after everyone had been sent away for the day. The sky was very beautiful—red and purple. Maharajji was definitely in a samadhi. It was not a silent one, but it was surely some sort of samadhi. As he leaned way back he said, "Are there skies like this in America?" And, somehow, I knew that there would be some connection with this moment when I was back in America. Today I thought of that.

॥ॐ॥

On one occasion, KK invited me to join him and his cousin ML in an evening drive out to Kainchi to deliver some lamps and supplies that had been purchased at Maharajji's instructions for a forthcoming holiday ritual. This opportunity was a delight, for never, when Maharajji was present, had I been allowed to be at the temple at Kainchi in the evening after the gates were closed.

It was a quiet time of deepening dusk and all was gentle and silent. Maharajji was sitting alone on his outdoor tucket when we arrived. ML and I joined him while KK went about his business of storing the things that we had brought. For once there was no banter or conversation of any kind. This was what I had really yearned for—the opportunity to meditate in Maharajji's presence—for the constant drama of words and apples that usually surrounded Maharajji kept all consciousness focused on the physical plane. Although the yearning to meet him on the other planes was always strong and persistent, when the drama was in progress I lacked the discipline to ignore it thoroughly and draw my mind within, to focus on the ajna (third eye) in such a way as to bring consciousness to other planes.

Now all was silent; this was the opportunity. I sat in the lotus position and brought my attention to my forehead. Almost immediately I entered into deep meditation and felt the physical plane drifting away. At this point I was vaguely aware that Maharajji had suddenly lain over on his side and was snoring. I recall a vague surprise, because from the position he was in it seemed obvious that he was not really asleep. There was little time to reflect upon this, however, for suddenly my body was shaken by violent and powerful shocks of energy, which literally made my teeth rattle. The shaking seemed to grow in intensity and the focus on my forehead faltered as the attention was drawn

*down to the shaking body. Immediately Maharajji sat up, turned to ML, and
said, "Ask Ram Dass how much money Steven makes."*

*I heard the words from a great distance and also heard ML's reply that he
didn't want to disturb me because I was meditating. However, Maharajji
insisted, and ML gently shook my knee. I could feel great resistance in me to
"coming down" and I tried to come down just enough to answer, "thirty
thousand a year," hoping to be allowed to go back "up." But once down, the
experience was over. It was, however, enough to show me that my discipline
of mind wasn't sufficient to work with the huge energies that Maharajji could
release in me with but a snore.*

*Shortly afterward we were "jao'ed." Just at the corner of the temple I
looked back. There sat Maharajji in his blanket in the darkness, immobile as a
statue. There was something unearthly about him at that moment. It wasn't
the Maharajji of the warm intimate moments; it was the remote Shiva who sits
atop Mount Kailash in eternal meditation. This was that aspect of Maharajji
which, like the Himalayas, seemed vast and impersonal and touched a place of
great depth and innocence within me. This was the force that drew me. It was
love beyond love. (R.D.)*

*MEDITATE TO RAISE THE KUNDALINI.
THINK ABOUT GOD; IT WILL GO RIGHT UP.*

*TO SEE GOD, YOU HAVE TO HAVE SPECIAL
EYES. OTHERWISE YOU CANNOT BEAR
THE SHOCK.*

*When I was a little child he used to cover my head with his blanket. I used
to get some sort of vibration—from head to toe I would shiver. You can call it
sensation, but sensation is a cheap word for what I felt. I cannot express that
pleasure.*

*One Ma was talking about wanting to go to Chitrakut. Maharajji said,
"You want to go to Chitrakut," and he grabbed her by the wrist. The next*

thing she knew, she was in Chitrakut. Then, back at the temple again, she was groggy for eight hours.

At the mela, the first time Maharajji put Gurudatt Sharma into samadhi they had to watch him carefully, because he was in so much ecstasy they were afraid he would fall into the fire.

I put my hand on his head when I was bathing him, and my whole body got charged with electricity.

On our way to Jageshwar we stopped in Almora, and Maharajji asked me to meditate. I experienced the sensation of flying and thought of Mount Kailash before I lost consciousness. After some time I returned to normal waking consciousness, and we continued on. Later my wife and others reported having seen Maharajji and me in Delhi at that exact time. They wondered why we had left so quickly.

During one of his visits to our ashram, Maharajji asked one of his devotees to meditate. The devotee sat down and immediately went into samadhi trance. Maharajji asked the ashramites to look at his eyes and to shake him back to life. They tried without success, because he was like a stone. After ten or fifteen minutes, Maharajji turned to the devotee and shouted loudly, "Get up! Get up!" Immediately, the devotee opened his eyes and got up. Maharajji had never touched him. Later Maharajji asked the swamis of the asham, "Do you sit in meditation? Can you sit like that?"

Maharajji's process of teaching concentration and meditation was unique. He'd somehow shake you out of it the moment you began to feel some pleasure. I once asked him why he'd stopped my samadhi, and he answered that the

mind has its limitations, that I was in a physical body, and that these things
are achieved slowly, slowly—otherwise I'd become a lunatic. He understood the
capacity of your body.

जय

Maharajji never allowed meditation on him when I was in his presence.
Even now the worst mischief will disrupt my meditation if I try to concentrate
on him. But there is no dearth of bliss for me.

जय

Maharajji often foiled our attempts at meditation. Many times when we'd be
sitting there, someone would start meditating and Maharajji would send over
his two "meditation spoilers." One was his driver and the other a little boy
who was the driver's friend. He would send them over to shake people out of
meditation. One time we were all sitting there and he said, "Okay, meditate,"
and after about a minute he started telling jokes and making everyone stop.
Another time Maharajji called us into his office and told us to start singing. We
started singing but no one was really into it so after a while it died down, and
then he yelled from the other room, "Keep singing." We picked it up again
and it died down again, and he yelled, "Keep singing." And finally after
about three hours the singing caught on and got really great. When it ended
everyone just naturally fell into meditation, and as soon as that happened we
heard from the other room, "Take dinner," and we were all ushered into the
other room. We were never able to cling to that meditation space.

जय

I valued meditation very highly, so when I found out that an essence
meditation teacher was going to spend the summer rainy season in Kausani, a
small remote village in the Himalayas, I made elaborate plans to join with
three other Westerners for a quiet, intense summer of practice. When I told
Maharajji of my plans, all he would say was, "If you desire." Then he said,
"Go! I'll call you."
    The house in Kausani was perfect, and we settled in with great delight, our
summer meditation fantasy seemingly assured. We dug a toilet, took turns
fetching water and cooking, gazed blissfully at the Himalayas, and awaited the
arrival of our teacher, Anagorika Munindra.

It was at the beginning of the second week that we heard a few Westerners had arrived in the village and were staying at a small hotel below. We all agreed that they shouldn't be invited up to our house, for we should protect this space for the work we would commence with Munindra's arrival. But the Westerners continued to arrive in Kausani, and they were not at all pleased to be excluded from the mountaintop. After all, Maharajji had told them to come. He had said, "Go be with Ram Dass in Kausani. That's a beginner's course. Not for Ram Dass."

I was furious. Maharajji knew we wanted to be alone, yet he had deliberately sent what now amounted to twenty people. We decided to stick to our original plan, no matter what!

But we had underestimated the extent of Maharajji's lila, for on Friday of the second week a letter arrived from Munindra: "Due to several administrative matters I must take care of here in Bodh Gaya, I shall be unable to come to Kausani this summer." There went the fantasy. Once we had surrendered the fantasy of a quiet summer of meditation, we joined with the other Westerners who had arrived in the village, moved into an ashram across the valley, and had a productive and intense summer ashram experience.

We returned to Kainchi at the end of the summer, at the call from Maharajji. As we came before him for darshan he was laughing. He said, "Ram Dass teacher, Ram Dass teacher. Buddhist teacher never came. Ram Dass teacher, Ram Dass teacher," and he cackled and pulled on my beard. No doubt about it—the events of the summer had not been just a chance misfiring of our plans. There was a paw in the pie. (R.D.)

जय

Maharajji had instructed me to be by myself and not to speak much. He had also told me to focus upon my ajna and think of him; so one summer when we were in Kausani, some fifty miles from where Maharajji was, I remained in my room alone, fasting for five days. I had many pictures of Maharajji with me.

As I was beginning this retreat, I read a story from the Mahabharata about the Pandava brothers, of whom Arjuna was the most skilled. The brothers, so the legend goes, were jealous of Arjuna's skill and asked their guru why he was so much more proficient. The guru said, "There is nothing so special. It's just that he wants it more than you do." To demonstrate, the guru gave them the task of shooting the eye of a bird with their bow and arrow. Arjuna did the task easily. Afterward, the guru asked each of the brothers what they had seen.

One described the tree on which the bird sat; another described the bird and its coloring. When Arjuna was asked, he said, "I see the eye of a bird."

I wanted to see Maharajji the way Arjuna saw the eye of that bird. I needed only to make Maharajji my meditative focal point, for focusing on Maharajji would simultaneously focus the eye, the mind, and the heart. After a day or two, the pictures of Maharajji seemed to lose their value and I put them all away; yet I felt Maharajji's presence in the room. By the fourth day I felt him so close that it was as if he were standing right behind me.

The fasting made me emotionally very sensitive, so when I began to feel that he was no longer behind me and absent from the room I became very upset. Then I realized that the absence was of Maharajji as a separate entity; for what had happened in the course of those meditative days was that Maharajji had come closer and closer, until he had gone inside of me. I felt alone; not lonely, just alone. It was a feeling of strength and clarity and fullness, but also of aloneness and silence even in the presence of sounds. It was a little like being the last person on earth. When I finally emerged from the room and was with people again, the feeling slowly left me; but I now knew that in the path of merging with Maharajji lay my freedom. (R.D.)

KUNDALINI RESTS BELOW THE NAVEL. IT CAN BE RAISED BY THE GURU'S GRACE, BY THE GENTLE, SIMPLE TOUCH OF THE GURU'S HAND.

SERVICE

WHEN ASKED WHY he was surrounded by so many badmash, Maharajji said, "Only sick people come to a doctor." And like an old and trusted family physician, Maharajji was available day and night for his devotees, and he made "house calls." Thus Maharajji's own behavior was a perfect model for that sadhana he most encouraged in his devotees: selfless loving service. For the householders, who composed the largest percentage of his devotees, Maharajji did not generally encourage severe austerities, nor extensive meditation practice, nor complex rituals. Rather, he guided us to *karma yoga,* a way of coming to God through living life as an act of devoted service. In this way Maharajji mirrored the teachings of the greatest devotional literature, as in the Ramayana, the Bhagavad Gita, and the Bible. But Maharajji made it clear that hard work alone was not the essence of the matter. Rather, it was work carried on with remembrance of God; that is, work done with love in the presence of God's grace.

One man worked so hard in the ashram that he almost never had Maharajji's darshan. But late one evening it so happened that, one by one, all the devotees left and Maharajji was alone on his tucket. The man then went over to sit with Maharajji. Maharajji appeared surprised, since the man never seemed to have time to have darshan. So Maharajji said to him, "What would you like?"
The man merely answered, "Atma-gyan [knowledge of the self]."
Maharajji replied, "Service to all is atma-gyan."

Maharajji would sometimes quote the Gita about purifying the heart: "You can get one-pointedness through work; the Gita says and then you get insight."

SERVE THE POOR AND REMEMBER GOD. YOU BECOME ONE WITH CHRIST.

"Did Maharajji give you any special teachings?"
To this, Brahmachari Baba smiled sweetly and said, "He taught me service."
We were all silent for some time after that.

Maharajji asked HC how he thought a man succeeded in the world. HC said by diligent, sincere work. Maharajji countered, saying that God's grace was also necessary. Without God's grace no amount of hard work will succeed.

Once I asked Maharajji how it is possible for a man to remember God all the time. He told me the story of Narada (the celestial sage) and the butcher: Vishnu (one of the aspects of God) was always praising the butcher and Narada wondered why, since the butcher was always occupied and Narada spent twenty-four hours a day praising Vishnu. Vishnu gave Narada the task of carrying a bowl of oil, full to the brim, up to the top of a mountain, without spilling a drop. The task completed, Vishnu asked how many times Narada remembered Vishnu. Narada asked how that would be possible, since he had to concentrate on carrying the bowl and climbing the mountain. Vishnu sent Narada to the butcher and the butcher said that as he works he is always remembering God.

Maharajji said then, "Whatever outer work you must do, do it; but train your mind in such a way that in your subconscious mind you remember God."

ᵱᵤ

Maharajji had often instructed me to remain alone, to have little to do with people, and at the same time to serve and feed people. Once I was staying in my room because he had said I should eat alone and not spend time with others. That night a Western couple had a fight, and later Maharajji looked accusingly at me as he asked them, "Where was Ram Dass? Why wasn't he there to help you?" (R.D.)

ᵱᵤ

I asked Maharajji about my sadhana, and he said, "To serve human beings is the only way for your salvation. You need not do dhyan *(meditation) or* puja. *Serve all living beings."*

> WHOEVER WORKS FOR GOD, HIS WORK
> WILL BE DONE BY ITSELF.

WORK IS GOD. WORK IS WORSHIP.

> THE MIND SHOULD ALWAYS BE ENGAGED
> IN WORK.

Maharajji, how can I know God?
"Serve people."

ᵱᵤ

Maharajji, how can I get enlightened?
"Feed people."

Maharajji, how can I raise kundalini?
"Serve and feed people."

Maharajji opened us to the true joy of service as a way of being with God. It's interesting how critical people get around us because they don't understand why we work so hard, so joyfully.

Maharajji allows you the privilege of doing his work.

Said one devotee, "It's an honor to be allowed to serve Maharajji.

About Anger and Love

MASTER OF ABUSE

Maharajji REACTED in a variety of ways to those of us plagued by anger; and all of those ways sooner or later brought the anger to the surface and helped us begin to let go of it. Sometimes a devotee would become the object of a continuous barrage of abuse from Maharajji. The abuse, coupled with the underlying love, was a great panacea for even the most hidden and deep-seated anger. For others it seemed as if situations just developed around Maharajji that forced anger to the surface like a badly inflamed boil. And at just the right moment, Maharajji would be there with the necessary word or glance to release the anger—and the necessary cup of milk to soothe the soul after surgery.

For two years, Maharajji made Dada do many things as part of the temple management that he avoided at home. And throughout, Maharajji would abuse him to his face and behind his back, from morning until evening. In the course of this training Dada learned to control his anger. After two years Maharajji asked Dada's wife if he got angry anymore, and she replied, only very rarely.

251

Maharajji told Dada that if he were Dada's wife, he would have thrown Dada out a long time ago.

Maharajji turned to Dada and said, "You are a fool." Dada agreed. Then Maharajji said, "You are not a fool." Dada agreed.

That Dada had become quite philosophical about Maharajji's abuse of him is evident from a conversation between them. There was a constant sound of gunfire nearby and Maharajji asked, "What is that?"
Dada answered, "They are just firing blanks, Baba."
"What do you mean, blanks?" Maharajji asked.
"That's what you do, Maharajji," Dada answered.
"Oh," said Maharajji, "I also go on firing blanks," he said delightedly.

"Dada is a master of arts," said Maharajji.
Dada replied, "And you are a master of abuse."

When Maharajji was so bad that he made the Ma's cry, he said to them, "Only if you are strong enough to hear my abuses can you face the world."

> *THE PERSON WHO IS CLOSE TO ME CAN BE SCOLDED.*

> *A SAINT NEVER GETS ANGRY.*

> *I COULD NOT GET ANGRY WITH YOU, EVEN IN A DREAM*

One day when we Westerners had been sent to the rear of the temple grounds, as was usual during the day, I decided (for sentimental reasons) to go upstairs in the building I had lived in in 1967 and sit in my old room. One of the windows of this room looked over the wall into the front part of the temple, which was otherwise not visible from the back. As I idly looked out one of these windows, my attention was caught by a sight that transfixed me at the window but also made me stand well back, so that I could not be observed from outside.

Down below, at the window of Maharajji's room, a devotee who worked in the temple and served often as our translator was crying profusely. He was obviously talking to Maharajji. Then he got up and walked back toward the rear of the temple, still in tears. When he was gone from view, Maharajji appeared in his doorway and came out into the courtyard. He stood looking like a mad lion or elephant, and though I couldn't hear him it was obvious that he was yelling and turning this way and that with great fury. Everyone in the front courtyard seemed to be cowering. It didn't seem "dharmic" to me. Maharajji had, after all, specifically said to me that a saint never gets angry.

Feelings of betrayal rushed through me, for here was Maharajji obviously in a rage. So he wasn't a saint either. What kind of guru was this? He said one thing and did another. I myself now became enraged and felt, for the first time since 1967, my heart turning cold toward Maharajji; and the thought came to me that apparently I'd have to leave Maharajji and go it alone. I stumbled back downstairs, deeply disappointed, and sat with the others but said nothing. Later I learned that right after the scene that I had witnessed, Maharajji apparently walked back into his room, called Dada, and in a very conversational tone asked, "Did Ram Dass see me get angry?" Dada said he didn't think so. But Maharajji insisted that I had and sent him back with a message.

When Dada found me sitting sullenly, he said, "Maharajji wants to know if you saw him get angry."

"Yes," I said.

"Well, he said to tell you that if you have any questions they will all be answered later." And he left.

A few moments later the crying devotee appeared, bag in hand, to tell us that he had been banished from the temple, supposedly, as we later learned, for letting forty pounds of potatoes go bad in the storeroom. He said tearful good-byes and left. Now this fellow was not particularly competent, and though he was sweet he was rather a nuisance. Normally I would not have been unhappy to see him go, for he was constantly trying to ingratiate himself with the Westerners. Under these circumstances, however, I suddenly felt compelled to support the underdog. I got up and followed him out to the front of the temple.

Just going out to the front unbidden was already an act of insurrection. And as this crestfallen fellow was leaving the temple gate I purposely went up to him, embraced him, and gave him some money and a note with my address in Delhi if he needed anything. Then as he left I walked defiantly back through the temple, like the showdown scene from the movie High Noon. *Everyone realized that I had sided against Maharajji.*

All day I waited, but no clarification was forthcoming. As usual, we were not called to the front of the temple until a few minutes before the departure of the last bus. At the time one of the couples was having some marital difficulties, and Maharajji spoke directly to them. He said they must see God in each other and give up their anger. I sneered inside, remembering the scene I had just witnessed. Then he paraphrased the words of Kabir: "Do what you do with another person, but never put him out of your heart," and as he spoke he looked directly and forcefully at me. The words burned into my heart and I heard them in a moment as applying to the married couple, to Maharajji's behavior with the devotee, and to my own reactions to the scene I had witnessed. Once again I had gotten caught in the mellow-drama and had forgotten to remember the illusion—and behind it, the love. He never said anything else about this incident, which made what he did say all the more powerful. (R.D.)

ॐ

At times Maharajji's behavior reminds me of a story Ramakrishna tells of a saint who asked a snake not to bite but to love everyone. The snake agreed. But then many people threw things at the snake. The saint found the snake all battered. "I didn't say not to hiss," said the saint.

ॐ

I was getting so angry at Maharajji because I was sick of hearing him say that I was good. I was so tired of the words, "Bohut accha." Once he went on for ten minutes telling this man how good I was, and I just got up and left. I could hear him screaming this "bohut accha" like a mantra as I walked away.

I went back and sat by the havan, and Maharajji later came back there and called me over. I was still angry. I was thinking, "Why can't he leave me alone; I want to sit here by myself!" But I went over anyway. And he said, "Oh, no. She's angry. She has to drink some milk." So he had some milk brought and I had to drink it.

ओम्

Whenever I would get very angry, Maharajji would have someone bring me warm milk, or sweets, or some cardamom pods to chew. He said these things soften anger.

ओम्

I once found myself becoming very angry while at Maharajji's temple. Most of the anger was directed against my fellow Western devotees. Although there were perhaps some justifiable reasons for the anger, the fever pitch to which it had risen at the end of the two weeks was surprising, even to me. It was at that point that I walked to the temple and arrived late.

All the Westerners were sitting in the usual row on the porch, on the opposite side of the ashram courtyard from where Maharajji was sitting. From here they could watch him from a distance while they were taking prasad (lunch in this case). When I arrived and sat down, one of the Westerners brought over a leaf plate of food that had been saved for me. And at that moment the fury broke and I took the leaf plate and threw it. From across the courtyard, Maharajji watched.

Almost immediately I was summoned to his presence, and I crossed the yard and knelt before him.

"Something troubling you?" he asked.

"Yes," I said, looking over at all the Westerners. "I can't stand adharma (those behaviors which people manifest that take them away from God). I can't stand it in them (pointing to the Westerners), and I can't stand it in me. In fact, I can't stand anybody at all except you." And as I looked at him, I felt that he was my only safe harbor in this darkness of my soul, and I began to cry. No, not just to cry but to wail. Maharajji patted me vigorously on the head and sent for milk, and when I could see through my tears, I saw that he was crying, too.

He fed me the milk and asked me if I loved him. I assured him that I did. Then, when I had composed myself sufficiently, he leaned up close and said, "I told you to love everybody."

"Yes, Maharajji, but you also told me to tell the truth. And the truth is that I just don't love everybody." Then Maharajji came even closer, so that we were practically nose to nose, and he said, "Love everyone and tell the truth."

The way he said it left no doubt about the way it was to be. For a fleeting moment I had an image of a casket—apparently symbolic of my death—but it

*was shaped in a way that was unlike my body. It seemed representational of
this conversation in which, in effect, I was protesting that,* who I thought I
was *could not love everyone and tell the truth, and Maharajji was saying,
"When you finish being who you think you are, this is who you will be.
When you die you will be reborn to love everyone and tell the truth."*

Then he said, *"Sometimes the most anger reflects the strongest love."*

*Looking across the yard at those Westerners, toward all of whom I self-
righteously felt anger, I saw suddenly that the anger was at one level, while
immediately beneath that, at a slightly deeper level, was incredible love—two
planes of relationship in which a person might say, "I love you but I don't like
you." And if Maharajji's instructions were to be carried out—and there was no
doubt that they were, for he was my guru for better or worse—the anger would
have to be given up to make way for the love.*

*Then Maharajji offered me a bargain: "You must polish the mirror free of
anger to see God. If you give up a little anger each day, I will help you."
This seemed to be a deal that was more than fair. I readily accepted. And he's
been true to his end of the bargain.* (R.D.)

॥ॐ॥

*I was once very angry at another devotee in the ashram, and I went directly
to Maharajji, who was sitting on a stone by the roadside, for help. I knelt
before him and put my head at his feet. He placed his hand on my head and
kept me in that position for the entire darshan. When it was time to go, he
helped me up. My knees were bruised and deeply marked from the coarse
gravel I had been kneeling on. I had not felt it the entire time. My anger was
gone.*

FORGIVENESS IS THE GREATEST WEAPON, BECAUSE A SAINT SO ARMED IS UNPERTURBABLE . . . HE CAN GIVE UP ANGER IMMEDIATELY.

*A young fellow once came and Maharajji asked him how he was, and he
said, "Oh, Maharajji, I've overcome anger." Maharajji said, "Oh, very
good!" and kept praising him.*

*At the time, there was another fellow present who had been asking
Maharajji for many years to come to his house, but Maharajji had never come
because the boy's father didn't believe in sadhus or saints. But now Maharajji
turned to this boy and said, "Do you still want me to come to your house?"*

The boy said, "Yes, but let me arrange it with my father." Maharajji said, "Go and then we will all come." The visit would mean, of course, that the place of honor in the house would be given to Maharajji so the father would have to sit someplace else.

Finally, the whole party went and Maharajji sat on the tucket belonging to the boy's father. Then Maharajji leaned over and looked the father in the eye and said, "You're a great saint." But in Hindi he used the very personal form, which you use only to very intimate friends and to people in the lower caste. So it was really an insult to use that form to the old father. The old man got upset but held himself together. A little time passed and Maharajji leaned over again and said, "You're a great saint." By this time the father's face got red and he was getting worked up, but he still kept control. A few minutes more went by and Maharajji leaned over and said the same thing again. This time the father completely lost it. He got up and started screaming at Maharajji, "You're no saint, you just come in and eat people's food, you take their beds, and you're a phony."

At this point the young fellow who had overcome anger leaped to his feet, grabbed the father by the collar, and started shaking him, saying, "Shut up, you don't know who you're talking to. He's a great saint; if you don't shut up I'll kill you."

At this point Maharajji got up, looked around bewildered, and said, "What's the matter, what's the matter, don't they want me here? We should go—they don't want me here." So he got up and started walking out, and he turned to the young fellow as he was going out and said, "It's very difficult to overcome anger. Some of the greatest saints don't overcome anger."

The fellow said, "But Maharajji, he was abusing you."

"That's right, he was abusing me. Why were you angry?"

THE LANGUAGE OF THE HEART

Maharajji loved to have the Sunderakand chapter from the Ramayana read aloud. At one point in the story, a message is brought to Sita (wife and devotee) from Ram (husband and God), from whom she has been separated. Ram is telling of his torment in being separated from such a pure devotee: "One's agony is assuaged to some extent even by speaking of it; but to whom shall I speak about it? For there is no one who will understand. The reality about the chord of love that binds you and me, dear, is known to my soul alone; and my soul ever abides with you. Know this to be the essence of my love." When this section was read, tears would roll down Maharajji's cheeks, and often he would become immersed in a state of bliss.

It was just this quality of love that bound us to Maharajji. Within and beyond the apples, the kindnesses, the kidding, the comings and goings, the abuses, was the love. Now and then he spoke of love, but always, he *is* love.

One devotee said, "He knows the language of our hearts."

Maharajji would quote Kabir: "It is easy to dye your cloth, but it is hard to dye your heart."

One evening in Kainchi one other devotee and I were sitting with Maharajji. The other devotee was reading the newspaper to Maharajji in a dull monotone. I thought to myself, "Maharajji, how can you bear this boring man? Why do you put up with him at all?" Slowly, I began to experience the most incredible love welling up in my being, greater and greater love until I felt my heart would burst. Just then Maharajji simply put his hand on my head, and the sensation stopped. When I tried once more to recapture it, I couldn't. I looked up at Maharajji and he was smiling at me, filled with compassion. I felt like weeping.

THE HEART NEVER GROWS OLD.

I desired to have Maharajji come to visit my home but kept putting off asking him. I had told Dada of my desire, hoping that he could help me to invite Maharajji. I had just met Maharajji for the first time a few weeks before. One day I was standing outside the window where Maharajji was, when he called me in. Just he and Dada were in the room. As I entered, I felt myself transcend into some other state of consciousness and was aware mostly of a great opening in the region of my heart chakra—but it was as a gaping, empty blackness. I could barely see with my eyes or hear with my ears, and I'm sure my mouth was hanging open. My eyes went unblinking.

The two were talking. Maharajji would look at me and speak to Dada, and Dada would translate what was said. Maharajji was saying he couldn't come visit me because the people in the village where I was staying were all very wicked and they had no love for him. Then he sent me out of the room. Afterward, when I returned to my more habitual consciousness, I felt as though Maharajji meant that he could not come visit my heart, as it was filled with worldly desires and had no room for love of him—and that as a result of that darshan, he had cleared out my heart so that he indeed could come flooding in.

> *CLEANSE THE MIRROR OF YOUR HEART AND YOU WILL SEE GOD.*

EVEN IF A PERSON HURTS YOU, GIVE HIM LOVE. THE WORST PUNISHMENT IS TO THROW SOMEONE OUT OF YOUR HEART . . . YOU SHOULD LOVE EVERYONE AS GOD, AND LOVE EACH OTHER. IF YOU CANNOT LOVE EACH OTHER, YOU CANNOT ACHIEVE YOUR GOAL.

> *KUMBHAK [RETENTION OF BREATH] CAN BE ATTAINED THROUGH BHAKTI [DEVOTION] ALSO. WHEN THE EMOTION REACHES CLIMAX, THE BREATH STOPS AND THE MIND BECOMES FIXED.*

Such peace and love I never got from anyone in the whole world, not from mother, not from father, not from wife, not from anybody. Extraordinary.

> *NEVER HURT ANOTHER'S HEART.*

A SAINT'S HEART MELTS LIKE BUTTER. NO. IT MELTS EVEN MORE THAN BUTTER. BUTTER ONLY MELTS WHEN YOU PUT IT NEAR THE FIRE, BUT A SAINT'S HEART MELTS WHEN ANYONE ELSE'S HEART COMES NEAR THE FIRE.
> *—MAHARAJJI QUOTING KABIR*

When asked to relate some stories of Maharajji, a devotee said, "I've been with him only a short time (twenty-eight years), so I don't know any stories. What therefore can I tell? All I know is that he gave my family a special kind of love, which, because it lies beyond words and form, cannot be expressed.

ॐ

"Why do you love me?" Maharajji asked a woman.
"I don't know, Maharajji."
Maharajji repeated his question again and again. Finally he said, "You love me because I love you."

ॐ

A devotee asked, "Will our love for each other interfere with our love for you?"
Maharajji replied, "If love is pure, it interferes with nothing."

ॐ

A Western devotee of Maharajji went to have the darshan of Deoria Baba, a reknowned and respected saint of north India. When the devotee returned to Maharajji, she told him that the saint had said Maharajji was an incarnation of love.
"Why, that wicked man! What does he know? Who does he think he is?" shouted Maharajji in response to the compliment.

ॐ

Said one devotee, "Maharajji was love incarnate. No religion, only love."

LOVE IS THE STRONGEST MEDICINE. IT IS
MORE POWERFUL THAN ELECTRICITY.

A devotee asked, "What do we do if we feel darkness or separation?"
"If you love God enough, there will be no separation," replied Maharajji. "If you love all, there can be no demon."

LOVE ALL MEN AS GOD, EVEN IF THEY HURT YOU OR
SHAME YOU. BE LIKE GANDHI AND CHRIST.

What if you fear God more than you love him?" asked a devotee.
"Fear of God is just another kind of love," answered Maharajji.

I COULD HAVE BEEN SUCH A GREAT SAINT
IF I WEREN'T SO COMPASSIONATE.

KEEP ME IN YOUR HEART.

Like the Wind

MAHARAJJI WAS MOVING, always moving—from one city to another, from one house to another, from one room to another, from one position to another. Until the final years of his life he was in continuous movement. Like a river. Or, as he said of himself, "I am like the wind. No one can hold me."

There was no way to capture Maharajji—he had much guile in escaping. When Maharajji was in a group and wanted to leave, he would say that he

needed to go to the bathroom, and he'd run away. Later we old devotees figured out this ruse and he had to find new ones.

ॐ

I think I cried and laughed—and sang—all the time I was with him. I saw him seven or eight times in 1965, never for more than a day at a time and always in a different place. He operated differently back then. He was traveling back and forth across northern India from Calcutta, but he would be *off like a thief in the night in a devotee's Mercedes. He just never stayed anywhere for long.*

卐

Whenever Maharajji would get out of the car, his eyes would be incredibly open, sparkling. Everyone said that when he traveled in a car, he'd be very attentive, hanging halfway out the window, looking at everything. And when he'd get out of the car, his eyes would be wide open, looking around at everything. I remember Dada once laughing about a car ride with Maharajji. Dada said that Maharajji just wouldn't stop talking—wanting to know everything, asking about everything—just like a child. You had to give him total, constant attention. And he would give step-by-step instructions to the driver, all along the way: "Turn right, turn left, turn around, go back."

卐

We left about two hours early to catch the train. Still, he said, "Oh, we're going to be late, we're going to be late! We should have left earlier!" Maharajji was talking like that constantly—"Oh, der ho gai, der ho gai—it's late, it's late!" This time he was just frantic. Everyone was sitting there, unable to say anything. Maharajji was saying, "We should have gotten our tickets earlier. We won't get on the train . . ." It was so funny! We got there about an hour and a half early.

卐

HC said that on the long train rides when the Mothers were traveling with Maharajji they would often sit around him. Maharajji would sometimes sit on the floor of the private compartment and they would chant for hours in rhythm to the clacking of the train. One favorite (which even now I've heard a Mother reciting as she worked) is from Kabir: "Dina Bandhu, Dina Nath, Mere dore tere hath [Compassionate friend, compassionate Lord, my puppet strings are in your hand]."

卐

Maharajji was right next door to us on the train. Around three o'clock he came pounding on our door, hammering on it with both fists. I knew immediately it was he. I leaped up and threw open the door to find Maharajji was standing there with his arm along one edge of the door and his other hand *on his hip. He said, "Kya time ho-gaya [What time is it]?" It was almost time (3:30 A.M.) for us to get off. In Mathura station everyone was asleep on the floor, and as we stepped among the sleeping people, Maharajji said, "Sub sota hain [Everyone's asleep]. Sub sota hain." He kept looking back and forth, saying it over and over. "Kyon [Why]? Why is everyone sleeping?"*

Shiv Charan said, "Baba, it's 3:30 in the morning. Bohut der ho gai [It's very late]. . . ."

I was thinking, Well, we're all asleep, you know how it is. Asleep in illusion. It was a beautiful moment. Especially beautiful was his waking us up. That was the only time that ever happened to me. Maharajji wakes you up with "Let's go!"

Maharajji would often have tickets purchased for one destination and, then, knowing that the devotees would wire ahead, get off at a station preceding that stop. Maharajji would say about Ananda Mayee Ma, another great saint whose travel schedule was published and who always had crowds around her, "It's terrible what her devotees do to her, keeping her locked up within the eight gates," referring to the way in which they kept her a captive of their love.

Maharajji is like Ganga: It flows down to Haridwar and they build a pilgrimage center, but the river is not concerned about the pilgrimage center. It just flows on. At Allahabad the same thing, and again at Benares . . .

Maharajji was visiting the city of Bareilly when a devotee told him that he had to go to England for a few days on business, and he asked Maharajji to accompany him there. Maharajji said, "Let's go!" They went by air and spent three days in a good hotel. After three days, Maharajji insisted that they return immediately to India. The devotee argued that his work wasn't finished. He'd need only two more days. Maharajji said, "No, let's go." Then a telegram arrived saying that the devotee's wife was very ill. They left that night. Afterward, when asked about the trip, Maharajji would laugh and say, "I went. I drank milk and ate fruits."

Maharajji once accompanied his devotee, the Indian ambassador to Saudi Arabia, on a Haj, a pilgrimage to the sacred Moslem shrine at Mecca. They flew from India to the capital city, Jeddah, and stayed in the Indian embassy. From there they visited the sacred places of Islam. Maharajji later told people that when some Moslems discovered he was a non-Moslem, he was beaten. "Then I came back right away," he said.

ॐ

A guard who was in charge at the Indian-Tibetan border said at one point that Maharajji had crossed the border, gone into Tibet, and returned.

ॐ

Who can say why he goes to these places or what he does there?

ॐ

I had become very comfortable in the hotel in Nainital. I had my "cave"—a small room on the top floor where, with Indian prints and holy calendar pictures, some books and candles and incense and a heater, I had made a cozy retreat into which I anticipated burrowing for several months. But when it was finally "just right," the edict came from Maharajji: "Tell Ram Dass he should go now. He shouldn't stay so long in one place. He can return again." The next day we left for Delhi.

At other times he'd say, "The whole universe is your home." And: "All are your family." Once when we wanted to stay with him he said, "You don't need to stay here. The light is everywhere." (R.D.)

> FOR A SADHU TO STAY IN ONE PLACE
> MEANS TROUBLE. A MOVING YOGI,
> AND A MOVING RIVER . . . IMPURITIES
> AND SEDIMENTS AND FILTH CAN NEVER
> SETTLE THERE. IF I STAY HERE,
> ATTACHMENT WILL FORM.

Previously, before Kainchi was built, Maharajji used to visit Nainital frequently. He often came to our home in the government house either in a car or a dandi (litter). *All the family, neighbors, and many Nainital devotees would gather. Maharajji would eat a meal, then go. Whenever he came, there was a sort of bhandara. Food was prepared and people brought sweets and so forth. In those days he was always roving about—sometimes in Nainital, sometimes Bhowali, here, there. People were always after him, taking him home.*

जय

Maharajji came to Ajmeer to my father's house. He said, "Give me a dhoti. I want warm water, and I want dal and chapattis. I'll eat them in your kitchen."

जय

Mrs. Soni first met Maharajji when she was only about twenty-four years old. She was very shy. Maharajji was at a neighbor's house, and when she went for his darshan she brought along her three toddlers. As soon as she entered, Maharajji said, "I'm going to your house." She kept quiet. In her heart she didn't want him to come, because she felt too shy. Other women urged her, saying that people begged him to come to their home and he wouldn't come, and here he was asking to come to her home. Still, she didn't want him to come. Finally Maharajji said, "Get up! Let's go!" and off he went to her house. Fortunately it was some feast day, and she had prepared the traditional foods. Maharajji ate everything he was offered.

जय

In speaking of the yatras (pilgrimages), *R said that Maharajji would always sneak away to visit devotees when traveling in the south. He said Maharajji would never speak of them. "He has devotees everywhere. You can't know how many and where they all are."*

जय

I first met Maharajji in about 1930, when I was a schoolboy. Father was a great devotee. Maharajji visited our family in Faizabad (near Ayodhya). After my father's retirement, I became superintendent of police of jails. Maharajji would come visit wherever I happened to be posted—Agra, Bareilly, Kanpur, Lucknow, and so on. One room in our home was always kept vacant for Maharajji. From the 1930s on, I detected no drastic change in Maharajji's

appearance. We prepared his favorite foods daily—loki (squash) vegetable,
mung dal—in case he should come. When Maharajji didn't come, we would
take it as his prasad.

ৡ৸

For more than twenty-five years Maharajji visited our home in Lucknow.
He came at least once a year, for a few hours or a few weeks. He was both
guru and grandfather to everyone in our family. All the children were born and
raised under his guidance. He referred to them as his own children, and they in
turn were very free with him.

ৡ৸

It was such a pleasure to take Maharajji to a house. He didn't neglect
anyone in the house—he would play with the kids . . .

ৡ৸

I asked what it was like to be a child around Maharajji. She answered,
"Oh, he became a child himself. It was so wonderful. I used to bring him milk
and press his legs. I would just sit there by the tucket. We never knew when
he would come to our house or when he would leave. He would just arrive.
Sometimes he would leave in the middle of the night, and so, in the morning,
we would look into his room and it would be empty—except for devotees
sitting there." And she laughed, especially as she thought of the devotees
waiting there.

ৡ৸

Maharajji seldom used to stay more than a few hours in any one place.
Sometimes devotees would press him into staying overnight or even a few days
and he would relent. When he finally left the place, he would heave a deep
sigh of relief and say, "Oh, I've come out of the jail." Maharajji once stayed
for six days in the home of a devotee. When he left he said, "Oh, today
the force of desire has released me. That fellow had locked me behind bars."

ৡ৸

Once we invited Maharajji to visit our house, and he said he would come.
We made our house ready, cleaned it, and laid out the special things for his

visit—prasad and all. For five days we waited for him but he never came. Later when we saw him again we asked why he hadn't come, and he said, "I didn't feel like it."

ॐ

A man said to Maharajji, "You've promised for years to visit my home and you have never come. I'm not going to come to see you anymore, because you won't visit my home."

Maharajji said, "Oh, I didn't understand! It's your home. I had thought it was my home and so I didn't need to visit."

ॐ

In 1937 Maharajji came to the home of a family of devotees. He paced up and down the verandah for a while, then looked into the big room that was the office of the head of the family. He asked that the office be vacated. "You take another room—leave this one for me." He remained in the room for three to four months, coming out only for an hour, both morning and evening. He allowed no one to come in.

ॐ

Maharajji would suddenly appear at a devotee's house, any time, day or night. Once in the middle of the night in the early 1940s he came pounding on the door of a devotee's home. He roused the man of the house and told him he was being chased by other devotees. They would leave him no peace and so he was asking for shelter. The man said, "How can I help you? They will come here as soon as they miss you."

"It will be all right," said Maharajji. "I'll hide under your bed. Lock the doors and windows, give me a mat and a blanket, and when they come, tell them you haven't seen me." The man did as he was told, and when they came he abused them soundly for waking him, and then he angrily sent them away. Maharajji slept under the man's bed, pulling the bedsheet down to the floor to hide himself. The man awoke at 4:00 A.M., and not seeing Maharajji, he looked in another room and then another. Although the doors and windows were still locked, Maharajji was nowhere to be found. Later he learned that Maharajji had returned to the house from which he had escaped the night before. Concerning the locked doors and windows, Maharajji only said, "Oh, I didn't want to disturb you."

ॐ

Maharajji would take to the shortcuts and jungle roads whenever he had to hide from his followers. There remains no culvert in the area under which he has not passed at least part of a night—especially those between Gethia and Bhumiadhar, because he used to run away from Nainital to Gethia every night. Back and forth he went. He would make devotees anywhere, and anyone would be turned into a devotee—in this art, he was an expert—but when the time came to leave, he'd leave his new devotee.

卐

At Bhumiadhar, after everyone had gone to sleep, Maharajji would go out to the road and sit in the middle of it with two or three people. As others would awaken, they would join the group. Then Maharajji would have them stop a truck, and he'd hitch a ride a few miles down the road and the process would start all over again.

卐

Brahmachari Baba began reminiscing about Maharajji's exploits in the Kumoan Hills. He gestured enthusiastically, pointing out places in the vast panorama before us as we sat below the Bhumiadhar temple. He spoke quickly, one description following another: "That's the tree he used to sit under before there was ever a temple here. It was like a darbar (a king's court). So many people came to see him. We would walk all over these hills, never staying long in any one spot. Maharajji would sleep anywhere. He'd lie down on those cement pilings by the side of the road to sleep and would tell me to stay awake. If I happened to drift into sleep, he would immediately chastise me and then go back to sleep. This would go on for days on end. He wouldn't let me sleep and we'd travel everywhere. Wherever he went, so many people would gather and trail along. The Mothers would come whenever they could. There were many feasts because of the Mothers."

卐

I had been given an inside room in the home where Maharajji and I were visiting. Late in the evening Maharajji said to the older couple whose house it was, "What are you doing letting a young man sleep inside there? How do *you know what they are like? These days, you cannot trust young people." So they finally moved me to an outer room. About two hours later Maharajji came and woke me, saying, "We must go quietly so they won't awaken." He explained that this was why he had had me moved to an outside room. Maharajji would insist on opening the doors, so that they wouldn't squeak.*

We went down the road in the dark, holding hands. We came to a crossroads where a rickshaw walla was asleep. Maharajji started to cajole him sweetly to take us in the rickshaw, but the walla refused. After some persuasion he finally agreed, and then Maharajji started to barter about price, one anna at a time. The walla finally agreed to make the ride for twenty-six annas. It took at least twenty minutes. Finally Maharajji asked me to get down and wait while he and the walla went on farther. Maharajji went to some house and then returned and had the walla take us to the train, which was just ready to depart as we got there. At the station, Maharajji gave the walla his blanket and a lota and twenty or thirty rupees. The rickshaw walla cried.

राम

Maharajji was in the hills going from one place to another when a devotee from Almora found him. He said that Maharajji had stayed away from their place for so long, and now that he'd been found, he wasn't going to let him go so easily. He took Maharajji home, fed him and gave him a room upstairs, and said he was locking Maharajji in the house for the night so that he wouldn't run away. After the family had gone to bed, Maharajji said to JB, "Let's go!" Maharajji had JB take off his dhoti and tie one end to the house and throw the other out the window. First Maharajji, then JB, climbed down and ran away. Outside the city they came upon a small hut with a small lamp burning. Maharajji knocked and a little old lady answered and started abusing Maharajji for coming so late. She said that she was expecting him hours ago and had food all ready at that time. Maharajji went in and ate.

राम

He was a nomad, you see that. He would go on roaming about. . . . He would visit the devotees. You don't go to him. He comes to you.

The Family Man

ALTHOUGH HE MOVED about constantly, Maharajji was still a family man on many levels, though preeminently it was God's family with which he identified.

ALL WOMEN ARE MOTHERS AND SISTERS, AND ALL MEN FATHERS AND BROTHERS IN GOD'S FAMILY.

> *THE WHOLE UNIVERSE IS YOUR HOME.*
> *ALL ARE YOUR FAMILY.*

The way in which Maharajji said such things often conveyed the impression that he, who intimately understood reincarnation, was sharing with us a literal truth about our relationships with one another across births.

On the more mundane level, Maharajji was very much like a grandfather, especially to the Indian devotees. And as such he frequently gave counsel about family matters. The gist of this counseling was clearly to keep the family unit strong by properly honoring the roles involved.

A WIFE MUST SERVE GOD BY SERVING HER HUSBAND.

Maharajji most often instructed women to be loyal and patient, that this is what kept the marriages together, no matter whether a man was bad or good. For example, a wealthy family came with a modern daughter dressed in a pants suit (unusual in India), who had left her husband. Maharajji said in front of everyone, "Yes, he was wrong, but you shouldn't have been so impatient and gotten so angry." Maharajji was very hard on the young woman. He felt that if cultural changes occurred such that women no longer held the family together, all would be lost. He said, "This is why we don't have divorces."

WOMEN ARE HIGHER THAN YOGIS IF THEY ARE LOYAL TO THEIR HUSBANDS.

"You don't even care about your old father," Maharajji said to a devotee. "Every day you should take sweets to your father. If a man has a father and mother, he needs no God. It is easy to pray to a murti but hard when the murti speaks back." Then he made the man hold his ears (an Indian form of promising, similar to "cross your heart") and promise that every day he would attend to his father and bring him sweets. The next evening the father came to Maharajji. "What is this?" Maharajji said, "Your son loves and serves you and you do nothing for him. You should make your son a new suit. He is your devotee."

राम

Maharajji said that mothers were next to God, and he made them in this form in order to share himself, because only God and mother can forgive all faults.

राम

(The mother of one of the Western devotees visited India and was asked what she experienced with Maharajji.)
I felt that I had a certain "status." The word status is such a negative word in my life that I hate to use it, but I guess perhaps it applies. There was some kind of respect because I was a mother, which I felt was accorded to me by Maharajji. I had never gotten this from anyone else, certainly not in America. It was very nice.

I know that Maharajji also gave such respect to Krishna Das's mother. The sanctity of motherhood was emphasized. All women are mothers. Intellectually I have felt that there are good mothers and bad mothers and the fact that you've given birth to someone doesn't really say much. Yet, with him, the feeling was right.

जय

If my mother did not have her cloth over her head, Maharajji would say, "No, Ma. That is not the way," and he'd fix her cloth.

जय

Often I would see old women feeding Maharajji directly. He said, "I can feed men, but women must feed me because all women are the Mother."

जय

"You are angry with your wife. You do not treat your wife well. She is Lakshmi! You should not treat her so badly," said Maharajji to a devotee.

जय

M's son-in-law went to Kainchi to have darshan, but Maharajji wouldn't talk to him. Finally he asked, "Where is my daughter? You've come alone to enjoy the hills. Go back and bring my daughter!" The son-in-law left and returned later with his wife.

WITH INDIAN YOUNG people his relationship seemed to be more that of a grandfather, guiding in worldly matters yet still touching with the spirit.

Maharajji would come and sit in my room, and I'd never go there because I was afraid he'd tell everything and I didn't want my parents to know.

जय

K played like a child when she was with Maharajji. Though she had loving devotion to him, Maharajji chastised her, saying, "You don't read the books, and then you get angry with me for your bad marks in school."

Maharajji told a student to worship his mother every day if he expected to pass exams. He didn't do so; nor did he pass the exams.

The son of one of the Ma's said that Maharajji always gave him worldly rather than spiritual guidance when he was young. He said that he had not been interested in spiritual things then, but that now he has some spiritual feelings and remembers Maharajji often.

Some students came and looked at Maharajji with cold expressions and started to go away. Maharajji called to them and said, "You are enjoying in your way, and I in mine." Though they wanted to leave the temple, they were reluctant to go. They wandered around confused. After some time, they came back for another darshan. Now their faces were softer and more animated. His work with the heart was so subtle.

YOUNG MEN ARE LIKE LIONS.

Maharajji spent some time at our house in Haldwani when I was nine or ten. Whenever I would come in, he'd say, "My daughter has come, my daughter has come." The day he left I was very sad; he wouldn't even look at me. That night I was so upset that I couldn't eat supper. At 4:00 A.M. there was a knock at the door. Mother saw that it was Maharajji and let him in. He told my mother, "I came back just for my daughter. You have four chapattis and some vegetables that she didn't eat. Bring them and we shall eat together."

An old man was brought to Maharajji for the first time, but he hadn't wanted to come. As he came in Maharajji said, "Stop beating your son so much. It is not going to make him any better." The man had in fact been beating his son a great deal. Only his wife had known, and after he left Maharajji he chided his wife for telling. But she hadn't. When he then went to slap his son, he would hit him once and then find himself slapping his own face. This continued until his own face was black and blue. After that he stopped beating his son.

To THE ELDERS who were living with their children, Maharajji often repeated: "Maun! Naun! Kaun!" which translates as "silence" (i.e., don't grumble or complain); "Salt" (i.e., don't point out faults or make judgments, such as, "there is not enough salt in the food"); and "corner" (don't interfere in family life. Stay out of the world and in the corner).

Maharajji often played the role of arranger of marriages. Of the few who already seemed married to God, he was protective, helping them escape the parental pressures to marry. But for most, he encouraged and even bulldozed them into the marital state.

Rabu said that he wouldn't marry, but when Maharajji told him he had been saving this girl for him for five years, Rabu married her.

जय

One of the Ma's sons was adamant about not getting married, and the Ma came to Maharajji for help. Maharajji met the son on a bridge and put a blanket over his head, then said, "He'll get married. He's now prepared." And he did marry.

जय

Maharajji once told a devotee to call his neighbor over. She was a doctor, a Christian woman whose husband had died, leaving her with three young daughters. As soon as she came into the room, Maharajji said, "Your daughter hasn't been married yet? You met an eligible young man in Kerala? His family wants twenty thousand rupees? You can't give twenty thousand." She replied that this was so. The next day Maharajji again called her. "Now you should go. Approach the boy's family again. They won't ask for money. Give them whatever you can. They'll accept." She went to Kerala. The boy's father explained that money wasn't important, that what they wanted was a good wife for their son, and the wedding was arranged at minimum cost to the woman.

जय

*A traditional Indian woman and her daughter, both obviously disturbed,
were waiting for a moment alone with Maharajji. But just as they arrived,
Maharajji said in front of everyone, "Look, she should marry the dark one
because she isn't very pretty. Your daughter isn't pretty and if one who isn't
pretty marries a handsome man, he'll always have eyes for others. Let her
marry the dark one." MS, another devotee there, was so embarrassed for the
women that she said in her mind, "Oh, Maharajji."*

ॐ

*My aunt had pock marks and wasn't very pretty. She was sad because she
had not married. Maharajji said to her, "You are mine," embracing her. Filled
with bliss, she no longer desired to marry. Then a month later she became
engaged to a very nice man.*

ॐ

*In my youth I had taken a vow not to get married, from the day my aunt,
who had raised me, died. My family tried to get me married, but I was
adamant. When I was between the ages of twenty-five and thirty, Maharajji
would tell me not to get married and told people that I was tubercular or had
cancer, and that I was dying. In my thirtieth year, Maharajji asked me, "Do
you want to get married?"*

*"No," I answered. Maharajji then admired my shirt and asked to have it.
He asked what sort of shirts I had before I started college, and I replied that I
had only one old, torn shirt, but it served the purpose. Maharajji then asked
how many I had now, and I said twelve. When asked why I had so many, I
replied that as a teacher in public school, I had to maintain a certain code of
dress or I'd be fired. Maharajji said, "No, no it is not this. Now you want to
get married. You could have done with one shirt. If I ask you to marry, what
will you do?" I told him, in that case I'd have to marry, but the responsibility
would be Maharajji's. For eight days Maharajji continued to press for my
marriage.*

*On the eighth morning, Maharajji set off to catch the train. On the way to
the station, he turned off the road to a young woman's house and beckoned me
to go in with him. There was kirtan going on and Maharajji was sitting in the
puja room. I was called in and so was the young woman. Maharajji asked if
I'd marry this girl, but I refused. Maharajji said, "If I ask you to?" I replied
that the responsibility would be Maharajji's. First Maharajji said, "I'll not do*

it." Then he said, "All right, all right. I'll solemnize the marriage!" He put tilaks on our foreheads and said, "There, I've got you married! Do you accept it?"

"Yes."

Later Maharajji said, "Don't think that I or you have done this. God plays the lila in his own way. No role of mine, none of yours. It was to happen!" My wife and I have been very happy, for over twenty-five years.

॥ᵘ

Siddhi Ma one day described the marriage lila of one of Maharajji's long-time devotees. On the very day of this man's marriage (which Maharajji had arranged and insisted upon, to the man's objection), the man sat before Maharajji and would not leave him. But Maharajji insisted so forcibly that at last the man was taken and dressed in groom's garb and seated on a horse for the ride to the bride's home. As he was riding through the jungle he spied Maharajji wandering there, and he leaped off his horse and ran to him. Again Maharajji forced him to return and continue with the marriage. (The man, whose children are now being married, reports that this marriage was a spiritual boon and freed him from many misconceptions. Only after marriage, he reports, did his sadhana truly begin.)

On hearing this story, another devotee told of a man whose marriage was all arranged, and on the wedding day the groom's procession passed by Kainchi. The groom saw that Maharajji was there and so stopped off, with the intention of obtaining his blessings before continuing on. To his surprise, Maharajji instead detained him, refusing to let him continue to the bride's home. And the man never married.

ALTHOUGH MAHARAJJI was formal and traditional in his reactions to Indian marriages, he obviously recognized vast cultural differences in the marriage mores of his Western devotees. Some he pressed continually to marry, asking them again and again and offering to them as a partner, one choice after another. In a few instances he took two relative strangers and announced that they were now married or should marry.

Sometimes Maharajji talked about a certain union so much with two potential partners that they psychologically accepted the match as a fait accompli. Then Maharajji would never mention the matter again and the marriage would not happen. Sometimes, when such an arranged marriage didn't seem to "take," he dissolved it with alacrity.

Three times, Maharajji asked me if I wanted to get married. The first time was with Ian. Every evening after darshan we'd walk the two miles up that beautiful Kainchi Valley to our houses in Ninglat. Ian was such an astral being that when I was with him everything was magic—roses and winged fairies. One night when Ian came over to my house there was just a lot of sexual energy in the air. I turned it away since it really wasn't the time or the place. But after he left my whole body was alive with desire. I just lay there with it and tried to think of Maharajji. The next morning the minute I entered the temple for darshan, Maharajji called me right into the room, where he was sitting with Dada. Maharajji asked me, "Do you want to get married?"

I said, "No."

He said, "Do you want to marry Ian?"

"No, no." I wasn't horrified; there was simply no question in my mind. I hadn't even made a connection between this darshan and the night before. Maybe there wasn't one. But as Maharajji was asking me he looked deeply at me, as if to study my whole being, and then he turned around to Dada and said, "She's very good." And then he hit me on the head and said, "You're very good. Don't get married. Jao." I started to get up and then he said, "Sit down." He hit me on the head again and said again, "You're very good. Don't get married. Jao," and again another time before I left.

The second time he asked me whether I wanted to get married was after I had hitchhiked from Vrindaban to Kainchi with Carlos Vishwanath. It was an overnight trip and we had slept on the platform of some train station. When we arrived in Kainchi, Maharajji pulled me into his room right away and asked, "Do you want to marry Vishwanath?" Again, there was no question in my mind. So Maharajji said, "Accha, good. Don't get married. Jao."

The third time occurred when another devotee playfully said to Maharajji, "Saraswati isn't married yet. You haven't married her off yet. You should marry her to Ravi Das [Michael]."

Maharajji said "Accha? That's very good. Bring her here." When I appeared he asked me, "Do you want to marry Ravi Das?" The devotee started laughing.

I said, "But Maharajji, he's like my father." So Maharajji said, "Accha, very good. Don't get married," and he sent me out again. Then he called in Ravi Das and asked him the same question about me. Ravi Das's reply was, "Maharajji, I only want to marry you."

Maharajji kept asking me if I wanted to marry. I kept answering that I only wanted to marry him. Then he'd say, "But how can you fulfill your desires if you marry me?"

हरि

We had a saying in those days: "Don't bring your date to see Maharajji, because he might marry you off."

हरि

During my first darshan with Maharajji, I walked in with an old friend of mine I'd known in America. Just as we neared the gate, the friend grew frightened and said, "I can't go in there with you. We have to go in alone. He might marry us."

हरि

When Maharajji arranged the marriage of J and K, he told them that marriage was nothing to celebrate. Marriage, he said, meant that you were fettered by the feet to the world.

MAHARAJJI WAS A family man at yet another level, although most of his devotees never heard about it during his lifetime and did not believe it when they did hear. Apparently he was betrothed at the age of eight, before running away from home to become a sadhu. Although he never returned home, the woman to whom he was betrothed as a child performed much tapasya and prayed that he would return so that her life as a woman could be fulfilled. He did return temporarily and fathered two children with her, although he never remained with the family as a householder. Yet the family, which now includes several grandchildren, reports that Maharajji always watched out for their material comfort and always arrived to fulfill the ritualistic functions demanded by his role as father and head of the household. They all consider him primarily as their guru.

The Touch of Grace

In INDIA, WHERE there is no social security for old age, one's sons become one's security. When a man and a woman marry, the wife comes to live in the husband's home, so that he remains with his family. Thus to Maharajji came many people who yearned to have a child, and most particularly a son. Maharajji was known to be able to make fertile the unfertile and to determine the sex of a child. Most often he didn't interfere, but every now and again he granted what was considered a great boon.

When my wife and I started our family we had three daughters. This was not of concern to me, but my own mother became very anxious for a grandson. Maharajji told me that I would have a son. I said that I didn't wish for a son, and he said, "You don't wish for a son, but your mother does. Now you will have sons. Many sons. If you wish for sons, you will have them. If you wish, you will have sons and sons and sons." When my wife was again pregnant, about seven months, Maharajji was in Kainchi and he said, "Well, Siddhi Ma! Shiv Singh has a son! A son is born there." But he was not born yet.

Two months later our son was born. We put him on Maharajji's lap: "Maharajji, this is your fruit."

283

He blessed the boy and said, "You will have sons now. God has no scarcity of sons in his regime. You will go on producing sons now. Now, no daughters. Sons and sons."

ᵊ

You need not necessarily have faith to receive grace. Maharajji once said to a tourist couple who had come to Kainchi from eastern Uttar Pradesh, "You have three daughters. You want a son. All right. Bring me ten bags of flour."
"Maharajji, how should I send it? I'm from far away."
"I know you are from far away. Go to Haldwani to this shop and they'll arrange it."
The man went to the shop and arranged that ten bags of flour be sent. The total cost was such that he had only enough for gas and expenses to get home. They later had a son.

ᵊ

A lawyer and his wife who had not had children came to Maharajji for help. He gave the man a guava and said to give it to the wife and they would have children. The man thought how his brother's five children seemed as though they were his own. What did he really need children for? So he put the guava on his puja table. A month later he gave the guava, still in perfect condition, to a friend who also had no children. The couple ate it, and now they have three children.

ᵊ

A man who had no children came to Maharajji, who said, "You build a well here at the temple and you will have children." So it happened. I met that man's son, who himself now has two sons. Maharajji had told the father, "You construct a well and your boat will keep floating," meaning that the family line would go on.

ᵊ

Once a chauffeur was driving Maharajji up to Nainital to visit some devotees. When he came to a steep hill the chauffeur debated with himself whether to push the car to excess, in order to make the hill. He didn't want to break the car, but because he had Maharajji in the front seat he decided to try it. When they arrived, Maharajji said, "You don't have any children."
"No, Maharajji."
"How long have you been married?"
"Nineteen years."
"Here, eat this apple. You'll have a child."

Ten months later his wife had a son. The chauffeur said, "For such a little thing, Maharajji would do a big thing."

BUT IT WAS NOT only for children that Maharajji bestowed his touch of grace. His touch healed, brought economic prosperity, and spiritual growth as well.

A very ill relative, a young boy who had been quite strong, had been committed to a hospital, and his situation deteriorated to the point where doctors gave up hope for saving his life. When Maharajji came to the hospital room he touched the boy on the head and remained with him for a short time. The hospital staff and patients assembled to have Maharajji's darshan, so Maharajji distributed prasad and left for Kainchi. The boy began to recover immediately. It was like a second birth for him.

The brother of J said, "We were doing kirtan and we expected J (who drank to excess) to come and quarrel with Maharajji. He came rushing toward Maharajji and from the first touch of Maharajji he was changed. He stopped drinking, and hasn't drunk since, and that was some years ago.

Mrs. P said, "I didn't want to go see any gurus, and so decided I'd just go and take pictures, but I arrived to find that the door wasn't open. Later someone told me just to walk up and down in front of the door and Maharajji would open it. Suddenly Maharajji opened the door and said, "Go away!"

I replied, "I'm not going."

"Oh, my goodness, you are a very stubborn woman. What do you want?"

I replied that I wanted a photo. He said all right, but I replied, "No, you have to come outside. It's too dark in the room."

Maharajji replied, "The photo will come out." I argued with him, and Maharajji again said, "You are very stubborn. Do you want to become a doctor?"

I said, "Even in my dreams I couldn't become a doctor, because I am such a second-rate student."

Then Maharajji touched me on the head and spoke some mantra. Shortly after, I was admitted to medical college where I got top distinctions.

A certain man was staying in the ashram whose wife had recently died and whose business ruined. Maharajji called for this distressed man and asked him

to play his flute. The man played "Raghupati Raghava Raja Ram," and
Maharajji sat still, with tears flowing from his eyes. Maharajji took the man
alone into a room, and when the man came out he was happy. He said that
Maharajji had touched his foot to his head. Maharajji told a devotee to give the
man some money and send him home. Maharajji's blessings have sustained the
man and his family ever since.

गगग

One day in 1968 Maharajji sent word that a group of nine of us would go
for a ride in the Land Rover. After one stop at an apple orchard, we went up
into the mountains to a rest house owned by the forestry service. The servants
there obviously were expecting us and were delighted at Maharajji's presence.
Maharajji went immediately into the building, which appeared to consist of one
large room, and Gurudatt Sharma went inside with him. We all sat out on the
lawn, then Gurudatt called me. I ran in and found Maharajji sitting on a tucket
and I knelt at his feet. Only the three of us were present. Maharajji looked
closely at me, then closed his eyes for a moment and said, "You make many
people laugh in America."
   I thought of my lecture style, which consisted of much humor, and I replied,
"Yes, I guess so."
   "You like to feed children."
   (H'm. That was a strange one.) I love to cook for people and I certainly
like children, so I said, "Yes, I guess so."
   Then he reached toward me and tapped me three times on the forehead.
   The next thing I recall is Gurudatt Sharma leading me by the arm out the
door and the brilliance of the light outside. A few minutes later we all piled
back into the Land Rover and returned to the temple.
   What was that all about? Was it an initiation? What had happened to me? I
recalled the story of Ramakrishna touching Vivekananda on the chest with his
foot and putting him into samadhi, until Vivekananda yelled, "But what about
my family?"—for they were dependent upon him. At that point Ramakrishna
removed his foot and Vivekananda returned to normal consciousness.
   Was this a similar event? Many months later, in a letter to me in America,
Hari Dass said, "That day you were in a very high state. When you came
outside, tears were streaming down your cheeks." I don't remember that at all.
   Over the years since then, I have asked many devotees about that incident
but have never received a clear answer. Some said it was a boon; others pointed
out that Maharajji was in the habit of masking important initiations so that
they looked like nothing had happened. Another devotee told me that the guru
could awaken the kundalini energy in a devotee with a touch. The matter is

still not clear. At the time it only seemed to increase my confusion—but that was Maharajji's way. (R.D.)

तीम

I had been teaching in America but felt that my impurities were contaminating my teaching, so when I came before Maharajji in 1971 I asked that he make me pure enough to serve him in sharing the dharma in the West. At the time he hit me on the head and said, "You will be." That seemed like a true boon and I accepted it as such. But some months later when I was still in India I continued to be aware of and often overwhelmed by my impurities. So again I asked Maharajji to make me pure. At that time he looked me over carefully and said, "I don't see any impurities."

Well and good for him to say that—after all, he saw God in everyone—but I wasn't satisfied. I wanted to feel pure. At any rate, I persisted in complaining. Then one day I was called into a back room, into which I had never been before, where Maharajji remained at night. Maharajji was on his tucket and S. L. Sah, who was a great Ramayana student and had become my deep friend and trusted teacher, was also present. Maharajji asked me what I wanted, and I said that I just wanted to be pure enough to serve him. Then he went under his blanket. There were strange movements under the blanket followed by some snoring. I felt deep peace, and curiosity as well. Then he came out from under the blanket and tapped me on the head and said, "You will be." Later, SL said that under the blanket Maharajji had been doing mudras (specific tantric body movements designed to bring about certain effects).

Shortly before that incident Maharajji was reported to have said to KK about me, "I'm going to do something for him." Perhaps this was another of those underplayed initiations. Nobody seemed to know; Maharajji didn't say; and I still felt impure.

On the last day I was with Maharajji, I said, "Maharajji, you promised me that I would be pure enough to do work in the West and I don't feel that I am."

Maharajji looked mildly interested in that observation, then handed me a mango which he had been holding and said, "Here, eat this."

I had often heard about Maharajji giving boons to people, sometimes by means of a piece of fruit. At the first opportunity I went into the latrine to eat the mango so that I wouldn't have to share it with anybody. I debated whether to hold on to the seed to get more mango boons, but finally I discarded that plan as being too "clever."

It is now six years since that day, and slowly, very slowly, the impurities are falling away. (R.D.)

तीम

Krishna Das (Roy Bonney)

Krishna Play

IT SEEMS AT ONCE surprising and obvious to note that Maharajji was quite different in the quality of his relationship with men and with women. With men he hung out and gossiped, scolded, and guided—as friend, father, and sage. With the women, on the other hand, in addition to those roles, he seemed frequently to assume roles like that of Krishna (one of the forms of God in the Hindu pantheon), as child and playmate and lover. Such play on Maharajji's part of course created some consternation and confusion among devotees and also grounds for criticism on the part of people who did not like or trust Maharajji. But for the women devotees who were directly involved with Maharajji in this way, his actions served as a catalyst to catapult them to God.

WITH WOMEN

Once, when Maharajji was entering a room, the Mothers decided to hide behind the door so he wouldn't see them. He said, "Where are they? How could they leave? How can they leave me? They cannot leave me. How can I go on? How can I bear to be without them?" He was trying to pull on a sock. Finally they had so much pity, they rushed out to him.

†पु

When Maharajji went to another plane of consciousness and came back, the Mothers would kid him like a daddy coming home from work: "What have you brought us, Maharajji?"

†पु

Several Mothers went to the temple for darshan, only to find Maharajji and a male devotee sitting behind a barbed-wire fence. Maharajji said to them, "Oh, you women say that Baba is nothing and only has his feet rubbed by women—but now you see you can't get behind the wire." The man was rubbing Maharajji's feet and began reciting a verse from the Ramayana. One Ma answered his song with another verse from the Ramayana. This pleased Maharajji and he asked them to come closer. Then the Ma said, "You have come as an incarnation in mortal form into the world for us!"

†पु

One man said, "My wife just wanted to sit and be with Maharajji. She didn't want to talk. She was too shy."

†पु

R's wife was very reluctant to speak of Maharajji and her feelings about him. But she had a loving look on her face, and with her eyes and small nods she responded to comments. When asked if Maharajji ever seemed like her own child, she looked especially warm, and she nodded, smiling.

†पु

We'd be sitting outside and Maharajji would pull my hands under the blanket and make me massage his legs, almost pulling me under the blanket. I loved touching him, but I was not sure how far you can go in touching Maharajji. I'd be working on his feet and calves, and he'd grab my arm and pull my hand up to his thigh. So I'd do his thighs for a little bit and then my hands would start wandering down to his calves again, because all of a sudden I'd look around and see all these people staring at me. An Indian woman would be gasping, and I'd get real embarrassed, so I'd start working on his feet again. Then his hand would come sliding down and grab mine and pull it up again.

He would often perform this puzzling ritual with me. And if I tried to explain it to myself, no sooner would I have the thought than he'd turn to me and yell "Nahin!" and then go on with his conversation.

राम

One Indian widow who had no children came to Maharajji, worried about who would take care of her. Maharajji said, "Ma, I'll be your child." She started to treat him like a child and then he said, "You know, Hariakhan Baba used to suck the breasts of women. I'll sit on your lap." And he sat on her lap and he was so light and small, just like a child. He sucked on her breasts and milk poured out of them, although she was sixty-five. Enough milk came from her to have filled a glass. After that she never missed not having children.

राम

I felt a great deal of fear of Maharajji and experienced a kind of awkwardness with him, wanting so much to do the right thing yet afraid that I wouldn't know what that was. He called me into his room in Kainchi one day. (Of course it always happened on the days when you really needed it.) He had me close the doors. He was up on the tucket, I was sitting on the floor, and he leaned down to hug me. I reached out to hug him back and he meant for me to come even closer. He said, "Come closer, come closer, you're not close enough." And he just lifted me off the ground, onto the tucket, and into his arms. He put his arms and his blanket all the way around me. He absolutely covered me with his blanket and with his being. He swallowed me whole! I melted—all my fears, all that stuff totally vanished into the sea of Maharajji. I was completely out of my body, totally immersed. So that's how he answered all those questions: Just by one hug!

I was kneeling before Maharajji when he grabbed at my sari and started pulling at it. Then he was holding my breasts and saying, "Ma, Ma." I felt for the first time as if I were experiencing an intimate act free of lust.

There are stories about gurus doing things with women. But somehow around Maharajji there was a feeling of such purity that people could tell me anything he had done, and it never shook my total trust in him at all. It was clear that he needed nothing; he had no desires of his own.

I believe that he would do things with women for whom the sexual part of their lives was not straight. In retrospect, it looks as though it served a very direct function for them.

We were singing in front of Maharajji and I was massaging his arm when suddenly a sexual thought with regard to him came to my mind. I was embarrassed, because he was looking into my eyes. So I immediately quit massaging his arm and started writing Ram in Hindi with my finger on my own arm, over and over again—still holding his gaze the while. At that point the thought faded. Maharajji reached over right then and pulled gently on the ring I was wearing at the time in my nose, turned my head sideways, and pointed out my nose-ring to an Indian nearby. "See," he said sweetly, "she's very good."

The first time he took me in the room alone I sat up on the tucket with him, and he was like a seventeen-year-old jock who was a little fast! I felt as if I were fifteen and innocent. He started making out with me, and it was so cute, so pure. I was swept into it for a few moments—then grew alarmed: "Wait! This is my guru. One doesn't do this with one's guru!" So I pulled away from him. Then Maharajji tilted his head sideways and wrinkled up his eyebrows in a tender, endearing, quizzical look. He didn't say anything, but his whole being was saying to me, "Don't you like me?"

But as soon as I walked out of that particular darshan, I started getting so sick that by the end of the day I felt I had vomited and shit out everything that was ever inside me. I had to be carried out of the ashram. On the way, we stopped by Maharajji's room so I could pranam to him. I kneeled by the tucket and put my head down by his feet—and he kicked me in the head, saying, "Get her out of here!"

I was unable to move for the next three days, but after that I felt perfectly well again. And I had worked through a lot of my reactions to that darshan: revulsion, confusion, and so forth.

That was the first time, and I was to be there for two years. During my last month there, I was alone with him every day in the room. There was a progression of comprehension. He seemed in one way to be turning me into a Mother, helping me to understand that sex is okay. Sometimes he would just touch me on the breasts and between my legs, saying, "This is mine, this is mine, this is mine. All is mine. You are mine." You can interpret it as you want, but near the end in these darshans, it was as though he were my child. Sometimes I felt as though I were suckling a tiny baby. Although he didn't change size physically, he seemed to become very small in my arms. It was a beautiful transformation.

त्रम्

Maharajji had called me into the small room in the Kainchi ashram and asked me to sit on the tucket with him. He then began calling me "Ma, Ma," and said to me, half in English, half in Hindi, "Meri Mother, meri Mother." As he did so, it seemed as if his body had shrunk to the size of a baby's in diapers before my very eyes. I held him in my arms and rocked him like a baby.

त्रम्

I was sitting on the floor looking at Maharajji and he was on his tucket looking back at me, when he started talking to me in a way that I could understand totally everything he was saying. Then he pounded on the tucket, because he wanted me to sit up there with him. And I was trying to figure out where to sit. How were you supposed to sit on the tucket with him? He pounded on the tucket closer to him, and so I moved over a little bit and then I decided, well, go for broke, and I sat right in front of him, cross-legged. I was understanding everything he was saying, but as soon as my mind would start working, naturally I wouldn't understand anything.

Then he kissed the palms of my hands, grabbed me, and pulled me toward him, hugging me. The famous hug. Then it was as if I were looking through his eyes. I could see everything in the room, including everything behind me. I seemed to be sitting inside him, totally immersed inside him. I don't know how long we were in there.

जय

Maharajji was the only being I've ever met who would seem to do anything to get you free. It wasn't as if he had an image to maintain; his teaching was beyond any form or structure. Every other teacher is either a Hindu or a Buddhist or something else, but Maharajji wasn't like that.

जय

Just before Maharajji left his body an old woman came to the temple with her children and grandchildren. She put her hand on Maharajji's head and gave him a blessing of very long life. She did it twice in Sanskrit: "May you be blessed with many years of long life."

Maharajji was crying. "Did you hear what she said, did you hear what she said?" His delight was that of a child.

WITH MEN

MAHARAJJI OFTEN SPOKE to the male devotees about women. Through many conflicting statements he seemed to be spelling out a most subtle teaching.

*One of the cosmic questions he asked me, totally out of the blue, was,
"What is a woman?"*

> CHRIST AND HANUMAN SAW ALL
> WOMEN AS THE MOTHER. YOU
> HAVE TO UNDERSTAND THE MOTHER
> TO REALIZE GOD.

*About a school for girls being built, Maharajji commented, "Educate the
girls and they will educate society."*

ON THE one hand, he said:

SEE ALL WOMEN AS MOTHERS,
SERVE THEM AS YOUR MOTHER.
WHEN YOU SEE THE ENTIRE
WORLD AS THE MOTHER, THE
EGO FALLS AWAY.

> A PURE WOMAN IS BETTER THAN
> A HUNDRED YOGIS. WOMEN ARE
> MORE OPEN TO LOVE GOD.

IT IS NECESSARY TO BE
BRAHMACHARYA [CELIBATE], BUT THAT
CAN BE LIVING WITH ONE WOMAN.
A PURE WOMAN SATI [WIFE] CAN
TAKE YOU TO GOD IN A MOMENT.

WHILE, ON the other hand, he also said:

> WOMEN AND GOLD ARE STUMBLING
> BLOCKS ON THE PATH TO GOD.

A WOMAN IS A SNAKE; YOU
SHOULDN'T EVEN TOUCH HER.

Perhaps it was a matter of, "If the shoe fits . . ."

Once a devotee expressed his feeling that it was embarrassing to have such attractive women around, and Maharajji replied, "Your vision should be faultless."

श्री

A devotee was embarrassed when Maharajji came to his room at the university and discovered a pin-up calendar on the wall. Maharajji asked who she was, and the devotee said no one, going to turn the picture to the wall. But Maharajji stopped him, saying, "She's a Ma. Don't dishonor her."

श्री

I had almost no sexual thoughts the whole time I was in India. It wasn't being suppressed; it just wasn't pertinent at that time. When we'd go back to the hotel, I wouldn't spend much time with other people. I didn't notice women as women at all, though perhaps some of the men did.

I don't remember Maharajji doing the kind of teachings with men as he did with the women. I don't remember any direct sexual teachings. He would talk about women and gold a lot; about how lust was poison, and how one of the greatest poisons for yogis was lust.

When I was in the middle of an affair with a man I was traveling with, Maharajji put a quick stop to it. The first time we saw him after the affair, Maharajji told us to be brahmacharya.

श्री

Usually since I spoke Hindi we would just rap together about this or that—sort of "man to man." And often he'd let me take photographs. Sometimes, though, he'd just reach down and pull me up into him, into the Cosmic Hug.

One morning after I had been physically intimate with another devotee, we were with Maharajji. Not expecting to be with Maharajji so soon, I felt much guilt in the close juxtaposition of the two events. Maharajji pointed to this other person and said to me, "To that one you are giving your best teachings." Then he told us to be brahmacharya and he turned to other topics. I was left guessing. (R.D.)

At all the temples, women and men slept separately unless they were married. One night Maharajji sent one married couple and a single man and woman to stay at a two-room forestry guest house we sometimes used. I assumed that the Westerners would appreciate the temple policy, the women sharing one room and the men another. (At that time I was feeling responsible for the Westerners' behavior.) The next morning I found out that a man and woman had slept in each room. I was angry with them and told them that they were insensitive to this culture. We were all immediately called to Maharajji, who asked how everyone had slept, and, turning to the people who had stayed at the guest house, he asked them who had slept in what room. They told him and he simply said, "Very good."

Maharajji repeated a number of times, "Ram Dass should not touch women. Women are like a snake for Ram Dass." Apparently he was well aware that I, for one, could not see all women as the Divine Mother; in fact, my own fear of women had led me to seek out relationships with men. His warning didn't help in this matter.

But his strongest injunction, which he repeated over and over again, with much finger-pointing, was, "Ram Dass, kanchankamini [gold and women]." Each time Maharajji would say this phrase—often used in the literature and by other saints such as Ramakrishna to warn people about the pitfalls of attachment to sex and money—I would review the ways in which I was still clinging to those desires. And though the desires were deep, deep within me, it was apparent that they were on a collision course with the desire for enlightenment and that sooner or later they were bound to lose. But I guess I was (am?) like the abbot of a monastery who prayed, "God, let me be free of desires so I can be like the desert fathers—but not just yet." I wanted to play with the sex and money just a bit more.

But Maharajji wouldn't relent. Often I would be called from the back of the temple compound many times a day. Each time I would kneel before Maharajji and he would look pointedly at me and intone "kanchankamini," and then send me back. It almost sounded as if he were warning me about something specific, but at that time I interpreted it as a general admonition to get on with it. I tried a variety of ways to free myself from the bonds of lust. I offered the lust into the fire in various rituals and asked God through a variety of religious metaphors to take this attachment from me. But apparently I was not ready to be free, for the attachment to these desires remained.

In 1974 I met a woman spiritual teacher who explained to me that she was sent by Maharajji (astrally) to help me with my inner work. The major part of our work together turned into sexual tantric practices. It proved very helpful in loosening the bonds of attachment to desire with which I had been struggling.

In the course of our work together she seemed to have a difficult time staying in her body. Her consciousness kept floating away. Because it had been suggested that the precious metal gold would help to "keep her down," I decided to buy her a bracelet and ring of gold. It was in the jewelry store that I recalled Maharajji's repeated admonition to me about "women and gold." Shortly afterward I felt that much of my fear of women had been dissipated through this relationship, allowing my attachment to lust to be loosened so that I would get on with my spiritual journey, and I left those teachings. It felt like Maharajji's grace had brought me to this woman, and it was through his grace that I left her. (R.D.)

॥॥

Maharajji once visited us while a sculptor was staying in our house. All over the living room were huge sculptures and paintings of nudes. I was a bit concerned that Maharajji might not like them and wanted him to go straight into the bedroom, but he sat on the sofa, looked around, and admired everything. He said, "How wonderful! These are good." He began to talk like a connoisseur, putting me at such ease that I forgot all about the nudity. He appreciated, admired, and asked questions about the art pieces. "Where does the

*wood come from? How do you do it? At what time do you do it," and so on.
Maharajji could fit into any situation.*

SEXUAL ENERGY IS THE POWER
TO CREATE GOD. IF YOU RAISE
THE ENERGY THEN YOU CAN FEEL
AND MEET BRAHM.

Take It to Delhi

THE EVER-SO-subtle relationship between the guru and the devotee is much dependent upon faith. The deeper the faith and trust the devotee has in the guru, the more readily are spiritual qualities awakened in the devotee through the guru.

In the spiritual literature, the true surrender is spoken of as the surrender that is no surrender. That is, one opens—through faith and trust—to a method such as a guru only when such faith resonates with truth at the depths of one's being. Then there is a readiness for such opening. If one is still rooted only in intellect or emotion, any act of surrender is but

another act of ego and can, based on misjudgment, lead to horrendous consequences. So one cannot *choose* to surrender to the guru. But when the devotee and the guru have met at the depths of being, then such surrender is not actually surrender to another person but, rather, surrender to one's own God-nature.

There is a story concerning surrender told by Maharajji's devotees about another saint, Sombari Maharaj, very highly regarded by Maharajji, who had lived at an earlier time.

It seems that he gave one of his devotees two potatoes and instructed

301

him to eat both of them. The instructions were very firm. The man
went down near the stream and began eating one of the potatoes.
Shortly thereafter a very poor old man came along and begged for the
other potato, saying, "You have food and I have none." The devotee
could not refuse and so he gave the second potato away. When he returned, Sombari Maharaj abused him roundly for not doing what he had
been told. The harangue ended in, "So it was not your *bhagya* [more
than luck, perhaps destiny] to take the second potato." Later the man
became very successful in the world but not successful in his final spiritual efforts in life—for that was the *second* potato.

Such a story, which seems to pit charity against surrender to the guru,
is a hard teaching indeed. However, we must learn finally to surrender
self-conscious charity in order to become charity itself.

Some of the stories concerning the total faith and resulting surrender
of the Indian devotees around Maharajji are awesome indeed, and some
of their failures of faith are equally awesome. Maharajji didn't make it
any easier for any of us devotees, because he continually sowed seeds of
doubt about himself to undercut any flickering faith we might be devel-
oping. Still, we watched as our doubts became consumed into an ever-
deepening trust. He seemed to be leading us to the realization, once
expressed by Ramana Maharshi, that "God, Guru, and Self are One."
Thus we found that trust and opening to Maharajji led us only to a
deeper part of our own beings and a deeper faith in ourselves.

MAHARAJJI SOWS SEEDS OF DOUBT

*I recall once bringing to Maharajji a new Westerner, someone I liked and
whom I wanted to be impressed by Maharajji—that is, I wanted Maharajji to
do his "tricks." Maharajji looked at him and said, "You come from Canada?"*

"No, Maharajji. I come from the United States."

*Maharajji nodded as if he had now placed him and said, "You have three
sisters."*

"No, Maharajji, I'm an only child."

*By this time I was getting very uncomfortable. But Maharajji kept it up,
questioning him incorrectly about his journey and his work and then dismissing
us. The fellow looked at me as he left, and said, with slight pity, "I'm sure
your guru is very nice." He never returned. (R.D.)*

जय

We were in Delhi in the fall of *1972* at the home of the inspector general of forestry in India, a long-time devotee of Maharajji. Many people were coming and going, among them a woman with a slightly haughty air. When she arrived she pranammed to Maharajji and then said, "You remember me—we met at so-and-so's house."
MAHARAJJI: "Eh [What]?" looking confused.
WOMAN: "Oh, Maharajji, you said this and that. You must remember."
MAHARAJJI: "Kya [What]?"
The woman was miffed because she had come with important friends and was clearly trying to impress them. Finally she and her party left. Maharajji sat up immediately and told us about the woman's father, grandfather, marital situation, and biography.

जय

Maharajji said to a nineteen-year-old boy who had come with his family, "You failed, you failed."
"No, Maharajji! I didn't fail! I got a second."
"You failed. Do you think a second is any good?"
Then Maharajji added, "No, you didn't fail, you got a first, but you don't deserve it. You are failing because you are arguing too much with your father and mother instead of studying, and you don't deserve it but you got a first. But from now on, you must study."
Maharajji was very fierce. Mrs. Soni, whose friends these were, was very embarrassed because she knew the results had already been published in the newspaper and that the boy had received a second and that these were final results. The embarrassment of your guru making a mistake (seemingly) is torture. The family all thought that Maharajji was a nice man, but the boy himself was condescending about him. Mr. Soni sent a driver to take the boy and his parents home, and when the driver returned he had a note saying that the impossible had happened: Four exam papers had been recalled and the boy's paper had been regraded—he had received a first.

जय

Maharajji once said to me, "A very high woman who loves you much is coming to India." I thought about that and became more and more confused, for the only high woman I knew who loved me was Caroline, the woman with whom I'd been living prior to coming to India, and she certainly was not planning such a trip. There was nobody else. What could this mean? Was Maharajji fallible? Had he simply made a mistake? It was not until 1970 that the matter was cleared up, when Caroline admitted that she had in fact traveled to India while I was there in 1968 but had visited temples to study architecture and hadn't wanted to bother me. (R.D.)

राम

On my second visit to India in 1971 I had met Maharajji at Allahabad. After a few days he sent us on to Delhi. As we were leaving, Maharajji said to me very quietly, "I'll meet you in Vrindaban." He didn't specify when, and I didn't ask. After all, if he said he'd see me in Vrindaban, then he'd see me in Vrindaban.

We spent about a week in Delhi and then decided to go on a pilgrimage of Shiva temples in the south. This trip would take us through Vrindaban, where we could see Maharajji and get his blessings.

We left Delhi and stayed the night in Mathura, preparatory to seeing Maharajji in Vrindaban the next day. With much fruit and many flowers we arrived at the temple in the early morning. The pujari explained that Maharajji wasn't there and it was not known when he would arrive. Even knowing of Maharajji's notorious reputation for unpredictability, I was disappointed, for he had said, "I'll meet you in Vrindaban." And I knew that by the time we returned from the south sometime in April, Maharajji would, in all likelihood, be up in the mountains, since the plains in which Vrindaban was located would already be turning unpleasantly hot. What could he have meant?

At the temple that morning I was sitting listening to some old women carrying on the continuous chant of "Hare Krishna, Hare Rama" that was heard there from early morning until late evening. A small bird flew overhead and dropped a piece of straw, which landed on my lap. Perhaps that was Maharajji and he was giving me a gift. Or perhaps I was once again just grasping at straws.

After offering the fruit and flowers before the murti of Hanuman, we went on our way, and at the end of the pilgrimage we proceeded north. On the journey a great dialogue took place as to the route we should follow: If we were to go to the mountains to Nainital there was a direct route; but to go via Vrindaban was more circuitous, requiring an extra day. We were now well into April, and most likely Maharajji would be in the hills. But then, he had said he would see me in Vrindaban, and I could still taste that disappointment when we didn't find him there on the way south. I was in favor of going directly to the mountains, but I was outvoted and we went on toward Vrindaban.

Again we spent the night at Mathura and the next morning brought fruit and flowers, though this time in slighty less abundance, because our expectations of finding him were weak indeed. We dallied in the marketplace to enjoy freshly squeezed fruit juices and finally, at about eight-thirty, headed for the temple. When we arrived it seemed ominously deserted. We parked before the main gate and went in. The pujari met us. After we pranammed to him we asked if Maharajji was here.

"Oh, no," he answered, "Maharajji hasn't been here for weeks. He's probably up in the mountains now. He's not here." Our collective heart sank, but we offered the fruit and flowers to Hanuman, and after no more than five minutes in the temple we hastened back to the car, thinking that if we drove without stopping we could be in Nainital by evening. Just as we were closing the car doors, a small Fiat sedan raced down the road and stopped next to us. The driver looked vaguely familiar, and next to him sat Maharajji, who got out of the car and walked into the temple without taking any notice of us.

We rushed over to the car to find Gurudatt Sharma, Maharajji's frequent traveling companion, sitting in the back. Sharma-ji is usually friendly but quite tight-lipped about Maharajji's business, but we did manage to extract from him that they had been in a distant city the previous evening. At 2:00 in the morning, Maharajji had awakened him and the driver and said, "Come on. We must hurry. We have to be in Vrindaban." They had driven all night and arrived in Agra at about 7:00 A.M. Then Maharajji said, "We still have some time. We can visit so-and-so." And after a short visit, again Maharajji rushed them on to Vrindaban. After all, he said he'd see me in Vrindaban. (R.D.)

THE FAITH OF THE DEVOTEES

I don't go to other saints, since I have got Maharajji. I don't need anyone.

ॐ

If you remember Maharajji, nothing bad can happen to you. If you forget him, you may have fear.

ૐ

Maharajji was in a car and they came to a bridge. Coming the other way were these oxen pulling carts of sugar cane, completely blocking the bridge. The driver slowed up, but Maharajji said, "Why are you slowing up?"

The driver replied, "Well Maharajji, I can't go through."

Maharajji told him, "Go!" The driver protested, and Maharajji replied, "Close your eyes and go!" So the driver closed his eyes and pushed on the gas, and when he opened his eyes there they were, on the other side.

ૐ

Whoever came near him, he graced. If you had pure faith, he'd do whatever you needed.

ૐ

It was he who forced the faith upon me, not me who gathered it.

ૐ

Shiv Singh was to go home from Kainchi one afternoon, but Maharajji said not to go. The next day he again told him not to go, and again the third day. "Dada, what should I do?" asked Shiv Singh. "I have a contract outstanding for an apple orchard. It's very competitive. There is one lakh of rupees involved. If I do not go, I won't get the orchard." For five or six days Maharajji kept him in Kainchi. Shiv Singh again spoke to Dada: "Now the contract is lost," but he did not have the courage to tell this to Maharajji.

Maharajji finally chastised him: "You have left home for so many days. You must go and do some work." Maharajji made Shiv Singh feel guilty for loitering. He left and four days later he returned, happy. In the interim, there had been a hailstorm: Some damages had brought the price of the orchard down to half the original price, and Shiv Singh had bought it.

॥ॐ॥

If you have any needs, don't ask man for help; ask directly to Maharajji. Maharajji will do everything.

IF YOU HAVE ENOUGH FAITH, YOU CAN GIVE UP MONEY AND POSSESSIONS.

On a train she took to come for a visit my sister-in-law spoke of Maharajji to the women sitting near her. One south Indian woman got very excited and insisted on coming home with her to meet him. She was a very mysterious, high-society lady. She behaved as though she were one of our family and would even go into my wife's room and take her good saris to give away to other women. The woman stayed with us some seven days, but still Maharajji had not come, so she went to Kainchi. When Maharajji finally came to our house, she was with him. The Nainital devotees and also the Lucknow ones where she had visited all complained how she had moved in on them and given away their valuables. Maharajji asked why I had allowed her to stay at my house. I said that Maharajji had sent her. Whoever Maharajji sends is welcome in my home—I cannot turn away Maharajji's guests. Maharajji denied sending her. I countered, "How could she have come without your knowledge?" (How could she? Maharajji knows everything, it is his house. Of course he had sent her!)

This Maharajji did not deny but countered instead with, "But she gave away your valuable things!"

I replied, "They could not have been so valuable, so necessary, if we no longer have them. They must have been useless things, or we would still have them—is that not true?" Maharajji remained silent. What could he say? The other devotees were surprised that Maharajji acknowledged that he is aware of and responsible for all such things.

॥ॐ॥

Once there was a departmental exam in my office. I was forty-three years old and felt that I was too old to try, because I didn't want to fail in front of my family. The first paper I did half-heartedly and spoiled it. Maharajji was not here. When I returned from the examination, Siddhi Ma was standing on the porch of Dada's house, and I knew Maharajji had come. I went in to see him and put pen and pencil at his feet. Maharajji said, "Are you appearing for the examination?"

"Yes."

"You'll pass." Before the second exam, Hubba and Maharajji were on the roof. I told them I was appearing in a second exam. I was weeping. "Why are you weeping?" Maharajji asked.

"I am afraid of failing."

Maharajji sat us down and said, "You'll pass."

Then Hubba said, "Go. Have faith."

But in the exam there were five questions and I spoiled four-and-a-half. After the third paper I saw Maharajji. He asked me how well I had done. "Immensely good," I lied. I thought, "How is it possible that I can lie to him?" Three months later the results came down and I had gotten through.

ॐ

A man had an abscess on his eye that even surgery couldn't cure, but he later told Maharajji, "When I read the Chandipath (a book of mantras about the Mother), the eye healed on its own."

Maharajji acted with disbelief, saying to the Mothers and everybody, "Do you believe that he just read the Chandipath and the abscess healed? Do you believe that? Is that possible? Could that have happened? Ma, what do you think?"

ॐ

Again and again over the years, Maharajji has taught me to have faith that he will guide me through my own heart. I need only listen to that higher intuitive sense. That's when I feel him the most. Here is an example of how he taught me this:

Among the sadhus in Vrindaban was a handsome young sadhu who spoke some English and who had befriended many of Maharajji's Western devotees. He would take them on pilgrimages around the town, showing them out-of-the-way temples and special holy places. In the evenings the Westerners sometimes joined him for chanting. I was invited time and again, but I felt no desire to participate; being near Maharajji each day was enough for me. The rest of the time I was content to wander about and think of him and what had transpired during the visit that day.

But this young sadhu kept sending messages inviting me to the gatherings, which I kept declining. One evening a Westerner arrived bringing a leaf plate full of food that the sadhu had sent to me. This attention made me uncomfortable. I felt distrustful of his motives, and simultaneously I felt distrustful of my own motives in distrusting him. Perhaps I was inwardly competitive with him.

Soon afterward we were all told to go to Allahabad, a city some two hundred miles distant. There we were housed in a devotee's home and each day we visited Maharajji, who was staying at Dada's home about a mile away. On one occasion three of us arrived at Dada's home in a rickshaw. The house was surrounded by a fence with a gate and outside the fence was a single tree. As we drove up, sitting under the tree was the young sadhu from Vrindaban. The two Westerners who were fond of him jumped off the rickshaw, ran up, and pranammed to him. After I had paid the rickshaw, I came up to the gate. At this moment the sadhu rose and we bowed to one another. I couldn't understand why he was sitting outside the gate. If he had come to see Maharajji why wasn't he inside with the many others? Perhaps he was of a sect that could not enter a home. Or perhaps he needed to be invited in. Now that he had stood, was I supposed to invite him in? I couldn't very well ignore him, go in, and leave him there. And yet something in my heart—that same discomfort I had had about him back in Vrindaban—held me back from inviting him. My distrust of his purity made it impossible for me to bring him to Maharajji.

We stood there facing each other and I was transfixed by indecision. Then suddenly an Indian man emerged from the house and with much honor and delight welcomed the sadhu and took him inside. Immediately I concluded that this sadhu was indeed pure and that my reticence was my own impurity, and so I skulked into the house and sat in the front room, half-heartedly singing with the others. The sadhu was nowhere to be seen. Shortly afterward I saw him among the singers and then I didn't see him anymore. My own heart was heavy with guilt for allowing my own competitiveness or whatever it was to parade through me as an intuitive reflection about another's impurity.

Then I was called back to the kitchen area, where Maharajji sat surrounded by Indian devotees. I fell at his feet and he hit me on the head and said to the Indians, "Ram Dass speaks well, he's a good lecturer, but he doesn't understand people." These words were translated and I realized that Maharajji was not going to let the scene that had taken place outside pass unnoticed. I could only agree with him and wallow more and more in my guilt and feelings of impurity. Again and again Maharajji repeated the same statement, that though I could speak well I was no judge of other people. Everyone agreed and looked at me with loving pity. I agreed again and again, most wholeheartedly. Finally, when Maharajji had milked the moment for all it was worth, he said, "Yes, he does not understand people. He would have brought that sadhu inside. And that man is not pure—he wants things of his devotees." And with that he gave me a fierce hit on the head and laughed delightedly. My head spun, and through the clouds of guilt, self-doubt, and self-pity, suddenly came the brilliant sun of comprehension. Maharajji was, in his inimitable way, telling me that this time I had been right. He was teaching me to trust my heart. (R.D.)

THE SURRENDER OF THE DEVOTEES

Maharajji used to quote from the Ramayana, where Ram says to a devotee "Friend, why are you worried? Surrender by my power all thoughts to me, and all your priorities will determine themselves." He quoted this the day he left Nainital for the last time.

ॐ

An important man came to see Maharajji but kept checking his watch because he had a meeting with a minister of finance. Maharajji kept delaying him and the man grew more and more nervous. Finally, when he would undoubtedly be late, Maharajji let him go, and the man rushed to the place only to find that his meeting had been postponed.

ॐ

Usually when Maharajji stayed at my house for seven or eight days, other devotees would also be there, but this night there were none present. It was midnight, and I was tired, but Maharajji still wanted to talk so I was pressing his feet. Then he started to snore. I thought he was asleep and I decided to go to my bed. I quietly started to get up, when out of his snoring he said, "Suraj, where are you going?" So I sat down again. Again and again, the same thing happened. Finally, I determined not to go to sleep but to stay all night. At that moment, Maharajji said, "Suraj, go and sleep."

राम

I was once in the state of mind that I was going to do whatever Maharajji said, as a sadhana. Instant obedience to his word! At the time I was living up the hill behind Kainchi. Since it was twenty minutes straight up to a small village there, I always had to leave darshan early so I could get up before dark when the snakes come out. Once we were all sitting around Maharajji, in a wonderful, loving darshan. The bus had not yet come. And Maharajji turned to me and told me, "Jao." Here I was in strict obedience, yet it was still light; all the others were still there, and he was telling me to go immediately up the mountain. I was very slow to leave that afternoon, and he was watching my struggles with twinkling amusement.

राम

At Dada's house Maharajji was telling us all to go to different places. Sitting in front of me was Vishwambar, with whom I'd been spending a great deal of traveling time, even prior to coming to India. Maharajji told Vishwambar to go to Benares. I didn't want to go there because I wanted to spend some time alone. But when I came up, Maharajji said, "Go to Benares."
    I said, "Couldn't I please go to Ayodhya?"
    He said, "No, go to Benares." I was so foolish that I thought I could still go to Ayodhya, even though he specifically told me not to. I went to the train station and got a ticket on the Faizabad Express, which goes to Ayodhya. I rationalized that since it is kind of a triangle, I could go to Benares by way of Ayodhya. I got the ticket for the train that was to come in on track 10 at 3:00 P.M. I went to track 10 in plenty of time, but when, by 4:00 P.M., no train had come, I decided to question somebody. The conductor said that the

Faizabad Express had come in on track 8 today; it had been announced in Hindi, which I don't speak. So I'd missed the train.

Just as I was standing there wondering what to do next, a train pulled in behind me. I turned around to look at it and saw, on the side of the cars, "Benares Express." So I went to Benares. Now Benares is a pretty big place, with lots of hotels, but I went to a cheap one recommended by a friend and checked in, and as I sat in my room, I heard someone singing the Chalisa (hymn to Hanuman). It turned out to be Vishwambar. So I surrendered to that, and we spent a week together, during which we were very close.

जय

We were in Delhi at a party held at the home of the Sonis, who were old devotees of Maharajji. Mr. Soni was the head of the forestry department of India, and the party had not only devotees but people from the government and family members as well. It was an old-style cocktail party, and Mrs. Soni was passing a tray of canapes. As she came up to me, she said, "I had a dream the other night and I woke up from it and knew that Maharajji wanted me to tell you something."

"Yes?"

And then looking at me with her dark beautiful eyes, and speaking in a manner and tone that was completely out of context of the cocktail party, she said, with the deepest intensity, "You know, Maharajji demands complete surrender." A moment later, as if waking from a dream, she sweetly asked, "Won't you have one of those canapes? They are especially good." And she moved away. (R.D.)

जय

We were up in the mountains visiting with Maharajji at Kainchi. The eight-year-old VW bus was doing yeoman's service each day, moving the Western devotees from Nainital down the mountain to Kainchi each morning and back up each evening. Soon there were too many for the VW and some had to go by public bus, but still twenty or so managed to squeeze in the VW or on the rack on top, and, as VWs do, it smiled gamely and did its thing. But one day, just at the town of Bhowali, the VW stopped. It wouldn't start again. So we left it there and the next day told Maharajji. And he said,

"Take it to Delhi." All the way to Delhi, a hundred and ninety miles away? That seemed absurd to me. Couldn't someone local fix it? All he would say was, "Take it to Delhi."

That evening back in Nainital I spoke to the Sah family who owned the hotel. They knew of a mechanic, and I arranged for him to go and see the car. A day later he looked at it but could not start it. So again I told Maharajji and again he reiterated, "Take it to Delhi." Then I told him that in Almora, thirty miles away, was a German economic project and they used VWs and had a service man. Maybe I could get him to come over. Maharajji said, "Take it to Delhi."

I wrote to people in Almora asking them to contact the German repair center, and after letters back and forth that took the better part of two weeks, it became clear that no incentive would get the mechanic to come to Bhowali and that they weren't even interested in looking at it if I got it to Almora. I told Maharajji all this, and you can imagine his response: "Take it to Delhi."

So again I went back to the mechanic in Nainital and again he went to look. This time he got it running and drove it up to Nainital, but on the outskirts of town it stopped and he could not get it going again. Enthusiastically, I reported this progress to Maharajji, but his instructions had not changed.

It was now more than four weeks since the breakdown and it became evident that the Nainital mechanic just couldn't fix the car. Since there was nothing else to do, it was decided to "take it to Delhi." A truck was rented, complete with Sikh drivers, and the car was loaded aboard. With Krishna Das as passenger, they left for Delhi. Krishna Das told hair-raising tales of the journey—of the drinking and of moving the VW from one truck to another, and so forth—but finally it got to the repair man at Delhi. The VW was rolled off the truck and the repair man walked over, opened the engine compartment, took one look, connected one wire, and the car started and ran perfectly.

After that the term that came to be synonymous with my lack of surrender was, "Take it to Delhi." (R.D.)

THE KARM-UPPANCE OF NOT SURRENDERING

JUST AS ONE tells a child not to do something even when the consequences of the act are all too obvious, so Maharajji would warn or in-

struct people about this or that. But as the child insists on doing the act and one watches the inevitable effects that follow the cause, so Maharajji's devotees would often ignore his words and Maharajji would watch . . . and allow. Now and then he would say, "I told you so."

Once Maharajji upbraided a man who had just come to visit a friend at the temple, telling him to take food in his truck and go home immediately. The man's feelings were hurt because he thought Maharajji was insulting him. It was late at night so he slept in his truck outside the temple. When he got home, he found that his house had been robbed during the night.

जय

When Maharajji and a party of devotees were staying in the holy town of Chitrakut for a month, he took them one day to the hut of a sadhu who lived on minute quantities of a rare jungle root. He never ate food. Maharajji asked the sadhu for a piece of the root, and the sadhu offered a tiny piece. Maharajji shouted, "Don't be so stingy. Give more. I know you've got more." The sadhu gave two large pieces of the precious root. Maharajji broke these into many small pieces and gave a little piece to each devotee except one, whom he told that the root would do him great harm. The devotee pleaded for just a tiny piece of what was now Maharajji's prasad, so Maharajji relented and gave him a piece.

That same evening, Maharajji and his devotees sang kirtan—"Sri Ram Jai Ram, Jai Jai Ram." Maharajji sang the loudest. The devotee who had been warned not to eat the root became violently ill, left the party, and went to his room. After a short time, Maharajji came to the devotee's room, pulled him to his feet, and brought him back to the kirtan. He again felt sick and returned to his room. Maharajji again came and brought him back. The kirtan went on until the early hours of the morning. By this time, most of the devotees had fallen asleep, but Maharajji continued to sing. Finally Maharajji allowed the sick devotee to return to his room and fall asleep. When he awoke, he found Maharajji sitting beside the bed. "Are you all right now? I told you not to eat the root. When I was sick, you slept all night; when you were sick, I stayed up all night praying."

जय

Late one night at the Kumbha Mela in Allahabad, Maharajji was in his tent giving darshan. The next day was the most auspicious time of the decade to bathe in the Sangam. Maharajji's devotee, a police official, was placed in charge of security and crowd-control for the millions of people. This night he was with Maharajji, when suddenly Maharajji got up and said, "Let's go." Late at night they drove Maharajji to the train station, where they waited for a west-bound train to come. The policeman and others tried to persuade Maharajji to stay for the auspicious day. Maharajji said he wouldn't and told them to be very careful the next day, for there was going to be a catastrophe.

Maharajji left and the people returned, having taken his words lightly. That morning at 4:00 A.M. at the Sangam, thousands of people were thronging to bathe at the special moment. A parade of naga babas (naked sadhus) was going in when the masses of people in the back started surging forward and the people in front were blocked by the parade barriers. Many were killed and hurt in the stampede.

ऊँ

Once in Lucknow, Maharajji suggested that several devotees accompany him to visit someone who lived in another part of the city. Maharajji suggested that they walk, and immediately they set off; but at the first corner the devotees sighted a horse and carriage and suggested that they ride. Maharajji refused, saying, "I won't sit on it." The devotees insisted, arguing that there was no other conveyance available and that their destination was far away. Maharajji relented and sat on the seat facing the back; the driver and the two devotees sat in the front.

The moment the horse was prodded to start, it jumped up on its hind legs, lifting the front of the carriage. Since Maharajji was in the back he easily stepped off onto the road. The horse continued to rear and kick, nearly turning the carriage over and terrorizing the passengers in the front seat. Maharajji said to them, "I told you that we shouldn't sit on this tonga. You wanted to get on. Now do you want to get off?"

ऊँ

I had the good fortune to encounter Maharajji at Ganj in June 1963. When he inquired about me, I told him that I was coming from Rishikesh and was on my way to Vrindaban. Then he said, "Your Gurudev [guru] is sporting verily like the Lord of Vrindaban himself. But he will be stopping all that soon. You take your guru to be the Lord himself, don't you? Go back now." And he arranged money for my journey, but I didn't quite understand. Only after several days did I learn about the illness of my holy master from an English daily. Immediately I rushed back to Rishikesh, and within a fortnight of my arrival, Gurudev attained mahasamadhi *(died). I later had occasion to meet Maharajji, and he asked me whether I had gotten back to the ashram in time. And I gratefully said yes.*

तुम

HR, *who had developed cataracts on his eyes, went to see Ananda Mayee Ma, who told him that he should go to Aligarh to have them operated on. But when he saw Maharajji in Lucknow, he was told to go to Sitapur and have the operation there. HR followed Ma's instructions, had the operation, and lost his sight in both eyes. Afterward he would still come to visit Maharajji, who would say, "Why did you go to Aligarh when I told you to go to Sitapur?"*

तुम

At the time of my wedding, I came to Maharajji and he asked me how I would proceed there. I told him by bus, but he countered, "No, take the train." I was stubborn, for there was a wedding party and all the plans had been made, so I refused. Then Maharajji asked me for the bus route. He requested that I change the route and stay overnight and tell him exactly the time I would leave in the morning. I did as he said in following these plans, but still I went by bus. During the bus trip, the bus rolled over twice, and though there were loose metal trunks rolling around inside, no one was hurt. We all had to climb out the driver's window. When we returned, Maharajji sent a jeep and welcomed us.

तुम

One devotee said, "If you are in the presence of a saint, it is very difficult. If you disobey him, there is definite suffering."

तिप

I recall one day being with Maharajji when he was told that someone had used his name to raise money for a school that was not a pure venture, soliciting the money without Maharajji's permission. His reaction was vividly burned into my consciousness and has given rise many times since to images or nightmares. He said, "I shan't do anything to him. But for what he has done he will whirl around the universe for aeons."

तिप

A man who had served Maharajji became arrogant and humiliated some of Maharajji's devotees. Maharajji was so angry he just sat there huffing and making growling sounds like a monkey. He called the man into his office, and the next thing people saw was this large man being thrown out the door, landing five feet away on a stone. The devotee failed to appear to do arti, as he had done previously. The next day, Maharajji was out on the road when a car passed with the man and wife inside. She pranammed but he wouldn't look. It is said that Maharajji commented sadly, "He will never come back to me." Later the man took to drink.

तिप

A hunter had made fun of Maharajji to his friends, saying that he could get some meat for the baba, though he knew that he was vegetarian. Later, when the hunter's friends became devotees of Maharajji, the hunter tried to see Maharajji. But for five years he never was able to be at the right place at the right time, although his wife and children had had darshan. Finally one of the Mothers who stayed with Maharajji interceded, and Maharajji said, "All right." Then he was able to find Maharajji.

तिप

Many years ago, at one annual mela in the village of Neeb Karori, a baba got angry and cursed Maharajji. Maharajji had showed him up by pouring a continuous stream of milk from a lota. The following year a cyclone came to

*the village as a result of the baba's curse, and every year after there was a
storm. But the villagers knew that if they took Maharajji's name, nothing bad
would happen. Maharajji, it is said, cursed him: "God will punish you by
cutting your tongue in pieces." A few years later, that baba was found dead in
Farrukhabad with his tongue cut.*

卐

One day at Neeb Karori a man came to Maharajji complaining that he had
no son. He promised to have a temple built and a well dug, and Maharajji
indicated that God's blessings were with him. After the birth of a son the man
did nothing. Maharajji commented, "What do I have to do with this matter?"
Soon after, this man's house burned to the ground, destroying all his
possessions and money.

卐

An old man in a town where Maharajji had been staying had become blind.
People were talking to Maharajji about healing, and Maharajji said, "Samarth
Guru Ram Das cured his mother from blindness, but there are no saints like
that anymore." Then Maharajji asked for a pomegranate, had it squeezed, and
drank the juice. He then put his blanket over his face and they saw that
underneath there was blood coming out of both his eyes. Maharajji told the
blind man that if God restored his sight he should retire from business and
devote his life to spiritual pursuits. The man's vision was restored shortly
afterwards.

The doctor came and examined the eyes and said, "This is impossible! Who
did this?" They told him it was Maharajji and the doctor rushed to the railway
station to find him. Maharajji was already aboard the carriage and the doctor
jumped on and pranammed, and Maharajji kept saying, "This is the doctor
who cured the man's blindness. He is a very good doctor, a very good doctor."
But after three or four months, the old man couldn't resist and went back to
work and almost immediately lost his vision again.

卐

A large number of Westerners were being housed in an empty house belonging to one of the Indian devotees. We filled it with our bodies from wall to wall. Each day we would make our way to Dada's house where Maharajji was staying; there we visited with him and were lavishly fed with meals, many sweets, and much tea. But then Maharajji stopped seeing us. Each day we would go to Dada's house and be fed; but without Maharajji's darshan, it lost the source of the appeal. Although I loved being with him, I didn't mind so much for myself—but there were many Westerners who had just recently arrived, and a number of them had not yet even met Maharajji. Day after day they waited, following us from house to house, but I could see that soon they would tire of this game and leave. However, there was nothing I could do.

Then one day I was called to Maharajji's room and told, "Ram Dass, commander-in-chief, don't bring anyone here tomorrow until six at night." I had my orders, and when we returned to our quarters I announced that we would not go to Maharajji the next day until six. The next evening all the new people and most of the old devotees arrived, as ordered, at six. We found that some of the old devotees had ignored my instructions and arrived at four. These people had been fed; but more important, they had had a long visit with Maharajji. And when we arrive at six, though we were fed, we were not allowed to visit him.

Late that evening I was again called in to see Maharajji. This time he seemed angry with me and said, "Ram Dass, today people came at four. Tomorrow I don't want anyone to come until six." Again when we returned to our quarters I made his wishes known, specifically making them clear to those who had ignored me.

The next day it was worse. Not only did the original miscreants go at four, but now the mutiny was spreading, and other old devotees joined them. At six I arrived with the new devotees, who still assumed that my orders were to be honored, and a few of the old devotees who were sticking with me. And again we were faced with the same situation. The group that went at four got a long darshan with Maharajji and we got none. I was beginning to get angry.

The next day no such instruction was forthcoming, and we all came early but we were kept singing in the living room while Maharajji stayed with the Indian devotees in the kitchen. After some time a message came that Maharajji would see the women, and they all rushed out of the room to have his darshan. After some time, during which we were to continue singing, a message came that half of the men were to come for darshan. Of course, all wanted to go, but the meek and the righteous and some of the newer people remained behind with me, weakly carrying on the singing while we jealously listened to the laughter and talking in the other room.

Then the message came that Maharajji would not see anyone else that evening. And I became furious at this arbitrariness. That some of the new devotees who were kind enough to wait should not have darshan seemed grossly unfair, and I sought out Dada and expressed my perturbation. My anger was not masked, and Dada said, "I think you'd better tell Maharajji yourself."

"I will," I said.

Dada went into Maharajji's room and soon I was called in. There were only the three of us. Maharajji looked at me and asked, "Kya?"

I knew of course that he knew what was in my mind, and I was in no mood for games, so I said, "Maharajji, you know my heart."

But he wouldn't be deterred from having me explain, and he just reiterated, "Kya?"

I said, "Maharajji, you aren't being fair." And I proceeded to tell him of these new devotees who couldn't see him. When I finished my explanation I sat back on my haunches, waiting. I guess I felt I deserved an explanation and was waiting for one. After all, Maharajji wasn't living up to the rules in my guru guidebook.

He looked at me quizzically, looked at Dada as if he didn't understand, then he reached forward and gave a yank at my beard and said, "Ah, Ram Dass is angry." That was all. And then he looked directly into my eyes and we held the gaze.

During those moments I saw clearly my predicament. Maharajji had not acted "rationally" or at any rate "fairly," and he wasn't apologizing for it, either. I had a choice. I could get up and walk out of the room and leave him, in which case I would be left with my righteousness—but no guru. Or I could surrender to his irrationality and unfairness, knowing that he knew and I didn't. I bowed down, touched my head to his feet, and surrendered again. (R.D.)

VISA KARMA

FOR THE WESTERNERS, the "play" with Maharajji frequently focused around matters of visas and permits. As guests in a county already burdened with millions of hungry people, we low-budget spiritual seekers were not the most desirable component of the tourist population. So we spent significant amounts of time every three months in out-of-the-way villages and cities, ferreting out friendly immigration officials who would extend our visas.

Maharajji was a court of last resort, who, if the chips were down, might send us to some devotee somewhere, perhaps a police chief in one city or a government minister in Delhi, and mysteriously the visa extension would appear . . . usually. But sometimes Maharajji would send a devotee here or there and nothing would seem to work. Maharajji would thus seem totally ineffectual when pitted against the stony resistance of the visa department, and the devotee would be shipped back to America or else off to Nepal to reenter India at a later date.

The visa dance just seemed to enhance the doubt and confusion as to the relative powers of the worldly versus the spiritual kings. Most of us saw it, however, as more of Maharajji's playing with our clinging and as one more situation in which we had to learn to surrender.

When I asked him what to do about getting a visa, he first told me to go to Kanpur. Then he said, "No, don't go to Kanpur. Go to Mathura. No, go to Lucknow." He told me three different places to go in about two minutes. Then he said, "It doesn't matter where you go, because they're going to throw you out anyway"—which, of course, they did.

त्तय

Once I became worried about my visa and started to press Maharajji. He was in the "office" and Dada and I were talking to him through the window. I kept asking, "Where shall I go? It's almost expired. Where shall I go? What shall I do?" Maharajji wouldn't tell me anything, but while I was pressing him, he just put his head in his hands. Dada could see what was happening and he whispered to me, "Get out of here. Leave right now or he may send you back to America. Get away from the window."

Later, of course, it all worked out—one of those miracle stories of just catching the train as it was pulling out on the last day of my visa; being told at the visa office it was impossible to renew; my bursting into tears; and the officer saying, "There's one thing I can do." I stayed on in India for two years. As the Tao Te Ching says, "In action, watch the timing."

त्तय

When I came to Maharajji I had overstayed my visa three months. But everything just flowed. I didn't have any problems at all with the visa office.

त्तय

It was time once again to apply for a permit for a six-month extension for the VW bus. The first six-month permit that I had obtained, the previous spring, had been a week-and-a-half's worth of hassle and had cost hundreds of dollars. Now the VW was tired, and so was I, and I wanted just to give it to the Indian government. But Maharajji would not hear of it. Rubbing my nose in my material attachments, he kept insisting that the permit should be extended. So I found myself fighting with the ministry of finance to keep a car that I didn't even want. And explaining to them that I was doing it under orders of my guru found me few sympathetic listeners. The permit extension, which normally might be expected to take a few days, took almost three weeks. It required no less than twenty-three signatures, the final one being that of the minister of finance himself. That meant a member of the prime minister's cabinet had to sign personally to allow me to keep one battered 1964 VW bus for six more months. Of course, this was in addition to the duty that had to be paid, which by now equaled the value of the car.

During the first few days, I used reasoning and firmness and "justifiable anger" as the tools to make the system spit out the permit extension. But none of that worked. Once, after getting up and storming out of an office with an exit speech about "no way to treat a guest in your country," I went back to my hotel and realized that by blowing up I had just lost a point, because there was no way around that particular office. So the next day I had to go back and apologize.

And so it went. Once, the person whose signature was needed was attending his nephew's wedding for a few days; at other times the application paper had been misplaced, or they couldn't agree on the tax, or I needed two independent assessments of the value of the car . . . It was necessary to go to the offices each day or the application would get lost in the bowels of that huge bureaucratic monster already totally constipated with folders and papers ominously piled from floor to ceiling. There was no way to leave Delhi.

What a teaching about possessions! No matter how convenient the car might be, it certainly wasn't worth all this . . . car-ma. I could hear Maharajji laughing at my "pile of bricks."

There was, however, an interesting serendipitous teaching in all this. While we waited for the clearance for the car we were staying at a delightfully run-down, semi-hippie hotel. At first we lived out of our backpacks, expecting each day to be free to leave Delhi and get back to a "holy place." But as the days went on in this exasperating process, we began to settle in. More and more Westerners passing through Delhi found their way to our room until, each day, there would be a satsang of thirty or more of us, and we would chant and meditate and talk about the spirit. Soon people were bringing Indian bedspreads as wall hangings, and pictures and fruit. The wife of the owner of the hotel was even preparing ghee for our puja lamps. Finally we were so much in the spirit that it no longer mattered if we ever left Delhi. And at this point, my visa application was filed, the permit for the car came through, and we were free to leave for Vrindaban. (R.D.)

Sadhana

MAHARAJJI BEGAN his spiritual work very early in life. He told one devotee that as a small child of seven or eight he would skip school to go
into the jungle to do tapasya. Wisps of information suggest that he had
been born into a landed family who lived in a stone house, but that he
had left the security of his home very early to wander about as a sadhu.

During those years he traveled about dressed in only a single dhoti,
and he took his food and water in a discarded fragment of a broken clay
water jug, which he wore on his head like a cap. At this time, he was
known as "Handi Walla Baba [the baba with the broken clay pot]."

At some stage, he passed time near Aligarh and Manpuri, where he
performed spiritual practices by sitting for some time in water. The local
residents knew him then as "Tikonia Walla Baba." ("Tikonia" means a
triangular-shaped reservoir.) Probably about this same time he began to
pass time in the town of Neeb Karori (from which he later got the name
by which we knew him). There he stayed for some time in various underground caves, coming out sometimes during the hot season to sit in a
ring of fire in the hot sun.

It was not until the 1930s that he began to appear regularly in villages

325

in the foothills of the Himalayas and northern plains. Early on, he would play with the children and then disappear into the woods. Later he started to allow Indian householders to take him into their homes to feed him. These people were quick to recognize an extraordinary presence in him, and they began following him for his spirit and healing powers.

He was often seen visiting temples dedicated to the deity Hanuman; later he instigated the building of many such temples by his devotees. He seemed to be on a continuous religious pilgrimage and encouraged others to visit the holy shrines around India. His special affinity for Hanuman and Ram was reflected in his continuous repetition of these names of God and in the stories he both told and asked to have read to him. Yet despite his predilection for Ram and Hanuman, he honored all aspects of God and found the true spirit in all forms of worship.

Obviously he had undertaken severe austerities during his own sadhana. Yet he later said that such practices were not necessary. He honored those who undertook such practices but for the most part encouraged his devotees to feed and serve people, live dharmically, and, above all, to remember and love God.

MAHARAJJI'S SADHANA prescriptions were tailor-made for the individual devotee to whom they were directed.

At one point I asked Brahmachari Baba if Maharajji taught him tapasya, and I gave examples of the tapasya Maharajji is said to have done himself, such as sitting up to his neck in a lake and sitting in the summer noonday sun surrounded by four fires. Brahmachari Baba immediately said, "No. Only ordinary things such as various yoga-asanas [postures] and meditations and pranayams." With a little more questioning, he said, "Maharajji told me to be maun [silent]. I was silent for three years . . . after that Maharajji told me to do the standing tapasya—that is to say, I must never sit or lie down, but remain always on my feet. This I did also for another three years. I performed this tapasya at Bhumiadhar before the temple complex was built. I had a special contraption to support my body for sleep. Sleep would come and my legs would swell up very big. Maharajji also told me to be phalahari [to eat no grains, only fruits and vegetables]. This I did for some eight years."

श्री

For many years before I met Maharajji I was searching, going here and there, studying this and that. I began following strict yogic codes—*brahmacharya, 3:00* A.M. *risings, cold baths, asanas, and dhyan. It was during a period when I had given up coffee and tea that I met Maharajji. Tea was being offered to all of us, and I didn't know what to do. I said nothing but did not accept a cup of tea, and Maharajji leaned over to me, saying, "Won't you take tea? Take tea! You should drink the tea. It's good for you in this weather! Take tea!" So I drank the tea. With that one cup of tea, all those strict disciplines and schedules were washed away! They seemed meaningless and unnecessary; the true work seemed beyond these things. Now I do whatever comes of itself.*

जय

When some devotees questioned him about hatha yoga (physical method of attaining union with God), Maharajji told them: "Hatha yoga is okay if you are strictly brahmacharya. Otherwise it is dangerous. It is the difficult way to raise kundalini. You can raise kundalini by devotion and by feeding people. Kundalini does not necessarily manifest as outer symptoms; it can be awakened quietly." To another one he said, "If you are going to stand on your head, take butter. If you eat impure food, don't do the headstand. Impure food goes to the mind and affects it."

जय

Some Westerners who come to Kainchi from Rishikesh practiced the whole hatha yoga regimen, swallowing dhotis, putting string up the nose, and so forth. Maharajji urged them to stop being so fanatic about that, saying, "I did all those things myself. It's not the way."

YOGA IS NOTHING. YOU CAN ATTAIN SO MUCH WITHOUT IT.

Maharajji used to say that equanimity in every aspect of life will take you to the higher path. He would say that the ogres who follow the left path, eating human flesh from dead bodies at the burning ghats and other polluted foods, if they concentrated on God they were therefore not corrupted. Physical corruption can be there, but what is important is the mental state.

WITH DESIRES, HATHA YOGA DOES NOT WORK.
TODAY NO ONE REALLY KNOWS HATHA YOGA.
IT CAN'T WORK THROUGH BOOKS. THEY
USED TO FAST AND USE HERBS.

A Western devotee thought she wanted to take sanyas (renunciation), and Maharajji instructed her to gather all the accouterments. She got the cloth, had it dyed orange, and got a mala, sandal paste, and stone. After she had all the tools and had prepared herself emotionally, Maharajji never mentioned the ceremony.

जय

Reading the Gita in front of Maharajji, a devotee paused and asked Maharajji to tell him what was the quickest method to see God. Maharajji laughed and asked the man if he knew how to swim, and the devotee replied that he did. Maharajji said that, in that case, he should bind his arms and legs and tie himself to large boulders and throw himself into deep water. "Then you'll see God right away." Maharajji laughed. Becoming more serious, Maharajji continued, "Arjuna never saw God in that way. I've never seen God. He cannot be seen with these two eyes. Only after years of practice and hard work can you hope to see him."

WHEN A MAN HAS REACHED THE POINT WHERE HE
CAN SIT IN MEDITATION FOR SIX MONTHS, THERE
IS NO NEED OF EATING, NO NEED OF LATRINE OR
OF REST. ONLY ONE DROP OF AMRIT [NECTAR] FROM
THE TOP OF THE HEAD TO THE BODY KEEPS HIM
ALIVE. IF A TIGER EATS THAT BODY THERE IS NO
CARE, BUT ONLY WHEN THE LIFE COMES BACK TO
THE BODY WILL THERE BE PAIN.

We Westerners would pass the day pursuing our usual pastimes—eating, sleeping, drinking tea, gossiping, and moving about. Maharajji often jokingly listed these five behaviors as all that Western devotees were good for. Actually we also meditated, studied, sang kirtan, and washed clothes.

Athough most of us considered our primary spiritual method to be our relationship to Maharajji as our guru, he seldom admitted it. He continued to throw dust in our eyes.

Maharajji always kept telling me that other people were my gurus. At first I took him seriously. But finally I'd just say, "Maharajji, they may be upa-gurus [teachers along the way], but you are my Sat Guru [ultimate guru]. You are my guru whether you like it or not." He just laughed. (R.D.)

"How do I know if a person is my guru?" a devotee asked Maharajji. "Do you feel he [guru] can fulfill you in every way spiritually? Do you feel he can free you from all desires, attachments, and so forth? Do you feel he can lead you to final liberation?"

Asked to tell how he had met Maharajji, a devotee smiled with amusement and answered in this way:

Once a Bengali gentleman I met at a mela was having visions of a baba every time he took a bath in the Ganga, and he was looking for this being at the mela. "He is my guru," the man told me. The Bengali described the baba, and I showed him a picture of Maharajji. The Bengali said, "That's the one." It was arranged for him to meet Maharajji some time later when Maharajji was in town. The Bengali gentleman came before Maharajji and asked Maharajji when Maharajji and I had met. At first Maharajji didn't answer. Finally, after the man had asked several times, Maharajji said, "We have been together for innumerable lives." Later, Maharajji asked me, "Was that the right thing to say? Isn't it true?"

IT IS NOT NECESSARY TO MEET YOUR GURU ON THE PHYSICAL PLANE. THE GURU IS NOT EXTERNAL.

WHATEVER MAY BE GURU—HE MAY BE A LUNATIC OR ANY COMMON PERSON. ONCE YOU HAVE ACCEPTED HIM, HE IS THE LORD OF LORDS.

The first time I saw Maharajji a disciple had brought him here. I came to Maharajji for his blessing for some illness and I said, "I'll make you my guru!"

Maharajji replied, "But I'm not your guru. By God's grace, you will be all right. Your master is someone else."

The next day I asked Maharajji who my guru was, saying I was anxious to meet him. I said to him, "If you can make me healthy, you must be my master."

Maharajji said, "No. I'll make you healthy. Just pray to God. Your master is another—Swami Sivananda." I went to Rishikesh and met Sivananda. I told him what Maharajji had said and Sivananda accepted me as a disciple.

There was a great mahatma who had spent thirty years in a cave in the lion pose (on his knees, back arched, tongue protruding, eyes crossed). When I saw him I told him that Maharajji was my guru. He said that Maharajji is a great mahatma, but made it clear to me that Maharajji never keeps disciples. When I asked Maharajji if a certain sadhu was his disciple, Maharajji said, "What are you talking about? Of course not. This is a personal matter. It is a result of one's own yearning to become a siddha mahatma."

Although he wouldn't admit that he was our guru, now and then he'd say something that made it pretty certain. Once he said to me, "Stay in the ajna chakra [point between the eyebrows] and think only of me." (R.D.)

MAHARAJJI AGAIN and again sent us on specific pilgrimages. For us, it often felt as if we were merely being sent "away," but perhaps there was more. Pilgrimages to holy places have never played a very large part in American life. A few Christians and Jews have visited Jerusalem, and some followers of Islam have made the pilgrimage to Mecca. But while we often do not call them "holy places," many of us have received spiritual sustenance from such places as the Lincoln Memorial and from trips to the mountains and oceans. In India, pilgrimages to holy temples and places of great spiritual power have always played an important part in cultural life. For people who have families and jobs and thus cannot live in spiritual retreats, the most usual forms of spiritual practice are doing charitable acts and making pilgrimages. And Maharajji very much encouraged such pilgrimages through example and instruction.

When Maharajji and Dada were walking along the mela grounds, Maharajji said, "Saints have been coming here for thousands of years. Dada, take the dirt and touch your head."

जय

We were going with Maharajji to Chitrakut. As we entered the boundaries of the sacred place, Maharajji sat down, looked around, and said, "This is the place where Ram and Sita moved here and there." After he had moved a little further over the dry earth, a thorn pierced Maharajji's foot. He bent down and pulled out the thorn, saying, "Many such thorns must have pricked the Lord's feet." He said this in such an emotional way that it brought tears to the eyes of all the people there. It was just a small thing but so charged as to affect everyone very deeply. Later, when we had all returned to our senses, we laughed at our tears, unable to understand what had brought them on.

जय

Maharajji once told a devotee to be sure to take off of his shoes in holy places because the vibrations of a place can thus be transmitted up through the feet.

जय

Before meeting Maharajji, I had made a pilgrimage to Amarnath Cave in Kashmir. In this cave there is a lingam (phallic symbol of Shiva) made of ice that changes its size in relation to the cycles of the moon. The cave is supposedly left over from a previous yuga (age), hundreds of thousands of years ago, and in it Shiva and Parvati (his consort) stayed. It was a rainy day when we got there, and I was so saddle sore from two days' climb on a horse that I didn't feel anything. Much later, in discussing pilgrimages, Maharajji said to me:

"You went to Amarnath Cave?"
"Yes, Maharajji."
"But you didn't understand it."
"No, Maharajji."
"You will." (R.D.)

॥ॐ॥

Accompanied by the Mothers and a few devotees and servants, Maharajji stayed in the Amarkantak dharmasalla for eleven days. Each morning after breakfast, they went to the various sacred places in the area—the temple, Kapildhara, Dudh-dhara, Sonmuda, and so forth. Often they wandered in the jungle, and Maharajji would visit with an old sadhu who lived there alone in a cave. The sadhu had a white beard and long jetta (matted hair) and extraordinarily long fingernails. He prepared rotis and fed them to Maharajji with his own hands, along with fresh milk from his cow. Maharajji commanded everyone to bathe in the sacred reservoir of Narmada Mata. He then took off his clothes and, holding the hand of a devotee, submerged three times under the water, shouting, "It's very cold, very cold!" as he came up. He immediately threw his blanket back on.

MAHARAJJI USED names to awaken us to our deeper selves. First we were Joan, Jeff, Joe, Danny, and Barbara—and then we were the whole Hindu pantheon.

The naming of the Western devotees reflected the difference in Maharajji's lila with men and women. While many Western men were given Das *[servant] names—such as Ram Dass, Krishna Das, Balaram Das—as far as we know, no women were called* Dasi, *the feminine counterpart. Nothing Maharajji did was without meaning, yet the subtlety of this distinction is hard to interpret.*

Women were instructed to perform acts of service as frequently as were the men, and regardless of the individual name given, Maharajji often called each woman simply, "Ma." Whatever our ages or conditions, we became Mothers, the role that has always encompassed loving service.

Yet perhaps that was not the aspect he wished to stress most; perhaps we

*most needed to see ourselves as goddesses, as the shakti whose first service is to
her lord—who is God.*

जय

One day during a period of confusion, I was complaining that Maharajji
was ignoring me and that he was never going to give me a name. Balaram got
very excited and said, "Oh, ask him, ask him. Lots of people ask him. I'll ask
him for you. This is a good excuse for you to be with him, a good excuse to
talk to Maharajji." Even though I thought I should wait until he gave me a
name, I asked Balaram to feel it out.

The very next darshan, Maharajji said, "She wants a name." I was so
embarrassed, that I no longer wanted a name—I just wanted to run and hide.
Then Maharajji gave me a name, saying "Rukmini!" He said it very harshly,
and I was very cool to it. It just wasn't right. I felt he hadn't given it freely,
that he'd been pushed into it. I was very upset.

I didn't tell anyone about it, and I was really unhappy for a few days.
Maharajji of course sensed my confusion about it, called me into the room,
looked at me, and with such sweetness said, "Mira, Mira." I wanted to melt.
The name sounded like music to me.

जय

When he gave me my name, I felt it as a sort of thorn. It was on a day
when I was feeling full of self-pity and out of place in the satsang. He gave me
the name, "Priya Das," beloved server. I always felt that a lot of it was in
response to my own state of mind at the time.

जय

One day Hari Dass wrote on his slate that Maharajji had given me the
name Ram Dass. I asked if this was good. He said yes, that it was a name for
Hanuman and meant "servant of God." Since then I have found that name to
be very much a reminder of my path—that I am slowly growing into the name.
(R.D.)

I was standing alone by Hanuman when Maharajji appeared around the corner of the temple. Leaning on the railing next to me and looking at me, he said, "General Mahavir Singh," and disappeared. I was stunned.

One morning a few days later we were all out on the road, where the pavement was all hot and sticky. He came and sat down, so everyone else sat down next to him and got their nice clean clothes completely filthy—a number of people experienced considerable anxiety about that—and in the midst of talking with people he turned around and looked at me and said, "What's your name?" Rather sheepishly, I answered, "General Mahavir Singh." He looked at me and crooked his head and smiled. And he said, "Nahin! Ab se, Krishna [No! From now on, Krishna]." Then he paused for a moment and said, "Krishna Das."

For MAHARAJJI, remembering God and repeating a name of God was the royal way. God was always just a breath away and appeared again and again on Maharajji's lips.

THE BEST SERVICE YOU CAN DO IS TO KEEP YOUR THOUGHTS ON GOD. KEEP GOD IN MIND EVERY MINUTE.

ALL IS GOD'S WILL, BUT MAYA PREVENTS YOU FROM KNOWING IT'S ALL GOD'S WILL. HE GAVE US EYES, EARS, NOSE, MOUTH. BUT HE ALSO GAVE US THE WISDOM TO USE THEM TO ATTAIN GOD.

KEEP GOD IN YOUR HEART LIKE YOU KEEP MONEY IN A SAFE.

HE WHO KNOWS GOD KNOWS EVERYTHING.

RAM RAM RAM RAM RAM RAM RAM RAM RAM RAM RAM

Once a devotee asked Maharajji what mantra he should use. "The mind can't concentrate. Use any mantra—use it, use it," repeated Maharajji.

नाम

Maharajji taught me the utter simplicity and the power of mantra by actually immersing me in a situation and then rescuing me with God's name. So that I would not miss the teaching, he would repeat it three times. For example, one morning as I sat before him, massaging his feet, I found myself suddenly in the depths of depression and remorse. It was so unexpected that I was totally caught up in it, neither questioning its source, nor seeking to transcend it. Then, from within me, as if it were the voice of another, I heard the quiet repetition of God's name. In my desperation I latched on to it, and to my surprise the depression lifted and all was as before. I sat quietly massaging his feet.

Then, once again, I was plunged into a state of anguish, and again I was consumed by it. Once again, as the voice from within began to repeat God's name, I latched on to it and the depression lifted. I laughed within myself at the strange occurrence, only to find myself yet again deep in suffering. This time, however, I turned immediately to mantra. I no longer identified with the mind state, for it was like a passing cloud. As I repeated the mantra in my ear, I looked up at Maharajji. He was smiling, twinkling at me. Maharajji used this same silent technique of teaching to show me not to identify with sexual thoughts.

नाम

Around 10:00 A.M., a man came to my home and said that Maharajji was calling me from the Ganga, and I immediately went to find him, accompanied by a young boy. At the Ganga some devotees said he'd gone for a walk toward the Sangam and had been gone for two hours—too long for such a short walk. They said he must have returned to my house. I said, "No. He sent for me to come here. He must be here." After some time the boy begged me to give up and return; twice he did this, and both times I insisted we continue. The third time, I felt in a quandary. I could neither go forward nor turn back. Out of concern for the boy I could not continue, and out of desire for Maharajji I could not turn back. I stood helpless.

Just then the boy called out, "There he is!" And there was Maharajji in a boat just beside us on the Ganga, with two other men. The boat came ashore and Maharajji got out and questioned me about the entire story, asking for all the details. Then we walked to where the other devotees were standing. Once

*there, Maharajji sent them all away except for me. He again questioned me for
every detail of the story—receiving the summons, coming to the Ganga,
walking along in search, the boy's pleadings—but this time Maharajji insisted
that I tell him what was in my mind at the moment of quandary with the boy.
I replied, "Why, I turned to saying Ram, Ram."*

*Immediately, Maharajji leaned over and whispered in my ear, "Just take
Ram's name and all desires will be fulfilled." He had created this entire
situation to teach me that!*

 राम

*I would sit in meditation saying the name of Ram into the night. One
morning at darshan, Maharajji was giving out prasad. It had been so long since
I had gotten any that I had almost given up even thinking I would get some.
Somebody was passing it out and he dropped some in my lap, and Maharajji
said, "Give her more, give her more. She should have more because she says
Ram, she says Ram. She's taken the name of Ram." I was so happy because
he knew! He really knew!*

राम

*When I was eighteen I asked him to give me a mantra. He said, "What! I
don't know anything about these mantras. I only know Ram." Then I handed
him a photo of himself and he wrote "Ram" all over the back of it. Such
personal acts were so special. Look! I carry it with me all the time.*

राम

*He gave mantras to my wife and children before me. When he gave me a
mantra I thought to myself, I won't take it because I'm not fit for it; I'm too
full of sin.*

राम

*I had a shirt that Sihu embroidered with RAM RAM RAM all around the
collar in purple thread. I was alone at the tucket and Maharajji came out in the*

middle of the afternoon. He saw this shirt and grabbed it. "Look at this!" he said to some Indians who had come for darshan. "Look at what's on his shirt! It says RAM RAM RAM RAM RAM RAM RAM." Then he chided the Indians, "India's really good for him! Why don't you people like India? Look at how good it is for him! It says RAM RAM RAM RAM RAM. He came all the way from America! It says RAM RAM RAM RAM RAM. Why don't you like India?"

ॐ

I can't resist telling of the time Maharajji told Naima and me to go around the back at Kainchi to where some young naga babas were—and to do full dunda pranam to them. At that time, we were both wearing special Ram tilaks. There were some five sadhus hunkered around a fire and smoking a chillum. It was very smoky and their naked bodies—but for langotis (loin cloths)—were ash-covered. They took very little notice of us, even as I performed dunda pranam. What they were saying among themselves was that all you needed was to take Ram's name and you would have no difficulties in this life. The example one of them gave was of plunging into the icy cold water of the Ganga up at Gangotri. All you had to do was take Ram's name, and it was not difficult at all. All the babas were wearing the same tilak that I was wearing.

ॐ

Maharajji sent a baba to get malas in the market at Vrindaban. This baba scolded a certain devotee, saying, "You are a haughty one. I bought malas and now you think Maharajji will put one on you." Then Maharajji said to this devotee, "Take a bath and do puja." Maharajji then put a tilak and rice on the devotee's head with his own hand and put a mala around his neck. The devotee said, "Now, Maharajji, you must give me a mantra." Maharajji did.

ॐ

There was a Ma who in her youth was devoted to Ananda Mayee Ma. After some time, she met Maharajji and became very close to him but was confused as to who her guru was. Maharajji came to her in a dream and gave her a mantra. She was in bed and had to get up and write it down. He said, "This is a mantra from Ma." Later, Ananda Mayee Ma confirmed that it was the right mantra.

जप

Annapurna had the desire to be initiated into a mantra by Maharajji. Maharajji arranged a whole ceremony, initiating her formally: a mantra, a mala, all of it.

जप

After Maharajji had left his body a devotee had three dreams. In the first one, Maharajji gave her a mantra. In the second dream he told her how to use the mantra with OM (the cosmic syllable) on the inbreath. In the third dream, after the June feast, he said that she had worked very hard and had done more than she should have.

जप

Maharajji spent long periods inside his room during the last two years. He wanted to hear God's name both inside and outside all the time. We used to spend time with him in the room. Everyone thought that we must be having a good time, but actually he was mostly silent, with closed eyes, listening to the Westerners singing kirtan outside. Now and again he would open his eyes and look around. "Anything to say? Do you have any questions?" he'd ask us. Then he'd again drift back to this other plane.

जप

On Krishna's birthday celebration in 1973 all the Westerners fasted and did kirtan. At midnight they did arti to Maharajji. Through the closed window he kept telling them to "jao." Still they stayed, singing sweet kirtan. Finally he opened the window and tears were streaming down his face. He sat still and listened for a long time. It began to rain, as if God were raining down flowers—a very auspicious sign.

PEOPLE ARE QUICK TO TAKE A CHAPATTI
BUT SLOW TO TAKE THE NAME OF GOD.

Maharajji had a pundit chanting the Shrimad Bhagavatam (one of the great holy books) daily at the temple for a month. I couldn't understand what he was chanting, but I could feel the pundit's devotion in my heart. Every now and again he would intersperse the story with a few refrains of the Hare Krishna mantra. Maharajji asked me, "What is he saying?"

"Maharajji, he is saying Hare Krishna, Hare Rama."

"Ah!" Maharajji was delighted. "Ram Dass has heard the essence."
(R.D.)

राम

While I was touring with a swami in southern India, he had given me mantra diksha *(initiation) for a very powerful Shiva mantra that he said would give me vast wealth and vast power. I was fascinated and did the mantra day and night for many weeks. As a result of the mantra I began to travel outside of my body. Five years earlier, Maharajji had asked me if I wanted to fly and predicted that I would, and now I found myself flying out of my body. Sometimes when doing the mantra I would be taken out of my body and onto another plane, where I would meet the swami. After this had been going on for over a month, I was in a cave in Surat, meditating. But I couldn't stop doing the mantra. I was once again taken out of my body, but this time on the astral plane I was brought to a room where Maharajji was sitting.*

I was ecstatic and rushed to his feet. He sat on his tucket, wrapped in a blanket. Then he pulled the blanket up over his face and I heard him blow three times as if extinguishing candles. I felt simultaneously, with each blow, my body inflate as if it were an inner tube at the air pump in a filling station. At the conclusion of the third inflation, the scene disappeared and I found myself once again back in the cave . . . but the mantra was gone—not in the sense that I couldn't remember it but, rather, because it had lost its compelling quality. It no longer possessed me; I no longer had any desire to repeat it. Maharajji had taken it away. (R.D.)

राम

One woman devotee did mantra from childhood. Fifteen days before
Maharajji left his body, he called her in and said, "Here is a new mantra. Do
this."
"Maharajji, how can I change now?"
He said, "Touch my feet." Since then she has done only that new mantra.

राम

In 1968 when I was leaving for America, Hari Dass gave me his mala that
he had worked with for years. The beads were large and dark from handling
and were made from the stem of the sacred tulsi plant. At the time, he told me
that Maharajji had given him the beads many years earlier. Oh, how I
treasured those beads! I wore them daily and slept with them at night, using
them as a constant reminder of the Shri Ram mantra that was at times like a
lifeline connecting me to the spiritual oxygen I craved.

And then one night in 1971 when I was back in India, a group of us were
walking up to the Hanuman Garh temple, which is about a mile from
Nainital, where we were staying while visiting Kainchi. We had various
drums and cymbals and were chanting as we went. I was playing a set of
cymbals, and apparently the cymbals caught the string of the beads and broke
it. It was evening and in the darkness I failed to notice as one after another of
the beads fell along the wayside. When I did finally notice, twenty or more of
the sacred number of one-hundred-and-eight beads were missing. I was heartsick
and searched the next day along the road but found none of the beads.

I had never seen big beads like those before and didn't know how to go about
replacing them, so I asked Maharajji. First he denied ever having given them
to Hari Dass, though I didn't believe his denial; then he said those beads were
no good anyway. He said I could get the right beads from Sita Ram Baba in
Ayodhya.

In Allahabad many months earlier, Maharajji had instructed me to see a
holy man named Sita Ram Baba, of whom I'd never heard. Apparently that
had been a foreshadowing of this moment.

I had never visited Ayodhya, the seat of Ram's kingdom, and the thought of
getting "special" beads from a "special" baba at the instructions of the guru
was the delight of a spiritual materialist (like me).

Within a day I was on a train bound for Ayodhya.

The first matter of business upon arrival was to find the right Sita Ram
Baba. Maharajji had said he was old, so it should not be too difficult. But as I
roamed the streets in the tonga with my bad Hindi, it was not so easy. After

several hours I was directed to a house a mile or so out of town. A fellow in his twenties standing at the gate said that Sita Ram Baba was his uncle but was taking rest—perhaps I could come back later. But, like Hanuman, I was not to be deterred and said that I would sit outside until he would see me. It was very hot outside but my resolve was firm.

Apparently the boy told his uncle, for within a few minutes I was ushered in. Sita Ram lay on a hammock, and he was very old indeed. His nephew said he was one hundred and twenty-eight years old and he looked every day of it. His skin was transparent and his hands skeletal and his voice but a whisper. He acknowledged knowing Maharajji and said that I could return at sundown. I was disappointed for I was eager to get the beads and get back to Maharajji, and it almost looked as if Sita Ram was too old and feeble to help me anyway, but there was nothing to do but wait.

So I left, deciding to visit the famous Hanuman murti in Ayodhya. But as the tonga started down the street and had gone perhaps fifty meters, I looked back and there was Sita Ram Baba literally running after the tonga. He jumped aboard and said we would get the beads now. I was delighted yet concerned lest the ride be too much for the old man. Now that he was up and moving, however, he seemed to be stronger and filled with more life force.

But the next disappointment came when we arrived at the shop where the beads were supposed to be. It was closed. He said there was nothing to do but return in the evening, so we turned to go back to his house. But about a hundred meters down the road we met the shopkeeper, and Sita Ram prevailed upon him to return to the shop. Once at the shop, I felt the goal was in sight. The shopkeeper showed Sita Ram Baba several malas, but in each case, though I thought them beautiful, Sita Ram Baba rejected them as not "the ones." Then he spoke at length to the shopkeeper, who suddenly lit up and went to a desk and opened a tiny drawer that was in a dusty and unused corner. I was thrilled, for it was just like all the occult books had said such things occurred.

But the beads he brought out were cheap-looking, garishly painted in orange or green, and had been crudely carved with Sanskrit symbols of Sita and Ram on each bead. I had seen such cheap beads in many places and was always put off by them. But Sita Ram said that these were "the beads" so I bought three strands for about fifty cents each and smiled gamely. Then I returned Sita Ram to his house, thanked him, caught the afternoon train, and returned to Maharajji's feet the next morning.

When I arrived, Maharajji asked about the beads and I laid them before him. All he said was, "Those aren't the beads. I'll have to get them for you myself." But he never did. (R.D.)

In INDIA, RITUALS have always played an important role in maintaining the spirit. But too often these same rituals stifle the very spirit they are designed to preserve. For Maharajji, rituals were to be honored yet kept in perspective.

A fire ceremony was to be held at Kainchi, with Maharajji present in the temple compound. I decided to sit through the entire nine-day ceremony to see if I could erase my past reactions to ritual (which were primarily negative) and open my heart to this process. For if Maharajji was instigating this, there must be a good reason for it.

The major participants in the ceremony were two Brahmin priests and two laymen-householders, both of whom were old devotees of Maharajji. The days wore on slowly. It was hot by the fire, and the repetitiveness, the heat, the fatigue, the intensity, and the visual power of the scene slowly opened me emotionally, until I felt as if that edifice were a spaceship carrying all of us within it higher and higher.

During the first six days, Maharajji never attended the ceremony but was constantly apprised of its progress. On the seventh day, when the ritual had truly taken on a life of its own for me and had begun to hold me deeply, he suddenly started to yell from the opposite side of the compound, where he was sitting. It seemed that he was calling in a strangely jarring manner to one of the householder-laymen who was a major participant in the ritual. For almost seven full days these four men had been going without stop and here was Maharajji disrupting the entire process. Seemingly without a second thought the devotee got up and went to Maharajji. My concentration was broken, so I followed after him to see why Maharajji had called this man from the ceremony. I found the man handing out prasad, small packages of puris and potatoes, to the local children who came every day to the temple to be fed. There were dozens of other devotees who could have done this, but Maharajji chose to call this man.

Later, still confused and somewhat resentful toward Maharajji for disrupting what had finally become a sacred ritual for me, I spoke to the man who had been called away. He simply said, "Maharajji is beyond all ritual." (R.D.)

ॐ

We were attending a yagna (fire ceremony), though we always preferred contact with Maharajji over all these rituals, because his darshan is the greatest

puja. But he would always tell us, "Go there, you devil, wicked man, leech!"
And whatever he really wanted was not difficult for us to do. He asked one
devotee if he'd like to sit in the puja, and the man replied that he'd rather not.
Maharajji said, "You are a miserly fellow. All those pundits are there and you
think you have to pay them. No! I'll pay them." This touched the man's
heart, and the next morning he took his seat at the yagna. Offerings were
being made to the fire, with chants of "Swaha! Swaha!" "Hap!" Maharajji
shouted. "What does this swaha, swaha do for them? Go out and distribute the
food! What is the use of throwing things into the fire?"

तम्

He was always very considerate with everyone. Although he never told
anyone to go do puja or rituals, he encouraged them to do it if it was their
habit. I regularly did some puja in the morning, but when Maharajji came to
visit, serving him became the puja. But every day Maharajji would leave the
house in the morning to visit the home of other devotees or on some walk, thus
giving me time to do my puja.

तम्

I used to keep a complete fast on the day and night of Shivaratri (day for
honoring Shiva), not even taking water or even sleeping. I would stay up the
whole time doing puja to Lord Shiva. One year by chance, Maharajji came to
Nainital the day before Shivratri, and we ended up at the home of one devotee
who had prepared special food for Maharajji's visit. Maharajji told everyone to
eat, and when asked why I wouldn't eat, I said that it was a fast day. He
said, "Why fast? Carry on! Eat!" I told him that I would eat only with his
permission. He said, "Yes! Eat!" then I took food from him. He said, "You
do your puja now." I asked for his blessings to go, but he replied, "No, you
do it here—here, in front of me." I started my puja.
Maharajji sat there talking and people kept coming and going. Three or four
people who had never recited these prayers before were so charmed that they
also began to recite. Maharajji turned to me and said, "Oh, you are just
showing off. What is the use of fasting and all these rituals? The Lord is
within you. You can't remember him until his grace is there. If his grace is

there, everything is there. Always remember him and try to acquire him. And if his grace is there . . ." Then he sat still for two-and-a-half hours. The whole atmosphere was charged. Each year I had been very fastidious about that particular day, fasting, praying, and so forth, but this time he broke that.

On other occasions he wouldn't allow me to do my puja. I told him that I wouldn't do it if he wouldn't allow me, but that I also wouldn't eat until the puja was done. Then he shouted, "Close the door, you wicked man! Finish your puja! What is this puja and this troubling the Lord? Praying and fasting? Can't you remember the Lord for a second? What good is this puja? I don't understand!"

ﬆﬄ

Every morning and evening at the temple, rituals would be performed that included the use of a red paste and grains of rice. After the ceremony the pujari would place a bit of this paste and a few grains of rice in the middle of each person's forehead. The high point of the ceremony for the old priest would be the placing of the tilak on Maharajji's forehead. Maharajji would of course be talking to people during the whole process and, invariably, just as the old pujari would apply the paste with great seriousness and concentration, Maharajji would turn his head to talk to somebody else and a smear of red would go completely across his forehead. The pujari just could never get Maharajii to sit still for the rituals.

EQUALLY AS IMPORTANT as fire ceremonies are the ceremonial baths in the sacred Ganges River. Maharajji disrupted even these.

Two old men were en route to the Ganga at mela. It is considered a very holy thing to bathe in the Ganga at this time. Maharajji commented, "No, take your bath here. Everywhere is the Ganga."

ﬆﬄ

Once a devotee was on his way to the Ganga to take his ritual bath, when he encountered Maharajji. Maharajji sent him back without his bath, saying, "Serving people is better than a ritual bath in the Ganga."

OFTEN MAHARAJJI QUOTED:
"ALL ACTION IS PRAYER. ALL TREES ARE
DESIRE-FULFILLING. ALL WATER IS THE
GANGA, ALL LAND IS VARANASI
[ANOTHER NAME FOR BENARES].
LOVE EVERYTHING."

THE LESSONS Maharajji taught about rituals, like so much of his teaching, were fraught with the paradox that outdistanced the rational mind. He seemed concerned that the rituals be done properly, yet he broke all the rules. But as one devotee said, "When there was work, he would set aside the rituals, and the minute the work was completed, he sent you to do puja." But perhaps he also broke the rules, such as upsetting that fire ceremony, to show people that the thing itself was not the ritual but the spirit: Do the ritual to tune in, but don't get caught.

There were two old men who, having raised families and done their duties, had taken sanyas and were wandering about on foot. They spent many months at the Kainchi temple, and Maharajji had them singing "Sita Ram" for several hours each morning. When it was time for them to leave, Maharajji called them in front of him and, in what appeared to be outrage, yelled at them for beating an iron pan in front of the murtis during arti. (In the scriptures, iron is not to be used in the temples.) Maharajji told them that they didn't know how to behave properly and so he threw them out. As they turned to walk away, Maharajji broke into a grin and sang in a high falsetto voice, sweetly, "You beat the gong, and I threw you out."

राम

A man brought in his baby for Maharajji's blessing, but all Maharajji did was to pat the child on the head. The man was angry and said he wanted Maharajji to perform the proper blessing ceremony. Maharajji retorted that he didn't know that ceremony, that he'd blessed the child, and if the man wanted the proper ceremony, he would have to go to someone who knew it.

राम

Once the Westerners had prepared to do a great puja to Maharajji, planning to wash his feet in all the proper ingredients in order to make amrit. They had divided up the tasks among them and were quite excited about it. When Maharajji came out he was wearing socks. He made them perform the ceremony using his index finger instead.

तम्

When Maharajji's Vrindaban temple was completed, he told B to be pujari there. The young boy was not a Brahmin (as priests traditionally are) and knew nothing of pujas and rituals. Maharajji called in a pundit and told him to teach the boy the prayers. Then Maharajji sent him to the bazaar to buy a sacred thread and tulsi beads. Maharajji put these on him and told him to do the puja to Hanuman, that now he had become a pukka pujari *(first-class priest).*

Maharajji had gone out one day, and J, the man who had built the temple, came and questioned B as to his caste, his knowledge of Sanskrit, and so forth. B answered that he was not a Brahmin but a Thakur *(a lower Hindu caste). J was upset, and just then Maharajji appeared and called him away. J complained to Maharajji, and in the big hall in front of many people a discussion followed. Maharajji then asked B if he knew Sanskrit; if he could read the Bhagavad Gita. B said no and Maharajji retorted "Don't lie." Maharajji told J that B knew the eighteen chapters of the Gita by heart. J then asked to hear chapters eleven and twelve. Maharajji threw his blanket over B's head and hit his head a few times. Then B began to sing the Gita in the best Sanskrit, impressing all the Brahmins. J broke down and threw himself at Maharajji's feet. B remained pujari for a year and a half. Although he never again recited the Gita, when that boy would perform a puja he was in such communion with God that much peace would come to all.*

As a protector of the dharma, Maharajji not only kept devotees from getting lost in the rituals, but also he was quick to point out spiritual deception, fraudulence, and materialism when he would find it.

Once at a mela, Maharajji and a devotee passed a sadhu sitting as if in deep meditation, with a lota next to him. Maharajji said, "He's a deceiver." He told a young boy to steal the sadhu's lota. As soon as the boy took the lota, the sadhu came out of meditation and jumped up. Maharajji yelled to the boy, "Drop it, drop it, or he'll beat you."

†꘏

"Come on," *said Maharajji to a devotee. "I'll show you a very big mahatma. You'll have darshan [here he was being sarcastic] of a very great saint." Maharajji and the devotee traveled by car to the ashram of this baba, and Maharajji led the devotee to a young man clothed in saffron silken robes and smoking a cigarette. When this man saw Maharajji, he threw his cigarette away and pranammed to him. They sat down and the sadhu went into his room and brought out a very expensive blanket. (Maharajji was wearing an old, very plain blanket.) The sadhu removed Maharajji's blanket and wrapped the new one around him.*

"What's this?" *asked Maharajji.*

"It's a new blanket, a very beautiful, expensive one. That millionnaire's mother came and gave it to me. It was kept for you, Maharajji. Here it is. It's a most excellent blanket. Don't give it to anyone."

Maharajji didn't take a second to get up. He threw off the expensive blanket and said, "You are a sadhu? Can there be distinctions between blankets? This is good and this is bad? A blanket is a blanket!"

He snatched his old blanket and said to the devotee, "Come on. He's a sadhu and he sees a difference in blankets. What can he see in men?" *Maharajji left for the car, mumbling,* "What's this? Hap!" *They got into the car and drove away. Maharajji was very different from the ordinary sadhu.*

†꘏

A devotee was describing some dishonest sadhus. Weeping, Maharajji said, "Look what they have done in the name of dharma."

> THE EYES OF A SAINT ARE ALWAYS
> CONCENTRATED ON THE SUPREME SELF.
> THE MINUTE HE IS AWARE OF HIMSELF,
> SAINTHOOD IS LOST.

One person loaned some two thousand rupees to a sadhu and it was not returned. Maharajji said, "When you loan money to a saint, don't expect to get it back."

MAHARAJJI WOULD QUOTE: "JUST AS YOU FILTER WATER, HAVE A WORKING KNOWLEDGE OF GURUS."

Staying with V's cousin was a big sadhu from Lucknow, who was reputed to be very clever and to be able to make predictions by looking at the palm of one's hand. V showed his hand to the sadhu, who predicted good things but a short life, no more than sixty to sixty-five years. V wasn't happy. Later Maharajji asked him what had happened, saying, "Don't lie, tell me. You think your age will only be sixty-five. No. no. I'll tell you—not less than eighty-five. Whenever sadhus come, show them great respect and feed them if possible. But don't let yourself get too involved with them."

ॐ

Maharajji spoke of a companion from his early days: "He was so high, yet his maya was so strong."

ॐ

The chief of police of Kanpur, a devotee of Maharajji, came to Maharajji one day with a warrant for the arrest of a baba, who was also very fond of Maharajji, on charges of desertion from the army and illicit dealings in Kanpur. Maharajji told the police chief not to serve the warrant. After all, the man was now a sadhu and shouldn't be held responsible for desertion. Maharajji later scolded the baba: "What are you doing? You pretend to be a sadhu and yet you are still doing this business. Leave it."

The baba left Kanpur for Nainital, where Maharajji was also going. With his very imposing figure and a beautiful singing voice, the baba quickly gathered a following from whom he collected a lot of money. Maharajji called the baba to him and rebuked him, telling him to leave it all and run away, but the baba continued to use and manipulate money and power. He married twice, leaving children with both women before running away from them. Until that time Maharajji had been kind and sympathetic toward him, always asking how his "swami" business was doing. At this point, however, Maharajji rebuked him for his lecherous activities, and the baba, breaking with Maharajji, never returned.

तम्

*Traveling in the south Maharajji and SM came to an ashram, and
Maharajji went into a gate and saw a Krishna murti under a tree, not being
properly cared for. He said, "You stay, but I am leaving. A murti is the same
as the living God and it must be treated that way—I don't want to be where
somebody thinks that they are higher than God."*

Because there was so much spiritual fraudulence all about, Maharajji
was joyful and honoring when he found people of pure spirit.

*One devotee said that every time they passed a temple while driving in a
jeep, Maharajji would stop the jeep and pranam, and for every sadhu that
passed, Maharajji would bring his hands together too, under his blanket.*

तम्

*I took some swamis, including a famous singer, to have Maharajji's darshan
in Vrindaban. Before I could introduce them, Maharajji said, "I know them.
Call them here. They must have some tea. He wants to sing bhajan." I had
never told Maharajji about this famous south Indian singer, who was
accompanied by five south Indian women. Maharajji called for tea, then took
me alone into his room and said, "He's very good. Would it trouble him to
sing for me? His singing would give me great pleasure. Would it trouble him to
sing kirtan?"*
I replied, "Baba, what trouble would there be in your place?"
*Maharajji came out and asked the swami to sing. The swami sang some
bhajans about Radha (Krishna's beloved and devotee) and Krishna. He felt a
strong connection to Maharajji. "Now you are tired," Maharajji said. "You'll
eat sambar and rasam [southern food] here! Mas! You'll make food here?"
Maharajji laughed. The women couldn't understand Hindi. "Speak up! Tell
me! Will you come here every day for meals? Sambar, rasam daily."*
*I told Maharajji that we couldn't stay in the ashram since we wanted to
move around and visit the temples of Vrindaban.*
"Accha! Then do this—come every day and take prasad here!"
We came to see Maharajji daily, and each time he tried to fill us up with

prasad. He took special care of this swami, saying, "He's a very good mahatma. This sort of saint you won't meet."

जय

Swami Sivananda was considered one of the great saints of India. He left behind him many disciples and a great ashram in Rishikesh. Maharajji would now and then visit the ashram unannounced. Each visit, some incident would occur that would be long remembered at the ashram. Sometimes the head of the ashram would prepare food for Maharajji with his own hands. Once Maharajji called for a swami who was very old and revered. This swami honored only the memory of the great Sivananda and would not even bow to anyone else. As he came near Maharajji, Maharajji shouted "Veda Vyas [a great historical saint in India]! Veda Vyas has come!" At this, the swami's entire demeanor changed and he did full dunda pranam before Maharajji. In some deeper way they recognized one another.

FOR THE HIGHEST SAINTS MAHARAJJI held the greatest reverence and love. When one was privileged to hear him talk of such beings, it was like hearing him speak of members of an intimate and loving family. Just the quality of his voice as he spoke or remembered or reflected conveyed the depth of the connection. He spoke this way of such as Christ, Ramakrishna, Hariakhan Baba, Tailanga Swami, Shirdi Sai Baba, Ramana Maharshi, Nityananda, Ananda Mayee Ma, Sombari Maharaj, Deoria Baba, and Sivananda, among others.

A picture of Shirdi Sai Baba was given to Maharajji and placed at his feet. Maharajji immediately sat up and took up the picture. "It doesn't belong there. He was a very good baba," Maharajji said and put the picture by his head.

जय

There was a great saint named Gangotri Baba who lived permanently on the snows of Gangotri in the Himalayas. Maharajji was known to visit with him. One can't say who was whose devotee. Beyond a certain point, the behavior of saints is inexplicable.

टाम

Once in Allahabad, the head of a five-hundred-year-old Gorakhnath sect, begun shortly after the time of Shankara, came to see Maharajji, and Maharajji made Dada and others touch his feet. The man was very humble and said, "Here I am before the saint of saints and you call me saint."

टाम

Maharajji once said, "Once I was going by Ramana Maharshi. He got up and tried to follow me but I ran away."

टाम

Maharajji said I should not go alone to the Kumbha Mela. I was with him, holding onto his blanket so I would not get lost. A ragged man came up to Maharajji and put his arms around him in a very familiar way. They began to dance, arm in arm, singing "lillyri" over and over again. It lasted about two minutes. It's the only time I've seen Maharajji dance. I tried to touch the man's feet because I had heard that Hanuman and other great rishis attended the mela, but I could not touch them. It was such ecstasy that I couldn't. Then the man disappeared. I have always regretted not forcing myself to touch him.

टाम

Maharajji had gone through Behariji temple and out the back and into a house, where he asked for food. In the street someone was yelling, "One roti!" and Maharajji called him in. It was a sadhu who only begged for two rotis a day. Maharajji asked him, "Where is your roti?" Maharajji took it and ate it. Maharajji said the man was an Iraqi who had come to Vrindaban forty years ago, but the man didn't seem of this world to the devotees who were present.

टाम

Once a sadhu came into the temple carrying a trident and covered with ashes (which are characteristic of Shiva). Maharajji ran right up to him and did obeisance, and the man disappeared.

जय

Another time, a man came late at night and asked for a lantern at the temple gate. Dada went and gave him the lantern because his car had broken down, and then the man came back and returned the lantern. The next day Maharajji said, "Did you invite him into the temple for food?" They hadn't. He said, "You fool! Don't you know who that was? It was Sombari Maharaj [a saint long deceased]."

जय

KK worked hard at the bhandara. Maharajji later told him he had had the darshan of Sombari Maharaj there. KK was angry because he hadn't realized it. Maharajji said, "Why should you know?" and the anger disappeared.

जय

Maharajji went with one of the Ma's to visit a new murti of Vaishnavi Devi being installed, and it was still in the packing case. Only the face showed. Maharajji talked to the murti and the Mother clearly saw the murti blink. That is the true consecration.

जय

Rabu was sick and had lost his voice. Maharajji told him to do Devi puja (prayers to the female aspect of God) to Durga for four days. As the last line was recited, Maharajji opened the window and called out, "I've told the Mother [Goddess Durga] and all will be well with you now."

जय

Maharajji's love of Christ was unearthly. When he was asked, "Who was Christ?" Maharajji answered:

HE WAS ONE WITH ALL BEINGS AND HE HAD GREAT LOVE FOR ALL IN THE WORLD. HE WAS ONE WITH GOD.

YOU MUST ACCEPT THE TEACHINGS OF CHRIST AND FOLLOW THEM. CHRIST SAID TO BE LIKE A LITTLE CHILD—NEVER THINK OR SPEAK ANYTHING THAT COULD HARM ANYONE.

NO ONE BELIEVES IN CHRIST, BUT I DO.

HE WAS CRUCIFIED SO THAT HIS SPIRIT COULD SPREAD THROUGHOUT THE WORLD. HE SACRIFICED HIS BODY FOR THE DHARMA. HE NEVER DIED, HE NEVER DIED. HE IS ATMAN (THE SOUL), LIVING IN THE HEARTS OF ALL.

You never knew what a devotee's statement would evoke. A boy came one time and asked, "Maharajji, did Jesus really get angry?"

As soon as Maharajji heard the word "Jesus," tears came to his eyes. He was sitting up when the question was asked, and he leaned over on his elbow and tapped his heart three times with tears coming down from his eyes. There was total silence for a moment. Maharajji had brought the reality of Christ into everyone's consciousness, and he said, "Christ never got angry. When he was crucified he felt only love. Christ was never attached to anything; he even gave away his own body." And at that point everyone was crying—we had gone through the complete Passion of Christ. And all of a sudden he sat up and said, "The mind can travel a million miles in the blink of an eye—the Buddha said that."

"Why was Christ so maligned?" Maharajji was asked.

"It is so with all saints, but they see only love in everyone. You should not speak, hear, or see evil. You should see love everywhere and in everyone. See the good in all."

Maharajji once went to Catholic mass and took prasad there. Maharajji, T, and BD were all in Lucknow on Christmas morning and decided to go to Jesus' puja. As they approached the church, Maharajji had BD go in first (as he was a Westerner). Maharajji was of course barefoot, wearing his blanket and dhoti. BD knelt down before the font of holy water and someone there sprinkled water on his head. T and Maharajji followed this example. They attended the ceremony, and when time came for Communion, they received the Sacrament in their hands.

Once a devotee asked Maharajji how Christ meditated. Maharajji sat up and closed his eyes for some time. Tears began to stream from his eyes as he sat in silence. Then Maharajji said, "He lost himself in the ocean of love."

MAHARAJJI HONORED purity of spirit, no matter what the tradition or lineage. He kept drawing us back from our concerns about individual differences, back beyond the forms, with his oft-reiterated remark, "Sub Ek [All one]!"

*ALL RELIGIONS ARE THE SAME. THEY ALL
LEAD TO GOD. GOD IS EVERYBODY . . .
THE SAME BLOOD FLOWS THROUGH US
ALL, THE ARMS, THE LEGS, THE HEART, ALL
ARE THE SAME. SEE NO DIFFERENCE,
SEE ALL THE SAME.*

*YOU MUST HONOR SHIVA THROUGH LOVE.
RAM AND SHIVA ARE THE SAME. RAM
WORSHIPPED SHIVA, SHIVA WORSHIPPED
RAM, THEY ARE ONLY ONE.*

*IT IS DECEPTION TO TEACH BY INDIVIDUAL
DIFFERENCES AND KARMA. SEE ALL THE SAME.*

*YOU CAN'T REALIZE GOD IF YOU SEE DIFFER-
ENCES. LEARN TO FIND THE LOVE WITHIN.*

*A Moslem devotee invited Maharajji to attend a religious festival at his
home. The whole family and many of their friends gathered together to sing
Sufi songs and to hear readings from the Koran. Many Moslem mullahs
(priests) and scholars attended the festival to perform the rituals and read the
scriptures. When Maharajji arrived, the devotee escorted him to the place of
honor in front of the scholars. They immediately ceased their singing and
complained to the host. They said that they couldn't continue the rituals in the
presence of a Hindu. Maharajji verbally abused them for their prejudice and
narrow-mindedness. He quoted from the Koran and from some great Sufi poet-
saints on the oneness of all religions. Maharajji asked for some prasad. When it
was brought he distributed food, sweets, and money to the scholars. Happy
again, they started their chanting. Maharajji accompanied them for many
hours, singing "La Il Aha El Il Allah Hu."*

*THE BEST FORM IS TO WORSHIP GOD
IN EVERY FORM.*

*YOU MUST ACCEPT EVERYONE AND SEE IN
THEM THE LORD. THERE IS NO OTHER
NEED FOR A SAINT.*

EVERYONE IS A REFLECTION OF MY FACE.

Hanuman

O<small>F ALL THE</small> holy books in India, the Ramayana was by far Maharajji's favorite. And within the Ramayana he was particularly fond of the chapter entitled "Sundarakand."

In Lucknow this old man always came to see Maharajji, and Maharajji would always ask him to recite from the Ramayana. "Sing this part! Sing the part where . . ." and so forth. The man would sing and Maharajji would eat his meal. Maharajji would never sniff or anything, but tears would stream down his face like a child. The Sundarakand was his favorite part.

When the Ramayana reading was in Kainchi, he'd open his window just a little to listen to it.

T<small>HE SUNDARAKAND</small> concerns the exploits of Hanuman, an extraordinarily charming, wise, powerful, and loving monkey whose sole preoccupation was to serve God in the form of Ram. Maharajji never tired of hearing and repeating the adventures of Hanuman as described in the Ramayana and in a special prayer to Hanuman, the Hanuman Chalisa.

Maharajji used to quote from the Ramayana such things as, "I bow down to Hanuman, whose praises can only be sung by Ram. The stories of Ram are so beautiful that the birds of doubt are chased away."

ᛏᛅ

He loved to hear the Hanuman Chalisa sung by the Westerners early in the morning. He was very happy with it, and in the middle he'd start joking and make everyone laugh.

ᛏᛅ

From the very beginning, he loved the Hanuman Chalisa very much. In the early days, when a big mob gathered, he would tell them all to sit down and recite the Hanuman Chalisa. When they were all involved in it, he'd get up and go somewhere else.

To be in Maharajji's presence when such stories were repeated seemed to turn these stories into an awesome living truth.

Ordinarily when we read the Hanuman Chalisa, nothing particularly struck us. Sometimes Maharajji would say, "Is it written that Hanumanji will live forever . . . that he was for all time? How?" Maharajji would say only this much and put everyone into a thoughtful state. Maharajji put a spark to the reading.

ᛏᛅ

Once when we were sitting with Maharajji at Dada's house, a devotee was reciting from the Ramayana. Tears streamed down Maharajji's cheeks, and then he went into a very blissful samadhi state. We were all overwhelmed by the quality of the moment. When the reading stopped Dada suddenly got up and led Maharajji into the other room and closed the door.

MAHARAJJI NOT ONLY honored the story of Hanuman but over the years had encouraged devotees in many places in India to construct temples for the honoring of Hanuman. Some of these temples are small and located in devotee's homes, and others are large public ones to which hundreds come each day. It is not possible to determine how many temples were constructed at Maharajji's inspiration, if not his direct instigation. For someone so aware of the pitfalls of ritual, it seems strange that in his later years he should be so identified with temples. However, everything connected with the temples, starting with the very construction, held subtle teachings. Every temple involved much drama of one kind or another about such aspects as the acquisition of land. And these difficulties embroiled many devotees in processes that in each case intensified their own ultimate faith in the spirit.

The big temple at Nainital is constructed upon a spot where previously there was dense jungle, inhabited by wild animals. Part of the place had been used as a burial ground for very young children (who are not cremated). Local people believed the site to be haunted by ghosts. When Maharajji visited the place and indicated that he wanted to build a temple there, the local officials put up a lot of resistance. Nobody thought that a Hanuman temple could ever be built there.

Maharajji just camped by the side of the road. Each day many devotees would walk out to the spot to be with him. Slowly, slowly the vibrations of the place changed. Once he pointed to a mule shed, which was the only structure near there, and said, "Here there will be a big temple and people will come from all over the world to it." Everyone laughed because it seemed absurd. Then after some time, Maharajji had Hari Dass Baba bring to the place a small murti of Hanuman that he had made, and it was duly installed. That was the beginning of what is now a large temple complex on the top of a high hill to which people come from all over to have darshan.

राम

The large Kainchi temple is built at a spot where Sombari Maharaj, a great saint of that area, had lived in a cave. The cave still remains at the back of the temple and there is a strong feeling of continuity of spirit there.

Once Maharajji, Siddhi Ma, and Jivanti Ma went at night to the site that was later to become the temple at Kainchi. While the Ma's sat by the roadside, Maharajji crossed over the river and didn't come back for four or five hours. When he did, he said, "I hear the sound here. We shall have a temple."

ॐ

When Maharajji was asked why he didn't build an ashram at a particular-holy place, he answered that it was not for such as him to do. This was a very old, old temple site. He would not want to disturb the vibration already set up.

ॐ

In our city, the place where the temple now stands was where people would relieve themselves. It was very dirty. Maharajji came, blew a conch shell to purify the place, and stayed there. People gathered and cleaned it up and built a temple.

ॐ

Maharajji frequently used to visit the old Hanuman temple in Lucknow, situated on the banks of the Gomati River. The temple was built before 1960 by a devotee of Maharajji at his request. Maharajji would sit there and give darshan, and though the temple became famous, puja and bhandara to celebrate its opening were never done. Once M asked Maharajji about this, and Maharajji replied, "No, no. Not this temple. We'll have a bigger temple."

One day while driving Maharajji to someone's house they passed by an old bridge which was being replaced by a big new one. Maharajji pointed toward the bank where the construction was going on and said, "There we'll have our temple!" There was no question of doing anything. Later, when driving to Kanpur, Maharajji suddenly shouted, "A wonderful temple has been designed in Lucknow."

Two years later there was a change in government and an old devotee became minister of public works. He came to Maharajji and suggested that the old temple was too small. Maharajji said, "As you like." A few days later the man came by with a fine model of the present temple. Maharajji said, "Yes, make it."

When the new bridge was completed, the old one was abandoned. At the same time, the river began to consume the old temple. The government suggested destroying it, but Maharajji said that a temple shouldn't be destroyed, that nature should run its course.

The government bought the temple for thirty-five thousand rupees as *compensation. Maharajji asked the minister how much the new temple would cost, and he said eighty-five thousand rupees. When asked where the balance would come from, Maharajji said, "It will be made!" Six months later the government had given most of the money, and the owner of the contracting company offered to pay the balance. Then the temple was built on land that was also given by the public-works minister. Two years ago the Gomati flooded and took off the back half of the old temple complex.*

THE MOST IMPORTANT teaching of these temples, however, is that they all contain statues of Hanuman. These statues, constructed of stone or cement, were invested through prayer, mantra, and chanting with the spirit of Hanuman, and thus they became murtis and were treated in the same way that one would treat the actual Hanuman.

As the years passed, Maharajji came to spend more and more time at these temples in the course of his wandering, and this tended to strengthen an association in the minds of the community between Hanuman and Maharajji. This association went back to the earliest stories about Maharajji, far predating the construction of the temples.

Exactly what the association between Maharajji and Hanuman is, plays endlessly in the minds of devotees. He talked about Hanuman continuously and named many of us with one or another of the names used to refer to Hanuman, including those names of God to which the word "das [servant of]" was attached; and he instructed many on the path of service and devotion that would bring them ever closer to Hanuman.

A man asked Maharajji, "What should I do for sadhana?" Maharajji said, "Don't bother your head about that, just keep repeating Ram as Hanuman did." This man was an old devotee, now retired from his livelihood work.

SERVE AS HANUMAN SERVED.

SOME DEVOTEES regard Maharajji's focus on Hanuman as due to Maharajji's being a member of a traditional devotional sect in India, in which the relation of devotee to God is like that of servant to master—with Hanuman the perfect embodiment of that form. This sect focuses its devotion upon Hanuman, the monkey-God depicted in the Ramayana as serving God (in the form of Ram) with totally concentrated one-pointedness. His exploits, which reflect this devoted service, bring him into such intimacy with God that he becomes known as the "breath of Ram itself."

Other devotees see the deep intimacy that was often evidenced in Maharajji's dealings with Hanuman as reflecting a bond between them far transcending the usual devotional forms.

When Maharajji was staying at Neeb Karori, it is reported that he spoke to Hanuman directly, as if he were right there.

जय

Maharajji would visit an ancient (eight-hundred or thousand-year-old) Hanuman temple at Aliganj in Lucknow. He would sit there under a giant shade tree near Hanuman for long periods.

जय

There used to be treacherous landslides along the ridge that later became the Hanuman Garh temple site. Maharajji told K that all this would stop when Hanuman came; he would protect the place. Since the temple was built, there have been no more landslides.

जय

Maharajji invited a famous pundit to come to Kainchi and recite the Shrimad Bhagavatam. This man was used to reciting before large and very receptive crowds, and he complained to Maharajji that on this occasion he had to recite to only a few illiterate villagers. Maharajji gently rebuked him and said, "Don't worry. Hanumanji is listening."

जय

A forest fire in the hills came dangerously close to the temple but stopped just at the perimeter of the grounds. Maharajji said, "The monkey army protected us. They put out the fire."

जय

At the consecration of the Hanuman murti at Kainchi, Maharajji stayed away most of the day. Late in the afternoon he said to a few devotees, "Let's go have darshan of Hanuman. Get a pail of milk. We'll give him some milk." A crowd started to gather around the room, but Maharajji had the door closed, with only three or four devotees inside.

One of the devotees thought, "I have always wanted to see how a murti is fed."

As the devotee thought this, Maharajji turned and said, "Everyone turn around and face the wall and close your eyes." They all did this, but the same devotee wanted so badly to see that he thought of opening his eyes anyway. As he thought this, Maharajji said, "And if you open your eyes you will be blinded." Suddenly they all felt a change of energy in the room. They experienced through closed eyelids a brilliant light and heard the sound of drinking. When they were allowed to turn around they found the pail empty, a tiny puddle of milk on the floor, and some milk dripping from Hanuman's mouth. Maharajji told them to collect the milk on the floor and give it out as Hanuman's prasad.

MAHARAJJI OFTEN told the following story, which some devotees suspected was about himself:

In a small village there was a tiny Hanuman temple to which the local people would come. The practice is for a devotee to bring some sweets and offer them to the murti by giving them to the priest, who then takes the sweets into the room or alcove where the murti is and draws a curtain. Then he offers the sweets to the murti with appropriate mantras. After this the priest usually takes a few of the sweets and sets them aside to be given later to the poor neighborhood children. The rest he brings back to the devotee-donor as prasad, which the devotee then eats as a blessing from Hanuman.

It so happened that the old priest in this village was called away by illness in his family, and he left a young neighborhood boy who loved to be around the temple to take care of the temple while he was away. Soon some devotees came and brought sweets, and the boy took them as he had seen the priest do and went behind the curtain. Even though he had never been with Hanuman when the curtain was closed, he offered the sweets to the murti. But Hanuman wouldn't take them. The boy became upset and demanded that Hanuman take some of the sweets. He even picked up a stick and began to beat the murti. Suddenly all the sweets disappeared from the dish. The boy returned to the devotees, joyfully explaining that Hanuman had accepted their offering. The devotees, who were used to receiving back a portion of their gift, concluded that the boy had decided to keep all their gift for himself, and beating the boy, they sent him away. When the old priest returned and was told about this incident, he said, "All my life I had hoped to become pure enough so that my offerings would be accepted by Hanuman. But I never was. This young boy had that purity and was so blessed."

राम

On Maharajji's last day at Kainchi, he stopped for two minutes in front of Hanuman and folded his hands. He was wearing only a dhoti. It was completely silent. This was only the second time, said one long-time devotee, that he had ever seen Maharajji do this. The other time was at the consecration of the murti.

FOR MOST OF US, however, the link we experienced is even more intimate than these stories suggest. For us, Maharajji *is* Hanuman.

Hanuman's qualities are described in the various texts about him as follows:

I bow to the son of the wind-god, the beloved devotee of Sri Rama, the chief of the monkeys, the respository of all virtues, the foremost among the wise, a fire to consume the forest of the demon race, possessing a body shining as a mountain of gold and a home of immeasurable strength. (Tulsidas, Sri Ramacharitamanasa, English translation [Gorakhpur, India: Gita Press, 1968], pp. 595–596)

राम

Who is this monkey Hanuman? Rama let him loose in the world. He knows Rama and Rama knows him. Hanuman can break in or break out of anywhere. He cannot be stopped, like the free wind in flight. Hanuman can spot a tyrant, he looks at deeds not words and he'll go and pull his beard. Disguises and words of talk cannot confuse a mere wild animal. . . . Hanuman will take your sad tune and use it to make a happy dance. Strong is his guard . . . the Son of the Wind. (William Buck, Ramayana [Berkeley: University of California Press, 1976], p. 427)

ॐ

Hanuman is no monkey, but some god in the form of a monkey. No one can equal him. He is brave and kind, self-radiant, a befriender of the meek, strong and intelligent, and a knower of time and place (adapted from Tulsidas and Buck).

Hanuman must be reminded of his own powers, for he has no self-consciousness.

"Listen, O mighty Hanuman; how is it that you are keeping mum? A son of the wind-god, you are as strong as your father and a storehouse of intelligence, discretion, and spiritual wisdom. What undertaking in this world is too difficult for you to accomplish, dear child? It is for the service of Sri Rama that you have come down upon earth." The moment Hanuman heard these words he grew to the size of a mountain, with a body shining as gold and full of splendor as though he was another king of mountains. (Tulsidas, p. 593)

ॐ

You assumed a tiny form to reveal yourself to Sita—then became immense and terrifying to burn Lanka. (Hanuman Chalisa)

ॐ

"But my son, all the monkeys must be pygmies like you, whereas the demons are mighty and great warriors. I have grave misgivings in my heart on this score," said Sita.
On hearing this the monkey revealed his natural form, colossal as a mountain of gold, terrible in battle possessing great might and full of valour. (Tulsidas, p. 608)

ॐ

He entered the grove, ate the fruit and began to break down the trees. He later said to Ravana, "I ate the fruit because I felt hungry and broke the boughs as a monkey is wont to do."

Ravana laughed and said, sarcastically, "We have found a most wise Guru in this monkey!" (adapted from Tulsidas, pp. 610–614)

H<small>IS</small> APPETITE for love is insatiable.

*Sita, the Mother of the Universe, wishes to feed Hanuman because of her intense love for him. Hanuman begins to eat. And she keeps cooking more and offering more and he keeps eating more until the pantry is empty. She borrows food and cooks more, but he keeps saying, "More, Mother, more!" Finally her mother-in-law brings trays of cooked food to help her out, but Hanuman won't eat it even though it is brought out by Sita. With his discriminative power he knows the difference and says, "No, Mother, this is not cooked by your hand."
(a folk tale)*

ﬗ

*Hanuman's eyes filled with tears as he recalled the Lord's virtues. He ever enjoyed the nectar of the Lord's story. His only desire was to be allowed to remain as a devotee of Rama. Again and again the Lord tried to raise him up; he, however, was so absorbed in love that he would not rise. When Rama asked him what he wanted, Hanuman answered: "Grant me unceasing devotion, which is a source of supreme bliss."
Ram answered: "So be it." (adapted from Tulsidas and Hanuman Chalisa)*

ﬗ

Hanuman says to Ram: "A monkey's greatest valour lies in his skipping about from one bough to another. That I should have been able to leap across the ocean, burn the gold city, kill the demon host and lay waste the Asoka grove was all due to your might; no credit, my Lord, is due to me for the same." (Tulsidas, p. 620)

ﬗ

Then with his sharp fingernails Hanuman tore open his breast and pulled back the flesh. And see, there was written again and again on every bone, in fine little letters . . . Rama Rama Rama . . . and in his heart were Ram and Sita. (adapted from Buck and Tulsidas)

ॐ

Hanuman, all joy comes to those under the umbrella of your grace, and the work of the world, however difficult, is made easy. (Hanuman Chalisa)

ॐ

Then like a storm Hanuman drove away low spirits, like a light he brought courage. (Buck, p. 223)

ॐ

To me who was being drowned in the ocean of desolation, dear Hanuman, you have come as a veritable bark. (Tulsidas, p. 607)

ॐ

By your very sight, O dear monkey, I have been absolved of all sins. (Tulsidas, p. 600)

ॐ

"O, Hanuman."
"My King." Hanuman knelt before Rama.
Rama said, "As long as men shall speak of you, you will live on earth. No one can equal you. Your heart is true; your arms are strong; you have the energy to do anything. You have served me faithfully and done things for me that couldn't be done."
"It's nothing," Hanuman said, "I am your friend, that's all." (Buck, p. 426)

ॐ

Still today, high in the pine forests lives Hanuman. He will always be listening wherever Ram's name is spoken; he will listen endlessly to his old adventures and his own true stories. So take care. He is here. (Buck, p. 432)

How like maharajji all this is . . . Maharajji who playfully gathers and throws fruit; whose extraordinarily long-armed body changes shape and size, at one moment becoming tiny as a mosquito and at another, vast as a mountain of gold; who moves continuously from place to place with surprising agility and awesome strength; who is a vast ocean of compassion for his devotees; who does not seem to know or acknowledge his own extroardinary powers; but who never forgets his total love of Ram.

As the devotees see it . . .

One day I was sitting with Maharajji on a wall near the Kainchi temple. A pundit was reciting from the Ramayana to a nearby audience, when I suddenly became very uneasy. Maharajji grabbed me by the hand and took me over to the Shiva temple and we sat down in front of it. I looked at Maharajji, but what I saw was a huge monkey. That's all I remember. Others recall that at that moment we both disappeared. Several hours later Maharajji came walking back into the temple, yelling, "Where's Dada? Where's Dada?" A search was started and I was found upstream along the river, just coming back into consciousness. I don't remember anything else.

राम

Maharajji says that all the stones in Chitrakut are like precious jewels. SM, however, said, "Why collect stones, when you have Maharajji?" Just after that conversation, Maharajji was at the temple and had gone to the bathroom. Afterward SM helped him wash his hands. As he walked away there was an imprint of his wet foot on the small stones there. She collected these and put them in her sari. When her daughter came, SM told her to take them back and keep them at the house. Some days later she returned home and opened the box where she kept the stones. On each stone there was some imprint of Hanuman. Her husband didn't believe her so he got a magnifier and, sure enough, there they were. Later the box and stones all mysteriously disappeared.

राम

One day Maharajji was in his room while Dada was in the kitchen. Maharajji yelled, "Dada," and Dada ran to the hallway and found Maharajji standing outside his door with no blanket, his dhoti hanging down in the back like a tail. His body was of tremendous size, filling the hall. Dada fell at his feet and Maharajji went back into his room.

Once many people were sitting around Maharajji. He seemed to be in an exalted state, and a small girl was there sitting at his feet. Suddenly she began to weep. People asked her why she was crying. She said, "I can't say! I just saw Ram and Sita there inside Maharajji's chest." She then proceeded to describe the garments Sita wore and how they looked. Maharajji kept silent.

Seeing Maharajji would put some devotees into samadhi; others would then ask him to put them into it, too. Once when this happened Maharajji got angry, but later, during his bath, he started to scratch his back, and those devotees saw fur on his back and heard him growl like a monkey. They were all filled with ecstasy.

A certain man, every time he came near, would take one look at Maharajji and pass out cold. When they would revive him, all he would say is, "All I saw was a huge monkey."

"Maharajji's body pulsed with Ram," said a devotee.

On one occasion, one woman said to her husband, "I hear something in the next room." Their bedroom was near the room that they keep for Maharajji, but at this time he was not staying there. They went in to see what was causing the noise and found tracks just like Maharajji's footprints, all the way up the wall to the ceiling.

राम

SM said she once saw Maharajji's body with Ram written on every cell.

राम

Maharajji was once in Haridwar and planted himself on the doorstep of a sanyasi. This fellow developed a dislike for Maharajji and unsuccessfully tried to chase him away. One day the sadhu was preparing some very fine sweets with raisins, almonds, and so forth. Maharajji was watching and making comments. The sadhu said that he wouldn't share them and told Maharajji to go away, but Maharajji stayed right there. When the sweets were ready, the sadhu went to the Ganga to bathe, leaving Maharajji to guard the house. When he returned he found most of the sweets gone. Maharajji said that they looked appetizing, and so he had to try one; they were so good that he had kept eating them until they were almost gone.

राम

Dada, a professor of economics, described how he graded exam papers until late at night in his study at home, then went to bed. The house was securely locked and Maharajji was several hundred miles away. When Dada awoke in the morning, he found scrawled across the top paper the words राम राम राम *(Ram, Ram, Ram). It was apparently just Hanuman at play.*

SOME devotees not only saw Hanuman in Maharajji, but heard him as well . . .

At a reading of the Ramayana, when the reader asked what section he should recite, Maharajji said, "Recite the part where I am talking with Vibhishan." (It was, of course, Hanuman who spoke with Vibhishan.)

राम

Once in the midst of a discussion about the Kainchi temple, Maharajji said: "Do you think I'm collecting properties and becoming a landowner? I have absolutely no attachment to anything. I could leave everything just as I did Lanka." (In the Ramayana, Hanuman burned Lanka.)

Once, at Dada's, Maharajji was feigning sickness and had the doors of his room locked from outside. Later he was seen running down the street. When questioned about how he had gotten through the locked doors, he said, "The monkey became as small as a mosquito and flew out the window."

"Maharajji, you can do anything. You are Hanuman."
"I'm not Hanuman. I can do nothing . . . I am everything. I can do anything for anybody."

MAHARAJJI SAID, "EVERYWHERE I LOOK
I SEE ONLY RAM, AND THAT'S WHY I'M
ALWAYS HONORING EVERYTHING."

I DO NOTHING. GOD DOES EVERYTHING.

Hanuman, bestow your grace upon us,
Divine Guru
O, Son of the Wind, reliever of suffering,
embodiment of blessings,
live always in our hearts.
                              —Hanuman Chalisa

Krishna Das (Roy Bonney)

Jao!

I had heard about him in America and saved my money so that I could make a pilgrimage to India to meet him. I arrived at the temple with fruit, which somebody had told me to bring as an offering. The gatekeeper let me in to the back, where I saw him sitting on a wooden bed, wrapped in a plaid blanket. There were a lot of Indians and Westerners sitting on the ground around him. I was a little nervous so I went along the side of the courtyard up to the bed and put down the fruit while he was looking the other way. I bowed the way I saw someone else doing it, and when I raised my head he was looking right at me. Everything just stopped for a minute. Then he said, "Jao!"

My Hindi was poor but I knew that word! It was the one I used to get rid of the beggars who had crowded around me in Delhi. It meant "Beat it!" or "Get away!"

I was stunned and went through disbelief, embarrassment, anger, and guilt. I didn't know whether to laugh or cry. Here I'd come all this way from America and the first thing he'd said to me was "Beat it!" But then I thought, "Okay. You know best." And he threw me back one of the pieces of fruit and said "Jao" again. Only this time it was okay; this time I heard something else. It wasn't "Get lost!" but "Everything's fine. I love you. Go."

373

Now I can see that it all happened in those few minutes. He did whatever needed to be done; I got what I needed to get. All the times afterward when I was with him were wonderful, but they were just frosting on the cake.

THE VARIATIONS IN Maharajji's use of the word "jao" were infinite—from a bellow (sometimes preceded by "Ap [You]!" for the recalcitrant) to a tender, "Jao, Ma . . ." as he gently patted a woman devotee bowing at his feet.

Usually as devotees would come before him during the day, he would hand them a piece of fruit or some sweets, or ask them a question or two, and then jao them. Others would be allowed to sit with him while he gave darshan off and on through the day. It is interesting that a word seeming to imply rejection—"go away"—could be said with so much love that it came to mean "go with blessings" or "go with grace" or "go with my love."

There was jao to another part of the ashram; jao to take food or rest; jao to go carry out some indicated duty or service; jao that might be postponed, if one could think of a good question—or even ignored, if some distraction occurred, such as new arrivals. There was the jao of disgrace and banishment for some misdeed (often followed by a giggle once the culprit had passed out of earshot).

The word became Zen-like in its all-encompassing quality and, when roared inexplicably at first sight of a devotee entering the ashram, totally Zen in its effect.

Jao could be for a moment or forever—to the nearby city of Nainital for the night or, most dreaded by the Westerners, *maha-jao* (great jao) to America. Jao could even be questioned, if one was willing to play that perilous game. For a jao might be disputed successfully; but also a jao of a week to go visit Holy Benares might, on the response of a groan, be transformed to a jao of a month for a pilgrimage to Rameshwarem at the southernmost tip of India. Never was it simply "Go!" but always, "Go with love."

We were sitting on the hill opposite the ashram with some binoculars watching Maharajji, who was sitting on the roof of the building in the back of the ashram compound. We saw an Indian man who was trying to be with Maharajji sneak up along the stairs, hold his head really low, and rush across the roof toward Maharajji. And even from that distance, though we couldn't hear, we could certainly see the jao and the man go right back down again. "Oops, there he goes!" We were up there smoking dope and eating yogurt and having darshan with binoculars. When Maharajji found out that he was being watched with binoculars, he looked through them and he liked them.

तुम

We'd be sitting with Maharajji and he'd tell us all to go, and I'd be the only one to get up and go. My whole training was to do just what the teacher said. Then I'd be the only one outside. Everybody else would be inside laughing and talking with him as if he had never said jao. Chaitanya used to brag about how many jao's he'd survived, like battle scars. But I had a very hard time hearing the jao and not leaving. Then I would hide behind something and see if he really meant it. Later I saw that sometimes he'd say it to you and you knew he meant it; other times he'd say it and it wasn't the same.

तुम

Once Maharajji was jao'ing us all to Delhi for a week to hear Krishnamurti, or "Ram-Murti" as Maharajji would call him. I didn't really want to go, so I was hiding out, but as I came around a pillar I ran right into Maharajji, who was standing there alone. He looked at me and his whole body started to shake and he let out deep sobs: "Oh-ho-ho-ho," as if he were wracked with grief, crying crocodile tears. And he kept sobbing out the words, "Delhi, Delhi." Of course I burst out laughing and ended up going to Delhi. One of the things Krishnamurti said with great soul-force while we were in Delhi was, "I abhor all gurus!" Perfect!

तुम

After a month on pilgrimage in southern India, we returned to Allahabad in the early morning hours, anticipating another long gentle round of being with Maharajji. When I came into his room at 6:30 in the morning his first words were, "Has your visa been renewed?"
"I don't know, Maharajji. I made application."
"No, it hasn't. Jao! Go to Delhi."
"Now?" I was a bit taken aback to be thrown out before I'd even been welcomed home.
"Go by the 9:30 train this morning."
Once this devastating piece of business had been transacted, Maharajji

became tenderness itself, rolling around on his tucket, handing out the rudraksha beads we had brought from Rameshwarem temple, and playfully pulling my beard and patting me. Although I tried to get him to change his mind about sending me away, I found myself back on the train at 9:30.

In Delhi Maharajji had arranged for me to receive help from a minor official in the government. And so began another round of entanglement in bureaucratic red tape. The prospects seemed to go from bad to worse. Earlier in the fall I had tried to take care of the visa extension with KK, up in the mountains. He had arranged for me to speak with the head of the visa bureau in that community. Those proceedings had gone awry and now made the work in Delhi more difficult. These machinations with KK, more or less behind Maharajji's back, were not ignored by Maharajji, who kidded me mercilessly about how KK was now my advisor, my guru, and if I had not tried to get the visa done through KK, everything would now be all right.

As the end of February approached and the visa situation looked hopeless, I suddenly recalled the previous February when I had first seen Maharajji on this visit to India. "How long do you want to stay?" he had asked.

"Forever."

"March?"

"You mean next month?"

"All right, a year from March."

And now, early in March a year later, despite all the apparent attempts of KK and Maharajji to help me, I received my "quit India" notice from the government. There was no doubt about it: Maharajji was using the government to do his dirty work. All I could do was laugh and surrender once again. He had covered every angle.

Generally I tend to cry in the presence of purity or dharma. I'm not quite sure why that is, but the feeling is that such purity is too much to bear. I also cry when I am ecstatically happy and, in rare instances, when I am very depressed. At the leave-taking from Maharajji I cried and cried, and, again, I'm not really sure why. Mrs. Soni felt great concern about my crying and said, "Don't cry. You will be able to come back—won't he, Maharajji?"

Maharajji said, "He can come in a year . . . or six months." But I wasn't really crying because of sadness; if anything it was from joy, for Maharajji had instructed me that serving people was my dharma. My work was clear. And he seemed to be telling me to get on with it.

Maharajji said two more things that day that I can remember. First he said, "I will always be in communion with you." And the second thing was "Jao."
(R.D.)

*DUE TO INDIVIDUAL KARMA, PEOPLE
MUST BE SENT AWAY FROM A SAINT.
HOW THIS IS DONE VARIES. WHEN THE
TIME FOR THE ASSOCIATION ENDS,
THE SEPARATION MUST OCCUR.*

*Within a month, I went back to America, with absolutely no regret. I was
really happy to be going. Maharajji could give you that kind of energy, so that
you really didn't mind leaving, so that you were really exuberant about going.*

*I SEND PEOPLE AWAY BECAUSE ATTACHMENT
HAPPENS BOTH WAYS.*

*I WILL NEVER ALLOW ONE OF MY PEOPLE
TO ESCAPE FROM ME.*

The Great Escape

WHAT WAS TO be Maharajji's final day at Kainchi was spent in darshan, kirtan, and prayers. Both Indian and Western devotees were gathered. Maharajji was asking after everyone at the temple and elsewhere. Twice he put one of his Indian devotees into samadhi and brought him out of it by throwing his blanket over the man's head. At one point he said to those gathered, "He is your guru. He is young and I am old. He will live and I will die!" Everyone laughed. He then had the Westerners sing to Hanuman. There were tears in his eyes. The Indian women did arti before him, and one and all received a tilak upon the forehead.

Then he went to bathe and eat and hinted that he was leaving for four or five days. When he came out of his room he went to the temple and paused before the murti of Hanuman, holding his hands together in pranam silently for two or three minutes. Again he stopped and honored each of the murtis at the temple in turn. While crossing the bridge out of the temple compound he met an old devotee who was a photographer. Maharajji gave him an old photo and told him to copy it and distribute it freely. He instructed that the daily feeding be stopped and the Mothers taken to Nainital. Then he said softly, "Today, I am released from Central Jail forever." As he approached the car that was to take him to the station, the blanket slipped from his shoulders to the ground. A devotee tried to put it back on, but Maharajji said, "Leave it. One should be attached to nothing." Others folded it and placed it in the car.

Just at the moment when he sat in the car, an old woman arrived from the nearby village of Bhowali. Maharajji said, "Ma, I've been waiting for you." He touched her on the head and said, "I'm going." He was gay and full of humor.

The driver of the car was another old and trusted devotee. He reports that during the ride to the railway station, he became aware that Maharajji's feet had become extremely big. "I was afraid," he said.

Maharajji kept saying to him, "What is destiny? What is going to happen? Tomorrow we don't even know." They got to the station early for the train, so they sat in the car for two hours. Maharajji pointed out a beautiful rainbow and said, "Look at that natural beauty. How beautiful is God's creation, man can never make anything so beautiful."

Tickets had been purchased to Agra for him and for Ravi, a young devotee. On the train Maharajji did not close his eyes all night and kept waking the devotee and saying, "I'm not tired, talk with me." Ravi asked him to drink the milk which the Mothers had sent in a thermos, but the milk had turned bad. "Throw it out," Maharajji said, "Throw the thermos out, too." Ravi didn't want to, but Maharajji did so himself, saying, "Throw it out, I will not need it anymore." He spoke of many things and many people through the night. He said, "I've come on earth only for the spreading of dharma."

When they reached Agra, Maharajji jumped from the train while Ravi trailed behind with the baggage. Instead of following the platform, Maharajji jumped from it easily, crossing six sets of tracks and jumping up on the main platform. Ravi caught up with him at the ticket-taker who had stopped Maharajji for his ticket. Then Maharajji bargained with various rickshaw drivers: one wanted three rupees (about thirty cents), which Maharajji argued was too much. Finally a price was fixed and they set out, only Maharajji knowing the way. En route, Maharajji pointed out a house and said, "Their son has gone to America and the family feels very sad. Sons don't serve their fathers anymore." When they arrived at the house, he told Ravi to give to the rickshaw driver the milk bucket filled with Ganga water that Maharajji always carried with him. Again he said, "Have no attachment for anything."

Except for one hour when Maharajji went to see a heart specialist (he had complained of pains in his chest), he remained at S's house from 6:00 A.M. to 9:00 P.M. that evening. The specialist said that Maharajji's heart was fine and that he just needed rest. At 9:00 P.M. he left for the station to meet the train that would take him back up to the foot of the mountains at Kathgodam. He was accompanied by young Ravi and another devotee, D. After some time he told Ravi to go and sit in the next compartment. Ravi went there but was thought to be a thief by the occupants, who yanked the chain and had the train stopped. Ravi was taken up and placed in the police van that was a part of the train. Ravi persuaded the police to ask Maharajji at the next station if Ravi was with him. Maharajji was very loving to Ravi and said, "We'll get off at Mathura and I'll make a call to the DIG [Deputy Inspector General] and set things straight." At Mathura, not far from Agra, they got off the train. Some people bowed to him. He then sat down on the steps of the station after leaning against the outdoor latrine. D went to get a taxi, while R waited with Maharajji.

Maharajji then lay on the steps and began convulsing. His eyes were closed and his body was cold and sweating. D fed him some pills and Maharajji said, "Turn off the lights." He asked for water and to be taken to nearby Vrindaban. He was carried by stretcher to the taxi and laid across the back seat. During the ride to Vrindaban, Maharajji seemed unconscious for most of the way, though now and then he mumbled things they could not understand. They took him to the emergency room at the hospital. In the hospital the doctor gave him injections and placed an oxygen mask over his face. The hospital staff said that he was in a diabetic coma but that his pulse was fine. Maharajji roused and pulled the oxygen mask off his face and the blood pressure measuring band from his arm, saying, "Bekar [useless]." Maharajji asked for Ganga water. As there was none, they brought him regular water. He then repeated several times, "Jaya Jagadish Hare" [Hail to the Lord of the Universe]," each time in a lower pitch. His face became very peaceful, all signs of pain disappeared. He was dead. No one at the hospital had recognized him. The hospital staff left the room. Ravi and D carried Maharajji out and placed the body in a taxi and took it to the Hanuman temple. (It was about 1:15 on the morning of September 11.)

HC said that in September 1973, shortly before Maharajji's mahasamadhi, he felt such a longing, such a craving to go see Maharajji. He and his wife went to Kainchi just two days before Maharajji left. "It was no strange thing—not a miracle," he said of this coincidence. But he said that when he got there, it made him think very deeply. The experience was "exceptionally something else."

During this visit, Maharajji foreshadowed his leaving by saying to him,

"Ask whatever you want—then I am going to go." HC said that all that was in his mind evaporated. He asked nothing, nor did he catch the hint.

ᵀᵐ

Oh, Maharajji told us all that he was going to leave this world. One time he said to us that when he leaves, he will leave us all laughing! Then he said that when he leaves Siddhi Ma, he will leave her weeping. As he said this, Siddhi Ma began weeping so much. But Maharajji said she shouldn't worry—he wouldn't let anyone harm her, that she would become radiant with his love.

ᵀᵐ

A friend of HC's said that Maharajji also clearly hinted to him of the coming mahasamadhi. Maharajji said to the man, "What can I do if God calls me back?"

ᵀᵐ

It is D's feeling that for the past two years Maharajji had been almost constantly in deep samadhi and completely forgetful of the world. The functions of talking and behaving with people were going on automatically while Maharajji wasn't in this world. He was forgetful even of the body's necessity to urinate and would pass all day without doing it. Then he would finally be reminded and would run, sometimes urinating as he ran. His dhoti and blanket weren't tied properly. Formerly, they were so neat and tight.

ᵀᵐ

On the Saturday before he left, he told me, "This is the ghost plane. Everyone has to die. People weep for their selfishness. Even the dying person weeps for his family. These are nothing, this is foolishness."

ᵀᵐ

Mrs. S was very worried about Maharajji's heart condition, so B got Maharajji alone to ask about it by flooding the car's carburetor when just the two of them were in it. He said, "Maharajji, the car is flooded and it will take one of your miracles—or I'll ask you a question and if you answer it directly, maybe the car will start. Are you really sick?"

"No, I'm not."

B then said, "Do me one favor. If you are, will you tell me?" Maharajji put his hand on B's head.

Exactly one month before Maharajji left his body, he said to a group, "My heart stopped last night." He said this twice, but someone giggled, which made B angry so he didn't pursue the matter. Then Maharajji said it a third time, but there was so much activity going on around Maharajji that B could not discuss it. Then B had to go to Europe. He returned a few days before Maharajji left his body. He planned to go for darshan when he remembered that he had promised to do something for another man, and he thought to himself that if Maharajji could do service for thousands, then he could serve this one other person. He went and served the other man instead of going for darshan, and so he didn't see Maharajji before the mahasamadhi.

राम

That last day, Maharajji allowed everybody to wash his feet and drink as much as they liked of the remaining water. He was very pleased. Then he said, "I'm not going today." But after a half hour's rest, he said, "No, I am going. Get the car." Then T said he had to check Maharajji's pulse, and Maharajji said, "Are you becoming a doctor, too?" T checked it and found no pulse.

He said to Maharajji, "Maharajji, if you keep playing tricks . . ."

Maharajji replied, "All right, fifteen seconds and no more." This time the pulse was perfectly normal. That last day, he was very happy and joyful, quite contrary to other times, when he would leave a place without appearing to know anyone.

T and D were talking to each other, saying, "He's too happy. This is contrary."

Maharajji said, "When you go to your house, you are happy."

राम

One day in 1971 or 1972, Maharajji was presented with a diary. From
that day on, he would fill two pages with handwritten "Ram" each day.
"ᵗᵗ ᵗᵗ ᵗᵗ ᵗᵗ   . . ." He asked that the diary be kept in his room. From
then on he was left alone for an hour each morning while he wrote in his
diary. When he traveled the diary went with him. By September 9, his last
day in Kainchi, he completed the entry, then proceeded to date the next page
September 10 and wrote "Ram" on it. Finally he wrote September 11 on a
clean page and did not write any "Ram" there. He then gave the book to SM
and said to her, "Now this is your book. You write in it."

ᵗᵗ

B had made a tape of Maharajji chanting, but Maharajji said, "You aren't
to let anyone hear it for two years." That was exactly two years before he
died.

ᵗᵗ

A few days before Maharajji left Kainchi he said to SM, "The temple must
be inside the ashram."
    She said, "You don't need another temple. You have five temples here
already." He just laughed. Now the Samadhi temple fills the courtyard where
the Westerners used to sing kirtan to Maharajji.

ᵗᵗ

On the morning of September 8, Maharajji called for me and we talked
privately for three-quarters of an hour on various subjects. After that I saw him
again at four o'clock in his room with two or three others. He was saying to
us, "All those who come into this world must go. Nobody will stay here.
They must go. Knowing this, why do people at the time of death go
"Whooooo, whooooo" (he feigned great weeping)? Why do they cry? They
should go gladly. They should go laughing. They shouldn't cry." After some
general talk he said, "Now I shall go. I won't stay and I won't give darshan
anymore to anyone."
    One devotee asked, "Maharajji, where will you go that we people will not
be able to get your darshan?"

"Oh, too far! Too far!" Maharajji replied.

"Where?" the devotee asked again.

"Oh, there . . . near the Narmada River," Maharajji said. (The Narmada River starts in Amarkantak, traditionally from the throat of Shiva.) The bus driver came shortly after that to take away all those people who lived elsewhere. Some man had just arrived and asked for a private darshan, but Maharajji said, "Baba Neem Karoli is dead! Who will you talk to now?"

The man laughed and said, "All right, if you order me to go then I will, but I'll return at eight in the morning and talk with you then!"

Maharajji said, "All right. You come. If I'm alive, I'll talk to you."

Outside in the courtyard the Westerners were singing and had begun to shout in unison the traditional salutation, "Sri Sri Sri One Thousand Eight Neem Karoli Baba Santa Maharaj ki jai!" Inside, Maharajji commented, "Baba Neem Karoli is dead! Now their voices will have to reach there," he said, pointing heavenward.

जय

Maharajji said to me, "Dada, I shall run away. What is attachment, to a saint?"

जय

Just a few nights before he left his body, there was a lot of activity in the ashram. He was jao'ing everyone. I was over at Hanuman, just singing for a while. When I looked around, everyone else had left the temple. Maybe they'd all been jao'ed, or had gone to the back of the ashram, but the temple was empty. I looked and saw Maharajji sitting there; nobody else was around. I went up to him and pranammed, and of course he jao'ed me. But I have never gotten such a sweet jao. It was the sweetest jao in the world. He called me "my daughter"—"hamari beti." And his look was just like pools overflowing with love.

"My daughter . . ." I could barely get up to my feet. It took a few minutes to get up. He didn't say jao again, just gave me that through-and-through look of total compassion. I felt that during those last few days he was taking on a great deal of karma. You could see so much anguish in his face.

It was strange those last few days. An Indian man used to come and do pujas, and he'd pass out while singing Ram. Maharajji was in the man's room one afternoon. There was such a crowd that I couldn't really see what was going on, but I could hear the man screaming in anguish: "Nath! Nath [Lord! Lord]!" I didn't know what it was. Perhaps he had some inkling of what was shortly going to happen. Maharajji was just sitting there while the man was screaming. You knew something was happening but of course you would never admit the possibility of what it really might be.

Dwarka Sah asked me if I had been in Kainchi for the last darshan, and as I hadn't, he told me some of his personal experience that day. After Maharajji had gone into the "office" for rest, Dwarka, feeling very heavy with sleep, had fallen asleep outside the door. He was suddenly awakened by Maharajji bursting out the door. Maharajji called to him, "Dwarka! Stand up!" Maharajji took his hand, and another devotee, R, took Maharajji's other hand. Together the three of them walked to Hanumanji's temple, where Maharajji stood in silence, hands folded in pranam, for a full two minutes. During this time his blanket fell off, and Dwarka picked it up and rewrapped it around Maharajji. Maharajji then went before Lakshmi-Narayan, and then before Shiva, standing again in silence for a long time before each temple. Then he began walking swiftly out of the temple grounds, and as he was crossing the bridge his blanket again fell off. This time he would not allow it to be put around him. He got into a waiting car and took Ravi with him, leaving Dwarka behind.

When we parted, Maharajji said to me, "If I don't meet you in this form, I'll meet you in another form."

In the summer an ayurvedic doctor from Delhi had come to visit Maharajji and to spend two weeks at Kainchi. Even before he was fully unpacked, Maharajji sent him home with no explanation. Maharajji had five boxes of apples put in the man's car and said, "Go immediately." The man was confused and angry. Maharajji also said, "This is the last time I'll see you."

Back at home the doctor received an unexpected opportunity to earn seven thousand rupees during the week when he would have been away. But he was afraid he was going to die, since Maharajji had said that he would not see him again, so he wrote his will and arranged all his affairs. Then in September, when he heard that Maharajji had died, he said, "Good." Later, when he went to the Delhi temple, he fainted, because he saw Maharajji in place of the Hanuman murti. This happened to him twice.

At the last group darshan he was sitting up on the tucket, rocking back and forth as if to get up, and we'd all think, "Oh, no, don't get up"; then he'd sit back down and we'd all think, "Oh, good." When he'd start to leave again, we'd think, "Oh, no! Don't go!" When he'd sit back down, you could just feel it in the air—"Oh, good, he's going to stay a while!" It was a long darshan. When he finally left there was something very reluctant about the way he walked. And I remember that we were just exhausted after that darshan.

After that darshan the focus of Draupadi's movie camera swooped up to the sky, to the top of the temples, which expresses the imagery we were left with then. You wanted to throw your hands up. It was intensely joyful, yet totally exhausting. After that it was very, very quiet. I rarely slept in the afternoon, but this time we all slept. We awakened to find that Maharajji had left. I think Janaki said she saw him pranam to the murtis before he left.

AFTER HIS DEATH in Vrindaban, Maharajji's body was placed on a large block of ice on a verandah of the ashram. In the evening it was paraded through the streets in a litter atop a car. Thousands watched the procession, which was complete with brass band and processional lights. At about 9:00 P.M., in the courtyard of the temple, Maharajji's body was placed on the funeral pyre.

Translation from Vrindiban newspaper, September 12, 1973:
The cremation ceremony of the earthly body of the famous and "wonder-working" saint, Baba of Neem Karoli, was performed with all the necessary religious ceremonies at his dwelling place, the ground opposite to the Sri Hanuman temple.

While he was going from Agra to Nainital he suddenly became unwell, and after that he died of heart failure.

Before the cremation, the dead body of the baba was carried in a procession in a decorated carriage in the city. The question of the place where the last rites should be performed was solved by the Pagal Baba (Sri Lila Nand Thakur), who said that Vrindaban is the king of holy places. He further said that there cannot be any better place than this. The old Mother who came from Kainchi ashram insisted that the cremation take place either at Kainchi or at Haridwar. The pyre remained burning up until three o'clock in the morning. By then a good number of devotees had reached there to pay their last homage. There was deep sorrow in the ashram and the devotees kept coming.

The president of the All India Congress Committee, Dr. S. D. Sharma, reached Vrindaban at 6:00 A.M. and remained sitting near the cremation place for quite some time. He has been a devotee of the baba since 1957. He has advised the ashram people to collect the literature regarding the baba's life and activities. A committee has also been formed. September 22 has been fixed as the date of the community feeding. The ashes have not been put into the Yamuna. They will be buried in his Samadhis. Some of his ashes have been preserved for immersion at several places of pilgrimage.

There is a controversy about the age of the baba. People say that his age may be between 250 and 300 years.

The inhabitants of Vrindaban were always against him. They always addressed him by the name of "Chamatkari Baba [miracle man]."

As soon as his American devotees heard the news of his death, there were a number of telephone calls from that country.

Big officials of India are coming to Vrindaban to pay homage.

जय

He numbed us in a certain way. We got to Vrindaban about 8:00 P.M. and they were just coming back from the parikrama (circumambulation of Vrindaban). That was when I saw his body on top of the car. And they brought it down for everyone to take a last look before putting him on the pyre. We all went to touch his feet. Something about it seemed really removed. It didn't feel like anything had changed—whatever had happened with his body seemed unreal.

I think it was just that sort of numbness that he put on us. You'd feel terribly sad and you'd cry, but there was some part of you that couldn't really believe it. But after time passed, you'd start to realize that though Maharajji is *still with us, his body was gone. At that time, though, even the idea that his body was gone wasn't real.*

कृष्ण

For the procession through the streets, Maharajji's body, covered with flowers, had been placed on the luggage rack on top of a 1955 Plymouth. As the car passed through the narrow streets, people threw coins from the windows of the houses along the way. Children ran after the car, catching the coins or retrieving them from the roadway. There was a loud band playing. We felt numb in the midst of the confusion. But just as the car went by us, we spied in the rear right-hand-corner window, three decals: one of Mickey Mouse, one of Donald Duck, and one of Goofy. Seeing them changed the entire meaning of the occasion. We recalled how our friend Wavy Gravy had always said that death was Donald Duck. It felt as if this was Maharajji's secret message to us.

कृष्ण

One old devotee spent the night sitting beside the fire in which Maharajji's body was burning, singing "Shri Ram, Jai Ram" at the top of his lungs. He said he saw Maharajji sitting above the fire and on each side of him were Ram and Shiva. They were pouring ghee on his head so that he would burn better, while overhead were all the devas (gods) throwing down flowers. Everyone was so happy!

कृष्ण

A Ma saw Maharajji sit up in the fire and look at her, pointing while leaning on his elbow in his characteristic way.

कृष्ण

I've experienced the deaths of people close to me before, but this was really different. Maharajji's presence was just so much stronger. We did the parikrama around Vrindaban that evening and the next night, too, but we were suspended in some way. I couldn't eat or sleep. It was the strangest thing.

I was hanging there, waiting for him to come back, waiting to see him walk down the street or sit on his tucket.

ॐ

S said it was Maharajji's lila that nobody around him at the time he died could realize that if they had spoken with true heartfelt devotion to him, "Get up, Maharajji, you are not dead," he would have done so.

THE NEWS OF Maharajji's death came with extraordinary swiftness to those of us who had left India, and the reactions were as varied as to any other part of his lila.

During the summer of 1973 I was staying at my father's farm in New Hampshire, and was there in September when the telegram arrived. My father and my stepmother, looking rather concerned, met me when I returned from shopping in the village. Dad said, "This telegram just came from India. I don't understand it, but I copied it down word for word as the operator gave it to me."

"At 1:15, September 11, Babaji left his bojhay [sic] in Vrindaban. . . ."
The telegram went on with further details. My father asked, "What does it mean?"

"It means," I said, "that Maharajji died."

They immediately tried to console or at least commiserate with me, but their words seemed strangely irrelevant, for I felt absolutely nothing—neither sad nor happy. There was no sense of loss. Perhaps I was just numb. A couple with marital difficulties were waiting for me, so I went and sat with them and helped them unwind the tangled thread of their loves and hatreds. Every now and then in the midst of the discussion, my mind would wander and I'd think, "Maharajji isn't in his body. Isn't that strange," or "I wonder what will happen now?" But I pushed such thoughts aside and forced my consciousness back to the task at hand, for, whatever was to come, there was no sense in stopping service to others.

Throughout that day and many times thereafter I remembered the words of the great Ramana Maharshi. He was dying of cancer and in the past had shown power to heal others, and his devotees were now begging him to heal himself. He kept refusing, and they cried, "Don't leave us, don't leave us," to which he replied, "Don't be silly. Where could I go?"

After all, where could Maharajji go? I had him in my heart. I had been

*living with him moment by moment and yet not with his physical presence—so
did it really make any difference? I wasn't sure.*

*When the couple left I started calling other devotees in the United States and
Canada and asked them to call others. It was agreed that those within a radius
of three or four hundred miles would join me in New Hampshire. By the next
noon some twenty of us were gathered. It was a peculiar meeting. We were all
somewhat dumbfounded by the news and many were crying, but at the same
time we were happy to be together and felt Maharajji's presence very strongly
with us. We cooked a big meal, which we ate around the fire. But before the
food we went up to my room to sit before the puja table and meditate and do
arti.*

*While all of us sang the ancient Sanskrit prayer, we took turns offering the
light (in the form of a candle flame) by waving it before Maharajji's picture.
After my turn I went to the back of the group and watched. In the reflection of
the candlelight I looked at the faces of my guru brothers and sisters and saw
their expressions of love and the purity of their hearts. And finally I was able
to cry—not out of sadness at the loss, but rather because of the presence of that
pure and perfect love that is Maharajji and which I felt in this gathering of
hearts. (R.D.)*

जय

*I rapidly went through many reactions when I got the news. One of them,
strangely enough, was, "Oh, poor Maharajji." My very first reaction was
grief, which was cut immediately with the realization that nothing had
changed. ("Grief for what?") Then I went through all the rest of the reactions,
like, "What's it all about? If he's not in a body then why am I? Why am I
still playing this game, which is all centered around him. If he's gone, I don't
want to play anymore."*

जय

*When he left his body I was way off on Mount Shasta, somewhere alone in
the woods. There was another person there whom I had met at darshan. When
Maharajji left his body, the word spread fast, so that we all knew about it.
The man had gone into town to make a phone call and had found out and come
to tell me, even though I was way in the woods. And I've talked to a lot of*

other people who were in America at the time, and they had similar experiences; wherever they were, they found out almost immediately.

ʃᴛ५

That summer I spent traveling around, still reorienting myself to being back in America. The first of September I came down to San Francisco from British Columbia to visit my Sufi family of previous years in California. Within a day or two I started to feel vaguely ill and wondered if I was having some sort of recurrence of the hepatitis that had sent me home from India. But there was no fever, no trace of jaundice, in fact, nothing—I just felt terrible. Since this was the home of Saul, who was a hakim *(healer), I received every loving attention and was put to bed. Then after about a week, my "illness" disappeared as mysteriously as it had come. Two days later, a close* Gurubahin *(Guru-sister) phoned. "I'm sorry to be the one to tell you," she said. "Maharajji has left his body."*

At that moment I felt only chagrin and amusement—he's run away again! "That fucker!" was all I could say.

As I hung up the phone, Saul came in the front door. "Maharajji has left his body," I told him.

"Praise God!" he cried and gave me a great hug.

ʃᴛ५

It's hard to explain how the news affected me. It was similar to the way you feel when you get ripped off in India: Instead of feeling perturbed, angry, or sad, you feel relief, because it allows you to accept something that's happened. Later there were other feelings.

Before he left his body, I had a really strong sensation, which came one time in Vrindaban when Maharajji was sending everyone away. Just before he "jao'ed" everyone, he explained that we were all just worshipping a clay pot. "What will happen when the clay pot breaks?" he asked. He was sending everyone to different places, people were crying, and I felt that Maharajji wanted just to split, that he was finished with the body. I felt like it was going to happen that day, so when it did, it didn't come as a surprise to me. It was too strong a thing to have an outward reaction to.

THE BURNING OF Maharajji's body happened so quickly after his passing that few devotees had been able to get there in time, so many of them planned to attend the funeral bhandara to be held in eleven days in Vrindaban. About thirty Westerners decided to fly to India for this ceremony and for a later one, to place some of the ashes at the Kainchi ashram.

In Vrindaban hundreds had already gathered by the time we arrived from America. The immensity of the love and openness of all the devotees was awesome. All the petty differences between the devotees from the hills and those from the plains were forgotten, as were differences between East and West. All the jealousies and judgments that we had had toward one another, which Maharajji created and exacerbated at every turn, showing us again and again our petty reflections in his big mirror, were gone for the moment. We shared a common loss, and, more important, we realized that we had all been privileged to have had the recognizable darshan of God on earth. (R.D.)

One of the amazing things that happened was at the funeral bhandara, the final Vedic ceremony, about eleven days after death, in which traditionally the soul has passed through all the bardos *(planes of existence) and is free.*

They had covered over the entire courtyard with tents and at one end had built a small platform on which they were going to light the sacred fire. Just as they were lighting the fire, out of the clear blue sky, from the east, came this big black cloud. And it came fast. As it was approaching, the wind was getting more intense and the canvas roofs began flapping. I remember thinking at that time, "Maharajji, if this is a sign from you, it just isn't enough," thinking that if he were going to come in some other form, I still wanted total immersion, total darshan.

The cloud kept approaching and the wind got stronger and stronger, and suddenly we were in the midst of a violent windstorm! The canvas was ripping in shreds, the supporting poles were snapping in two, the sacred fire was leaping high into the air. It was so exciting, so ecstatic, that people were leaping up and down, hugging each other and crying. It was recognized very quickly as Maharajji's blessing. Then, after the storm passed by and things were going to go on, I was so filled with excitement that I went rushing into one of the rooms in the back. I don't know why I went there, but as I rushed in I awakened Molly Scott. She'd just arrived, never having seen Maharajji alive. I burst in, filled with the excitement of this storm, waking her up. She told me later that she woke up at that moment with an entire song, melody and lyrics, in her mind. "There is no death. I feel you all about me. In every breath, I'll never be without thee. In my heart, in my mind, in the flower, in the child, in the rain, in the wind [etc.—each verse is different], you are born anew. You are born anew." This is the song that came from that storm.

MAHARAJJI HAD SO often spoken to us about death that we had his own words to work with.

> *AS LONG AS THE TIME DOES NOT ARRIVE, ONE CANNOT DIE.*

> *THE BODY PASSES AWAY.*
> *EVERYTHING IS IMPERMANENT*
> *EXCEPT THE LOVE OF GOD.*

Maharajji used to say that bodies should be cremated because it minimizes the craving of the soul to get back into the body. The last possession has been given away.

ॐ

Maharajji once asked a devotee, "What is this body? What is it made of? What happens when you die?" Then he answered his own questions: "The body is made of five elements. The body dies but not the soul. Atman, the real man, does not die."

> *WHY ARE YOU WITH SUCH EGO?*
> *ONE OF THESE DAYS YOU WILL*
> *HAVE TO LEAVE THIS WORLD AND*
> *BECOME ONE WITH THE EARTH.*
> —MAHARAJJI QUOTING KABIR

Maharajji would say, "When the time will come," in reference to his death. But at other times he would say, "Am I going to die? Never! I don't die."

THERE WERE ALSO many stories about the way in which Maharajji had foretold or reacted to the death of his devotees in the past.

Maharajji said a woman in Almora would die, but her doctor, also a devotee, insisted she was in good health. Maharajji and the doctor went to

*dinner at her home. She went into the kitchen during the meal, choked, and
died. Maharajji cried and cried.*

†प्र

*Once Maharajji and Mr. Tewari were talking on the parapet at Hanuman
Garh. Maharajji looked up above him and closed his eyes for a moment and
told Tewari that a certain old woman devotee from down in the plains had just
died. Then he giggled and laughed and laughed. Tewari, who had known
Maharajji for many years, was taken aback and said, "You butcher! How can
you laugh at the death of a human being?" Maharajji looked at him in surprise
and said, "Would you rather have me pretend I'm one of the puppets?"*

†प्र

*Once Maharajji said that we are on a long journey, birth to birth to birth.
The people we meet in each birth, we are predestined to meet.*

*It is also predestined how long you will be with a person, so you shouldn't
get attached to trying to keep together or feel sad at loss. Realize that you will
one day be separated, and then you will avoid that feeling of pain.*

†प्र

*Maharajji was sitting with some devotees when he suddenly asked, "Who
has come?"*

"Nobody, Maharajji."

"Yes, someone has come."

*A moment later, the servant of one of his devotees arrived. Before the man
could say anything, Maharajji said, "I know he's sick but I won't come." The
servant was astonished because the man had taken sick just a few minutes
before and had sent the servant to get Maharajji. Everyone encouraged
Maharajji to go, but he adamantly refused. Finally he said, "Here, take him
this banana. He'll be all right." The servant rushed home with the banana, for
all knew the power that Maharajji often invested in a piece of fruit. The
banana was mashed up and fed to the man. Just as he finished the last bit, he
died.*

††५

A lady took Maharajji to her unconscious husband and asked him to place his hands on her husband's head. Maharajji hesitated and asked what she wanted.

"Your blessing!" she replied.

"You want me to give a blessing?" He repeated this question three times, stalling for time. "Mother wants me to give a blessing. What should I do?" he questioned a nearby devotee. The devotee encouraged him to give the blessing. "All right, I'll give blessing." Maharajji got up from his chair. At that moment, the lights went out and the whole house became dark. The lady rushed away to fetch a lantern. Maharajji turned to the devotee and said, "When God has given darkness to this house, how can I give light?" Then he ran from the house. The lady caught him. He said, "I'll come again. I'll come again." And he left. The man died that same night. Never before had Maharajji taken so long making arrangements to give a blessing. The man was meant to die and his wife was trying to force Maharajji to give a blessing that he might live.

††५

One old forestry man came sobbing to Maharajji and said, "My son has died and what did you do?" Maharajji said the son had cancer and it was God's will. "But you could have saved him," the man said.

"What God wills must happen," said Maharajji. The man left and Maharajji said, "When somebody has done wrong, the karma must come back—maybe the father or his children, but someone must pay."

MAHARAJJI'S REFUSAL to interfere with the karma of death was apparently not without exception.

I was sitting with Maharajji late at night by the side of the road near the Bhumiadhar temple, not far from Nainital, when up the road came a very strange-looking man covered in rags and ashes. He started to shout abuses at Maharajji, so I thought he must be drunk. He kept accusing Maharajji of giving too much protection to his devotees. "This time," he shouted, "you have gone too far! In six days, I will have him." Maharajji seemed very excited and told me to go to the temple and fetch food for the stranger. I ran to get it and as I was coming back, the man walked across the road and seemed to rise up into the air and disappear. Maharajji was shouting, "See where he has gone, see where he has gone!" But I couldn't see him anywhere. Maharajji then told me that the stranger was Death. Six days later one of Maharajji's closest devotees died.

AND YET HE himself had chosen to die, as he had lived, in a form which reiterated again—nothing special.

He did everything according to nature. A child stays, a young man moves about, an old man stays. He did, according to the laws of nature. If he wanted to, he could do, but I don't think he changed nature for himself. When he was sick he asked about medicines; when he was tired he used to rest. When he got old he died.

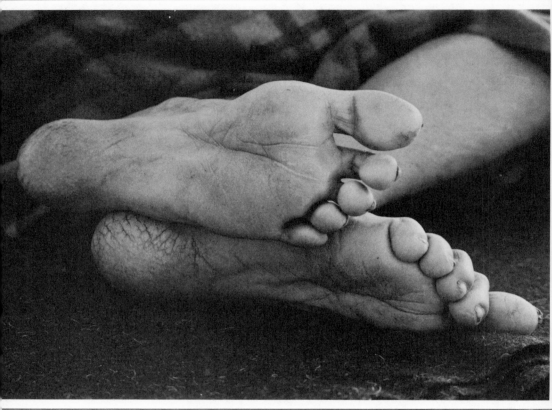

Krishna Das (Roy Bonney

Afterward

Maharajji went to the Shirdi Sai Baba temple in Madras. He sat there quietly. A woman with a baby sat crying before a picture of Shirdi Sai Baba, who had left his body many years before. Maharajji said, "You know what she is doing? She is asking him to cure her child, and he will do it because a guru never leaves his devotees. A guru is indestructible, immortal, and immune to old age and death."

WE DEVOTEES WHO knew Maharajji and were familiar with his lila are none too sure exactly what happened on September 11. We know a body was burned, but we are uncertain as to which of Maharajji's bodies it was. Perhaps he had just made a thought of himself solid, so that it could be burned. He taught us not to trust our senses and minds regarding him, and we have learned our lesson well. Now we are wary of accepting even the reality of a cremated body. Thus it is not too surprising to many of us when stories start to appear suggesting that all is not as it seems.

A few weeks after Maharajji's mahasamadhi, a stranger came to the Hanuman temple in Lucknow. He questioned the priest about the beads he

wore around his neck, and the priest replied they were tulsi beads that
Maharajji had given to him. The stranger said that he knew Maharajji and
thought that he was a great soul. He asked to be shown around the ashram,
and upon entering the bedroom kept ready for Maharajji, the man pointed to an
urn sitting on the bed and inquired about it. The priest realized that the man
didn't know about Maharajji's mahasamadhi. He told him that the urn
contained ashes from Maharajji's cremation. The man was shocked and he said
that this was impossible, since he had just seen Maharajji a few days earlier in
Amarkantak. He said that Maharajji had worn only a burlap sack around his
waist and no other clothing. Maharajji had told him that he had left his blanket
in Kainchi and that from then on he wouldn't wear expensive dhotis. He had
said that ashrams were prisons and that they caused attachment to creep back
into the minds of sadhus, who were supposed to have cleansed the mind of
attachment. Maharajji had said that he had run away from the ashrams and
that he'd never return. From now on he would live in the jungle and have time
to sing and pray without disturbance.

The priest was taken aback by the man's revelations. A moment later he
turned to question the stranger and he discovered that the man had disappeared.

ॐ

Maharajji told me two or three years ago that he would bring me three
things. He didn't, and I never reminded him because he does what he does. I
never asked him anything. Whatever he did for me came from his own mouth.
The three things that he wanted to give me were: rudraksha beads from
Pashupatinath, a Shiv-lingam from the Narmada River, and a special conch.

After Maharajji's death, a sadhu came and gave these to me. He said,
"These are being sent for you." This young sadhu came three times. The last
time he made it clear: "Everything is being done according to the orders of
Baba Neem Karoli!" Outside of these three visits, I never saw him, and he
came only to this house.

I never searched or inquired after the sadhu. If we inquire, that means there
is curiosity and that we want something, and that is not our duty. Whatever
Maharajji is doing, he is doing. The sadhu came to me and fulfilled the words
uttered from Maharajji's mouth. I suppose that it is he. Since that day I am
confirmed that he is with me.

You and I have some thoughts, and a third person fulfills them. How is it
possible? That power is working. The sadhu hardly looked twenty-one or
twenty-two years old. He last came ten days ago, in the morning. A great fire

*was raging out of control and I was rushing down the path when he came
walking up. He sat in my office and I called for tea. I told him about the fire
and even though the smoke could be seen from the house, he wouldn't allow me
to go.*

*I told the sadhu that Maharajji used to behave like this. He bowed his head
and smiled. I thought that most likely he was Maharajji and that's why he was
smiling. I told him that I had to go to the fire, but he wouldn't give me
permission. Then he told me, "I have sent Pawanasuta (a name of Hanuman)
there. He will control it. Hanumanji is there. Don't worry." About twenty-
five minutes later the fire was extinguished. He said, "You can go if you
want, but the fire is out." I went to the fire and he went another way. The
fire was out.*

*Prior to that day he had come before the Kumbha Mela, after which he had
told me that I'd get darshan. He wore Hanumanji's clothes (red)—one dhoti
and a small blanket. I told him that if Maharajji would give me darshan, he
would have to tell me that it is he. Maharajji, I said, had never kept anything
secret from me. I finally made my implication clear and the sadhu said,
"Everything is being done under his orders." If it is he, he should make it
clear.*

राम

*One family had been in the habit of making khir and placing it in a small
room before the picture of Maharajji. Once, several years back, the niece had
found the khir dripping down the picture, starting at Maharajji's mouth. Now,
some time after he left his body, khir was again made and left before the
picture. Later the family found that three-fourths of it was gone and that the
spoon had been used. The room is so situated that no one could have been in it
without their knowledge.*

राम

*A young fellow came weeping from Masiribhad in Rajasthan and when
questioned, said he had just been told that Maharajji had left his body two
years previously. But he didn't understand how it could have been two years
before, since only three months earlier Maharajji had arranged for the marriage
of his daughter and had come to the wedding.*

ᠤᠮ

Dada does puja to Maharajji each day by creating an extraordinary floral offering on Maharajji's tucket. On many days, after the puja is prepared and the room vacated, Dada returns to find indentations of footprints on the bedspread and some disarray. Maharajji has come and accepted the offering of love.

ᠤᠮ

One devotee, while reading the Ramayana on the occasion of Ram's birthday, felt Maharajji's presence. The next day when she opened the book, the name Ram was written in, just where Shiva says to Uma (his consort), "It's all illusion except the name of the Lord."

ᠤᠮ

In August 1977 I had walked to Kainchi from Nainital, since the rains had washed landslides onto the road. When I arrived, Siddhi Ma told me of a baba who had just left fifteen minutes before, who she said was so much like Maharajji in behavior and speech and feeling. He looked to be about sixty years old and very tall, over six feet. I stayed in Kainchi for some time and felt faith that somehow I would get a ride back to Nainital. Maharajji brought me to Kainchi and he would care for my return. At the gate I got a ride in a white car. Less than two miles up the road I saw a tall sadhu. I stopped the car and touched the baba's feet, saying nothing. The baba said, "We didn't meet at the temple and so we have met here." I enjoined the baba to come to Nainital, and, despite his protests of much business on the plains, he came. That evening at my home the baba asked a young boy if the boy recognized him—but he didn't wait for an answer and went on talking. Everyone who met the sadhu remarked how very much like Maharajji he talked and laughed. As the sadhu was leaving he told me not to try following him, that I wouldn't be able to.

ᠤᠮ

One night three of the workers at the ashram stayed up late talking about Maharajji. Around midnight they went to sleep. K slept on the verandah of

*the Hanuman temple, the chaukidar across from Maharajji's room, and the
cook outside the kitchen.*

*Some time after 1:00 A.M., the chaukidar was awakened by crying sounds—a
male voice—inside Maharajji's room. Yet the room was locked from the
outside. He was very frightened and so ran to K for help. K was in a deep
sleep and only after they had poured cold water on his face did he awaken. K
said he felt, upon awakening, as though he had the strength of fifty men. They
told him of the crying sounds and he felt completely calm as they were telling
him. He said that as he stood outside the locked room, listening to the sounds,
he felt no fear whatsoever—he knew with his whole being that it was all right.
He felt that inside that room was Hanuman (which to K is synonymous with
Maharajji). So they didn't unlock the door to look inside.*

NOW MAHARAJJI comes in visions to many of the devotees.

*There was a fairly wealthy man in Gujarat. He gave all his money away to
his daughters, came to Vrindaban, saw the Hanuman murti, and said, "I'm
never going to leave here." He became a cook in the ashram. He was the most
sincere, simple man imaginable, working from early in the morning until late
at night, scrubbing and cooking. He had never seen Maharajji but was deeply
devoted to him and told one of the Westerners that several times he had seen
Maharajji (in a transcendent form) in the ashram.*

*One such time it had been late at night and he was still working in the
kitchen. When he had finally finished his work, he just felt like sitting for a
while before the samadhi. While he was sitting there, he had felt someone tap
him on the shoulder. Turning to see who it was, he had beheld Maharajji
standing behind him, wearing a blanket but glowing in radiant white light. He
fell down at Maharajji's feet, and Maharajji touched him and made him cry.
He said that there were two other occasions when Maharajji had come to him
in this way. As this man was telling the story, he was crying and went over to
the spot on the ashram grounds where he saw Maharajji. "He was right here!
I saw him right here."*

राम

*One woman devotee was staying in the ashram after Maharajji's mahasamadhi.
Around 3:00 A.M. she awoke and went out of her room, and there, in a huge
form, at the entrance of the inner room of Maharajji's samadhi temple, was
Maharajji himself. Such a huge form! She was in a state of ecstasy on seeing
him and rushed back to her room to get kum-kum (red powder) to tilak him.*

When she returned outside he had vanished, but she was still in such ecstacy that she went over to the temple and wrote "Om Ram" on the wall of the samadhi building. It was just the ordinary kum-kum they use every day to write on the samadhi—and then they wash it off daily. But this time it didn't wash off—and it is still there. You can see it, and it's been over three years since she had this darshan. Whenever I return from a visit to Vrindaban, she inquires if it is still there. It always is.

तुम्

The day of Indra's mother's death was about a year after Maharajji left his body. She spent all afternoon at Kainchi talking about the flower Maharajji had given her when she was sick, which disappeared when she got well; how Maharajji had named her children; and so forth. Earlier in the day she kept asking, "Do you think anyone could see Maharajji's large form and continue to live?" That evening she was sitting with the other Mothers in Maharajji's room and suddenly she leaned over toward the bed as if she were doing a pranam—and died. Her fingers were still doing her beads.

तुम्

After Maharajji's mahasamadhi, a woman from Allahabad wanted to have his darshan. She was in Haridwar in bed with her husband when suddenly she sat up and started to speak incoherently. "He's come, he's here." She got very frightened and then she said Maharajji laughed and asked, "Why are you getting so frightened? Didn't you desire to touch my feet and massage my body like you used to?"

तुम्

In 1976 a devotee who had come to the temple wanted to go in to Maharajji's room, but the keepers wouldn't let him in. He started looking around for a key when he heard Maharajji's voice saying, "What nonsense are you doing? This is not the way. So-and-so is here. He will open the door." Just then that person came and let the devotee in.

तुम्

A local baba, when helping with the building of a temple for Maharajji, wondered how it would be built. Then he had a vision of Maharajji piling stone upon stone and saying, "I will build the mandir."

ॐ

After Maharajji died, a man and his family were passing by the temple, when their car broke down. They asked to be put up for the night. Just at this time, there was much concern at the temple as to where money would come from for the samadhi temple. All that night the man cried and felt he must do something for this temple. The next morning he gave all the money needed for the murti.

ॐ

My husband feels Maharajji talks to him all the time. Once he told my husband to get land and build a house; another time he told him that the local baba at the temple had no rice. My husband went immediately with supplies and found that, indeed, the baba had no edibles in his house.

For other devotees, Maharajji comes in dreams.

One afternoon in May around two o'clock, a year or so after Maharajji's mahasamadhi, I was deeply asleep in my room at the ashram. In a dream, Maharajji came to me and slapped my face five times and yelled at me to wake up immediately and water the trees in the ashram because they were dying of thirst. I indeed woke up immediately and my cheek was red and stinging as if it had just been slapped!

ॐ

Maharajji gave darshan to my wife in her dreams. He said that he was living in America now and that he was also working in a factory in Feradabad, where my brother is ailing.

ॐ

Once I had a dream, after Maharajji's death, in which he was taking me higher and higher into the sky. I was growing afraid and I said, "Maharajji, now I want to go back."

He said, "No." But I was so afraid. Then he said, "Okay, then you go back." And as soon as he said that, I woke up.

त्रम्

One night I dreamed that I was sitting with Maharajji again. All the Ma's were around, and I was just crying there at his feet. The next day I wept from love the whole day long.

Even without encounters on the physical plane, visions, or dreams, most of the devotees continue to feel Maharajji's presence and protection. But why should that be surprising? After all, Maharajji had again and again assured us that he would always be in communion with us and that we didn't need to be with his physical body.

One afternoon I was sitting across the temple courtyard from Maharajji. He was surrounded by devotees who were massaging his feet, laughing and talking about this and that, and sharing fruit and sweets. As I watched, the scene suddenly appeared to become static, as if I were watching a tableau. I felt a remoteness from it all. In my mind I thought, "My relationship with Maharajji is not in time and space. I don't need to be at his feet in physical form. It wouldn't really matter if I were to never see him again. He is in my heart." Just the thought made me feel guilty, but at that moment it all came back to life and I saw Maharajji turn and whisper to an old Indian devotee standing at his side. The man immediately came rushing across the courtyard, came up to me, and touched my feet. Then he said to me, "Maharajji told me to come over and touch your feet. Maharajji said, 'Ram Dass and I understand each other perfectly. His heart is open.' " At that very moment I knew that Maharajji had freed me from attachment to his form. (R.D.)

त्रम्

Once in Allahabad, Maharajji said to M Ma, "I must go. I have much work." She replied, "What work have you to do?"

"I have plenty of work to do, but I'll come soon."

Four months passed and he had not returned. The Ma's were talking about how Maharajji was not truthful. When they saw Maharajji again, the Ma's told him, "Baba, you speak lies."

"Why, Ma?"

"You said you would come, and it has been almost five months."

"I never speak lies. Where could I go? I am always here with you. Believe me, Mother, where could I go?"

ॐ

YOU CAN LEAVE ME. I WON'T LEAVE YOU. ONCE I CATCH HOLD OF YOU, I DON'T LET GO.

MS and I were discussing stories of how Maharajji is said to be alive and well in a rejuvenated body, that of a youth in Amarkantak. He said that actually what is important is to know that Maharajji is guiding us each moment. "I really mean that. I know it sounds like sweet poetry to speak in this way, but he is with us all the time. I say it from my heart."

ॐ

When he was in a body, I was always visited by him in dreams. Even now he comes in dreams, but they are not so vivid unless he has to instruct me in something. In the mornings when I sit close-eyed, I feel that he is in front of me. That used to happen and it still happens. I don't attach great importance to whether his body is there or not there. He is everywhere. When you meditate on him and think of him, he must come. He has always been here and will always be. There is no need to go anywhere special to find him. All places are equally good.

ॐ

From the first time I sat with him, I didn't have to be around him long before he was in my heart. He is in my heart all the time. I don't have a lot of pictures of him around. I don't often talk about him. He's still here—not in words, but in a feeling.

For months on end I'll forget about Maharajji's leaving his body, and then I'll have a very powerful experience of his presence. But I don't try to keep him in my mind anymore, which at one time was one of my practices. Yet sometimes spontaneously, or as a result of some input from somewhere, a real experience of his presence arises. And in that way, for me, it seems to be more a matter of grace.

Maharajji has been coming to me lately—as the father, which is exactly what I need now in my life. He comes as a huge teddy bear, who throws his arms around me and loves me in a very physical way—caressing and hugging—in a way that I've never known in my life before.

Still he is doing his work. We needn't do anything. Our problems are being solved by him. Physically we can't see him, but if we think and meditate, he is always with us. In my case I know that everything is being done by him. Still today if I have any problem, I meditate on him and he does it.

Just a few days back I was riding the bus from Bhowali to Nainital. As I was sitting there by the window I felt the warmth of Maharajji, as if he were sitting beside me. I went into some sort of trance and was talking to him. It wasn't until the bus pulled to a stop with a jerk that I realized I was having this trance.

My wife is from the Punjab and they greatly believe in family astrologers. Our astrologer said that her fifty-ninth year would be very difficult. A few weeks ago it began and she was not feeling well and was worried. While moving a packet of ash and flowers that had been given to her by Maharajji three years earlier at a yagna (he had scooped up the ash himself) she opened it and found inside a pearl ring she had never seen before. (It is believed that if you have a moon affliction in your horoscope, a pearl will help you.) Maharajji is there, so why worry? He will take care of everything.

                                    ༄

Just coming to visit the temple brought me back into his presence. Later, as we discussed this, one of the Mothers told me that Maharajji had said, "When a saint leaves his body, the temple becomes his body."

This year when I walked back into his room in Vrindaban, just as I crossed over the threshold, I felt as though everything I'd done in the last four years was irrelevant and meaningless. It was the same experience as having one of Maharajji's glances—it would bring you to right here, right now.

                                    ༄

During the return trip to India that I made this winter, as I was walking into the back part of the Vrindaban ashram, I was filled with the awareness that all the things I'd done over the entire past five years, including those that would be considered adharmic, were absolutely insignificant. I've read this in the scriptures, of course, but this was the experience—re-experience, I should say—that when you turn your heart totally to God, everything is forgiven; it is absolutely nothing. And that's what I felt when I went in there. I just sat for a long time in Maharajji's room. It felt as though the shakti from Maharajji's tucket were pouring off the blanket and into my heart, as if I were literally bathing in it, drinking the coolness of it.

                                    ༄

One cannot understand what he is. Physically he is not here, but he is listening to everything.

                                    ༄

It is very disturbing, you see. I start talking about Babaji and then it feels as if he is here or something. What can be done?

MAHARAJJI, LIKE THE wind, belongs to no one. People who never knew him when he was embodied also report seeing him in visions and dreams, sensing his presence, and feeling that they are called by him. Obviously his ability to touch people is not limited by physical contact.

> *WHEN PEOPLE THINK ON ME,*
> *I AM WITH THEM.*

There is no way to generalize how it has been for the devotees since Maharajji left his body. Each of us has gone on with life. Some of us cling to the memories of the form, the stories, the photographs, the rituals, the names, and each other. Others among us have let the form go, knowing that we need not necessarily cling to Maharajji, because he clings so strongly to us that, even if we tried, we could not forget. The legacy that he has left each person who acknowledges his existence is a faith deep within the heart. He reawakened that faith through mirroring for us a place in ourselves so deep that we rarely, if ever, had touched it before. It is a place of light, in which we truly share the brilliant, wondrous loving-living spirit. And seeing such a light has made it all different.

Before I met Maharajji I was doing the same things I do now, but out of orbit. He got me into orbit.

जय

I have seen the best entertainment. So I don't get any pleasure from the things of this world—fancy foods, cinemas, adventures. I have no will for them. One friend invited me to see the cinema in Nainital. I said, "Why? I have seen the biggest cinema here. That Nainital cinema will bore me. The biggest entertainment is Maharajji."

B**Y LEAVING US** with so few guidelines that are free of confusion, so few practices, he has protected us from getting caught in more superficial levels of our being. For example, we cannot hide in righteousness, because he was a rascal—nor can we hide in rascality, because his every act was dharmic. In no form can our egos hide, for Maharajji is always there, like Hanuman, to "spot a tyrant and pull his beard."

Sometimes I have flashes of it. I keep a couple of little pictures of Maharajji around the house. Every once in a while, when I'm rushing through things—like I'll get up late and have to rush to work, so I'll go speeding through the house—every once in a while he'll jump out and grab me. Either I'll see the picture and I'll think, "Whooo, right! Don't worry, I still remember"—or I won't see the picture but I'll have some kind of flash, like, "What are you doing? What's happening? Are you still there? Where are you? What's happening?"

When I was a young kid, I always dreamed of becoming a racer—cars, motorcycles, or whatever. And after Maharajji died, I began to race motorcycles. I would concentrate my energies on driving as fast as I could, but all that time I couldn't forget! No matter how fast I'd go, in a motorcycle or even in a plane, beyond that there is still the speed of light, and if you go that fast you don't exist anymore. That speed I could never reach. And that is the speed of Maharajji. He is like the speed of light.

Now the stories have been told, the form has come—and gone. And here we are, you and I and Maharajji, each just as real as our minds and hearts allow.

At this moment, as I write these words, I am here.

At this moment, as you read these words, you are here.

In this "here" that we share, beyond time and beyond space, Maharajji is.   Always.

I am like the wind
No one can hold me
I belong to everyone
No one can own me
The whole world is my home
All are my family
I live in every heart
I will never leave thee.

> *—from the words of Neem*
> *Karoli Baba, known as*
> *"Maharajji," adapted by*
> *Jai Gopal*

GLOSSARY

(Page numbers of first mention follow each term.)

adharma (255) *unspiritual way of life*
advait vad (140) *non-dualism*
ajna (241) *third eye*
akash (172) *celestial sky*
amrit (328) *nectar*
Annapurna (47) *Goddess of Grain*
annas (44) *small Indian coins*
arti (29) *worship ceremony of light*
ashanti (117) *not peaceful*
ashirbad (xi) *blessing*
ashram (6) *monastery*
atma (141) *God within*
atman (353) *God within*
ayurved (158) *doctor of herbal medicine*

baba (12) *title for an elder or holy man*
badmash (118) *rascal, troublemaker*
baraka (58) *blessing*
bardos (393) *planes of existence*
betel (189) *leaf chewed for digestive purposes*
Bhagavan (60) *God*
bhagya (302) *destiny*
bhajan (69) *devotional song*
bhakta (63) *devotee*

bhakti (259) *devotion*
bhandara (27) *feast*
bhava (25) *spiritual emotion*
Brahm (188) *the formless* (Brahma *creative aspect of God*)
brahmacharya (295) *celibacy*
Brahmin (12) *priest class in Hindu caste system*

chai (37) *tea*
chakra (7) *psychic energy center in the body*
chapatti (40) *unleavened flat bread*
charas (116) *hashish*
chaukidar (6) *gate-keeper*
chillum (xiii) *hashish pipe*
chimpter (222) *tongs*
crore (212) *ten million*

dacoit (46) *bandit, thief*
dal (44) *lentils*
dandi (267) *litter, palanquin*
darbar (270) *a king's court*
darshan (xiv) *spiritual meeting*
das, dass (332) *servant*

dasi (332) *female of das (servant)*
devas (389) *gods*
Devi puja (352) *worship of the Divine Mother*
dharma (141) *spiritual way of life*
dharmashala (93) *hostel, especially for pilgrims*
dhoti (50) *cloth used to cover lower part of a man's body*
dhuni (227) *camp-fire*
dhyan (248) *meditation*
diksha (339) *initiation*
dunda pranam (2) *full-length prostration*
Durga (127) *aspect of the Divine Mother*

Ekadashi (39) *lunar fast-day*

fakir (166) *sadhu*

ganja (227) *marijuana*
ghee (50) *clarified butter*
grihastha (220) *householder*
gur (214) *raw brown sugar*

413

guru (xi) *a liberated being who serves as a doorway to God*
Gurubahin (392) *guru sister*

Haj (266) *pilgrimage, especially to Mecca*
hakim (392) *healer, doctor*
halva (47) *grain dish made of wheat, ghee and a sweet*
Hanuman (11) *perfect servant of God*
Hanumanji (6) *familiar form of address of Hanuman*
hatha yoga (327) *physical method of achieving union with God*
havan (57) *smaller sacrificial fire ceremony, especially in a home*

jao (67) *go*
jelebees (39) *fried sugar syrup*
jetta (332) *long, matted hair piled on the head*
jhola (201) *shoulder bag*
juth (216) *impure, dirty*

Kali Yuga (140) *Dark Age*
kamini (208) *women*
kanchan (207) *gold, wealth*
kanchankamini (297) *gold and women*
kanna (37) *food*
karma (44) *effects of previous actions*
karma yoga (246) *using effect of previous action to attain God*
khichri (47) *rice and lentils*
khir (51) *sweet rice/milk pudding*
kirtan (24) *group singing of devotional songs*
Krishna (24) *an incarnation of Vishnu*
kumbhak (259) *yogic method using pranayam*
Kumbha Mela (47) *a great spiritual fair held every twelve years*
kum-kum (403) *colored powder for making tilaks*
kundalini (177) *spinal energy*
kuti (42) *hut*
kya (303) *what*

laddus (53) *sweet favored by Hanuman*
lakh (212) *one hundred thousand*
Lakshmi (208) *Goddess of Good Fortune*
Lakshmi-Narayan (24) *Narayan is an aspect of Vishnu, Lakshmi is his consort*
langoti (337) *loin cloth*
lassi (142) *churned yogurt drink*
lila (94) *play*
lingam (331) *phallic symbol*

loki (268) *squash*
lota (124) *water pot*

Ma (7) *mother*
maha-jao (374) *great jao*
Maharajji (xii) *great king*
mahasamadhi (316) *completion of the final incarnation of a realized being*
mahatma (152) *great soul*
malas (130) *prayer beads*
malpuas (51) *sweet fried bread*
mandir (210) *temple*
mantra (12) *method of yoga using repetition of words*
maun (326) *silent*
maya (196) *illusion*
mela (47) *fair, gathering*
mudra (175) *method of yoga using bodily form or gesture*
murti (28) *consecrated statue*

naga baba (315) *naked sadhu*
nahin (118) *no*

Om (338) *the cosmic syllable*

pakoras (97) *fritter*
pani (153) *water*
parathas (50) *fried flat bread*
parikrama (388) *circumambulation*
pattal (213) *leaf plate*
pera (38) *a sweet*
phalahari (326) *diet of vegetables and fruits*
pran (33) *psychic energy*
pranam, pranammed (6) *bow*
pranayam (232) *yogic technique involving breath control*
prasad (30) *consecrated food*
puja (11) *prayer ritual*
pukka pujari (346) *first-class priest*
pundit (104) *religious scholar*
puris (38) *fried flat bread*

Radha (349) *Krishna's beloved and devotee*
rakshabandhan (70) *protective ribbon*
Ram (32) *an incarnation of Vishnu*
rambans (157) *cactus*
Ram Lila (73) *celebration of the life of Ram*
Ram mantra (15) *repetition of the name of Ram*
rasam (349) *south Indian food*
rishis (140) *sages*
roti, rotis (45) *bread (same as chapatti)*
rudraksha (73) *seed used to make prayer beads*

sadhana (108) *spiritual practice*
sadhu (12) *renunciate*
samadhi (139) *spiritual trance*
sambar (349) *a south Indian food*
samskaras (159) *karmic effects of previous incarnations*
Sangam (32) *confluence of three sacred rivers*
sanyas (328) *renunciation*
sanyasi (196) *renunciate*
Sat Guru (329) *supreme guru*
sati (295) *wife, consort*
satsang (6) *community of spiritual seekers*
shakti (67) *psychic energy*
shaligram (222) *stone used in rituals*
shanti milta-hai (117) *peace is found*
sherabis (64) *winos, drunkards*
Shiva (12) *the destructive aspect of God*
Shivaratri (343) *holy day honoring Shiva*
Shiv-lingam (400) *phallic symbol of Shiva*
Siddha Loka (142) *dwelling place of highest celestial beings*
siddha mahatma (228) *highest saint*
siddhi (47) *psychic power*
Sita (257) *Ram's wife*
Sitaram (233) *mantra using the names of Sita and Ram*

tapasya (162) *austerities*
Thakur (346) *a lower Hindu class*
tilak (180) *forehead marking of religious significance*
tonga (194) *horse carriage*
tucket (9) *wooden bed*
tulsi (346) *sacred basil plant*
tyaga (208) *sacrifice*

ulfie (105) *sack-like robe*
Uma (402) *Shiva's consort*
upa-gurus (329) *spiritual guides other than one's Sat Guru*

Veda Vyas (350) *a great Indian saint*
vibhuti (147) *sacred ash*

wallas (32) *vendors, proprietors*

yagna (342) *a major sacrificial fire ceremony*
yatra (267) *pilgrimage*
yoga-asanas (326) *yogic postures*
yogi (42) *one who seeks union with God*
yuga (331) *age*